Judith Merril

# Judith Merril
## A CRITICAL STUDY

Dianne Newell *and*
Victoria Lamont

McFarland & Company, Inc., Publishers
*Jefferson, North Carolina, and London*

On the title page: "Judith Merril Gives Us Hell"—a sketch of Merril done by Margaret Atwood. Reproduced from *Aloud Magazine* (Judith Merril issue), October 1992, page 3, with the kind permission of Margaret Atwood.

LIBRARY OF CONGRESS CATALOGUING-IN-PUBLICATION DATA

Newell, Dianne.
 Judith Merril : a critical study / Dianne Newell and Victoria Lamont.
    p.   cm.
 Includes bibliographical references and index.

 ISBN 978-0-7864-4836-4
 softcover : acid free paper ∞

 1. Merril, Judith, 1923–1997 — Criticism and interpretation.  I. Lamont, Victoria.  II. Title.
 PS3525.E643Z75  2012
 813'.54 — dc23                                         2012018298

BRITISH LIBRARY CATALOGUING DATA ARE AVAILABLE

© 2012 Dianne Newell and Victoria Lamont. All rights reserved

*No part of this book may be reproduced or transmitted in any form or by any means, electronic or mechanical, including photocopying or recording, or by any information storage and retrieval system, without permission in writing from the publisher.*

Front cover image ©2012 Shutterstock; design by David K. Landis (Shake It Loose Graphics)

Manufactured in the United States of America

*McFarland & Company, Inc., Publishers*
 *Box 611, Jefferson, North Carolina 28640*
   *www.mcfarlandpub.com*

To Ursula M. Franklin
*metallurgist, physicist, pacifist, humanist, feminist*

# Table of Contents

*Acknowledgments* — viii
*Note on Archival Sources* — xvi
*Introduction* — 1

## Part One. The Postwar Fiction

1. Judith Merril and the Myth of the Frontier — 11
2. Atomic Frontier and the Advent of a Writer — 25
3. The Space Stories — 44
4. Alien Encounters — 65
5. Psychology and "Primary Communication" — 89

## Part Two. Shifting the Dimensions of Speculative Fiction

6. Merril in Dialogue — 113
7. New Waves and New Communities — 147
8. The Memoir — 179

*Epilogue: The Future of Judith Merril* — 208
*Bibliography* — 213
*Index* — 229

# Acknowledgments

This has been a rich and rewarding, not to mention intriguing, collaboration that began in the summer of 2002 at the Peter Wall Institute for Advanced Studies at the University of British Columbia. One of us, Dianne Newell, a professor in the Department of History at UBC, was a scholar in residence at the Institute that year; the other, Victoria Lamont, a young professor in English literature at the University of Waterloo, Ontario, and a former Peter Wall visiting junior scholar, had returned to the Institute for a reunion. At the Institute we discovered our complementary interests in women writers of genre literature. We saw a possibility for creating something special, a new angle on the role of modern American science fiction in the world. We agreed to toss around ideas over the winter and perhaps eventually to work on a joint paper regarding women's contemporary science fiction in the Cold War era. Several conference papers and publications later, we arrived at a logical conclusion: it was time to tackle a full-scale literary biography of Judith Merril, whose work had always been a special presence in our joint writing. When our publisher approached us in 2009 to explore our interest in writing a book on Merril, we decided the time was right.

We would like to say how thankful we are to the late Judith Merril for the fascinating and valuable archival, literary, and political legacy she left to the world. Merril was an extraordinarily prolific letter-writer and collector of books and magazines; fortunately, she made both her library and her personal papers available to the public. We owe a special debt to the Merril estate, particularly Emily Pohl-Weary, for unrestricted permission to copy and quote from the Merril papers; to Library and Archives Canada, for access to the voluminous collection of Merril papers and historic audio and video tapes housed in Ottawa, and especially to Suzanne Lemaire for her efficiency and valuable assistance; and to the Merril Collection of Science Fiction, Speculation and Fantasy (formerly the Spaced Out Library) of the Toronto Public Library, which houses Merril's original donation in 1970 of over 8,000 books and magazines, and personal papers and news clippings related to her work in the Merril Collection, as well as hundreds of reel-to-reel audio recordings of interviews, panels, and finished broadcasts taped by Merril during the 1970s and early 1980s.

We are especially grateful to Merril's granddaughter, Emily Pohl-Weary, who as co-author of Merril's published memoir, *Better to Have Loved: The Life of Judith Merril* (2002), agreed to be interviewed in 2004. As a principal in the Merril estate, she has been very generous with permissions. Newell's visits to the British Library in London, the Science Fiction Foundation Archive at the University of Liverpool, and the William Anthony Parker White (legal name for the writer and critic Anthony Boucher) Collection at the Lilly Library, University of Indiana, as well as her field trip to Tokyo to interview Japanese and American science fiction translators, publishers, and academics who knew and worked with Merril in the 1970s, have also proved very useful to the overall research on Judith Merril and this era of modern science fiction.

Dianne Newell would like to thank and acknowledge several former students in history at the University of British Columbia who provided intelligent and unique research assistance on Merril projects, co-authored essays on Merril, and, in some cases, worked with Newell's research collection of Merril publications, manuscript materials, and transcripts of audio recordings for their graduate research. These individuals include Michael LeBlanc, whose research assistance contributed to the conversion of the piles of original Merril audio recordings on reels from the 1970s at the Merril Collection to digital format. He also transcribed several dozen key interviews contained on those tapes. LeBlanc additionally wrote, under Newell's direction, an undergraduate graduating honors essay on Philip K. Dick's Cold War science fiction (LeBlanc 2002) and an MA thesis on Merril and Isaac Asimov as nonfiction writers (2005); a revised version of the latter won the international Science Fiction Foundation Graduate Essay Prize in 2005 (LeBlanc 2006).

Susan Roy, while completing her PhD at UBC and living in Toronto, spent two winters at the Merril Collection digitizing, inventorying, identifying, and annotating (thus listening to) Merril's nearly 500 old reel-to-reel audio tapes, which not only were in extremely poor physical condition, but the contents of which were also fragmented and rarely identified. Roy produced a complete electronic copy of all the original tapes and an annotated finding aid that in many cases identifies the source and supplies historical context for the works. She also served as official scribe for Newell's Peter Wall Institute workshop titled "New Angles on Science? Fiction?" that was held at the Wall Institute in 2002. A UBC Hampton Trust Grant awarded to Newell funded the bulk of the Merril tapes restoration project. The Merril Collection now houses, in addition to the large collection of original tapes, the digital versions and annotated finding aid produced by the Newell project.

A UBC Master's student in history, Jolene McCann, organized (and created an electronic annotated finding aid for) Newell's copies of Merril's correspondence, interviews, and supporting materials. Merril's move from the United States to Toronto in 1968, her intense involvement once there in North America's largest "free university" (Rochdale College), and her founding of the Spaced Out Library in the Toronto Public Library was the subject of McCann's MA thesis under Newell's direction (McCann 2006). McCann was awarded the Science Fiction Foundation Graduate Student Essay Prize for her essay on a topic related to her thesis on Merril and the Spaced Out Library (2008). She also co-published with Newell the essay "Judith Merril Moving In and Out of This World" (Newell and McCann 2009).

Jenéa Tallentire, during her UBC doctoral studies with Newell, co-wrote and co-published with her four biographical essays on Merril (Newell and Tallentire 2005a, 2005b, 2007, 2009), the last of which appeared in the Mendlesohn-edited *On Joanna Russ* (2009) that was short-listed for a 2010 Hugo Award for Best Related Work from the World Science Fiction Association.

Lastly, Kenichi Matsui, another UBC doctoral student at the time, organized and accompanied Newell on a field trip to Tokyo in December 2004 to interview science fiction writers, translators, editors, and publishers with whom Merril collaborated in the 1970s, and others who were aware of the impact of Merril's work in Japan. He also provided scholarly translations of her interviews and conversations in Tokyo, of several Japanese-language letters to Merril in the 1970s, and of a series of Japanese-language memorial tributes to Merril published in the 1990s. Dr. Matsui also was kind enough to check over the Japanese spelling and translation of titles into English for an earlier version of our book manuscript.

Victoria Lamont would like to acknowledge Ashna Bahgwanani for the many hours she spent in the Merril Collection poring over quotations and looking up countless references. Additionally, the University of Waterloo contributed funds for conferences and research travel, without which this collaborative project would not have been possible.

The opportunities to present our ideas on Merril, her science fiction, and science fiction circles have provoked in our collaboration many new ideas about and insights into Merril over the years. Conferences we have presented our Merril-based research at jointly, separately, or individually with others include "Discipline and Deviance: Genders, Technologies, Machines" (Duke University, Durham, North Carolina, 1998); 10th Biannual Swiss Congress on Women's History, Gender and Knowledge (University of Misericorde, Fribourg, Switzerland, 2000); "International Conference on the Nature of Gender and the Gender of Nature" (Kiel University, Germany, 2000); Academic Conference on Canadian Science Fiction and Fantasy (Merril Collection, Toronto, 2002 and 2003); Association of American Studies (Yale University, New Haven, Connecticut, 2003); the British Comparative Literature Association and Goldsmiths College conference "Autobiografiction" (Goldsmiths, University of London, 2003); Science Fiction Research Association Annual Meeting (New Lanark, Scotland, 2002, and University of Guelph, 2003); "A Commonwealth of Science Fiction Conference" (University of Liverpool, United Kingdom, 2004); Annual Meeting of the Portuguese Association of Anglo-American Studies (Lisbon, Portugal, 2006); "International Conference on Emotional Geographies" (Queen's University, Kingston, 2006); 28th Annual International Conference on the Fantastic in the Arts (Fort Lauderdale, Florida, 2007); and J. Lloyd Eaton Conference (University of California, Riverside, 2008 and 2011).

Newell also delivered invited papers on her Merril research while a scholar at the Institute of Social Change and Critical Policy, University of Wollongong, Australia (2002), and keynote lecturer at the Annual Joint Seminar of the Centre for Canadian Studies and Centre for Theory, Culture, Politics at Trent University, Peterborough (2005). She also presented papers on Merril and/or women and science fiction at the University of British Columbia: at St. John's College (1998), Centre for Women's Studies and Gender Relations (1999), Green College (2002), and Peter Wall Institute for Advanced Studies (2002 and 2007).

We are indebted to the Social Sciences and Humanities Research Council of Canada for a standard research grant (to Newell) to study Judith Merril and her circles, and to the University of British Columbia for several research awards related to Merril, including a Hampton Fund Award (2000–2003) and a Large HSS Grant (2004–2006); a Scholar-in-Residence Award from the Centre for Women's Studies and Gender Relations (Newell 1999); and, from the Peter Wall Institute for Advanced Studies, a Distinguished Scholar in Residence Award (Newell 2002) and a Director's Research Fund (Newell 2003–2010).

For invitations to present or publish our research, for access to archival records, and for interviews, we are grateful to the following people: Dr. Farah Mendlesohn, Middlesex University, London; Drs. Veronica Hollinger and Joan Sangster, Trent University; Lorna Toolis (who alerted us to the Merril papers at Library and Archives Canada), head of the Merril Collection, and her staff, Toronto Public Library; the staff of the British Library, London; Dr. Allan Weiss (who alerted us to the existence of the old Merril audio tapes at the Merril Collection), York University, Toronto; Andy Sawyer, science fiction librarian and course director, MA in science fiction studies, for sharing his expertise and for access to the Science Fiction Foundation Collection, Sydney Jones Library, University of Liverpool, and for fine hospitality; the staff of the Lilly Library, University of Indiana, Bloomington; Professor David Seed, University of Liverpool, for conversations and copies of his writings about science fiction, Merril, and the Cold War; and Professor George Slusser, co-founder and curator emeritus of the J. Lloyd Eaton Collection of Science Fiction, Fantasy, Horror, and Utopian Literature, University of California, Riverside.

The Japanese translators, publishers, academics, and writers in Tokyo who graciously agreed to meet and be interviewed regarding Judith Merril's work and reception in Japan include (named with family names last): Dr. Takayuki Tatsumi, who teaches American literature at Keio University, Tokyo; Mari Kotani, independent science fiction and fantasy writer and critic, interviewer of Judith Merril, and co-founder of the Japanese Association of Feminist Science Fiction and Fantasy; Komatsu Sakyo, the "king" of Japanese science fiction, a reporter, nonfiction writer, script writer, and award-winning science fiction writer; Takashi Ishikawa (journalist, writer, and critic), Masaki Yamada, Morio Kita, and colleagues; and Dana Lewis, an American magazine reporter and translator of Japanese science fiction and manga novels for many years, and a long-standing member of the Honaku Benkyo-kai gatherings of Japanese translators.

A great debt is owed to Hisashi Asakura, a prolific translator of English science fiction into Japanese, who passed away in February 2010. He provided invaluable services to Kenichi Matsui and Dianne Newell: in Tokyo, finding people to interview and setting up the interviews, accompanying Newell and Matsui to several of them, and allowing himself to be interviewed; providing Newell with a full set of the Japanese-language books of Judith Merril's work; and following up with advice on the translation into English of Merril letters and Japanese translators' memorials to Merril following her death. That he was a wonderful and loyal friend to Merril is clear from their correspondence. That long-standing friendship with Merril spilled over into Newell and Matsui's research visit in 2004.

Finally, we want to acknowledge the generous contributions of Lorna Toolis, branch head of the Merril Collection, Toronto Public Library, and co-editor of *Tesseracts 4* (1993), and Lisa Yaszek, associate professor, School of Literature, Communications, and Culture, Georgia Institute of Technology, and author of, among other works, *Galactic Suburbia* (2008). Toolis agreed to review an earlier version of the chapters in Part Two; the personal insights and anecdotes from her years as Merril's colleague and confidante have been invaluable to our understanding of Merril's later life and memories. Yaszek's thoughtful comments on an earlier version of the entire manuscript contributed significantly to strengthening both the structure and the intellectual framework of our work.

## Permissions

Permission to cite has been obtained for a number of previously published essays. Chapter 1 is a blended and considerably revised version of two essays: Victoria Lamont and Dianne Newell (2009), "Daughter of Earth: Judith Merril and the Intersections among Gender, Science Fiction, and Frontier Mythology," *Science Fiction Studies* 36 (1): 48–66, and Newell and Lamont (2005b), "Rugged Domesticity: Frontier Mythology in Post-Armageddon Science Fiction by Women," *Science Fiction Studies* 97 (32), part 3: 423–41. Chapter 2 draws on sections from Newell and Lamont, "Rugged Domesticity," and Chapter 3 draws on sections of Lamont and Newell, "Daughter of Earth," and "House Opera: Frontier Mythology and Subversion of Domestic Discourse in Mid–Twentieth-Century Women's Space Opera," *Foundation* 34 (95): 71–88. Chapter 8 is a blended, revised, and expanded version of two essays by Newell and Tallentire: (2007), "'For the Extended Family and the Universe': Judith Merril and Science Fiction Autobiography," *Biography: An Interdisciplinary Quarterly* 30 (1): 1–21, and (2005a), "Co-Writing a Life in Science Fiction: Judith Merril as a Theorist of Autobiography," in *Further Perspectives on the Canadian Fantastic: Proceedings of the 2003 Conference on Canadian Science Fiction and Fantasy*, edited by Allan Weiss, 19–33 (Toronto: ACCSFF). We also cite from Dianne Newell and Jenéa Tallentire (2009), "Learning the Prophet Business: The Merril-Russ Intersection," and (2005b), "Translating Science Fiction: Judith Merril in Japan," paper presented at Worldcon, Glasgow, posted by the Science Fiction Foundation (UK) on its website: http://www.sf-foundation.org/sites/default/files/imported/publications/essays/TranslatingSF.pdf.

We gratefully acknowledge the publisher's permission to cite from Judith Merril and Emily Pohl-Weary (2002), *Better to Have Loved: The Life of Judith Merril* (Toronto: Between the Lines).

## Dedication

Our special debt is to Ursula Franklin, professor emerita and fellow, Massey College, University of Toronto, who more than anyone (other than Merril herself) is responsible for this present book. Without Ursula Franklin,

Dianne Newell would never have known about or pursued an interest in Judith Merril and her circles in postwar science fiction; without Newell's extensive research into the history of Merril and other women in Cold War science fiction, Victoria Lamont would never have become involved in science fiction research; and without Lamont's expertise in the field of genre literature — Westerns in particular — Newell would not have entered into the realm of Merril's actual science fiction writing.

Ursula Martius Franklin is a Canadian metallurgist, research physicist, historian of technology, author, educator, pacifist, and feminist with a forty-year record of teaching at the University of Toronto. She immigrated to Toronto from her native Germany in 1949, twenty years before Merril arrived. Although they were very different individuals who lived quite different lives, Merril's and Franklin's lives were linked in many important respects. As activists, writers, and public intellectuals, their worlds intersected in Toronto after Merril immigrated there in 1968, especially around their well-developed anti-war and anti-censorship activism. Even before that, in the 1940s and early 1950s, Merril was writing powerful anti-nuclear war stories that focused on mothers, relationships, and families, and in the early 1960s, Franklin was investigating levels of strontium-90, a radioactive isotope in fallout from nuclear weapons testing, in children's teeth, research that contributed to the cessation of atmospheric weapons testing.

Franklin, however, is best known for her writings on the political and social effects of technology. She argues that the dominance of prescriptive technologies in modern society discourages critical thinking and promotes "a culture of compliance" (Franklin 1990, 12). Her highly influential and tough-minded book, *The Real World of Technology* (1990), is based on her Massey Lectures broadcast in 1989 as part of the Canadian Broadcasting Corporation (CBC) *Ideas* radio series. Merril was a freelance producer for *Ideas* in the early 1970s, the initial days of the program. Franklin's more recent book is *The Ursula Franklin Reader: Pacifism as a Map*, published in 2006 by Between the Lines, a small alternative press in Toronto. The *Reader* is a retrospective collection of her papers, interviews and talks on pacifism, feminism, technology, and teaching that, according to Franklin, owes much to the friendship and efforts of Michelle Swenarchuk, who nevertheless refused to be acknowledged as co-author. *Reader* has a reflexive, eclectic, and personal feel to it that is similar to that of Judith Merril's memoir, *Better to Have Loved: The Life of Judith Merril* (2002), which was co-authored by Merril's granddaughter, Emily Pohl-Weary, and also published by Between the Lines.

Having received her PhD in experimental physics at the Technical University of Berlin in 1948, Franklin in 1949 became the first female professor in the University of Toronto's Department of Metallurgy and Materials Science. In 1984, she became the first woman to be named University Professor, one of the highest honors accorded by the University of Toronto. A mountain of other awards and special recognitions in Canada has been heaped on her during her long, multifaceted, and illustrious career, including the Ursula Franklin Academy. The Academy is a small, publicly funded secondary school located in the Bloor West Village in Toronto that was named after her. Founded in September 1995, the Academy follows Franklin's vision of education. It combines innovation, high expectations, and strong relationships between the staff, students, and their families to create a "community of learners," offering integrated liberal arts and science packages and preparing students for academic programs at the postsecondary level. Merril, who in 1970 founded the Spaced Out Library at the Toronto Public Library with a donation of her own extensive collection of books and magazines, was similarly honored in 1990 when the collection was renamed in her honor as the Merril Collection of Science Fiction, Speculation and Fantasy (although she much preferred the original name). The Merril Collection is now recognized as the world's largest holding of science fiction and fantasy that is open to the public, with all the big, world-changing ideas that those genres imply. A noncirculating research collection, it has from the beginning played a catalytic role in forming a community of science fiction and fantasy writers and fans in Canada, and being a catalyst and innovator is very much what Judith Merril was all about.

A consummate mentor herself, Ursula Franklin offered two very large challenges when she and Newell spoke briefly in Vancouver in the spring of 1995: Franklin first suggested to her how critical it was that one look closely at the lives of talented but relatively unknown or forgotten women writers, especially those who chose Canada as their home, rather than heap further attention on the small group of female celebrities who are already well established in the public view. She then mentioned that, for example, there was a woman in Toronto who used to be a science fiction writer in the United States and was now curator of the science fiction collection she had donated to the Toronto Public Library. Her name was Judith Merril. Newell spoke with Merril by phone and then left the country for a year's sabbatical. She was able to read up on Merril's work and to speak with Merril in person at the 20th anniversary meeting of WisCon, the Madison, Wisconsin, feminist science fiction convention in May 1996, a year before Merril's death. Merril was a Special Guest at the meeting, flying around the place in a battery-powered chair, her body exhausted but her mind full of ideas and intellectual challenges for everyone with whom she came into contact. Newell and Merril hoped to meet that fall in Toronto or Vancouver, although Merril was skeptical about them seeing each other again. They never did, just as Merril, a believer in ESP to the end, had predicted.

# Note on Archival Sources

Archival materials cited in the text are not included in the Bibliography section. The in-text citations, when first mentioned, follow this pattern: document title, date, box#.file#, abbreviation. Abbreviations used in the text citations for archival materials are as follows:

- MP: Judith Merril Fonds, Library and Archives Canada, Ottawa.
- S&S: Street and Smith Publications Preservation and Access Project, Syracuse University Library, Syracuse, New York.
- White Mss: William Anthony Parker White (pseud. Anthony [Tony] Boucher/H. H. Holmes) Papers, Lilly Library Manuscript Collections, University of Indiana, Bloomington, Indiana.

# Introduction

Judith Merril was a central and socially radical motivating force in modern science fiction, first in New York City and its environs in the 1950s and 1960s, briefly in London in the mid–1960s and Japan in the early 1970s, and finally in Toronto, her home from 1968 until her death in 1997. Merril was born Josephine (Judith) Grossman on January 21, 1923, in New York. At the age of seventeen in 1940, she married Daniel Zissman and had a daughter, Merril, in 1942. As a twenty-one-year-old living on her own with her daughter in New York City in 1944, she discovered the gifted band of young science fiction fans and budding writer-editors of the Futurian Society of New York and began writing for publication. At first, she wrote for "low-brow" Western pulps and detective and sports magazines, but soon she was also writing for the top science fiction magazines. Divorced from Zissman in 1947 and taking her daughter's first name as her surname, Merril married the leading Futurian writer and literary agent Frederik Pohl in 1948, left her full-time editorial work with Bantam Books, and took up science fiction writing and anthologizing on a full-time basis. She had a daughter, Ann, in 1950 before separating from Pohl in 1951; they divorced in 1952. Merril continued writing fiction until 1963, by which time she was also a leading science fiction anthologist and editor. She married for a third and last time, to Daniel Sugrue, in 1961, separating shortly thereafter and eventually divorcing. She left the United States for Canada in 1968, becoming a Canadian citizen in 1976. She died of heart failure in Toronto on September 12, 1997.

Science fiction truly suited Merril, who was a lifelong social activist. While science fiction, broadly conceived, can be traced back through the past millennium, by the time Merril was writing science fiction after World War II — the period of the Cold War, atomic weapons, and the space race — it was still a marginal genre with a limited readership. But it also provided a unique, uncensored forum for social criticism, experimental expression, and oppositional politics. Merril took on successive, multiple roles as science fiction writer, anthologist, catalyst, editor, essayist, critic, and reviewer. She published several dozen science fiction stories and novellas, as well as two sole-authored and two co-authored books, in the 1950s; nineteen anthologies between 1950 and 1968, including the celebrated annual *Year's Best* science fiction series; and, between 1960 and 1985, five collections of her own stories and novellas. She also co-founded the New York Hydra Club (1947) for science fiction writers, editors, and publishers and the annual Milford Science Fiction Writers' Conference (1956) for professional writers. During the 1960s, she was the influential book editor for *The Magazine of Fantasy and Science Fiction* and, in 1965, a co-founder of the professional association Science Fiction Writers of America (later renamed Science Fiction and Fantasy Writers of America).

After her move to Canada in 1968, Merril took on additional roles as mentor, educator, radio and TV documentarist, editor, translator, and memoirist. She donated her science fiction collection ("Spaced Out Library") to the Toronto Public Library in 1970, where it was renamed in 1990 as the Merril Collection of Science Fiction, Speculation and Fantasy. Active in the 1970s with the free university movement and with American draft resisters, writers' organizations, and peace movements, Merril was also involved in translation projects in Japan, produced numerous programs on science fiction and related themes for the Canadian Broadcasting Corporation's radio series *Ideas*, and wrote and performed for TV Ontario commentaries for the *Dr. Who* series. A leading voice for the Canadian science fiction community in the 1980s, Merril founded and edited the first volume of Canada's science fiction anthology series *Tesseracts*—her twentieth and last anthology. She donated her sizeable collection of papers to Library and Archives Canada in the 1980s, and in the 1990s began writing her Hugo-winning memoir *Better to Have Loved: The Life of Judith Merril*, which was co-authored and published posthumously in 2002.

Remembered today as one of science fiction's best editors and anthologists, Merril was also an accomplished fiction writer. Although widely anthologized at the time, her stories have neither received the attention they deserve as groundbreaking science fiction in their own right (C. Willis 1992, 2003; Cummins 1992; Carey 2005; Yaszek 2008; Lamont and Newell 2009) nor, until recently, been the subject of a comprehensive, published bibliography (see Cummins 2006; also Stableford 1979 and Cummins 1992, 2001); nor have they been anthologized as a complete collection, though Elisabeth Carey has issued a compilation of Merril's "solo short SF": *Homecalling and Other Stories* (Merril 2005). While Merril's sole- and co-authored novels are long out of print, Carey has helped to rectify this unfortunate situation by reprinting

Merril's two collaborative novels with C.M. Kornbluth (as Cyril Judd) and her *Shadow on the Hearth* in a recent collection titled *Spaced Out: Three Novels of Tomorrow* (Merril and Kornbluth 2008).

This book offers a much-needed literary biography and critical commentary on Merril's science fiction, anthologies, essays, reviews, and leadership in the field in the United States, England, Japan, and Canada. Also included is the later reception of her work, especially the literary value and impact of her memoir.

Merril was writing science fiction in an era in which, as David Hartwell points out, science fiction authors were aware of their power to generate and spread ideas, to present alternate futures, and to influence the public consciousness through their writing: science fiction ideas were "in the air." Merril agreed:

> "Back in the Fifties," says Merril, "I used to talk about science fiction as being a sort of encyclopedia, in the sense of the French encyclopedia, which paved the consciousness-ground for the French and American revolutions. And I felt that this was very much what we were doing, that we were putting into print and into words ideas whose time was about to come, making it possible for people to be conscious of it" [Hartwell 1984, 110].

The fact that science fiction enjoyed this growing authority had much to do with the role science played in the 1950s as a new frontier that promised to reinvigorate American society through the anticipation of new territories for conquest (in space) and new resources (nuclear energy) to exploit. Hence, our readings of Merril's science fiction, which comprise Part One of this book, depend on our theory of American science fiction as a form of frontier mythology, which we explain in Chapter 1.

## The Many Roles of Judith Merril

The scope of this book extends beyond criticism of Merril's fiction. This book is also meant to serve as a far-reaching account of Merril's career, making it a valuable reference source for students and scholars of science fiction, women's biography and autobiography, women's contributions to frontier mythology, and women's activism. Our scope extends from Merril's earliest stories, published with the support of her Futurian associates in the 1940s, through her rise to prominence as a fiction writer and leading anthologist in the 1950s, and into the 1960s, when her literary output declined as she developed an insurmountable writer's block and became more interested in, and exceptionally successful at, anthologizing, reviewing, and reshaping American science fiction away from the conventional and into experimental writing and radical ideas that she referred to as speculative fiction: "SF."

We also consider reception by science fiction critics and fans during the "new wave" of feminist science fiction and criticism. In anthologies she edited in the mid–1970s to restore the status of "pre-feminist" women's early science fiction, and again in the 1990s to meet the demands of a new generation of feminist readers, Pamela Sargent suggests that women had difficulties sustaining their involvement in science fiction (1974, xiii), and that they were exceptional "pioneers, with few examples and female mentors to inspire and guide them" (Sargent 1995, 4). However, as discussed in greater detail earlier in chapter 1, more recent writings, in particular those by Connie Willis (1992), Farah Mendlesohn (1994), Helen Merrick (2003), Justine Larbalestier (2002a, 2006), Eric Davin (2006), Lisa Yaszek (2008), and Newell and Lamont (2005a, 2005b; see also Lamont and Newell 2009), point the way to a rich — if lost — tradition of women's science fiction that flourished in the 1940s and 1950s. Merril not only led in establishing this tradition but, as a role model and mentor, she also made a huge difference to other writers and readers of the period, female and male. By the time she was living in Canada and spending time in Japan in the early 1970s, she had established the sort of reputation and strength as a mentor and critic in speculative fiction with which to promote and influence communities of science fiction writers, fans, critics, publishers, and (in the case of Japan) translators of English science fiction in those two nations.

## Preview of the Chapters

This volume encompasses the entirety of Judith Merril's involvement in science fiction. It explores Merril's developing vision of science fiction as speculative fiction, a vision that emerged in the Cold War era, came to a head in the late 1960s, and took quite different forms in Canada and Japan in the 1970s and 1980s. Organized chronologically, the book is divided into two parts. Part One, "The Postwar Fiction," focuses on all Merril's fiction written during the 1940s and 1950s, while Part Two, "Shifting the Dimensions of Speculative Fiction," encompasses Merril's many additional roles in the field as collaborator, anthologist, and so much more. She wanted to change the world. The overall goal of this book is to supply a full, scholarly account of Merril's career in science fiction, placing her deservedly (with Isaac Asimov, Ray Bradbury, and Robert Heinlein) among the primary shapers of the field as we now know it.

Chapter 1 explains our critical framework for reading Merril's science fiction. Here, we argue that the Cold War period, when Merril was most active as a writer, saw a paradigm shift in the central mythology of American identity: the frontier myth. When a census in 1892 revealed that there was no longer an unbroken tract of "free" land in the American West, some observers saw this development as the end of the American Dream. With the potential of space travel and nuclear energy in the 1940s and 1950s, however, the promises of the American frontier — unlimited space and resources to fuel American expansion — were renewed. Just as women writers played an important but marginalized role in the production of the nineteenth- and early twentieth-century frontier mythology, we argue that Judith Merril's science fiction should be understood in the context of this larger trajectory of American frontier mythologists.

Chapter 2 explores the atomic frontier theme in Judith Merril's earliest fiction, as well as Merril's early career and radical politics in the 1940s and 1950s, in the context of discourses of atomic energy that drew from the deeply entrenched identification between nature and the feminine. Among these early stories of Merril's was the widely acclaimed "That Only a Mother" (1948) and her well-received novel *Shadow on the Hearth* (1950). This early fiction of Merril's was highly innovative in its departure from male-centered narratives of atomic energy as feminized nature, something to be harnessed and controlled. Instead, Merril imagined how individual women and ordinary families might be affected by the destructive power of nuclear energy.

Merril's pre–Apollo era space-travel fiction is the topic of Chapter 3; it overlaps with an account of her most prolific period as a fiction writer, 1952–1953, and her beginnings in 1956 as a noteworthy best-of-the-year series anthologist. This chapter also discusses Merril's need to keep and support her children from two divorces and considers how her situation as a mother informed both her productivity and the content of her near-future science fiction stories and novels. Merril privileged the role of the feminine in space travel and exploration by highlighting the importance of traditionally "feminine" virtues such as empathy, caregiving, and intuition in encounters with unfamiliar terrains and life-forms. Merril also suggested that constraints upon gender, sexuality, and reproduction — natural or social — were as subject to technological intervention and progress as the constraints of gravity upon the limits of human exploration.

Chapter 4 examines how another standard space-related theme, alien encounters, turns out in the hands of an anything-but-standard writer like Merril. Merril's alien figures call into question their underpinning ideologies of colonialism, race, and gender. Merril also explores links between women and alienness in stories such as "Rain Check" (1954) and "Exile from Space" (1956). Often focalized through the alien's point of view, Merril's narratives about aliens reverse the relationship between the "normal" subject and the "other" in order to expose the double standards and contradictions that often go hand-in-hand with inhabiting the female subject position.

Merril was fascinated by human psychology—psi, ESP, and telepathy in particular, and also their implications for human communication. Her stories on these themes are the subject of Chapter 5. Merril's stories of telepathy associate this ability with the feminine and represent it as a futuristic version of the forms of influence often attributed to women in frontier discourse. However, telepathy is not always a manipulative tool in Merril's writing: because telepathy breaks down the ego boundaries that isolate people from each other, especially men from women, it can help them communicate more honestly. Having experienced two difficult marriages and divorces early in her writing career, Merril had a very personal stake in this theme.

Merril's output as a solo writer, although significant, was relatively small compared to more prolific authors such as Asimov and Heinlein. However, when her additional activities and their impact are taken into account, her importance in the field of science fiction is undeniable. Part Two of our book details Merril's activities as collaborator, anthologist, and numerous additional roles in shifting the dimensions of science fiction.

In Chapter 6, we explore the crucial role of dialogue and collaboration in Merril's career. A collaborator by nature, Merril co-authored important novels with C.M. Kornbluth (as Cyril Judd) as well as short stories with him and several other prominent science fiction writers. She also promoted dialogues through her correspondence and push for professional standards in the field through workshops and in her work as an innovative anthologizer. With respect to the latter, we discuss her special, dialogic approach in determining what constituted a science fiction story and her distinctive style in framing the anthologies.

Although Merril stopped writing science fiction in the early 1960s, it was during that decade, discussed in Chapter 7, that she accomplished some of her best work as an editor, essayist, and influential reviewer for *Fantasy and Science Fiction*. This was also her London period, 1965 and 1966–1967, when she spent time with the editor and writers for the highly experimental British *New Worlds* magazine and produced her important collection of British "new wave" writing for American readers—*England Swings SF* (1968). Merril intentionally abdicated her leadership in 1968 and left the United States for a new, more socially and intellectually experimental life in Canada. This chapter also offers the first exploration of Merril's enthusiastic reception in Japan—where she spent time collaborating in the world of Japanese translation and avant-garde science fiction in the period 1970–1975, leading to her rekindled interest in science fiction as a revolutionary genre—and in Canada, her permanent home after 1968. In Toronto, she expanded her range of expertise as a communicator to become a documentarist and then emerged in the 1980s as an acclaimed founding figure in the Canadian world of science fiction and fantasy.

We come full circle in a sense in Chapter 8, which follows Merril's memoir project through the 1980s and 1990s. In failing health, she experimented endlessly with what stands, as we write, as the only book-length memoir by a female science fiction writer, and one of only a small number of autobiographies and memoirs ever produced in the science fiction field. To create this intricate and uniquely structured (and co-authored) study, Merril consulted her large collection of personal papers in Library and Archives Canada. Together with the extensive holdings of publications in the Merril Collection of Science Fiction, Speculation and Fantasy in Toronto, the Merril papers and works in print have been an invaluable resource for preparing this present book. Focusing on how Merril crafted her memoir around her correspondence and an eclectic range of other materials, we examine Merril's implied theories of life writing and the literary significance of her memoir — its representation of her lifelong drive to collaborate and experiment, to "change the world," and its success in recouping Merril's reputation as a science fiction writer and key innovator.

This volume is the first extensive account of Merril's contribution to science fiction from her early years as a science fiction author and anthologist to her later work as an editor and a critic, catalyst, and documentarist. Our most crucial goal, however, is to reverse the current erasure of Merril's contribution from the literary history of modern American science fiction. Our research has convinced us that Merril's undeniable impact on North American science fiction and speculative writing continues to resonate, yet she remains on the margins of most written accounts of post–World War II science fiction (when she is recognized at all). This striking exclusion suggests that something is amiss with the framework that currently shapes the literary history of women in American science fiction. On the one hand, a myth of the exclusion of women from science fiction before 1970 (which we discuss in detail in Chapter 1) cannot account for Merril's undeniable stature in the field, and so Merril does not figure prominently in feminist science fiction scholarship. On the other hand, Merril's accomplishments have been minimized in male-authored memoirs of post–World War II science fiction and in male-centered literary histories. Clearly, a more nuanced approach is needed in the study of science fiction as a gendered field that neither completely excludes nor completely welcomes women into its fold. This book works toward that goal through its attention to both the conditions in science fiction that enabled Merril's success and those conditions that have, over the years, led to her near-erasure from literary history.

# Part One

# The Postwar Fiction

CHAPTER 1

# Judith Merril and the Myth of the Frontier

Scientific research in space exploration and nuclear energy from the late 1940s through the late 1960s constituted a pivotal period in American history and culture because it had the potential to reopen the frontier "safety valve" of "free" land and other resources that, in the nineteenth century, had underwritten ideologies of limitless economic and geographical expansion. Following the 1890 U.S. Census, which reported that the western frontier was almost entirely settled, this foundational American ideal was relegated to fantasy until after the end of World War II, when the possibility of open frontiers seemed real again. This time, however, it was the Futurians, including Judith Merril, who became the new boosters — and critics — of frontier expansion. These links between science fiction and the American frontier have been explored by scholars such as Gary K. Wolfe (1989), David Mogen (Mogen 1982; Mogen and Mallett 1993), and, more recently, Carl Abbott (2005; see also Newell and Lamont 2005a). Patrick Sharp's *Savage Perils* (2007) traces frontier mythology through cultural representations of twentieth-century conflicts, including World War II and the Cold War nuclear frontier. Like Sharp, we see Cold War representations of the nuclear age as deeply implicated in a discourse of the frontier that can be traced to nineteenth-century theories of America's "exceptional" identity and we situate Merril's nuclear fiction in this context. To Sharp's analysis of the new, twentieth-century frontier, we add the frontier of outer space, in which Merril also played a pivotal role: If nineteenth-century westward expansion was an opportunity to regenerate civilization, as the historian Frederick Jackson Turner famously argued in 1893, Judith Merril deployed the new frontier of outer space to regenerate ideas about women and gender relations.

## Science Fiction and the Regeneration of American Frontier Mythology

Merril and many of her contemporaries began their careers as science fiction writers during a paradigm shift in the history of both American science fiction and American frontier mythology. While the Cold War sparked fears of an impending nuclear apocalypse, proponents of nuclear energy and space exploration were more optimistic about the future. These individuals countered that, for the first time since 1893, when Frederick Jackson Turner had famously declared that the American frontier had closed, new potential supplies of "free" resources emerged in the form of both energy and outer space. Real technological developments in both areas — the U.S. detonation of atomic bombs over Hiroshima and Nagasaki in 1945 and the launch of the German V2 rocket the previous year — shifted the stature of science fiction in American culture from that of the marginal pulp fantasy and escapism of the interwar years to a more authoritative, public discourse on the present, future, and alternative course of American history. Indeed, David Hartwell argues that the world since the 1940s has been "saturated" with science fiction ideas (Hartwell 1984, 111). Science fiction, we argue, became the new vehicle for a regenerated frontier mythology, predicated not on nostalgia for a long-gone frontier, but on the renewed possibility of a "safety valve" of limitless resources that would once again guarantee America's unique status as a nation of unlimited discovery, economic opportunity, and spatial expansion. Once regarded as sub-literary hacks, science fiction authors, led by the "big three"— Isaac Asimov, Arthur C. Clarke, and Robert A. Heinlein — emerged as cultural authorities whose writing spoke to future realities rather than juvenile escapist fantasies.

Our book is certainly not the first to make claims about a close relationship between American science fiction and American frontier myth. As Gary Westfahl (2000) observes, texts in which Westerns and science fiction explicitly overlap, dubbed "space operas," have long been denigrated as science fiction at its derivative worst (197). The term "space opera" is commonly understood as a pejorative label for a pulp magazine science fiction story typical of the interwar years that is too imitative of so-called horse operas or B-movie Westerns. However, a few critics have argued that the relationship between science fiction and the Western should be taken seriously. In his extended essay *Wilderness Visions: Science Fiction Westerns* (1982; see also Mogen and Mallett 1993), David Mogen examines the frontier experience in the work of a handful of prominent post–World War II male science fiction writers. Mogen speculates that the general belief about the frontier as being "an imaginary line between civilization and nature, or the uncreated future," explains why American science fiction so often conceives the future in terms of frontier analogies: "The frontier has simply moved to outer space, now that the historical frontier has been domesticated" (19). More importantly, he laments that "as yet there has been little discussion of connections between Westerns and science fiction that takes both traditions seriously" (8). Robert Murray Davis in "The Frontiers of the Genre" (1985) attempted to respond to this call, even suggesting that the commonalities and differences between the two genres produce a hybrid that allows authors to "play variations on well-worn themes," to "jolt readers out of generic expectations" (33–41). Recent postcolonial readings of science fiction by Sharon DeGraw (2009), Patricia Kerslake (2007), and John Rieder (2008) also acknowledge the genre's relationship to colonial and racial discourse, of which the popular Western was a central vehicle in the American context. Most recently, Patrick Sharp has argued that nineteenth-century myths of America's confrontation with savagery continue to underwrite the American identity well into the twenty-first century. Like Sharp, we argue for the particular importance of the Cold War period in the literary and cultural history of American frontier mythology, and of science fiction as a key vehicle for the circulation of discourses of a regenerated American frontier (Newell and Lamont 2005a, 2005b; Lamont and Newell 2009). Whereas women writers' instrumental contributions to nineteenth-century frontier mythology have, until recently, been overlooked in the paradigms that dominated scholarship on the frontier in American literature and culture, we want to ensure that women writers are included in the emergent scholarship of the twentieth-century nuclear- and space-age frontiers.

The future promised by the new, Cold War frontiers was double-edged. Although public anxiety about atomic technology was strong during the Cold War period, boosters of nuclear development, well documented by Spencer R. Weart (1988, 158–62), represented nuclear energy as an inflated version of a nineteenth-century frontier of so-called free land. For example, science reporter William Laurence prophesied in 1948 that "atomic energy could turn deserts and jungles into 'new lands flowing with milk and honey,' and, in sum, could 'make the dream of the earth as a Promised Land come true in time for many of us already born to see and enjoy it'" (quoted in Weart 1988, 158). Similarly, as David Wrobel has shown, economists, politicians, and other authorities during the nineteenth century argued that the frontier of "free land" meant that resources were there for anyone willing to claim a homestead (if they chose not to pursue that opportunity, the argument went, it was their own fault); hence economic prosperity was available to all worthy citizens (Wrobel 1993, 47). Science fiction was also rife with narratives of space colonization as a means of potentially escaping from social and economic pressures on Earth — sometimes from an atomically devastated Earth, a famous example of which is Ray

Bradbury's short story collection *The Martian Chronicles* (1950). Such narratives are extrapolations on the nineteenth-century concept of the American western frontier as a safety valve that relieved social tensions in the crowded American East. Indeed, the idea that expansion into outer space is the inevitable, fearless next step in American development remains prevalent in the present day within the rhetoric of such groups as the Space Frontier Foundation (SFF), whose website, as we write, is full of clichés from American frontier mythology, particularly its embrace of expansionist ideology and goals of limitless territorial and economic expansion:

> Our central goal is the large-scale permanent settlement of space. We believe people have the "right stuff" and that everyone will benefit from opening the space frontier. We believe that free markets and free enterprise will become an unstoppable force in the irreversible settlement of this new frontier, and that our world is on the verge of a truly historic breakthrough: cheap access to space [Space Frontier Foundation, home page].

That such groups see space colonization, rather than sustainability, as the solution to the problem of limited resources demonstrates the ongoing power of the frontier myth in American culture.

## Gender and Frontier Mythology

Central to American frontier mythology and its instantiation in science fiction are configurations of gender that are productive frameworks for understanding women's contributions to American science fiction during the 1950s and 1960s, the period of its consecration as a "legitimate" genre. As Annette Kolodny (1975) suggests in her feminist re-reading of frontier mythology, its central trope is that of the male explorer's penetration of a passive, feminized wilderness (6). Its "savage" inhabitants, also feminized (savagery and femininity are parallel categories in frontier mythology), are aligned with the landscape (nature) rather than with humanity (culture) (100) and are therefore a part of what must be tamed and domesticated in order for civilization to progress. The "master narrative" of science follows a virtually identical structure, with the pursuit of knowledge gendered as a masculine activity in search of its feminized object (Seed, quoted in Merrick 2003, 241).

In the postwar period, nuclear fission was represented through the same constructs of feminized nature that informed nineteenth-century frontier narratives: the explosive power at the core of an atom was likened to the savage nature lurking at the core of a woman. Like the nineteenth-century frontier depicted by historian Henry Nash Smith ([1950] 1970) and critiqued by

Kolodny (1975, 10–25), atomic energy was feminized — an offshoot of the classic identification between the maternal body and nature that Julia Kristeva (2000) suggests is foundational in Western culture. But the nuclear frontier was nature at her most unruly. As Kristina Zarlengo (1999) points out, the term "bombshell" (used to refer to sensuous women) was coined during the atomic age; the bikini bathing suit was named after the Pacific atom bomb test site Bikini Atoll, and pin-ups of scantily clad popular actresses were often literally attached to atom bombs and the planes that carried them. The passive yet sexually charged pin-up images of women such as the "anatomic bombshell" Linda Christian (as she appeared in a famous photo shoot in *Life* and in stock footage of disaster-formula B-movies) represented the explosive and potentially dangerous energy that lay dormant at the core of every atom (Zarlengo 1999, 946–47). Safely contained, nuclear energy would, like a good wife and mother, serve and regenerate mankind. One commentator of the postwar period equated nuclear technology with the regenerative power of the frontier, "a thing of sufficient challenge and possibility to give us endless incentive and the dignity that belongs to a race which pays its respects alike to Thomas Jefferson and Paul Bunyan" (quoted in Boyer 1985, 137). Uncontained atomic energy, on the other hand, was, like the undomesticated femme fatale, a threat to the very existence of civilization (Zarlengo 950). Commentators wrote that atomic war would "leave Earth 'a barren waste, in which the survivors of the race will hide in caves or live among ruins,'" and "obliterate all the great cities [and] bring industry and technology to a grinding halt" (quoted in Boyer 1985, 15). As we will show in Chapter 2, Judith Merril deploys this construction of femininity as contained, violent energy in her novel *Shadow on the Hearth*.

## *American Women Writers of Frontier Mythology*

In taking up frontier myths, American women writers claim authority over a central myth of American identity, the dominant forms of which represent femininity as an object, not a subject, of authority in the story of American development. It is not surprising, then, that women writers of frontier mythology tended from the outset to question dominant constructions of gender in frontier narrative. Kolodny argues in *The Land Before Her* (1984) that nineteenth-century women writers interpreted the journey west in terms of their domestic location. During what is sometimes called the Progressive Era (1880–1920), significant numbers of women writers, including Frances McElrath, B.M. Bower, and Caroline Lockhart, saw feminist potential in the Western's progressive and regenerative narrative arc (Lamont 2005, 31). For example, B.M. Bower's novel *Lonesome Land* depicts a western woman who learns self-reliance on the frontier, enabling her to leave an abusive marriage. It is in this historical trajectory that we locate the fiction of Judith Merril, who, like B.M. Bower and others, places women at the center of the frontier experience and deploys the frontier as a space in which to unsettle and revise traditional representations of gender.

The relationship that we suggest exists between women's Westerns and women's science fiction has been obscured by shifts in the cultural production of popular fiction in the United States. Various forces seemed to close down the feminist potential of the Western even as science fiction emerged as a new site for feminist experimentation. During the 1930s, popular fiction magazines became much more explicitly and firmly gendered than their predecessors. Fiction magazines such as Street & Smith's *Popular* originally attempted to appeal to a wide variety of tastes. Even Street & Smith's all–Western magazine *Western Story*, which debuted in 1919, addressed a mixed readership that included women in the editorial pages of its early issues ("Editorial Page" 1919, 128). Over the course of the 1930s, magazine publishers such as Street & Smith attempted to refine their target audiences, particularly in terms of gender; thus the Western was more aggressively marketed as male reading by male writers, while both women readers and writers were steered toward popular romance magazines for women such as *Romance Range*, which appeared in 1935 (Box 26, S&S). With the gendered branding of the Western in the 1930s, popular science fiction was the more welcoming vehicle for women writers of popular fiction who wanted to challenge gender norms, or at least not be defined as writers by their gender.

Although dominated by a masculine hegemony, American science fiction, as scholars of early twentieth-century science fiction have noted, may have been accessible to women because the genre encouraged transgression in terms of both content and production (Donawerth 2006, 26; Larbalestier 2002a; Newell and Lamont 2005a; Davin 2006; Yaszek 2004, 2006, 2008, 2009). By the early 1970s, Joanna Russ (1971b, 91) argued for the explicitly feminist possibilities of science fiction. However, Eric Leif Davin, Lisa Yaszek, and others have shown that historical accounts of science fiction before the feminist "second wave" (by everyone from Brian Aldiss, Martin H. Greenberg, and James Gunn to Sarah Lefanu and Shawna McCarthy) have suggested, incorrectly, that women had virtually no role in science fiction before the 1970s (Davin 2006, 2–3, 55–57; Yaszek 2008). "This exclusion narrative," Davin writes, "is nothing but mythology which has been accepted, unquestioned, in both academic and non-academic worlds" (2). And he adds, "But the genre never 'changed' to allow the entrance of women. The door had always been open and women had always been active participants" (57). Thus, in his recent study *Partners in Wonder* (2006), Davin provides the valuable work of surveying the writings of 203 known women science fiction authors from before 1960. Justine Larbalestier (2002a) has also documented a very large and enticing opening for women in science fiction created through the fan culture that grew up around the genre even before World War II, and that encouraged women's participation in the iconic science fiction conventions, fan magazines ("fanzines"), and letter columns in the science fiction magazines. Then there was a proliferation of science fiction and fantasy magazines, growing from a handful in the 1930s to over forty by the end of the 1950s, not to mention the shift in popularity in the 1950s from magazine fiction to paperback books. In addition to the specialty houses that published science fiction and fantasy, such as Ballantine Books and Ace Books, science fiction lists were established by half a dozen or more mainstream publishing houses, such as Doubleday, Scribner's, Random House, and Simon and Schuster (Larbalestier 2002b, 284–85; see also Yaszek 2008).

Brian Attebery suggests that other changes in American science fiction in the 1950s — such as the rise of a separate category for juvenile science fiction, thus leading to a separate category for an adult market — led to a partial breakdown in sexual taboos in the writing, which in turn made gender markings in science fiction more visible (2002, 6). This may help explain Merril's claim that she had in the late 1940s and the 1950s been specifically encouraged by magazine editors such as John W. Campbell Jr. to produce stories from a "woman's point of view," whatever that meant. Following World War II, Merril and dozens of other American women penned space operas and other subcategories of science fiction stories for magazines such as *Amazing Stories, Fantastic Universe, Future, If, Imagination, Infinity, Marvel Science Stories, Other Worlds, Planet Stories, Science Fiction Adventures, Space, Space Travel, Startling Stories, Thrilling Wonder, Universe Science Fiction, Venture, Wonder Stories, Worlds Beyond, Worlds of Tomorrow,* and, in the premier leagues, *Astounding Science-Fiction, Galaxy Science Fiction,* and *The Magazine of Fantasy and Science Fiction.* Science fiction was also published in mainstream magazines such as *Blue Book, Collier's, Esquire, Good Housekeeping, Playboy, Redbook, Saturday Evening Post,* and Canada's *Maclean's.* With the solidifying of gender categories for popular fiction in the twentieth century, adventuresome women writers in the 1940s and 1950s — occasionally (but not necessarily) writing under gender-ambiguous or gender-neutral names such as Leigh Brackett, M.A. Cummings, T.D. Hamm, F. Tennyson Jesse, D.E. Kaye, Dana Lyon, C.L. Moore, Andre Norton, M.J. Nuttall, Leslie Perri, M.F. Rupert, Idris Seabright, Wilmar H. Shiras, G.B. Stern, Francis Stevens, and Leslie F. Stone — would find in science fiction a strikingly similar form of cultural work to that of pre–1930 women Western writers.

## After Hiroshima: The Nuclear Frontier

If I return so insistently to the magnitude of the peril [...]* it is because I see in that our one great hope [...] as a vast threat, and a new one, to all the peoples of the earth, by its novelty, its terror, its strangely promethean quality, it has become, in the eyes of many of us, an opportunity unique and challenging [Oppenheimer 1946, 9].

[Gladys] walked over and picked up the chopper, trying to remember whether it had been hers, wondering if she had reached such a pitch of excitement that she could have thrown it unawares. The worst thing was being unable to remember. She didn't know whether she had used a knife. She raised her fingers to the hole in the wall, exploring its contours curiously, feeling what the chopper would have done if it had hit the man [Merril 1950, *Shadow on the Hearth*, 171].

The bombing of Hiroshima engendered in many members of the Anglo-American science fiction community a certain glow of self-congratulation for having predicted a world-changing scientific development. The British science fiction writer Brian Aldiss captures this "glow" in his introduction to *Hell's Cartographers: Some Personal Histories of Science Fiction Writers*: "Whatever else the A-bomb meant to Eartherly and all the rest of mankind, to a small handful of us it meant vindication. We who had been regarded as mad were proved dangerously sane. The Future had happened, and blown the lid off the Old Order" (1975, 2; see also Seed 1999; Bartter 1988; Larbalestier and Merrick 2003; Newell 2003; Newell and Lamont 2005b; Yaszek 2008). It was in this context that Merril had joined the Futurians in the mid–1940s. However, unlike other Futurians, Merril situated the nuclear debate in a woman-centered context, depicting in her novel *Shadow on the Hearth*, for example, a housewife who rises to the nuclear challenge by defending her home from looters during a nuclear attack.

In much science fiction of the atomic age, including Merril's, the post-atomic frontier is represented as the modern version of American civilization's ongoing cyclical encounter with savagery. For Richard Slotkin (1998), a *temporary* regression into savagery was, according to the myth of the frontier, a necessary prerequisite for ultimate progress, for the confrontation with savagery regenerated the civilized subject, who, through the experience, learned to recognize and subdue the savage within himself (12–14). During the Cold War era, Slotkin argues, U.S. interventions in the affairs of foreign governments, the McCarthy hearings into domestic threats to the Cold War order, blacklists, and loyalty oaths, along with other undemocratic initiatives to combat communism at home, were similarly justified — in both government policy debate and popular culture — as the period of regression that had been

---

*Most ellipses are from Merril's original text; bracketed ellipses throughout indicate omission of text from Merril quotes and quotes from others.

the prerequisite for progress since the earliest colonial encounters with American Indians (428–32). In this respect, little had changed between the 1820s and the 1950s: in James Fenimore Cooper's time, savagery was seen as lurking in the depths of his feminized, uncivilized landscapes and posing a perpetual threat to the women and children of an infant civilization; in the 1950s, the savage, regenerative power lurking on the nuclear frontier and at the core of every atom (and embedded in the era's new emphasis on youth culture) was a constant threat to the "normal" suburban American home and family.

## The New Reality of the Space Frontiers

> The sky is an endless dome of very clear and very blue glass. The innumerable sand hillocks of the desert are real only directly underfoot. The one you stand on is about 5 feet high and difficult to climb, and so are the others for 30 or 40 feet around. But beyond that distance they seem to be shallower and the dusty green sagebrush that grows on these hillocks does not look quite so dusty and dead. Underfoot you have whitish-yellow sand, brownish-yellow sand and the dusty green of the plants; in the distance there is just a faint impression of yellowish-white, overlaid with a greenish tinge [Ley 1949, 17].

A much more unambiguously optimistic strand of Cold War frontier mythology emerged when space travel became a real possibility in the American public imagination during the 1950s. Like the popular Western of the early twentieth century, science fiction in the 1950s constituted a response to a profound historical development: when the 1890 U.S. Census reported that the American frontier was "closed," the news was interpreted with foreboding by Frederick Jackson Turner. In his view, the western frontier was the source of America's power and uniqueness. Many classic Westerns of the twentieth century responded to this crisis of national identity with nostalgia for this "lost" frontier and cynicism about the future of a frontier-less American society. In the preface to his classic novel *The Virginian* (1902), Owen Wister lamented, "What is to become of the horseman, the cowpuncher, the last romantic figure upon our soil? [...] A transition has followed the horseman of the plains, a shapeless state, a condition of men and manners unlovely" (10). The same nostalgic loss is expressed in the well-known ending to Jack Shaefer's *Shane* (1949), in which the cowboy-hero's departure leaves us longing for his return:

> I strained my eyes after him, and then in the moonlight I could make out the inalienable outline of his figure receding into the distance. Lost in my loneliness, I watched him go, out of town, far down the road where it curved out to the level country beyond the valley. There were men on the porch behind me, but I was aware only of that dark shape growing small and indistinct along the far reach of the road [264].

Whereas the popular Western commemorates the lost frontier, the space frontier regenerates the frontier myth by providing limitless new territory for future conquest. Although narratives about travel to outer space were certainly nothing new by the post–World War II period, what *was* new was that space travel had become a scientific possibility. As Marina Benjamin explains in *Rocket Dreams* (2003), the 1950s was a period in which the conquest of space was regarded as not just possible but also inevitable. Classic works of popular science — such as *The Conquest of Space* (1949), written by the German American Willy Ley, and *The Exploration of Space* (1951), by the British science fiction writer Arthur C. Clarke — described space travel as the next logical step in the progressive technological track that America was already on.

A successful popularizer in the 1940s and 1950s of space flight, Ley, a rocket scientist, was an avid reader of science fiction, regular attendee at meetings of the Hydra Club, and contributor of essays and a regular science column to the top science fiction magazines of the day. For two years beginning in 1952, *Collier's* ran a series of articles in which top scientists, Ley among them, predicted that large-scale space colonization was imminent. In 1955, a television documentary produced by Walt Disney predicted that manned rockets would be tested within ten years. The Soviet Union's launch of the world's first artificial satellite *Sputnik-1* in 1957 led to a further surge in support for an American tax-funded space program, which would launch in 1963 (Benjamin 2003, 38–41). These developments fostered the perception that America was once again a frontiering nation; indeed, as Benjamin has pointed out, in the early years of the U.S. Apollo program in the 1960s, the Moon was deemed to be only a first step in the new era of space travel. One developer even attempted to found a suburb of Cape Canaveral, christened Rocket City, which was to service the future intergalactic space travel (Benjamin, 8). In *Conquest of Space*, Ley matter-of-factly set out the scientific basis for future space travel from the Moon to the outer reaches of the solar system. His opening paragraph, quoted at the beginning of this section, minutely describes a dusty desert landscape before narrowing in on the space rocket that is about to launch, signifying a seamless continuity between this western American, sagebrush-filled location and travel to outer space.

## *Domesticity and the Space Frontier*

American frontier mythology is underwritten by the gendered construction of its key categories: a feminized landscape to be conquered through masculine activity and ingenuity, which, paradoxically, ushers in an equally feminized civilization. Because men and women are positioned very differently in relation to this discourse, many critics have argued for attention to differences between men's and women's writing about the frontier. Early gender scholarship on women's writing about the American West — led by Kolodny —

suggested that, because of women's different position in American culture, their Western fantasies were, in comparison to male fantasies, more appreciative of the beauty of the landscape, less inclined to master it, and structured by narratives of peaceful domestication rather than violent conquest (Kolodny 1984, 3–13). Lillian Schlissel makes similar observations about frontier women's diaries, observing that they were more likely to depict indigenous Americans as helpful guides than hostile enemies (1982, 140). However, later scholarship on the topic, including Anne McClintock's *Imperial Leather* (1995) and Brigitte Georgi-Findlay's *Frontiers of Women's Writing* (1996), takes a more critical stance on the function of "domesticity" in frontier discourse, noting in particular its function in the western colonial project. These studies equate the domestic with the familial, home, and private sphere — realms typically gendered as feminine. Most significantly for the purposes of this study, Amy Kaplan in "Manifest Domesticity" (1998) argues for a destabilized, more dynamic and less essentializing definition of American domesticity that takes into account its role in nineteenth-century American territorial expansion. In nineteenth-century America, domesticity was not only constructed in relation to the unbounded public sphere — sometimes identified with the frontier — but also defined the relationship between the (domestic) nation and the foreign territories incorporated by its expansion. Nineteenth-century domestic discourse represented national expansion as a double maneuver involving both the domestication of alien territory and the assimilation of the "foreigners" incorporated into the nation as a result of that expansion. For Kaplan, the international dimension of female influence "helps separate gendered spheres coalesce in the imperial expanse of a nation by redrawing domestic borders against the foreign that lurk inside and outside its ever shifting borders" (602). In this context, domestic women's more sympathetic portrayal of American Indians (the indigenous foreign) can be read as a troubling manifestation of women's assimilating role rather than an expression of the shared experience of patriarchal and racial oppression.

Women writers of Westerns, such as Frances McElrath, invoked the "civilizing" power of women in narratives that held up women's authority as a solution to conflicts, an alternative to the violent confrontation between "good" and "evil" that marked the dominant version of the genre. In *The Rustler* (1902), Francis McElrath depicts a haughty eastern lady who travels west and, through her frontier experience, learns that her real authority as a woman lies not in her beauty and status but in her power as a social reformer of cattle rustlers. Popular Western writers also saw gender relations as part of what the westward movement would regenerate in eastern civilization; hence the familiar story, most famously recounted in *The Virginian*, of the snobbish schoolmarm who falls in love with a cowboy beneath her socially, but above her in terms of his "natural" qualities. Here civilization is regenerated in the sense that its central institution — the family — is returned to a basis in "natural" attraction rather than artificial social affiliations.

In science fiction narratives of space travel by Merril, these patterns are iterated in fascinating ways: whereas frontier mythology figured the regenerative westward journey as a return to natural law, Merril's narratives of the space frontier emphasized how science and technology would mean that gender roles and relationships were freed once and for all from biological determinism. Hence, her fiction speculates on the various ways in which social relations on a spaceship might be directed and managed using new social science tools from psychology and sociology in order to best serve the goals of space colonization. If, in the nineteenth century, the arrival of women marked the entry of civilization into the wilderness, Merril also saw women playing a central role in space colonization, but in more active ways than those shown in nineteenth-century frontier narratives, in which women typically are not the first to enter the frontier. For Merril, women's psychological makeup and reproductive role made them *more* suited than men to the confinement of space travel *and* enabled them to populate new worlds. At a time when many fans loudly objected to "feminine" content in science fiction (Larbalestier 2002a, 104–43), Merril, along with female science fiction writers such as Leigh Brackett, C.L. Moore, and Marion Zimmer Bradley, unabashedly figured the spaceship as a domestic, woman- and even family-centered space.

## Science Fiction and Colonialism

Science fiction criticism is only just beginning to grapple with the genre's legacy as a narrative of colonization and empire that, despite its claims to be a free-thinking, anti-establishment genre, reiterates many damaging categories of colonial discourse — including the oppositions between self and other, civilization and savagery, human and alien (or other), subject and object — in its figurations of alien planets and life forms. In American frontier mythology, the figuration of indigenous people as "savage" did not merely reflect colonial attitudes but actually did the work of colonialism by identifying indigenous people in ways that justified their displacement, extermination, or assimilation: as primarily animal in nature and therefore not rightful "owners" of the land they occupied, as remnants of man's savage origins whose demise was an inevitable aspect of the progress of "civilization," and, at best, as children in need of protection until they could be assimilated into the "superior" white civilization. At worst, they were considered not even present at all: the land, as in the case of Australia, was by colonial fiat declared *terra nullius*—"empty." Much popular science fiction, as Sierra S. Adare has noted, furthers this cultural work by imagining futures in which indigenous people play a stereotypical role at best, or are even rendered invisible (2005, 6–7).

The relationship between colonial constructions of indigeneity and the category of the alien in science fiction is abundantly clear, but nonetheless has not until recently been scrutinized in science fiction critique. Recent critical commentary on science fiction and colonialism includes John Rieder's 2008 study *Colonialism and the Emergence of Science Fiction*, in which he demonstrates that science fiction and colonial narratives are related in fascinating and not altogether straightforward ways.

Privileged Anglo-American women were complicit in the colonial enterprise during the nineteenth century because of their roles as loving inculcators of proper morals and values and also because of their "innate" skills at translation and communication: their very presence in the American West was represented as integral to the process of domesticating both the land and its "wild" occupants. Merril echoes this essentialist construct in stories that represent feminine figures as better equipped to communicate across boundaries of difference. In "Homecalling" (1956), a horrific-looking giant termite telepathically conveys its motherly love to an orphaned human child, and in *Outpost Mars* (1952, co-authored with C.M. Kornbluth under the joint pen name Cyril Judd), it takes a woman to telepathically detect aliens on Mars despite all the scientific proof to the contrary from Mars colony officials. And while Merril also shares with other science fiction writers of her day the seeming inability to imagine a future Earth that is anything but white and Anglo-American, her stories just as often turn the critical gaze onto the self rather than the other during cross-cultural encounters. Thus, Merril's human space explorers and colonists are often unable to understand or even recognize forms of intelligence that differ too much from their own self-image — often, as in "The Lonely" (1963), with disastrous consequences for their own survival. These discourses of colonialism overlap with those of gender in much of Merril's fiction. In two stories narrated from the point of view of alien visitors to Earth, Merril defamiliarizes her contemporary American society through an alien's attempts to adapt to and pass quietly within it. That these alien figures choose to "pass" as women further signifies an overlap between concepts of alienness and femininity that enables Merril to defamiliarize the position of women as "outsiders" in American society. Hence Merril explores and unsettles traditional patterns of both colonization and gender.

## Women and Literary History

The links between the history of American frontier mythology and that of postwar American science fiction have been obscured, first, by the sharpening of generic boundaries through the "branding" of popular fiction in the first half of the twentieth century, and second, by the denigration of "space operas"—narratives in which the relationship between Westerns and science fiction is explicit and that are therefore considered imitative and derivative, the "worst" of science fiction. As a result, we do not have a clear picture of the role that science fiction has played in a much longer tradition of representing American national identity. We have an even foggier picture of the important role that women writers have played as makers of this mythology, not necessarily because their roles have been marginal but more likely because women writers have simply not been memorialized—through reprints, anthologies, biographies, critical bibliographies, and so on—to the extent that male writers have been. (Joanna Russ's 1983 study of the erasure of women's writings in literary history in general, *How to Suppress Women's Writing*, has exposed a wealth of women's work that has been lost, erased from history, and its influence forgotten.) A case in point: B.M. Bower published over 40 Westerns over the course of her 40-year career and was as popular as her male contemporary Zane Grey. But when Bower died in 1940, only months after Grey, her reputation died with her, whereas Grey's work remained in print, was widely anthologized, and became the focus of scholarly studies of the Western form. Setting aside the question of how much this imbalance has to do with the quality of these authors' fiction, impact alone justifies considerably more attention to Bower's work than it has received since her death. The same pattern appears to be repeating itself in the wake of the death of Merril in the late 1990s: she simply has not received anywhere near the recognition of male contemporaries such as Isaac Asimov and Frederik Pohl, despite her undeniable achievements as a groundbreaking writer and influential editor, mentor, and experimentalist. In recovering the fiction of Judith Merril, the focus of the remaining chapters in Part One, we strive to arrest the process whereby women writers' contributions to American culture are erased.

CHAPTER 2

# Atomic Frontier and the Advent of a Writer

Fueled always by her activism, Judith Merril believed in the power (and obligation) of science fiction to imagine alternative or probable futures:

> When I was writing s-f, I was in a sense trying to translate visions of possible futures for people trapped in concepts of the past — or trying to translate what I perceived as realities of the present (by means of images of the future, cast in literary forms of the past!) to people whose present-realit[ies] were different from mine [Merril, "Essay on Translation," 4a (transcript), 1972, 32, MP].

A reality throughout her youth and adult life was involvement in political movements. Born into "an intense, but non-religious, Jewish background," with a mother who was a suffragette, an ardent, idealistic Social Democrat, and a New York Zionist, Merril experimented as a teenager at Bronx High School with the very social brand of Trotskyism that existed in the 1930s, joining the Young People's Socialist League (YPSL). She married a fellow YPSLer, Danny Zissman, in 1940 when she was seventeen and just out of high school. She parlayed that sense of resistance to imperialism into her science fiction and engagement with the New York Futurians in the late 1940s as well as the anti–Vietnam War movement in the United States and Canada in the late 1960s and 1970s. In the 1970s, she was active in the Toronto citizens' peace group Hiroshima-Nagasaki Relived, which was formed in 1975 on the thirtieth anniversary of the U.S. atomic bombing of Japan. In Canada, she was also involved in the free university movement and an alternative high school, the founding of a major public library for science fiction and fantasy, and the Writers' Union of Canada, as well as broader human rights issues such as the movement to aid U.S. draft resisters and anti-censorship campaigns. Merril saw science fiction as the ideal vehicle for engaging her politics in her creative writing. In Cold War America, she once recalled, the science fiction magazine and paperback novel "provided the only widely read medium for protest and dissent in a witch-hunted country" (1968 [1967], "Introduction," 5).

Merril had come to science fiction by way of the popular Western: aside from a few detective stories, both fiction and fact, written for *Crack Detective* (1945–1946) (mostly as Judy Zissman, her married name at the time, but also as Jo Daniels and "Georgie"), and fiction and fact stories for sports magazines such as *Big Book Sports, Sports Action, Sports Leaders,* and *Sports Short Stories* (as Ernest Hamilton or Eric Thorstein) (Cummins 2006, 41–42), Merril's earliest genre stories — both as a ghost writer producing "unusual fact" material on the Old West and as a writer, "pulp-style," of regular features for different books and magazines — were written mostly for the Western pulps. These narratives included tall tales out of the Old West, "Injun" stories, and stories of the "Real West," the "Working West," and the law (on the topics of frontier justice, vigilantes, and railroad wars).

For these regular columns, Merril wrote under various bylines: "Cowpoke," "El Amigo," "Georgie," "Judge Colt," "The Pilgrim," "Rawhide," and "Uncle Bob" (Cummins 2006, 59–60). Using the pseudonyms Ernest Hamilton and Eric Thorstein, she published a few dozen stories in *Blue Ribbon Western, Cowboy, Double Action Western, Famous Western, Real Western Romances,* and *Western Action* pulp magazines (Cummins 2006, 41–42, 46, 58–60). Given the connections between science fiction and the popular Western that we have argued for thus far, and her association with the Futurians, it is not surprising that Merril wanted to make the move from the pulp Western to science fiction. In the pulp Western, she was churning out text to make money; in science fiction, however, she was learning to craft a story, and she found in this genre a more powerful vehicle for activist politics, such as contesting patterns of gender in frontier mythology, increasingly manifest in the 1940s and 1950s in narratives about atomic technology.

## Nuclear Technology and Ideas About Women and the Home

Atomic bombs were revolutionary, not only militarily but also for their impact on Cold War domestic life, especially the role of the family, as research touched off by historian Elaine Tyler May's pioneering study *Homeward Bound: American Families in the Cold War Era* (1988) reveals. That research identifies a general expectation in 1950s America that parents, particularly mothers, would shoulder responsibility for creating normal families and stable homes to foster a Cold War consensus against various ideological and physical threats. Patriotism became equated with domesticity. Stephanie Coontz in *The Way We Never Were* (1992) argues further that in Cold War America, a stable, "'normal' family and vigilant mother became the essential 'front line' of defense to treason" (33). According to Kristina Zarlengo, of the several new and contradictory ideas of femininity fitted to the atomic age, the domestic female expert in civilian defense was as prominent as her opposite: the female bombshell. Public information campaigns encouraged all atomic-age mothers to imagine themselves as warriors in training, and women and children were hailed as the new class of soldiers—"deterrence soldiers" (Zarlengo 1999, 930, 940).

A portrait of the artist as a young science fiction writer. Merril in the mid–1940s. Reproduced from *Aloud Magazine* (Judith Merril issue), October 1992, page 7, with permission of the Merril Estate.

Women science fiction writers in the 1950s responded accordingly. In *Galactic Suburbia* (2008), Lisa Yaszek demonstrates how women science fiction writers, including Merril, Helen Reid Chase, and Alice Eleanor Jones, who privileged domestic settings and the mundane details of everyday life, did so not out of conformity to dominant ideologies of womanhood, but precisely because women's roles in the home had assumed central importance in debates about America's emerging technological identity (4–5; see also Yaszek 2006).

In this chapter, we further this reconsideration about what was once dismissed in the 1970s by a later influential feminist writer and critic, Joanna Russ, as "galactic suburbia" (1971a, 81) and "Ladies magazine fiction" (88), and by Merril's contemporary, Damon Knight, as the "sweat-tears-and-baby-urine variety" (1967, 120). We focus in particular on the double-edged promise of nuclear technology and its intersections with ideas about women and the home.

Merril describes in her own memoirs how she and other young mothers adapted to their husbands' absences during the war — and experienced a sense of liberation in the process — as they experimented with new family roles and structures that did not depend on male authority. When her first husband, Zissman, got drafted and shipped out with his naval unit toward the end of the war, Merril and her toddler found a place, together with fellow Futurian

Virginia Kidd, in an old tenement building west of Greenwich Village in New York, where they rented low-priced adjoining flats, knocking out the party wall in one of their closets to surreptitiously create an eight-room apartment that encompassed an entire floor of the building.

Sharing all the chores with each other and sending their toddlers to a neighborhood nursery school for working mothers, Merril and Kidd worked on occasional writing jobs at home to supplement their meager income as military wives, and they also worked at serious writing (Merril and Pohl-Weary 2002, 49–58). As was Futurian practice, they gave the place a Futurian clubhouse name: the Parallax. The Parallax became central to the Futurians for meetings and weekly communal debates and dinners, for which the two women did the planning and shopping; everyone else pitched in with the cooking, the cleanup and the cost. Merril remembered it as a sort of bohemian existence: "Living with Virginia was lots of fun against the backdrop of great intellectual stimulation, caring for children, coping with relationships, buying groceries, and all those things that are part of everyday life of a single working mother. [...] We lived a marvelous Parisian existence in our apartment" (56). Both Merril and Kidd left their marriages shortly after their husbands returned from military service — Merril and Zissman's relationship had changed, for she wanted to be a "working writer" and still thought of herself as a revolutionary, while she found that he had become more ambitious and conservative due to his time in the military — and both women quickly remarried Futurians (Frederik Pohl and James Blish, respectively) and launched successful careers in science fiction.

Merril's earliest science fiction capitalized on new roles for both women and science fiction in the emergent climate of Cold War. In mythological terms, American civilization was, in the aftermath of World War II, in a period of recovery from encounters with savagery. In the logic of frontier mythology drawn by Richard Slotkin and discussed in Chapter 1, savage acts of war were sometimes necessary to the regeneration of American civilization. Now, however, America needed to recover, and middle-class American women played a vital role in this recovery by cultivating the discourse of normalcy with which "fifties" middle-class American culture is widely identified. A return to normalcy — that is, a rational, reasonable state of mind in which the bodily instincts and primal emotions such as anger or grief are kept in check — would complete the cycle of regeneration.

Elaine Tyler May has documented the particular rise in authority during the Cold War period of "experts," particularly in the mental health professions, whose advice was often geared toward keeping sexual energy in check and maintaining a balanced emotional state (109–12, 178). Women were instrumental to this process both as wives to war veterans recovering from the trauma of war (64) and mothers whose influence over their children was both

Prominent science fiction writers in the Futurian Society of New York. From left: Lester del Rey, Evelyn Harrison, Harry Harrison, Isaac Asimov, Judith, Ann Pohl (in Judith's tummy), Frederik Pohl, Poul Anderson, L. Sprague de Camp, P. Schuyler Miller, New York, 1950. Reproduced from Judith Merril and Emily Pohl-Weary, *Better to Have Loved: The Life of Judith Merril* (Toronto: Between the Lines, 2002), page 275, courtesy of the Merril Estate.

profound and easily misdirected (93). However, this idealization of normalcy conflicted with other ideologies long associated with American frontier mythology, including individualism and progressivism, both of which privileged individual leadership and nonconformity. Normalcy was also at odds with the innovation and change necessary for American society to regenerate and progress.

## Merril's Contributions to the Atomic Frontier Theme

Merril's post-atomic fiction works through these tensions by focusing on the implications of nuclear technology for the seat of American normalcy: the middle-class home. Her celebrated first science fiction story, "That Only a Mother" (1948), deals with the threat that radiation-caused mutations will pervert "normal" biological processes. By this point, Merril was mystery and science fiction editor at Bantam Books and had just co-founded the Hydra Club in New York with Pohl, whom she would marry in November of the next year. Her novel *Shadow on the Hearth* (1950) takes place shortly after World War II, during the hours following an atomic attack on the United States, and stresses the idea that normal domestic routines and relationships should not be abandoned in the event of atomic war and radioactive fallout — they are a mother's crucial means of preserving civilization against the ravages of war. Both works are set in the near future. Both of them represent the atomic age as a period of regeneration following the savage war, and both construct normalcy in opposition to savagery.

## *"That Only a Mother" (1948)*

"That Only a Mother" is the celebrated short story that launched Merril's career in science fiction. Written about the mother of a child born deformed because of atomic radiation, the story was rejected as too scandalous by mainstream magazines, but was published in June 1948 in the leading science fiction magazine of the day, John Campbell's *Astounding Science Fiction*, to high praise; it became a classic in the field and remains one of Merril's most warmly regarded and most anthologized and translated stories, enshrined over the years in canonical anthologies along with stories by other members of what would become the science fiction establishment. Two decades after its original publication, Robert Silverberg selected it for the inaugural volume of his *Science Fiction Hall of Fame* (1970), Pamela Sargent chose it for her pioneering anthology *Women of Wonder* (1975), and, most recently, Robin Wayne Bailey included it in *Architects of Dreams* (2003). Frederik Pohl called it "a brilliant twisty-dismaying short story [...] that gets right into the glands and squeezes basic parts of the psyche" (1978, 173). And Lisa Yaszek's recent work on maternalist politics and postwar women's nuclear holocaust narratives places it on the front lines of women's nuclear war storytelling (2008, 114–17), by which she means authors who "combin[ed] two distinct twentieth-century literary traditions: the nuclear holocaust narrative and feminist anti-war writing" (113; see also Newell and Lamont 2005b).

Set during a relatively "clean" atomic war in a fictional 1953, a young military wife gives birth to her child while her husband — a nuclear engineer who has been working at the Oak Ridge atomic enrichment plant — is now away at war, in the midst of a widespread social panic over post–Hiroshima-Nagasaki, radiation-induced birth defects. The idea came to Merril in 1947, when she read a short article buried in the *New York Herald-Tribune* (and mentioned in her story) about the U.S. Army of Occupation in Japan denying rumors about infanticides occurring in the areas affected by the U.S. atomic bombs in 1945. The article reported that the rise in infanticide in Japan had no connection to the presence of atomic "fallout mutations" in that country

(Merril 1968, "Introduction," 7). This implausible claim set Merril's postholocaust story in motion: "[A lot of us were worried] about the much more insidious after effects — the cancers and leukemias that might follow years later for apparently untouched survivors; the lingering radioactivity; the sterility and mutations which might affect plants and animals and people in the aftermath" (1973, "Prologue," 5).

Part of Merril's story is narrated in epistolary form, through letters and telegrams exchanged between the main character, Margaret Marvell, and her husband Hank. In the letters, "Maggie" assures Hank that their newborn baby girl, Henrietta, is normal: "It's all there, darling, eyes, ears, and noses — no, only one! — all in the right places" (1948, "That Only a Mother," 91). Margaret's letters continue to document the child's progress, particularly her rapidly advancing verbal skills. By the age of seven months, Margaret reports that the child has all of her front teeth and can not only speak clearly but also sing. While Margaret responds to these abnormalities as if they are normal — advanced, to be sure, but normal — objective narration reveals a few months later the slightly more disturbing reality of a child with the helpless body of a ten-month-old, but the brain of a four-year-old. Despite constant news reports about nuclear-caused mutations in babies, and of crazed fathers committing infanticide in response, Margaret continues to see her own child as normal, and her doting mother's denial emerges as even more disturbing than the threat of atomic mutation itself. As Elaine Tyler May points out, Cold War mothers like Margaret, who doted on their children too much, were popularly considered to be as harmful as negligent ones (73).

When Hank finally returns to meet his now ten-month-old baby girl, we learn the extent of Margaret's apparent delusion: holding his baby for the first time, Hank discovers that she has no arms or legs. In shock, he asks Margaret why she hadn't told him of this in her letters, but Margaret does not understand the question. Hank is horrified: "*She didn't know. His hands, beyond control, ran up and down the soft-skinned baby body, the sinuous limbless body. Oh God, dear God—* his head shook and his muscles contracted in a bitter spasm of hysteria. His fingers tightened on his child—*Oh God, she didn't know*" (95).

The relationship between this story and frontier mythology is subtle, but significant. First of all, the nature of the child's mutations — an advanced brain coupled with an armless and legless body — are meaningful in the context of frontier mythology and the notion of species progression. In classic frontier texts such as James Fenimore Cooper's Leatherstocking Tales series, "advanced" humans are distinguished by superior intellects, while "savage" humans are identified with the body — they have more finely tuned instincts, and their bodies are generally more powerful. Civilized subjects make up for what they lack in instinct and bodily power through their intellectual facility with technology, particularly firearms. Hence, Cooper's iconic frontier hero Natty Bumppo is renowned for his marksmanship.

John Rieder has shown how this notion of embodiment gets taken up in early science fiction in the form of narratives about large-brained creatures with underdeveloped bodies, the precursors to robots and cyborgs, figures that represent in a disturbing way the ascendance of technology over humanity (2008, 113–17). Merril's "big-brained" baby is similarly as much a product of technology as of the natural union of Margaret and Hank — indeed, Hank's horrified reaction upon the discovery of his child's mutation mimics that of a stereotypical father discovering that his wife's child is not his own, which is certainly the case insofar as Hank's child is also the offspring of nuclear technology. That the child is a girl is a departure from the villainous and masculine aliens Rieder describes and troubles the "normal" distinctions between rational masculinity and natural femininity: If this child is more mind than body, then in what sense can she be female in terms of the dominant discourse of gender? Henrietta's "mutation" disturbs the very foundation upon which gendered identity is based.

More disturbing to Hank than the mutation itself is Margaret's inability (or refusal) to "know" about Henrietta's abnormal body and mind. One obvious reading of the story is that Margaret's motherly devotion overtakes her to the point of delusion, confronting readers, like Hank, with the uncanny specter of female hysteria. Thus, the release of atomic energy disturbs the natural order not only in terms of biological reproduction but also in terms of the behavior of mothers, whose devotion reaches an unnatural excess. At first, this seems to be the case: Margaret had difficulty getting pregnant in the first place, which she suspects was due to Hank's prior exposure to radiation. Once pregnant, "a dialogue takes place between Margaret's fears and hopes," as David Seed puts it, about the baby's condition, and the constant ellipses in Margaret's internal monologue suggest the "unverbalized fears" she suppresses (1999, 55). However, once the child arrives, Margaret's response to Henrietta's body is explicitly described not as a form of denial but as a lack of "knowing," which is a different order of perception than denial, in keeping with how Marxist theory describes our perception of naturalized social constructs: we see them as natural, as that which goes without saying, as "reality" itself. In this sense, Margaret is not so much deluded as she is interpellated into a different version of "normal" than her husband, one that is triggered by the condition of motherhood itself. She does not say anything to Hank about Henrietta's lack of arms and legs because, for Margaret, these details are normal — they go without saying.

Hank's reaction, on the other hand, is described as "hysterical," a term usually identified with the irrational categories of the feminine and the savage. His tightening grip on his child warns us that he too, like the fathers we have been hearing about in radio reports, is preparing to commit infanticide, which is also Seed's, Attebery's, and Yaszek's interpretation of Hank's intentions (Seed 1999; Attebery 2002, 101; Yaszek 2008, 115–16). Hank, not Margaret, is the hysterical one. When Hank's vision takes over the narrative in the end, the reader, having already seen Henrietta from Margaret's point of view, does not necessarily have to identify with his interpretation of Henrietta; indeed, his violent reaction to the baby is not necessarily any more rational than Margaret's. Hence the narrative calls attention to the provisionality of "normalcy" itself.

This is a story about not only the possible effects of atomic radiation but also the relationship between mother and child in the absence of the father's authority. This "freakish" social arrangement came dangerously close to becoming normal during World War II. Merril herself, as mentioned previously, like thousands of other American women, had been a single parent while her first husband served in the war effort, a situation mirrored in "That Only a Mother." In this light, Margaret's acceptance of her armless, legless, brainy child reflects the fact that, in Hank's absence, she has been allowed to determine for herself what counts as normal. Indeed, as the memorable opening line of the story makes clear, Margaret has had to accept Hank's absence as normal, as she "reached over to the other side of the bed where Hank should have been" (88). She and Henrietta develop a loving relationship that, because of Henrietta's ability to communicate, is based on equality and exchange rather than hierarchy and dependence. Margaret does not treat Henrietta like a helpless baby, nor like a mutated "freak," but like a rational, speaking subject. Indeed, when Hank returns from military service, Margaret regards *him* as alien and strange: "[So] many things to tell him, and now she just stood there, staring at a khaki uniform and a stranger's pale face" (94). While this is a story about "normal" bodies perverted by atomic mutations, it also raises the possibility that Margaret's female-authored perspective, in which Henrietta's differences are accepted and even cherished, is preferable to Hank's patriarchal response.

## Shadow on the Hearth *(1950)*

Like "That Only a Mother," Merril's novel *Shadow on the Hearth* plays with fundamental categories of frontier mythology that align nature, the feminine, and the primitive. Her use of frontier mythology is in keeping with popular Cold War representations of nuclear attack, which, as Patrick Sharp demonstrates, positioned it as a confrontation between civilization and savagery (153–69). *Shadow* is unique, however, in its domestic setting. In this work, the mother figure must descend into savagery in order to protect her two "normal" children from radiation following a nuclear strike on New York City. *Shadow* was Merril's first novel, published by Doubleday in the spring of 1950, and one of the first science fiction novels to discuss the potential effects of science on the lives of women, children, and families. Merril's conflict with her publisher over the title of the novel is representative of the gendered categories that constrained women's science fiction writing at the time: The "dismaying" title was chosen by the publisher in preference to several provided by Merril, "all of which pointed towards the idea of atomic war" (Merril and Pohl-Weary 2002, 99). The publisher also, apparently, took out the "fairly honest-adult treatment of sex" that Merril had included in the manuscript to reflect the background of "worry and intensity and fear" faced by, for example, Gladys and the male teacher-scientist she harbored in her home (Merril to Tony Boucher, February 10, 1952, 2.43, MP). Thus, despite Merril's objections, her publisher insisted on foregrounding the novel's idealized domestic setting, marginalizing the novel in relation to the broader arena of atomic debate that was Merril's primary target audience.

Certainly, domesticity is crucial to Merril's vision of atomic war in *Shadow on the Hearth*: she imagines it as the first line of defense when nuclear attack cripples public order and infrastructure. In the insulated confines of a well-ordered home, however, atomic attack, rather than leading to the abandonment of normal routines, reinforces their meaning and importance, for if atomic war is savage war, then normalcy, as previously discussed, is the most powerful means of defense against its consequences. Despite this domestic focus, Seed has shown how, in planning her novel, Merril was in dialogue with atomic science writers of the day — including John Hersey, author of "Hiroshima" (1946); David Bradley, who wrote *No Place to Hide* (1948); and scientists such as Philip Morrison, author of "If the Bomb Gets Out of Hand" (1946)—"in a selective and original way" (Seed 1999, 57–58; 2003, 126–27).

Merril's correspondence with Bradley in 1949, when she began writing *Shadow on the Hearth*, reveals her purpose and method in departing from the masculine norm for nuclear holocaust stories; she was inspired by her role at Bantam editing and marketing the 1949 edition of *No Place to Hide*. She grilled Bradley for information: What were the differential effects of radiation on children, adults, and old people, men and women, healthy or ill people? Merril told him that she wanted to write a novel for women readers that would contain technical information in a readable form: "Women LOVE to read about diseases ... and also about dangers to their children, homes, and family." Merril concludes that Bradley's *No Place to Hide* was, in truth, "a man's book, with little appeal for women," adding that "few women have read it or will, because the technique you used for relief from strain, the tropical isle stuff, fishing, etc., is men's reading exclusively" (Merril to Bradley, February 19, 1949, 44.10, MP). In contrast, Merril's heroine and her children find relief in setting the table for dinner, housework, and other domestic routines.

The effectiveness of Merril's novel is evident in the praise it received for, in Seed's words, "its understated method, avoidance of melodrama and unusually oblique description of nuclear attack" (1999, 57). While Seed and other contemporary critics respect Merril's novel for its originality in domesticating nuclear attack — hence the story's power and darkness — our close reading of the text provides an opportunity to examine something even darker and more revealing of the times: the way in which postwar concepts of normalcy were embedded in a much older American discourse of savagery.

While never mentioning the political situation that precipitated an atomic attack by a nameless enemy upon the archetypal American metropolis, New York City, *Shadow on the Hearth* focuses on the mythical role of the atomic bomb as the catalyst for regeneration of a domestic life that has become a little too easy. This is a modern iteration of the old paradox that civilization, the natural outcome of the frontier experience, threatens to weaken its citizens if they allow themselves to get too comfortable. The novel opens with the beginning of a normal day for Gladys Mitchell, a middle-class suburban housewife and mother, who is depicted happily negotiating the many demands of her husband and children. Merril herself did not identify with her heroine, who functions as representative of a domestic norm to which Merril did not aspire to conform: in a letter written shortly after the publication of *Shadow*, Merril told Fritz Leiber that she didn't "much care for women like Gladys, but [...] she was the inevitable personality through whose eyes the happenings could best be seen" (September 24, 1950, 38.8, MP). Gladys is indeed an idealized housewife of the 1950s, entirely satisfied in fulfilling that role. Once her husband, Jon, is safely off to work and her children are off to school, Gladys turns to the task of the family laundry. Although Gladys is bogged down in her domestic chores on this particular day, references to her housekeeper, Veda, and her washing machine remind us that normal, domestic life is easier than it used to be. Over the dishes, Gladys reminisces about harder times, when she and her husband lived in a crowded city apartment and "every penny that wasn't spent for necessities went into clean shirts and ties for Jon, or into the bank to build the dreams that had since come true" (*Shadow*, 7). Now her chief worry is whether she will be able to keep a luncheon engagement. "Everything's almost too good," she thinks to herself. "How long could things go on, getting better all the time?" (8).

This prelude to the atomic attack emphasizes its mythical role as the violent but regenerative event that Gladys unconsciously wishes for when she guiltily observes that things have become "too good." This meaning is symbolically reinforced through the comparison of Gladys, the devoted housewife and mother, and her neighbor, Edie Crowell, a well-to-do woman who is on her way to a society luncheon when the bomb hits, and who is later diagnosed with a fatal case of radiation sickness. Edie represents what can happen to suburban women when things are "too good": a socialite, she is childless, self-absorbed, a drinker, and prone to hysterics. The nuclear attack cleanses civilization of women like Edie, while invigorating the likes of Gladys, who foregoes the luncheon to get her domestic chores done; she, unlike Edie, is safely ensconced in the laundry room when the deadly blast erupts. Gladys's family is not entirely protected, however, for a teacher at school leaves a toy outside in the radioactive rain, resulting in her youngest child contracting a serious but treatable case of radiation poisoning. That this small oversight leads to near disaster reinforces the importance of the normal domestic routines that Gladys is determined to protect.

Like Bradley's *No Place to Hide*, *Shadow on the Hearth* explains the basics of atomic science, but through dramatization rather than exposition. Textbook-like, Bradley explains the different types of life-threatening radiation: "[Gamma rays] are ultrashort electromagnetic waves, closely related to X rays. Depending upon their energy, they have great penetrating power and constitute the main hazard from radiation outside the body" (171). Edie Crowell, Dr. Levy (a blacklisted atomic-scientist-turned-high-school-teacher whom Gladys hides in her home), and Gladys's little girl Ginny all contract various forms of radiation sickness, the science of which is represented in terms of its domestic meaning. When Dr. Levy is diagnosed with "a medium dose of gamma," Gladys asks, "What's gamma? What does that mean?" The doctor replies, "Oh. Well, as far as treatment is concerned, it means what he needs is rest, and if he could get some blood, that would help too" (239). Discussing the treatment of Ginny, the doctor explains, "We can't really treat the disease at all. [...] There's no way to deactivate an ionized cell. But if we treat the symptoms, just help the body through the worst of it, the damaged cells are eventually replaced" (254). Again, Merril represents atomic science in the domesticized terms of a mother's consultation with her child's doctor. Compare again to Bradley's exposition of the process of ionization:

> A radioactive particle or ray in passing through a medium [...] has numerous collisions with atoms of that medium and leaves behind it a wake of ionized fragments.... The great damage from neutrons, however, is not so much from the primary ionization as from the ionizing power of innumerable fragments of atoms left in its wake [179–80].

Whereas Bradley abstracts nuclear processes from the material bodies (the "medium") in which they take place, Merril brings the discourse of atomic science and atomic war into the home by focusing on its effects on the bodies of her characters.

As radiation attacks the normal workings of the human body in the home, so too does atomic attack destroy the everyday routines of human civilization. Since, in Cold War culture, middle-class women were primarily responsible for the production of normalcy in both body and mind, the savage war transforms them into domestic soldiers. Normal routines such as the preparation of dinner take on military importance: "She [Gladys] issued brisk orders, and the two girls obeyed swiftly, happy to seize on a pattern of behavior that they knew. It was a victory when Barbara so far forgot the world outside that she squabbled briefly with Ginny over the proper placement of the forks" (37). Later, Gladys "banish[es]" worrying thoughts about her husband's fate "by plunging into a fury of housework" (209). The home becomes a last line of defense against the savagery beyond its threshold: not only looters, but also an increasingly secretive and dictatorial government, embodied in the local "squadman" who flirts with Gladys despite having a wife and baby at home, the overzealous patrols who eventually shoot Gladys's husband as he struggles to find his way home after curfew, and government persecution of dissidents, which leads to the wrongful detainment of Gladys's housekeeper Veda.

Gladys's home becomes a literal battlefield in this savage war when she and the fugitive scientist, Dr. Levy, vigorously defend it from looters with an arsenal of knives, food choppers, rolling pins, and frying pans: "Gladys' rolling pin flew from her hand toward the first shape that loomed in the doorway. By a miracle of bad aim, it went straight by him to bring forth a yell of pain from someone right in back. A moment later Levy brought a heavy skillet down on the foot of the man in front, putting him out of the battle completely" (170). When the gas line in the basement springs a leak, a taken-for-granted household convenience becomes a dangerous and strange technology. Gladys's heroic attempt at what would otherwise be an ordinary household repair is depicted in the language of thrilling adventure stories of the pulp fiction era in which Merril wrote this novel:

> The box had made a lot of noise [...] the towel was off her mouth, but she was afraid to open it. She got her arms out from under her and yanked the towel back over her face. It didn't seem to do any good at all anymore. Gas was in her nostrils and her throat. Strangely enough, she wasn't dizzy anymore, but her eyes were tearing and they smarted. She set the box back in place. She seemed to be moving very slowly, but everything was getting done, quicker than she expected, too. She didn't quite understand it, but she supposed it was all right. She knew she had to turn that screw some more. It had been in one way, now she had to get it all the way the other way [126].

Being normal does not mean that Gladys is expected to maintain her usually placid and patient demeanor. The crisis unleashes pent-up energy and power in Gladys, reminiscent of atomic energy itself, which Zarlengo has shown was represented in the dual terms of domesticated and feminized nature ("good" atomic energy) and out-of-control female sexuality — the "bombshell" (Zarlengo 1999, 946–51). Throughout the text, Gladys conceals an inner turmoil in order to protect her young children as a well-controlled, good mother should do, but her volcanic composure periodically explodes in frustration and fury, such as when she reports the dangerous gas leak in her home: "No trouble in that neighborhood, lady," the official blandly reports. "'But there's trouble right here!' [Gladys] exploded. 'I'm right in the house, and I *know* there's —'" (*Shadow*, 121).

Gladys's unleashed power is evident not only in her ability to manage the household in the adversity of war but also in her changing relationships with her neighbors. She is normally able to stifle signs of her dislike for Edie Crowell, but not anymore. Angered by a hysterical phone call from Edie, Gladys "slammed the receiver down viciously, not trying to control the surge of anger. It seemed to make her stronger, helped her throw off the permeating weariness" (36). The sexually charged nature of Gladys's unleashed energy is signified when neighbor Jim Turner develops an attraction to her in the course of performing his civil defense duties — part police work and part community outreach — as a "squadman." Gladys's anger and sexuality signify her regression to the uncontained femininity of the primitive, from which she emerges as the regenerated domestic woman. Other characters are similarly regenerated: a chastened Edie Crowell recovers from her drunkenness and vows to join a temperance society; the atomic scientist, Dr. Levy, improvises a hot water burner for Gladys, proving himself "a right handy man around a house" (178); and Gladys's teenage daughter Barbara is sexually awakened by the heroism of the doctor who saves Ginny. These are examples of Slotkin's regenerative, savage war because civilized subjects are reacquainted, through war, with primal, gendered drives. This process reinvigorates American civilization by preventing the American subject from becoming effete, dependant on the supports of civilization, and alienated from the power and drives of the body.

Gladys's victory is complete when her injured husband Jon miraculously finds his way home just as it is announced on the radio that the war is over. The juxtaposition of the husband's arrival with the end of the war links the restoration of the normal, nuclear family to the military victory, making Gladys's rugged domesticity as symbolically important a weapon as the remote-controlled missiles that have subdued the enemy. Tellingly, an interview with Merril, as well as her own memoir, established that this unfortunate ending was without consultation, inserted by Doubleday to conform to the expectations of the Family Book Club. In her original manuscript, Gladys's husband Jon is killed near their home by civil defense patrollers (Seed 1997,

13; Seed 1999, 59; Merril and Pohl-Weary 2002, 99–100). Jon's death might have been too radical an ending for a story about a woman who survives nuclear attack just fine, without a man's protection. That stricture would vanish by the next decade, when Merril restored her original ending in the 1966 Roberts and Vintner edition of the novel.

The book garnered instant fame for Merril when it received a glowing review in the *New York Times*, which mentioned her writing in the same breath as H. G. Wells and George Orwell (Merril and Pohl-Weary 2002, 99). Anthony Boucher and J. Francis McComas, writing in *Fantasy and Science Fiction* (1950, 104), called it the leading novel of the past months, possibly even the "last years or even decades." *Galaxy* claimed that *Shadow* signaled "the maturing of science fiction"—that is, exhibiting less concern with introducing new science and more engagement with portraying "reactions to events growing out of probable scientific developments" (Conklin 1950, 141). Despite these accolades from the top science fiction magazines, Merril herself was not all that pleased with the novel; the "obvious (now) flaws and omissions" jumped out at her, she admitted in a letter to her writer friend, Leiber, but she was, nevertheless, "irked" by the many critics who thought the novel either too horrible or not nearly horrible enough (June 18, 1950, 38.8, MP). Motorola TV Playhouse purchased the story and adapted it for the ABC television network as a drama, *Atomic Attack*, first broadcast in 1954. These were television's early days; only twenty percent of American homes had the technology. *Atomic Attack* was expected to be sensational but was in the end a bit of a "fizzle," according to Merril (Merril and Pohl-Weary, 2002, 99). Certainly it has a different tone, even message, from that of *Shadow on the Hearth*. As Seed explains, the family in the television version is highly idealized, and the story is more "didactic," criticizes the national military campaign, promotes an "ethic of mutual help," (Seed 2003, 131) and ends with "a crude notion of triumph" (132).

In the late 1950s, Merril noticed that *Atomic Attack* was being shown in civil defense and Atomic Energy Commission programs, while *Shadow on the Hearth* itself was even being promoted in civil defense reading lists (Merril to Philip Wylie, August 19, 1958, 19.37, MP), the latter suggesting the novel's reinvention as a propagandizing documentary about the proper ways for ordinary people to defend themselves against the real possibility of an atomic attack, which is not at all how Merril had envisioned her novel. Recognizing how the subtle political critique had been virtually erased from the novel in its transition to television, Merril learned that translation from one medium to another was not a straightforward matter of transposition: "*Shadow on the Hearth* was a very political novel. It was written for political reasons, and one of the central characters was a physicist who understood atomic warfare and what it meant," she recalls in her memoir. To watch the television adaptation was, for Merril, "sort of like having a different lens on each of my eyes" (Merril and Pohl-Weary 2002, 100). Even at this early stage of Merril's writing career, she understood the idea and politics of translation from one medium to another, an insight that would prove important later in her life when she came to see herself as a translator in all that she did.

## "Death Is the Penalty" (1949) and "A Woman of the World" (1957)

In addition to her focus on mothers and their children, Merril also explored, in "Death Is the Penalty" and (as Rose Sharon) "A Woman of the World," the implications an atomic society might have for the politics of heterosexual romance and marriage. In terms of frontier mythology, marriage is the point at which humanity's natural sexual impulses are channeled into the civilized framework of marital union. Classic frontier stories such as Cooper's *Last of the Mohicans* and Wister's *The Virginian* end in a marriage symbolizing the beginning of a new society, created from the usually violent conflict between the expanding civilization and the savage forces (Indians, cattle rustlers) that oppose it. In "Death Is the Penalty," the conquest of the atomic frontier requires unprecedented state power, which extends into the most private lives of its citizens. Published in *Astounding Science Fiction* (1949), this text was written in the wake of the first Bikini Atoll tests, a series of atomic weapons tests conducted by the United States in the Pacific during the summer of 1946. It was a time when science fiction writers were just beginning to grapple with the implications of the nuclear age — particularly the still poorly understood biological dangers of nuclear technology and radioactive contamination that Merril probes in "That Only a Mother" and *Shadow on the Hearth*—and with the increasing secrecy and expanding state power that went hand-in-hand with nuclear development.

As in "That Only a Mother," Merril in "Death Is the Penalty" refracts her critique of nuclear development through domestic concerns, this time focusing on the militarization of the American private sphere and its frightening implications. The story revolves around a love affair between two scientists, Janice and David, whose affair violates laws prohibiting any liaisons between those who work on "restricted" science and those who do not. When they are caught by authorities, they choose death over separation and punishment. They are killed by futuristic weapons that use nuclear technology to turn them into blackened statues, or "permanents," effigies of their former selves caught in a last, loving embrace, kept on display as a lesson to onlookers.

"Death Is the Penalty" replays an old frontier plot in which lovers find themselves surrounded by an encroaching civilization that seeks control over their sexuality as part of its overall drive to control and contain nature. In *The Virginian*, for example, the novel's eponymous hero takes his bride into the wilderness for one last communion with nature before embarking on their civilized life. In Zane Grey's *Riders of the Purple Sage* (1912), the two lovers retreat into a secret mountain valley to escape the social forces threatening to divide them, and they choose to remain there permanently by deliberately triggering an avalanche that blocks the only way in or out. "Death Is the Penalty" similarly depicts lovers meeting in a secret swimming hole that straddles the boundary between the "restricted" and "open" domains of their respective research. The point of this story, however, is that the control nuclear civilization exerts over its subjects is pervasive to unprecedented (and even perverse) extremes.

Merril is particularly deft at using formal techniques to forge connections between readers of the 1950s and the possible futures she maps out for them. "Death Is the Penalty" is narrated in second-person point of view, positioning the reader as one of the onlookers viewing the "permanent" image of the lovers, participating in a guided tour. We learn that the "permanents" were left in situ after their death, and that the site of their sexual rebellion has since become a park — the fate of natural space, if it is to have any existence at all in a "civilized" context. "Boundaries" have since been erected around the "restricted" area where secret technologies are pursued, which physically prevent any contact between scientists on "restricted" and "unrestricted" projects. This setting takes to extremes the militarization of everyday life in the 1940s exemplified in civil defense programs and the secrecy of atomic research. The reader-onlooker contemplates the spectacle of Janice and David with the same nostalgia for the past invoked in 1950s Western films: "[Y]ou walk away thinking, and do not listen [to the guide]. You are wondering about the old days, when the things were wild and free — before Civilization, before the Boundaries — before even Security" ("Death," 64). This closing line positions Merril's readers to view their present in the same terms in which they have been accustomed to viewing America's frontier past — as a time when things were "wild and free." The difference is that readers in the late 1940s, when Merril crafted the story, were still in a position to intervene in the encroachment of a civilization that was taking its power too far by subordinating the very act of love to military priorities.

By the time Merril published her next nuclear story, "A Woman of the World," in *Venture Science Fiction* (1957), concerns about nuclear technology had shifted from its biological and social risks to the possibility of an all-out nuclear Armageddon. This narrative, as well as post-nuclear Armageddon narratives of the 1950s written by others (see Newell and Lamont 2005b), followed the teleological structure of frontier narrative by depicting post–Armageddon conditions in terms of atavism, or the return to primitive origins. "A Woman of the World" depicts a post–Armageddon, near-future Earth in the process of returning to "natural" conditions of lawlessness, in which a pocket of civilization has been relegated to a confined, armed, fortress-like rural community. The main character, Ellen Reeves, is a female member of this community who, along with a young male companion, schemes to leave it in search of a fresh start and freer existence. Their plan is to reclaim a piece of land and start a homestead together. After they make their initial escape, however, Ellen soon becomes irritated by her companion, Tommy, who proves to be an ineffectual leader—"a *good* kid.... Sure...." (81)—always wanting to stop for sex and having no clue of how to survive beyond the confines of civilization. The couple is accosted by a wild, bearded man as they explore a seemingly abandoned house. As Tommy and the wild man fight to the death, the semi-conscious Ellen comforts herself by saying, "*The best man ... best man always wins. So that* was all right" (82). When Tommy is killed in the struggle, Ellen disturbingly welcomes the wild man, who is about to rape her as the story ends. "A Woman of the World" was written and published as a commissioned companion piece to Les Cole's "A Man of the World," which narrates the same story from the point of view of the wild man who attacks Ellen and Tommy. The conversation between these two stories, and the significance to Merril of writing it under a pseudonym, will be addressed in Chapter 6.

"A Woman of the World" might be seen as reiterating ultra-patriarchal narratives of women who desire to be overpowered except for the fact that Ellen Reeves is not at all a sympathetic character. None of the characters in this story are, and so none of them represent a valorized position. The more important point is the alignment of nuclear and patriarchal society. As Susan Sontag would soon argue in 1965 (cited in Williams 2009, 250), and nuclear criticism would reiterate in the early 1980s (Williams, 247), nuclear armament was the outcome of patriarchal values followed to their furthest extent; hence, Merril's post–Armageddon world relegates both men and women to extreme versions of their traditional roles within patriarchy—as respectively savage beasts and masochists.

## Merril's Intervention in the Nuclear Debate

The power of Merril's stories about the atomic frontier lies at least partly in her intervention in the fundamental mythology that aligned the atomic frontier with the nineteenth-century American frontier. American readers were taught in popular literature and debate to understand nuclear technology and its implications for the future as part of the ongoing confrontation with savagery that constituted their very identity. At the core of this mythology are figurations of nature, gender, savagery, and civilization that Merril unsettles in her atomic fiction to various, subversive ends. The stunning ending of "That Only a Mother," for example, is predicated on Merril's skillful subversion of the classic identification of the feminine with the (primitive) body. In *Shadow on the Hearth*, a housewife becomes a frontier hero by accessing the energy and power that lies at the core of the feminine, be it atom or woman. In her stories about the possible future social fallout of nuclear energy, "Death Is the Penalty" and "Woman of the World," Merril attacks the patriarchal underpinnings of the frontier myth — the drive to dominate and contain nature — by exposing repression and war as the inevitable outcomes of this logic. Merril would bring this same attention to the deep structures of frontier myth in science fiction to her stories of the space frontier.

## Chapter 3

# The Space Stories

Human spaceflight was already a well-established subject in American science fiction by the time it became a real possibility in the 1950s, but with the 1957 launching by the Soviet Union of the world's first artificial satellite, *Sputnik 1*, the reopening of the frontier seemed to the public no longer mere speculation. Judith Merril wrote shortly afterward of this being a defining moment for America, perhaps something akin to the bombing of Hiroshima:

> The psychological shock wave that swept through this country in the wake of the first orbit of the Russian-made 1957 Alpha Earth Satellite—*Sputnik I*—was hardly less powerful than the one that ended the last "total" war with the explosion of the American-made atomic bomb in Japan. [...] For the first time in the experience of any living Americans, we had cause to wonder seriously whether it could be remotely possible that we, as a nation, might be in some way weaker or inferior to some other people ["How Near Is the Moon?" 1958, 222].

Merril seized upon the occasion of major cultural debates regarding space travel and new narratives of frontier expansion that speculated about a mythical future and alternative presents rather than idealizing a mythical past. Like many science fiction writers, both men and women, Merril's space-travel narratives borrowed from the popular American Western the familiar themes of exploration, adventure, conquest, and colonization. In this way, starting out as a producer of "unusual fact material" and writer of regular features for the Western pulps had been beneficial for Merril. When she turned to writing science fiction stories, Merril departed from the conventions of space-travel narratives, however, by creating female-, family-, and generation-centered stories of space exploration and travel (which she once cited as her favorite theme).

## Space Travel in the 1950s: The Shift from Romance to Realism

This chapter analyzes Judith Merril's space-travel stories, situating them in the context of space-frontier mythologies and gender ideologies of the 1950s. Space flight was the classic theme in science fiction into the 1960s, especially in cinema, culminating in Stanley Kubrick's *2001: A Space Odyssey* (1968), based on a story by Arthur C. Clarke and a screenplay by both Kubrick and Clarke. Merril once recalled that "[in the 1930s and 1940s] science fiction and space flight were almost synonymous: to be a fan of one was to be an enthusiast for the other; in some senses, the whole science fiction field, during the period of the ascendency of John W. Campbell's *Astounding*, was a great volunteer propaganda machine for space flight" (1968 [March], 39). Space travel remained one of the central myths in American science fiction until the actual U.S. Apollo 11 Moon landing in 1969 demystified the subject of the space frontier.

Before World War II and the Cold War, space-travel stories were heavily romanticized, and featured young adventuresome males as their heroes. For example, in Edgar Rice Burroughs's *A Princess of Mars*, the first of his "Barsoom" series of novels set on Mars, a Civil War veteran gets a second chance at heroism when he is magically transported to Mars, where he leads the rightful faction in a planet-wide war for supremacy and founds a new dynasty with the Princess Deja Thoris. In these stories, adventure was paramount; hence space travel is represented in fanciful terms with little importance attached to the science. Burroughs's space-hero, for example, is transported to Mars by some obscure form of magic or paranormal phenomenon. In one of the earliest stories of interstellar travel, E. E. Smith's (Lee Hawkins Garby's co-authorship is known but not acknowledged) *The Skylark of Space* (1928), the science behind the spaceship is explained in terms of ambiguous buzzwords. What mattered in fiction about space travel during the interwar years was not so much the science but the adventure, indicating the close relationship between space-travel fiction and its predecessor, the frontier adventure story.

The 1950s were pivotal in the cultural history of the space frontier: real technological advances in space flight in the 1950s meant that the space-frontier theme could lay claim to the level of realism demanded by John Campbell, the trend-setting editor of *Astounding* (Wolfe 1989, 254), and that space-frontier narratives now had the status of real social commentary rather than mere escapist, romantic adventure. Indeed, the closer international superpowers came to actual space travel, the more obsolete the romantic model of space travel from the first half of the century became. Thus, whereas the depiction of exotic worlds, even whole galaxies, was the focus of the "planetary romance" stories by Burroughs and the classic space operas by E. E. Smith and Garby (Wolfe 251–54), Leigh Brackett, and Edmund Hamilton, post–World War II space-frontier fiction increasingly exploited the ties between science fiction and frontier mythology to critique American society. Through stories of Earth's colonization of Mars, for example, Ray Bradbury's *The Martian Chronicles* (1950) projected America's imperial identity into the future, but in a far more critical light than that of Burroughs.

Merril, too, was a pioneer of the emergent, social realist trend in science fiction about the space frontier. Like her atomic fiction, Merril's space stories isolate and interrogate core categories and patterns in the frontier narrative. She also saw in the space frontier a rich opportunity to refigure conventions of sex, gender, and family relations, as well as female identity. In this respect, she deployed the concept of frontier as a space in which one could sort between what was natural and what was cultural as old institutions such as the family were tested in new environments.

### *"Barrier of Dread" (1950) and "Hero's Way" (1952)*

One of Merril's earliest space-travel narratives, "Barrier of Dread," published in *Future* (1950), is representative of the realist trend in postwar space-travel fiction. It addresses the fundamental contradiction of American identity that dominant iterations of the frontier myth attempt to resolve — namely, that the "American Dream" of unlimited economic opportunity and prosperity is based on the fantasy that resources are unlimited. "Barrier of Dread" depicts Earth's galactic empire of the future, an empire in which robots do all of the work, the space frontier provides resources for all, and war is unknown. However, the empire is rocked by the discovery that outer space is, after all, not infinite. The story concerns the efforts of the main character, the managing director of Earth's empire, to prepare his people for the profound shift in their culture and society required by the new reality of scarce resources. In the context of grossly exaggerated claims by space-frontier proponents about the potential of the space frontier to alleviate the problems of a small, crowded planet, this story provided a much-needed dose of sober second thought.

In the short but powerful story "Hero's Way," published in *Space* in 1952, another staple of the frontier myth — the rugged, masculine, frontier hero — is exposed as, in reality, the pawn of the state. In this story, the career as a professional space traveler (the term "astronaut" was not yet in formal use) is as glamorous as a career in professional sports, but also entails risks that authorities in the (space) Service are reluctant to discuss. In the beginning of the story, Brigadier-General Alex Halder addresses the newest cohort of space academy graduates before they take their final oaths of service in a televised ceremony. His address is actually a warning, expressed in the form of an anecdote about a recent star graduate, who returned from space suffering from sterility caused by alien radiation, leading his trophy wife to leave him in obscurity and robbing him of his dream of having a family. Halder hopes with this example to warn the recruits about the real sacrifices they are about to make. He speaks from experience, for we learn that he is also suffering from the effects of alien radiation, which has robbed him of his ability to speak without the aid of a battery-operated device. Unfortunately, Halder's warning falls on deaf ears as the graduates race to be the first ones to sign up for the Service as live cameras televise the newest cohort of future space celebrities, anxious to become "heros." The discourse of heroism, so deeply ingrained in frontier mythology, is exposed in this story as an ideological tool whereby the state recruits its subjects to do its work.

## Space Travel as "Traveling Domesticity"

Much of the new, socially conscious science fiction of the 1950s envisioned a future Earth governed by a single, Western-style world government — the culmination of America's Manifest Destiny. According to essays compiled in *One World or None: A Report to the Public on the Full Meaning of the Atomic Bomb* (Masters and Way 1946) — sponsored by the Federation of American Scientists only months after the end of World War II, and an immediate national bestseller — world government was the only viable form of government in the atomic age. In science fiction of the period, future Earth-centered galactic empires such as that found in Frederik Pohl and C. M. Kornbluth's *The Space Merchants* (1953) depicted outer space as serving the same safety-valve function that Frederick Jackson Turner's western frontier played in the nineteenth century: providing, in theory at least, the natural resources to fuel limitless industrial expansion and space for the excess population and, in the case of *Space Merchants*, the survival of huge transnational corporations (Wrobel 1993, 47). In Merril's work, scientists were frequently the central agents of this new frontier: whereas nineteenth-century pioneers have been mythologized as having tamed the landscape through sheer strength, character, and will, Merril's space explorers relied on specialized scientific and social science knowledge and training, intellectual ingenuity, and modern technology. In stories such as "Daughters of Earth," this emphasis on intellect over strength created more opportunities for female characters to join in the adventure of frontier exploration.

Merril took up these themes beginning in the early 1950s with the critical and imaginative approach that Carl Abbott would attribute to later "new wave" science fiction writers of the 1960s and 1970s (Abbott 2005, 250–51). She effectively challenged the prevailing science-adventure ("hard") mode of science fiction, with its concern for getting the science right. Looking back on the 1950s, she observed, "The industrial, political, and technological Space Age meant the beginning of a new period of exploration in the 'human factor,' as opposed to the 'hardware,' for both science and science fiction" (Merril 1968, "Introduction," 5). Merril was among the leading science fiction writers of the early postwar era who emphasized "soft" sciences as opposed to hardware: health sciences, botany, and the expanding and evolving fields of social anthropology, linguistics, sociology, and, most prominently, psychology (including the peripheral powers of the mind, such as ESP and psi). Hers were also among the earliest space-travel stories to represent unabashedly domestic themes, settings, and characters.

Just as domesticity, in the analysis provided by Amy Kaplan in "Manifest Domesticity" (1998), played a crucial role in nineteenth-century American imperialist discourse, it played an equally vital role in 1950s narratives of space colonization. In their science fiction about space travel, women like Merril powerfully interrogated conventional gender ideology and, in the process, advanced new images of women, families, and domesticity. As our previous chapter demonstrates regarding Merril's nuclear fiction, her "female" viewpoint is not merely a superficial addition to a "common science fiction theme," as Brian Stableford asserts (1979, 2016), but a substantially different vision of space travel than the predominant view — hotly debated within the articles in science fiction magazines — that women, love, and sex have no place in science fiction (Larbalestier 2002a, 104). As Elizabeth Cummins's (1992) excellent reassessment of Merril's short fiction argues, "Placing family issues at the center of her space travel stories was a bold assertion, a reevaluation of what really matters in human society" (206).

In Merril's fiction, the spaceship conflates the home-space with the workplace. On the various ships and space journeys in her stories, new social formations emerge to adapt, one way or another, to the requirements of space colonization, which involves scientific exploration and reproduction of the colony's population, both on board the ship and on colonized planets. The conditions and objectives of space exploration and colonization transform not only the relevance of physical sex differences but also traditional sexual mores and conventional structures of families, communities, and systems of communication. Hence, in Merril's space-frontier stories, women, children, and families figure more prominently than the individual male adventurer or hero, and work and domestic life are completely intertwined aboard the confining space vessels. Married couples who double as scientific teams perform both the reproductive and scientific labor necessary for the success of the colonial mission. Communal family structures involving surrogate parenting, or even polygamy, and matriarchies prove better suited than the patriarchal, nuclear family to the collective and sustained endeavor of space travel and colonization. Indeed, the vulnerability of the nuclear family in space is suggested by the stories "Dead Center" and "Wish Upon a Star," and also the novella "Homecalling," in which, as we shall observe, Merril's central human characters are children of dead or otherwise absent space-explorer parents navigating their situation without sentimentality and more or less on their own.

Merril's often radical rethinking of 1950s gender ideology furthered the work of early women writers of the American frontier such as Emma Ghent Curtis, Frances McElrath, and B. M. Bower, who also saw the frontier as a space for reworking gender categories. Sixty years earlier, Curtis published a Western titled *The Administratrix* in 1889 — well before the genre was supposedly "born" in 1902 with the appearance of *The Virginian* — in which a schoolteacher cross-dresses as a cowboy and experiences release from the constraints of "true womanhood." McElrath places the woman reformer at the center of *The Rustler* (1902), her account of cattle rustling in Wyoming, while Bower published one of the earliest literary accounts of domestic abuse — *Lonesome Land* (1912) — in American literary history. Merril's space-frontier fiction furthers this project: Women — individually and in collectivities, as mothers and daughters, and as scientists, artists, space travelers, doctors, and lovers — emerge as central characters, a feature hinted at by Virginia Kidd (1976), her close friend from the old New York Futurian days: "Back when women were being regarded as mere props to be rescued from bug-eyed monsters, Merril was addressing the question of what it might really be like to be a woman in the future, a woman in space" (10).

## *The Survival Trilogy: "Survival Ship" (1951), "Wish Upon a Star" (1958), and "The Lonely" (1963)*

In her Survival trilogy, Merril represents space travel as an inherently woman-centered endeavor because its conditions favor the attributes of women: Centuries of domestic confinement, for one, would make women *more* suitable than men for the loneliness and confinement of space travel — a premise tested and borne out in scientific studies conducted later in the 1950s, contributing to the formation in 1959 of NASA's Women In Space Early (WISE), a training program for women astronauts (Yaszek 2008, 160). Extrapolating on this premise, Merril suggests that, with the confines and scarce resources of the spaceship, communal, matriarchal social structures would be required for a successful intergalactic journey. Indeed, just as traditional frontier mythology represents frontiering as the process of regenerating a civilization, Merril sees the space frontier as a space in which to reinvent sex, gender, and familial relations.

In its exploration of sex and sex-role behavior in space, the short story "Survival Ship," published in *Worlds Beyond* in 1951, posits a voyage of space colonization planned around unorthodox sexual and family relations. The story depicts the well-publicized launch of the first-generation mother ship Survival, regarded as "the greatest spaceship ever engineered. People didn't think of the Survival in terms of miles-per-second: they said, 'Sirius in fifteen years!'" ("Survival," 61). However, heavy secrecy surrounds the identity of its crew: the "Twenty and Four" young, robust single male and female engineers who have won coveted places "with the object of filling the specially equipped nursery and raising a second generation for the return trip" (61). It turns out that the crew has been expressly conditioned to overcome the sexual mores of Earth to prepare them for the experimental "system" of children born to small groups of adults outside of "normal" family groups and raised communally. Those in charge of the expedition consist of the captain and twenty-one crew members — all women, we learn in the story's trick ending — chosen because

> we are stronger and, in our social placement here, more fortunate. We must be accustomed to the fact that [the men] are our responsibility. It is because we are hardier, longer-lived, less susceptible to pain and illness, better able to withstand, mentally, the difficulties of [a] life of monotony, that we are placed as we are — and not alone because we are the bearers of children [67].

The monotony and confinement of space travel and the necessity of reproduction make space colonization the purview of women rather than the male adventurers.

To create the surprise trick ending of "Survival Ship," in which all the authority figures on the journey are revealed to be women, Merril wound up eliminating most of the gender pronouns. This was deliberate. She was, she recalls, actually "trying to perform a simple literary exercise, to write a story which contained no personal pronouns," but that proved impossible to fully achieve (Author's note to "Survival Ship" 1973, 15).

The act of writing "Survival Ship" stimulated Merril to use it as the background for a story that would explore sex-role behavior: "How much of what we ordinarily consider 'feminine' or 'masculine' behavior is culturally determined, and how much is built into the genes? Certain science fiction conventions or 'games' could be marshaled to accomplish that, using an 'environment-shift' or a 'role-shift' and see where that goes" (Author's note, 16). She writes that she gathered ideas for many years for a book on an Earth matriarchy in the far future and also collected notes on a second generation of the original inhabitants of the Survival. She never did complete the planned book. But out of her collection of notes came a story about the matriarchy spawned on the voyage of the Survival published in *Magazine of Fantasy and Science Fiction* in 1958: "Wish Upon a Star."

"Wish Upon a Star" ended up as the second of what Merril saw as a loosely connected series of stories written several years apart—an informal trilogy on the voyage of the Survival—in which she charts successive generations of woman-centered expeditions. Her interest in the cycles of everyday life situates her fiction in the tradition of pioneer women's diary-writing, which offers us a very different version of the frontier myth from the male-authored tradition. In contrast to the adventure narrative's focus on the resolution of a conflict between hero and antagonist, pioneer women's diaries, and the domestic fiction that is a closely related fictional form, focus on the minutiae of everyday life and the inner psyche of those who live it (Schlissel 1982, 16). "Wish Upon a Star" is told through the eyes of a young teenage boy born on the Survival, the colonizing ship that, as we learn in "The Lonely," was launched during the "brief Matriarchy at the beginning of World Government on Terra, following Final War" ("Lonely," 133). Like the other boys, his job is to care for the younger children. After years in space, the women are still in charge of the voyage: "women were considered better suited to manage the psychological problems of an ingrown group, and to maintain with patience over many years, if needed, the functioning and purpose of the trip" ("Wish," 95). The few men on board, including the boy's father, have been "indoctrinated" into obedience of their female leaders. But as the ship is finally about to land on a seemingly habitable but unoccupied planet of the kind they were searching for, the boy ponders the possibility of a return of the "Earth-type" nuclear family and the masculine independence that traditionally goes with it, although this young teenager has no personal experience of any of these concepts and objects: "*House. Family. Inside-outside.* They were all words in the books. Hills, sunsets, animals. *Wild* animals. Danger. But now he wasn't afraid; he *liked* the thought. Wild animals, he thought again, savoring it. Houses, inside and outside; inside, the family; outside, the animals. And plants. The *sun*shine ... daytime ... and night" (98). By sympathetically depicting her young male protagonist's growing resistance to matriarchal rule, Merril complicates the reversal of the sexual hierarchy that she has thus far established in the story. The vision she offers of the future of gender relations in this 1958 story is not one of finality but one of uncertainty and possibility.

"The Lonely," published in *Worlds of Tomorrow* in 1963, completes the saga of "Survival Ship" and "Wish Upon a Star" somewhat pessimistically. The far-future history unfolds as written long after the period of the voyages; its very different narrative form—that of an exchange of memos and transmissions between two (apparently) male authority figures—indicates that patriarchal rule and culture on Earth have been restored. As opposed to the internally focused, private discourse of "Wish Upon a Star," the tragic fate of at least one of the mother ships is disclosed from the impersonal, institutional point of view of a memo from a senior anthropologist. The memo relates a broadcast from an alien civilization, the asexual world of Aldebaran IV, light years away, that witnessed the last days of the expedition: "[T]he first females born on the trip came to maturity ... could not conceive.... Three male infants were born to females of the original complement — less than half of whom, even then, were still alive and of child-bearing age" ("Lonely," 130). Despite this tragic end, we are reminded that four similar ships were launched, so the faint possibility of success remains even though Merril has called into question the viability of the experiment she set in motion in the first story of the trilogy. Such ambivalence is characteristic of the shift to realism in space-travel narratives of the 1950s and 1960s: space pioneers do not necessarily reap the free land and resources they seek — at least, not without a price.

## *"Daughters of Earth" (1952)*

Whereas the Survival trilogy entertains the idea of a future matriarchy in space, only to all but abandon this possibility in the last of these stories, Merril's 1952 novella "Daughters of Earth," published in *The Petrified Planet*, is a more deeply psychological exploration of what it might be like to be a woman in space. The focus is on the mundane details of everyday life, as well as on the adventure. "Daughters" is a foundational text in the Merril canon. It spans six generations of women (Martha, Joan, Ariadne, Emma, Leah, and Carla) in direct descent, with one generation staying close to home, and the next emigrating further than the previous travelers, eventually advancing the frontier into the far reaches of the galaxy, faster than the speed of light: they were "all different in their ways, but all of them daughters of Earth. They carried their rebellious heritage where they went" (1952, "Daughters," 202).

"Daughters" was a commissioned work, a "shared-world" novella, which was included with two other separate novellas written by different authors but addressing a common science problem posed to all of them. It was for the first volume of the John Ciardi — edited Twayne Science Fiction Triplet series. Publishing in the first shared-world anthology in genre science fiction represents another first for Merril: The Twayne Triplet series was a run of hardcover books that she regarded as "the first literary prestigious series of science fiction publications" (Jirgens and Francis 1991, 9). Asked to write a novella involving two specific types of planets, Merril focused on Pluto and, after prodding by the editor, who granted her an extended deadline, included the silicon planet the characters go to next in the story, Uller (see Merril's correspondence with Ciardi, 4.9, MP). This is how, Merril explains, she came to create cycles: "The cycle I was interested in and the one that the story is concerned with more, is the mother-daughter cycle of action and reaction, alternate generations [...] there are three daughters who go" (Jirgens and Francis 1991, 9).

As a story, "Daughters" was not what Merril had hoped for. She was somewhat hamstrung by a commitment to the editor's predetermined scenario whereby she had to create her story around two planets — one with a fluorine chemistry and the other with a silicon one. But it did represent her early transition into experimental writing within the genre. As she wrote in the summer of 1952 to a fellow writer and intimate friend, Fritz Leiber, she was juggling child custody issues with her first husband and her contentious divorce, with further child custody issues, from her second husband. She was also under considerable pressure to write, what with publishing deadlines to meet, two small daughters and a dependent mother underfoot, and bills to pay, but she had at least finished "Daughters of Earth":

> the silly-sil-story is not only done but typed, turned in, and *liked*.... The story is good on account of being (you should pardon please the conceit) awful goddam well-written; as a *story*, I'm afraid it leaves much to be desired. So here I sit, turning to termites and sex [stories] once more, with nothing to fret about except the bills that should have been paid [June 16, 1952, 39.3, MP].

Merril's comments to Leiber reveal that the "flaws" she detected in her own writing were not necessarily due to her limitations as a writer; rather, her experimental writings were less welcome in the popular American science fiction mass marketplace than "termites and sex," and financial pressures following her separation from Pohl in 1951 limited the number of risks she could take (and when she did take risks with sexual topics, as in "The Lady Was a Tramp," her personal circumstances forced her to take the rare, in her case, step of publishing science fiction under the shield of a pseudonym). Yet the creative and personal environment in which "Daughters" took off for Merril in 1952 was especially fertile: "This fall and winter, I guess, is/has-been a sort of coming-to-a-head period — much of my thinking, hoping, working of the past year-and-a-half is beginning to solidify or show results or something," she added, in her letter to Leiber.

Although Merril was not able to fully realize her vision for "Daughters" because of personal and professional pressures, it stands as one of the most important works of space-frontier fiction of the 1950s because of how it maps a story about generations of women onto a story of intergenerational space travel, deftly weaving together the psychological with the scientific. A particularly intriguing aspect of this story is its treatment of relationships between men and women in the context of the spaceship, a site where gendered and professional identities merge. Writing during the immediate postwar period, in which the workplace was once more very much a male-dominated arena, Merril envisions the spaceship as a co-ed workplace populated by professional couples whose skills complement one another. For example, on the ship of Emma Matlook Tarbell, the first ship of humans in search of a habitable planet, overlapping shifts of one married couple at a time are thawed out from their deep freeze every few months to constitute the ship's six-member crew. As a medical doctor, Emma is specially trained to thaw out the ship's inhabitants upon landing and is the unofficial specialist in obstetrics, while her husband, Ken, is a construction expert. As a sign that Merril does not in her fiction completely transcend 1950s discourses about gender and the workplace, she still privileges heterosexual marriage as the fundamental form of partnership between men and women, and she does not envision them working together on equal footing outside of that relationship. Nonetheless, her vision of gender relations and roles in space is a significant departure from the dominant paradigms in science fiction of her day.

The shift-partners live in a communal cubicle and interact, in a sense, with their frozen counterparts via a logbook filled with sociable observations. Shift changes are big events:

> Everybody was talking at once. The Tarbells would read the log for themselves, of course, and add to it, in the eighteen months to come. But for this first night, everything came out in a jumble of incident and anecdote, gossip and laughter: the no-doubt grossly exaggerated story of the error Jommy [sic] Bacon made three shifts back, before the Levines came out [of deep freeze] ... a joke written into the log by Tom Kielty, fourteen years ago, but still fresh and funny ... the harrowing account of a meteor storm written in the third year out ["Daughters" 1952, 218].

In this passage, the juxtaposition of the formally managed "log" and the spontaneous "anecdotes" signals the organization of social space into public and private realms, now conflated on the spaceship. "Soft" scientific technologies facilitate this social reorganization: the careful planning of a psychologist ensures that each "shift" of couples will be socially compatible as well as having complementary professional skills.

Whereas some other contemporaneous, familiar adventure narratives, such as Bradbury's *The Martian Chronicles* and Robert Heinlein's *Farmer in the Sky* (1950), stress the high frontier of space exploration designed to overcome various crises on Earth while paying some attention to home life and women's roles, even across generations (see Abbott 2005; Wolfe 1989), the intergenerational theme of "Daughters," sketched from the female perspective, depicts women's responses to space exploration as especially ambivalent and complex. The novella's six generations of "daughters" are among humanity's first interplanetary colonists. Motivating Earth's space program is the need to build a starship on a site located on the outer edge of the system, followed by travel to another planetary system in search of uranium supplies to create the atomic fuel for more advanced space journeys. Thus, Pluto is only on "the way out": a first "step to the stars" in an ever-advancing frontier ("Daughters," 206).

The novella's opening, Earth-bound focalizer (that is, the character whose vision is presented in the narrative) is Martha, who watches with mixed anxiety, sadness, and pride as her daughter Joan departs for Pluto. The next chapter is in the form of a letter from Emma, a fourth-generation descendant of Martha, to her granddaughter Carla, who is preparing for her chance to voyage further into space. This letter frames the remainder of the story, a third-person narrative about Carla's predecessors written by Emma, interspersed with Emma's epistolary asides to Carla. This form of narrative marks the story itself as a means of maintaining ties among generations of women otherwise separated in time and space: "I am putting this together for you ... a sort of goodbye present," Emma tells Carla in her letter. "There is little that you need; or that you will be able to take with you. But I can offer, and you can use, the accumulated experience of those who have lived longer or lived earlier" ("Daughters," 209). This desire to maintain connections to previous "homes" conflicts with each woman explorer's choice to leave. Joan Thurman, "a famous pioneer, one of the first-ship colonists" (211), rejects the "normal" life for a woman of Earth: "In the normal course of events [on Earth], she would have finished school that spring, taken her degree, and gone to work in industry until she found a husband. The prospect appalled her" (203). Joan's granddaughter, Emma, is driven to leave a settled Pluto for the planet Uller because of the sheer challenge: "new problems to conquer, new knowledge to gain, new skills to acquire" (213). Joan's daughter, Ariadne, meanwhile, is rooted in Pluto but also drawn to her ancestral home of Earth and fulfills her dream of "trips to Earth: she saw the sights and institutions, and made all the tourist stops, and came back home to die on Pluto" (214). Similarly, Joan's mother, Martha, stayed on Earth but once in her lifetime went to the Moon. Leah, Emma's daughter, is born on Uller but leads a group of dissenters to found a new colony elsewhere on the planet. At the story's close, Leah's daughter Carla leaves Uller on *The Ark*, a ship built for time travel. The point is that Merril's female space pioneers are neither superwoman adventurers nor tragic figures of sacrifice; rather, they are complex characters with conflicting desires for both the safety and familiarity of home and the unknown possibilities of the space frontier.

## Space, Sex and Reproduction

Nineteenth-century pioneers on the Oregon Trail often saw their journey over vast distances as irreversible and expected never to see their loved ones again. As exemplified in Merril's Survival trilogy and "Daughters of Earth," rather than invent machines to overcome the vast distances of space-time, Judith Merril assumed that many expeditions into space would take place over several generations. For Merril, however, this meant that innovative sex, reproduction, and child-rearing practices were as important to the success of space travel as any "hard" technological advancement. If humans could manipulate natural laws as fundamental as the structure of the atom or the laws of gravity, then certainly practices around sex and reproduction were laws of nature equally subject to human manipulation. Therefore, as we have glimpsed, much of Merril's fiction revolves around radically different sexual-social arrangements (though always within a heterosexual paradigm). Merril's speculations about the future of the family in space are grounded in issues that concerned women of her day, particularly the relationship between women's roles as mothers and as workers and professionals. While much of Merril's fiction endorses and even celebrates the ideology of motherhood — for which she would be criticized by later feminists — Merril was committed to her professional career as a freelance writer and editor. She underwent a debilitating abortion at the tail end of her brief marriage to Pohl, and in her memoir she talks about juggling periods of hemorrhaging and collaborating on her serialized books with C. M. Kornbluth (Merril and Pohl-Weary 2002, 106). Having spent considerable time as a single parent, Merril knew that paid work was not necessarily optional for women. Moreover, as the numbers of working and professional women continued to rise steadily throughout the 1950s, even as some popular magazines and television programs redoubled their idealization of mothers, Merril knew that fictional negotiations between marital status, motherhood, sex, and work would certainly appeal to her women readers.

Frontier settings enabled Merril to address these concerns. Nineteenth-century American frontier towns were known for the suspension of sexual mores as settlements struggled to establish themselves: prostitution was conspicuous (A. M. Butler 1985, xvi), couples lived together out of wedlock, women worked, and divorce rates were among the highest in the world (Riley 1996). Merril drew from this legacy to represent mores around sex, marriage, and reproduction on the space frontier as up for negotiation.

### *"Project Nursemaid" (1955)*

In her novella "Project Nursemaid," which appeared in *Magazine of Fantasy and Science Fiction* in 1955, Merril depicts a military space program designed to overcome the harmful effects of zero gravity upon the human body. Babies are adopted from women "in trouble"— given the illegality of abortion in this era, this point about unwed mothers was cloaked in coded language — and raised in a nursery on the Moon, where it is hoped they will grow up adapted to the conditions of zero gravity. In this story, growing up on the Moon was thought to be the only way humans would be able to fully adapt to lunar conditions. Professional "nursemaids" are also recruited to raise these "space-baby" resources, thus opening the way for lunar colonies. The plot revolves around the efforts of the male protagonist, Colonel Tom Edgerly, who manages the program, to find qualified nursemaids for the job and to counsel the (mostly) young women and couples "in trouble" who have agreed to give up their babies to the program. These tasks bring the colonel into contact with two groups of women who transgress the ideal female role of wife and mother: single women past their prime who, lacking their own children, apply for jobs as nursemaids on the Moon, and the women "in trouble" who have children out of wedlock. Both types of women were familiar to Merril's readers in the mid–1950s as representatives of "problem" women; space is the frontier safety valve she invokes to relieve the pressure they exert on their society's stability. She envisions a new, systematic form of child-rearing that simultaneously provides homes and a purpose to unwanted babies, saves the respectability of unwed mothers, gives "surplus" women something to do, and addresses a technological boundary (zero gravity) to progress in outer space. A willingness to experiment with the "natural" laws of reproduction rather than accept their "eternal" nature is at the heart of this story.

"Project Nursemaid" is also a deliberate merger of the most masculine of professional spheres — the military — with the feminine sphere of the nursery, which must have appealed to women readers who during World War II crossed these boundaries on a daily basis as they negotiated between their roles as mothers or future mothers and as workers. Merril focuses, however, on the point of view of the men who are confronted with an increasingly feminized workplace and assigned the task of running "Project Nursemaid." "It's a hell of a way to run an Army" (4) is the general's comment on the program, demonstrating how raising babies in the postwar era has supplanted training soldiers as his primary responsibility. We sense, however, that the project is failing. The general pressures Tom to hire a nursemaid soon, but Tom can find no one right — in his eyes — for the job because of its conflicting demands. He will settle for nothing less than the ideal candidate. In essence, he needs an adventurous woman — someone who desires both the adventure of space travel and the seemingly mundane life of a nursemaid, and who has both the characteristics of adventurer and nurturer. These prove to be conflicting attributes. One woman, an independent and successful businesswoman who announces her occupation as "madam," is rejected because Tom fears she will not meet the moral criteria of his superiors; another is too masochistic in her desire to make a sacrifice for her country. When he finally finds a suitable candidate, her qualities are telling: "She was wonderful, he thought, almost unbelievable, after most of the others who came in here: a woman, no more, no less — familiar, likable, motherly, competent, womanly kind of woman" (31). The rarity here is that a "womanly woman" would seek out, and be qualified for, a life in space, an exaggerated version of the belief that any desires and aptitudes beyond home and family were abnormal for women.

Ultimately, it is Tom Edgerly who changes his attitudes — both toward himself and toward the "perfect" balance he seeks between womanly and adventurous qualities. In the course of running Project Nursemaid he finds himself having to nurture and support the vulnerable young women who turn to his program for help due to their predicaments as unwed mothers. It soon dawns on him that men would make good foster parents for Project Nursemaid, and he finds himself in the process of signing up for the job (73–74). Edgerly has learned to let go of his idealized notions of motherhood, realizing that the outcomes of parenting are uncertain and subjective. This insight into motherhood, hardly news to Merril, would have been a welcome message of affirmation to Merril's women readers.

Completing the novella was in itself a reaffirmation for Merril of her continuing ability to produce powerful and important work. Tony Boucher loved the character Edgerly and accepted "Project Nursemaid" for the *Magazine of Fantasy and Science Fiction* with little in the way of revisions. This boosted Merril's creative energy at a time when it was running low. As she wrote to Boucher, the novella was the first writing she had done in over a year, between November 1953 and January 1955, but now she was fully "alert," and thought it was her best story to date (March 23, April 25, 1955, 2.45, MP). Writing to her friend Leiber immediately after submitting the manuscript, she revealed something of the agony of writing the story — of her writing drive accompanied by "a mood of intense masochism and sexuality, such as I have not experienced in 'real life' since I broke loose from Fred [Pohl]" (June 9, 1955, 39.8, MP).

The space frontier enabled Merril to address her own, unconventional experience as an unconventional woman, parent, and sexual being. In an environment that cannot accommodate the normative, nuclear family, whether on the mining frontiers of Colorado or in the weightlessness of outer space, new modes of social organization are needed. Thus, nineteenth- and early-twentieth-century frontier narratives are replete with stories of single male parents (McElrath's *The Rustler*), bachelor families (B. M. Bower's *Chip, of the Flying U*), and other alternatives to the nuclear family as the primary locus of sex, reproduction, and parenting. Merril's narratives of sex and child-rearing on the space frontier are part of this tradition.

## As Rose Sharon, "The Lady Was a Tramp" (1956)

"The Lady Was a Tramp," published in *Venture Science Fiction* (1956), is one of Merril's more provocative visions of sexuality in the context of space travel. "Lady" takes up the well-established tradition of representing the boundless frontier as no place for a "lady" (who belongs in domestic confines) but as a good place for prostitutes and other "bad" women. As if to express dissatisfaction with the very strictures on female conduct that prevented her from publishing in her own name, Merril penned a story in which a lone female medic commands authority over not only her own body but also those of the male crew. As medical officer aboard a merchant spaceship, Anita Filmord, a "hippy blond who was nobody's visiting daughter or friend," must for practical reasons be all women to the otherwise all-male crew of this necessarily "small ship [where] the payload counts" ("Lady" 44, 53). Her job as medical officer involves maintaining optimum physical and psychological health in the all-male crew throughout the dangerous maneuvers of jumping through "holes" in space into uncharted territories. Sex is just another physical need to be met, and thus just another item in the medical officer's job description. Anita delivers sex and seduction to the ship's crew with the same professionalism with which she meets their other medical needs. Anita is closely identified with the spaceship itself, which is dubbed a "tramp" ship:

> She [the ship] had been lovely once, sleek-lined and proud, with shining flanks; and men had come to her with hungry hearts and star-filled eyes, and high pulse of adventure in their blood. Now she was old. Her hide was scarred with use, her luster dulled; though there was beauty in her still it was hidden deep. A man had to know where to look—and he had to care [41].

This identification implies that the professional woman is, like the "tramp" ship, sullied and scarred by her involvement in the vagaries of commerce. And yet both Anita and the ship itself perform vital economic roles: the ship transports commercial cargo in space, while Anita's ministrations to the crew, including regular bouts of medicinal sex, keep the men working productively: "[He] drank from the flask when it nuzzled his lips, and swallowed the pills that she put in his mouth, and gave back what *she* needed: the readings and scannings and comps and corrections that went to the driver's seat, to the pilot's board" (56). As a scientist and a professional, Anita does not let her own desires interfere with the task at hand: "*Which one do you want?*" Terry, one of the crew, asks Anita, as she leads him to her cabin, to the "door where the light would be flashing red outside." "Which *one*? How could she possibly tell.... *Which one needs her?*" (56).

The story is told from the point of view of Terry, a newcomer to the ship, whose response to Anita's sexuality is aligned with conventions more familiar to Merril's 1950s readership. In this story, Merril intentionally experimented with writing from a male point of view, an accomplishment that was not lost on the prominent writer Robert Heinlein: "Is Rose Sharon actually female?" he asked the publisher of *Venture*, adding, "This writer seems to have actual background of field engineering and 'board-ship' psychology. If not, the accomplishment is all the more impressive" (Heinlein to Bob Mills, April 18, 1956, 7.55, MP). Once he discovered the real identity of the author of "Lady," Heinlein wrote to Merril about it several times over the years. What impressed him most was the creative imagination it must have taken to envision what it felt like to be "a still damp junior officer, all theory and no practical experience [...] and how it feels to get the nonsense knocked out of him" (Heinlein to Mr. and Mrs. Sugrue, October 7, 1960, 7.55, MP).

As the new IBMan officer, Terry is responsible for both manipulating the abstract mechanical brain whose function it is to permit the "dance of escape" (56) from the bounds of Earth and plotting coordinates for the crucial (and potentially fatal) space-warp jumps in space-time throughout the galaxies. "Tramp work was the toughest" (46), thinks Terry, who is tortured by the sight of the decrepit ship and the cocktail lounge–like atmosphere of life on board, by his sense of masculine competitiveness in the presence of its medic's obvious seductive behavior and her sexual intimacy with the men, and his need nevertheless to do well in this assignment in order to win a top post elsewhere. Resembling the lone male adventurer of conventional space operas, Terry's presence in the story highlights the threatening aspects of Anita's professionalized sexuality. Referring to her as a "bitch," "whore," and "tramp" (56), conventional terms for women who assert their sexual autonomy, Terry feels threatened by a woman whose sexuality is not owned and controlled by any one man. Anita's sexual authority is made possible by the fact that space travel deprives people of "natural" sexual outlets, making sexuality the purview of technological intervention rather than natural determinism. Traditionally reviled, the "professional woman" is now a highly prized expert. Similar situations exist in Westerns such as the 1939 John Ford film *Stagecoach*, in which the prostitute Dallas delivers a baby during a harrowing stagecoach journey. In this example, the shortage of "respectable" women creates a demand for the "womanly" skills that prostitutes are called upon to perform. In Merril's 1950s version of this plot, however, the professional woman retains ownership over her body and sexuality, whereas the prostitutes in many Westerns are openly exploited by men.

## Tragic Sacrifice

Merril's fictional oeuvre does not embrace the technological reorganization of the family and of gender relations without reservation. Two of her other mid–1950s space stories, "So Proudly We Hail" (1953) and "Dead Center" (1954), explore the potentially tragic implications of professional womanhood by depicting failed attempts of professional women to fulfill their traditional roles as wives and mothers.

Professional women have always posed a problem for American gender ideology because women are supposed to give of themselves freely, not in return for compensation. Consequently, narratives about professional women in both the nineteenth and mid-twentieth centuries try to resolve the contradiction between women's professional and "womanly" identities. In frontier mythology, professional women appear most frequently as teachers, less often as doctors — professions in which "feminine," nurturing attributes become skills that women are paid for. In Westerns such as Wister's *The Virginian* and Bower's *Chip, of the Flying U*, the professional woman eventually sacrifices her work to take up her traditional role as wife to the hero. In this way, these characters pose minimal threat to the established gender ideology.

By the 1950s, women were visible in more traditionally masculine professions. As Bonnie Noonan demonstrates in *Woman Scientists in Fifties Science Fiction Films* (2005), a central concern of science fiction cinema in the 1950s was the woman of science, whose role as a professional was represented as conflicting with her role as a wife and mother (99). The films Noonan describes resolve this tension through the visual language of the woman's sexual attractiveness, which is invoked to reassure film audiences that she is still a woman despite her professional abilities.

Merril also saw the professional woman as a conflicted figure. She addressed the tension between professional and "womanly" identity, not by sexualizing her female characters, but by emphasizing their internal struggle to balance the conflicting demands of their roles as professionals and as wives and mothers. While Merril deploys this technique in almost all of her stories about women and space travel, "So Proudly We Hail" and "Dead Center" merit separate discussion because both stories end with the scene of a rocket launch that is also a moment of tragic — though remarkably unsentimental — sacrifice. Thus, on Merril's space frontier, where professional women do *not* ultimately sacrifice their profession to their womanhood, some other form of sacrifice must be made. In other words, if the professional woman is unwilling to sacrifice her occupation for the sake of her family, then someone else has to fill her place on the altar.

## *"So Proudly We Hail" (1953) and "Dead Center"(1954)*

In these stories, as in narratives such as "Daughters of Earth" (discussed previously), Merril partially resolves the tension between women's roles as professionals and as wives and mothers by depicting marriages of professionals. Both are set in the very early days of spaceflight. In "So Proudly We Hail," strong, healthy, skilled married couples make up the majority of a sizable colonizing expedition to Mars, an arrangement that, to invoke Noonan's eloquent phrase, enables women to "[join] in the adventure" of space travel without compromising their ability to marry and risking the stigma of single womanhood (2). The considerable downside to this arrangement is that the professional couple's responsibilities are divided between those of the nation and those of the family, a theme reinforced in the story's title. Ultimately, the story calls into question the extent to which a harmonious merger of the private and the professional is even possible.

The professional couple in "So Proudly We Hail," Sue and Will, must meet the strict qualifications set by the militaristic authority in charge of the expedition. When Sue learns that, because of a minor health problem, she has been rejected by the space service, she conceals this news from Will because she does not want him to sacrifice his own dream of adventure in space. Not until the eleventh hour does Sue finally try to reveal that she is not going, but Will jumps to the only conclusion that he can think of: Sue's about-face must be due to an affair. Sue decides not to correct Will, so that he will continue his plans to join the expedition rather than choose to remain on Earth with her. By the time Will accidentally learns that Sue has been rejected by the organizers of the expedition and is not having an affair, it is too late for him to change his mind. On the morning of the launch of the expedition, Sue attends the launch ceremony. Overcome by grief, she throws herself into the flames of the launching rocket and is killed.

"Dead Center" ends more tragically with the deaths (in quick succession) of the members of an entire family. It is a tribute to Merril's skills as a writer that "Dead Center" is one of only a handful of science fiction stories ever to be selected for Martha Foley's annual *Best American Short Stories: 1955*. In this 1954 story, professional and "womanly" roles are again conflated through a gendered division of scientific labor between Jock, the husband and space traveler, and Ruth, his wife and the designer of ships that will take men to the Moon. Noonan observes in science fiction films of the period that young boys are often represented as victims of women's increasing social power, which robs them of their patriarchal inheritance (80). "Dead Center" similarly depicts a six-year-old boy, Jock and Ruth's son Toby, as the primary sacrificial victim of the professionalized family. Ruth, who was rich and famous when she met Jock, subsequently became a full-time housewife and mother. When Jock is lost track of during the first manned mission to the Moon (the story was written fifteen years before the first actual mission was completed), on a rocket Ruth did not design, she is cajoled into helping with the investigation to find out what went wrong and to rescue him. She is reluctant to reenter space work because of the conflict between her professional and marital involvement: as the engineer she must "think of what happened ... from the outside," but as Jock's wife, she can't help but "[remember] how it had been for *her*" (13). Ruth is also aware that Toby needs even more of her attention as he struggles to understand his father's disappearance, but she also finds herself increasingly preoccupied with the technical challenge and the public relations side of the rescue mission. This conflict between public and private desires and duties is the significant downside of the professional marriage.

Ruth's internal conflict must have resonated for American readers of the early atomic age, who, as discussed in Chapter 2, were encouraged by the U.S. government to view the home as the first line of defense in the event of nuclear war (McEnaney 2000, 11–39). Anxieties about the emerging militarized family of the 1950s permeate the crisis at the heart of "Dead Center." When Ruth does go to work on the mission to rescue both Jock and the space program, Toby, who is also a viewpoint character, mistakenly assumes that his mother is going to the Moon just as his father did. When he hears her in a public speech saying that "being Jock Kruger's wife was more important to her than anything else" (21), Toby takes it literally. But he is too young and too afraid to share his doubts and anxieties with anyone (other than the readers of the story). As the launch approaches, the sponsors of the mission, a partnership of private investors and the military, persuade Ruth to bring Toby to the launch as a public statement of her confidence in the program. Against her better judgment, Ruth agrees. While she is busy behind the scenes at the launch, she leaves Toby in the care of his grandmother. He had toured the rocket and asked Ruth a lot of questions: "She had never seen Toby so intent on anything. He wanted to know everything. Where's this, and what's that for? And where are you going to sit, Mommy?" (22). Believing that his mother is on the rocket, and terrified that she will disappear like his father, Toby sneaks away from his grandmother and stows away on the rocket; he finds "the spot he wanted" (23), in the dead center of the machine. Toby's body is discovered in the wreckage of the crash caused at the launch. The rescue mission is aborted. Ruth, we are told, dies of an overdose of pills. Jock is eventually discovered dead of starvation on the far side of the Moon: "They made an international shrine of the house, and the garden where the three graves lay" (25). Whereas women professionals in popular Westerns are the ones who make the necessary sacrifices to restore the social order that their very professionalism disturbs, the entire chain of events in "Dead Center" is set in motion when Ruth returns from motherhood to her profession, resulting in the sacrifice of her entire family.

## Merril's Radical Vision

Merril's perpetual focus on women, children, families, home, marriage, pregnancy, and other "feminine" themes, and her experimentation with new social structures, distinguished her work not only from male-authored fiction of the 1950s but also from most other prominent "pre-feminist" women science fiction authors, including Leigh Brackett, Katherine MacLean, and C. L. Moore, who, although innovative space-travel authors in their own right, did not so brazenly write about topics that were conventionally marked as "feminine" and "domestic," and eschewed by advocates of a more "manly" science fiction. Merril deployed the space frontier as a setting in which gender, sexuality, and reproduction, abstracted from their old, comfortable, "civilized" context, must adapt to new conditions. Indeed, if men and women could transcend the boundaries of space and time, surely the boundaries of sex and gender, family structure, and reproduction were permeable as well. Hence, Merril's space travelers discover (and create) new social worlds as well as new planets: the matriarchal dictatorship on the ship Survival, the asexual world of Aldebaran IV, the utilitarian sex of "The Lady Was a Tramp," the "space-baby" nurseries on the Moon, and the willing cooperation of the colonists on Uller. At the same time, Merril did not completely transcend old fears that woman professionals would disrupt the "natural" social order. If women professionals in popular Westerns were ultimately called upon to sacrifice their professions for the sake of their womanhood, in Merril's fiction, claiming an identity as a professional woman also has its price.

CHAPTER 4

# Alien Encounters

Since the nineteenth century, the ideology and practice of American expansion has been riven with contradictions between the racist ideology that justified it and the threat of the "impure" populations co-opted by it. Both the forced removal of the "Five Civilized Tribes" to Indian Territory during the 1830s and the annexation of half the territory of Mexico in 1848 were acts of territorial expansion predicated on constructions of Anglo-American identity as racially superior and therefore entitled, even destined, to occupy the whole of the American continent. As Amy Kaplan and Shelly Streeby have shown, these acts of territorial expansion, by co-opting populations constructed as "foreign" or "alien" into America's borders, threatened the very ideology of racial purity — and therefore superiority — that justified U.S. expansion in the first place (Kaplan 1998, 584; Streeby 2002, 20). Andrew Jackson dealt with the contradiction of the forced removal of the tribes to territories west of the Mississippi through what has been famously called the "Trail of Tears." Many opposed war with Mexico on the grounds that its people were a mongrelized race that would contaminate a racially pure America (Streeby, 112).

Both John Rieder (2008) and Sharon DeGraw (2009) have demonstrated the continuity of these nineteenth-century narratives of imperial expansion within foundational science fiction narratives of the early twentieth century, particularly exemplified by Edmund Hamilton's space operas with their battling Terran (Earth) heroes and evil aliens, and Edgar Rice Burroughs's Barsoom series, in which a Southern aristocrat is mysteriously transported to Mars while exploring Indian caves in Arizona. Like the imperialist adventure narratives that were popular at the time (Kaplan 1990), Burroughs's *A Princess of Mars* (1917) resolves the problem of "alien" incorporation through a romance between the American adventurer and an aristocratic female who represents the "best" of the alien group. The ancient, white-race creators of this civilization are extinct, having joined with other great races of early Martians "who were dark, almost black, and also with the reddish yellow race that had flourished at the same time" (64) to form Princess Deja's hybrid race, which is now at war both internally and with the green people. The hero, John Carter, becomes entangled in interracial conflicts among the different groups on Mars, heroically leads the "superior" Martian race to victory, falls in love with its princess, and conceives a child with her. Such narratives sustained America's identity as a frontiering nation following the closure of the frontier as well as reifying a racially white, American identity; as non–Anglo, nonwhite groups gained visibility and power in American society, science fiction narratives of alien encounters deployed the figure of the alien to shore up white male identity and supremacy (DeGraw 2009, 1–9).

## Normalcy and Paranoia in the 1950s

Merril's fiction critically demonstrates how this discourse of alienness was applied in the 1950s to a new, less visible host of enemies that would be created by McCarthyism. Merril also connected the alien "other" to an even longer tradition of woman as "other" in stories about alien visitors to Earth who adopt a female disguise to "pass" in Cold War society. Finally, Merril challenged America's colonial legacy and its continued stance of cultural supremacy through narratives that are sympathetic to the "alien" point of view and expose the fallibility of the colonial gaze — its propensity to misrecognize and misunderstand, and its desire to dominate, the "other."

### *McCarthyism: "Whoever You Are" (1952)*

In the 1950s, Cold War America engaged in a different form of expansion as it emerged as a dominant world power in both economic and military terms, and this expansion once again went hand-in-hand with anxieties about an alien presence within America's enlarged borders. Originally coined as a critical reflection on the anti-communist campaign of U.S. Senator Joseph McCarthy, the term "McCarthyism" came to describe the paranoia and excesses of the campaign, which began to wane in the mid–1950s. These anxieties became politically manifest in the McCarthyist persecution of communists, homosexuals, civil rights activists, and numerous other groups, who in the first half of the 1950s were routinely depicted as foreign threats lurking within national borders, and down the street, and under the bed. Because the targets of McCarthyism and Cold War paranoia were more ideological than racial (although Chinese, Hispanics, and racially based civil rights groups in America certainly suffered setbacks during the era of McCarthy [Marable 2007, 17], less easily categorized, and less distinguishable visibly, the threat they represented was twofold: one could be victimized *by* them or one could be accused *as one of* them, since that difference was not necessarily defined in terms of visibility, and indeed could very well be hidden in the guise of normality. Hence, white identity was not the guarantee of privileged identity in American culture that it once was. These anxieties about a generalized alien threat—and about the possibility of being subsumed by that threat—became manifest culturally in the proliferation of alien figures in Cold War American popular film and fiction, with which no other period in American culture is more strongly identified. The many forms that aliens took during the Cold War period reflect the abstract form that alien threats took in the Cold War imagination.

Merril's early McCarthy-era story "Whoever You Are" (1952) is a critique of the discourse of alien threat we have just described. This story imagines an expansionist, future galactic empire called the "Solar System." Scout ships, called "Baby Byrds," are routinely sent out from Earth to find new worlds to colonize (by what means is not explained), while the womb-like "electromagnetic gravatic Web of Force" defense system around the Earth detects and expunges alien threats. The relationship between expansion of empire and alien threat is clear.

When the returning Baby Byrd III is discovered to have aliens aboard and is immobilized by "The Web," a team is sent to board and investigate the ship. Although the original crew are missing, the search team discovers four incapacitated aliens. A note left by crew member George Gentile introduces the aliens as representatives of a benevolent race who are on a mission of peaceful exchange—who, indeed, are so trusting and benevolent in nature that they cannot understand why humans would keep them out of the Solar System in the first place. The note also reports, without much elaboration, that the captain, Malcolm, has committed suicide, and that the original crew has volunteered to remain on the aliens' home planet to free up space on the ship for the aliens to visit the Solar System as benevolent emissaries. Upon further searching of the ship, however, captain Malcolm's log is discovered, warning that the aliens are malevolent mind-controlling telepaths who have manipulated the crew into admitting them to the ship, and explaining that he will kill himself rather than allow the aliens to control his mind as well. So what manner of aliens are they, really?

The aliens on the ship are humanoid, looking remarkably like humans, only larger. Lacking any concrete evidence of the aliens' character or motivations, and unwilling to risk allowing the aliens to regain consciousness and explain themselves lest they unleash some unknown power, the various players in the unfolding drama have nothing to go on except their judgment of the character and sanity of the missing captain and crew, which in turn calls their own judgment into question in various ways. Some find Gentile's account plausible because "you can't tell with the brass when they get ideas in their heads" ("Whoever," 72), while others have a hard time understanding how or why the reputable Captain Malcolm would kill himself. The psychofficer is particularly suspicious of Malcolm's cynicism and attracted to the possibility of a race of aliens so loving that they are incapable of understanding any other kind of relationship with another civilization. This atmosphere of paranoia and uncertainty is not unlike that which existed in the lead-up to McCarthyism, gathering momentum as Merril wrote this story: like communism, the aliens represent, to some, an evil threat in the guise of benevolence. Earth's defense system is well set up to tackle conventional threats, not this alien "Trojan Horse." Such was the scenario described by J. Edgar Hoover in a 1945 speech in which he outlined the threats represented by Communism: "The Fascist-minded tyrant who we conquered on the battlefields is no different from the American communist corruptionist who now uses the trick of the confidence man until his forces are sufficiently strong to rise with arms in revolt." Whereas the fascist threat was easy to recognize, communism lurked beneath benevolent guises: The communist "poses behind a dozen fronts ... squirms and twists his way into those great American forces such as the church, schools, and the ranks of labor" (quoted in Fried 1997, 17).

If Edgar Rice Burroughs's aliens on Mars shored up the identity of the white male hero through their fixed, primitive identities, Merril's more ambiguously identified aliens on their way to Earth leave her male adventurers unsettled and self-doubting. As we have seen in Merril's story "That Only a Mother," such threats to masculine subjectivity lead to male violence. In "Whoever You Are," the ranking officer orders that the ship with the comatose aliens aboard be escorted to a holding area, with orders to destroy it on the first sign of a threat. Soon, Joe Fromm, the crewman from Earth who has been assigned to pilot the alien ship, reports that the aliens are attempting to communicate with him telepathically. That basic information is enough for the commanding officer to order the ship's (and Fromm's) destruction, on which note the story abruptly ends. Merril's story of an unspecified alien threat violently extinguished captures the increasingly paranoid discourses of alienness that underpinned McCarthyism, leading to knee-jerk persecution of an unclear, and perhaps totally innocent, alien threat.

## *Interspecies Romance and Marriage: "Pioneer Stock" (1955)*

Romance and marriage plots are a classic alternative to expunging an alien presence from the American "homeland." Overlapping proto–Darwinian discourses of racial difference, these narratives grapple with the "problem" of integrating races constructed as essentially different: the rational, enlightened white subject versus the savage "other." The ability, or more often inability, for such unions to produce fertile offspring signifies the potential for different racial groups to coexist within one society. In early nineteenth-century frontier narratives, sex and romance between Native and white lovers, such as Uncas and Cora in Cooper's *The Last of the Mohicans*, often ended in the tragic death of one or both lovers, which signified the impossibility of future reconciliation of Native and white populations. Only the racially pure (white) Alice and Duncan survive as the symbolic progenitors of the future American race. Some authors, including Ann S. Stephens (*Malaeska*, 1860) and Lydia Maria Child (*Hobomok*, 1824), depicted relationships between Native and white lovers that produced mixed-blood offspring; however, the outcomes of these narratives do not bode well for the future of Native American culture — the mixed-blood figure in *Malaeska* commits suicide upon learning about his Native mother, and in *Hobomok*, the mixed-blood figure matures in complete ignorance of his Native father, signifying the gradual disappearance of Native American people through assimilation.

Miscegenation became a common theme in science fiction from its early years, as described by Nicholls (1993c, 1089). Cloaked in the marginality, fantasy settings, and future orientation of the genre, Merril and her colleagues were able to explore interspecies romance without having to reconcile their fiction as closely as Cooper and Stephens did with social and historical realities. In such texts as Burroughs's *A Princess of Mars*, interspecies romance was depicted less ambivalently than marriages between Indians and whites in nineteenth-century frontier narratives. For example, John Carter legitimizes his leadership on Mars through his alliance with Princess Deja Thoris and conceives a child with her. In the Burroughs tale, the child of this union of alien and human survives, but this is by no means a critique of racial purity ideologies since John Carter and Deja Thoris are both aristocrats and thus racial equals.

Merril's "Pioneer Stock" (1955) was written shortly after Philip José Farmer's novella "The Lovers" (1952), renowned for being so controversial and ground-breaking at the time due to its graphic depiction of sex and love between human and alien — although Justine Larbalestier in *The Battle of the Sexes in Science Fiction* has exposed this story as decidedly anti-feminist (2002a, 138). Before Farmer's story, there had been no explicit sex in magazine science fiction (Nicholls 1993c). Merril recasts the human/alien dynamic in idealized terms in "Pioneer Stock." Humans interbreed with an alien race, the Dzairdee of Ganymede, whose females are physically unable to bear children outside of a completely loving and trusting relationship, a trait that is inherited by the golden-skinned human-alien offspring. The first offspring of a Dzairdee and a human signifies the rightness of the union and ensures the peaceful settlement of humans on Ganymede. Rather than disappearing through assimilation with the colonizing human race, the golden offspring of the Dzairdee and humans represent a new and different amalgamation of both species.

## Woman as Alien

In *Women Scientists in Fifties Science Fiction Films* (2005), Bonnie Noonan makes a compelling case that a distinct sub-genre of the 1950s alien invasion film — the giant insect film — linked aliens not simply to the generic threat of any number of marginalized ethnic, racial, or socioeconomic groups, but specifically to the threat of middle-class American women who had been empowered by their expanding public roles in wartime and were resistant to reverting back to their former domestic roles (74). Robin Roberts demonstrates equally strong links between women and aliens in 1950s science fiction (1993, 40–65). More generally, the perennial construction of woman as man's "other"—irrational and unbounded in both mind and body—invites comparison between women and aliens as they are represented in science fiction. As Peter Nicholls reminds us, most science fiction was written for men: "[T]o immature men, women often appear like an alien race, and much popular sf reflects a fear of their threatening foreignness" (1993c, 1088–89). Judith Merril was in this period a type of outlaw figure herself— divorcing, marrying again, giving birth, having an abortion, divorcing again, facing custody battles for her children, and encountering wicked writer's block and living with a married science fiction writer. She then struck out on her own to maintain her family and recover her professional reputation in science fiction circles, which by the late 1950s she had more than succeeded in doing.

In Merril's alien stories from the mid–1950s — "Rain Check" (1954), "Exile from Space" (1956), and "Homecalling" (1956) — the author links women and aliens, engaging conventions from both the frontier captivity narrative and science fiction traditions. In "Rain Check" and "Exile from Space," Merril depicts the experiences of aliens who visit Earth disguised as women and are eventually discovered and pursued by authorities on Earth. This is an inversion of the captivity narrative tradition, a famous example of which is the seventeenth-century captivity narrative of the colonial American Mary Rowlandson; in this tradition, the captive is usually a Western subject (often a woman) among stereotypically depicted indigenous peoples, who struggles to decipher the alien culture's mores, codes, taboos, and so forth, while frequently also having to contend with pursuit (see Derounian-Stodola 1998; also Carter 1997). Through her female alien women in "Rain Check" and "Exile From Space," Merril defamiliarizes American social structures and mores, particularly with respect to the positions and experiences of white women. In the novella "Homecalling," Merril transforms the figure of the giant termite queen on an unnamed planet into a protagonist who saves, rather than threatens, the lives of two orphaned children from Earth. All of these stories deploy the identification of woman and alien precisely to open up new ways of writing about women's points of view and about femininity as a concept.

## "Rain Check" (1954)

Told from the point of view of an escaped Martian captive on Earth, who has taken the guise of a woman, "Rain Check" (1954) uses this perspective to demystify American cultural categories and norms, including gender relations and mass-market representations of gender. Thus, this story exploits the potential for the alien figure to function as a position from which to critique the dominant culture, a tradition that can be traced to nineteenth-century Native figures such as Magawisca in Sedgwick's *Hope Leslie* (1827). As the alien narrator studies the behavior and dress of Earth (read: American) men and women in order to perfect "her" performance of femininity, the narrative exposes femininity itself as more performed than real and demystifies the unspoken assumptions that underlie the narrator's adopted identity category.

The narrator takes the disguise of a woman because she correctly perceives that the identity category "average man" is not the safe haven that Earthlings believe it to be in the context of Cold War–like paranoia: "If you wanted to get around on your own at a time like this, it wasn't the best possible shape to have" ("Rain Check," 135). Although the National Security Chief, Alan Landrin, instructs a meeting of civil defense officers to search for an average-looking man because "man is the best possible form for this environment here on Earth" (142), the narrator realizes that "woman" is the more effective disguise precisely because of women's invisibility with respect to the dominant culture and their perceived state of dependence in the public sphere. The narrator also counts on Landrin "overestimating my brain power, and [not] appreciating what I could do with my body" (126). Exploiting this situation, the narrator allows a civil defense warden named Mike Bonito, whom she meets at a restaurant, to essentially act as her chaperone, finding her a rooming house and escorting her there. While the narrator, through her analysis of Bonito's behavior, both manipulates and undermines assumptions about feminine dependence, she nonetheless misses other aspects of American gender discourse, such as the predatory model of sexual attraction that underlies male chivalry. Hence the narrator is confused by a "hungry, judicial look" (130) that frequently appears on Bonito's face, not realizing his unspoken expectation that she will return his assistance with sex: "He didn't leave. He just wandered around the room, opening and closing his mouth as if he was going to say something and then changed his mind each time. [...] Then when he turned toward me, he'd seem angry. But all he said, finally, was: 'Okay, kid, have it your way'" (136). Moments of cognitive dissonance such as this expose to the reader the contradictory nature of American gender discourse, which leaves the narrator perplexed but involves the reader in an in-joke with the author about the agenda that drives many acts of male chivalry. As these contradictions become increasingly clear to the narrator, she becomes more and more disenchanted with Earth: "I want to go home," she resolves in the story's last line (145).

Merril is particularly insightful in her representation of gender as performative but nonetheless embodied, anticipating a problem that theorist Judith Butler later addressed in two of her major works, *Gender Trouble* (1990) and *Bodies That Matter* (1993). In *Gender Trouble*, Butler articulated her now famous theory of gender as a repeated performance, through dress and behavior, of an identity category. It is the *repetition* of this performance that appears to produce gender as an essential core identity that *causes* gender behavior, but is *actually* the *effect* of repeated performances (J. Butler 1990, 178–80). In her later work *Bodies That Matter*, Butler addressed the critique that her primarily discursive model of gender failed to account for the materiality of the body. Forty years before Butler articulated her celebrated theory of performativity, however, Merril's fiction demonstrates her awareness of the complexity of gender identity as both an effect of discourse *and* a profoundly embodied experience: to perfect her disguise, the narrator in "Rain Check" looks to the women around her and to images of men and women on billboard advertisements to fashion the appropriate appearance, clothing, and accessories. Presumably, she must do so because she lacks the essential, core identity that would enable her to instinctively "be" a woman. Yet she is not very different from Merril's women readers of the day, who also learn how to be "women" by watching and imitating other women, as well as idealized women featured in advertisements; do Merril's women readers, therefore, also lack, then, an essential, female core?

Not only does the narrative expose the category "woman" as imitative and performative rather than essential, but it also emphasizes femininity as a performance that must be repeated. To sustain her disguise, the "shapeshifting" narrator must be vigilant. Hence the narrator periodically inspects her appearance: "I took a good long look at myself in the mirror. My hair was messy, and my lips weren't quite the same kind of red as the other woman I'd seen. I fixed that, and then remembered to take a comb and a lipstick to account for it" ("Rain Check," 133). A lack of attention to details such as facial features, lip color, cosmetic kit, and so on might compromise her disguise, reveal her "alien" nature, and expose her to capture. Again, Merril's alien narrator's position is not very different from so-called "real" women, who must also periodically inspect their appearance in comparison with a perceived standard represented by other women. Indeed, Mike Bonito makes this point when he says, "Ain't that just like a woman?" (134) after the narrator returns from one of her shapeshifting sessions. This predicament, although treated humorously by Merril, is not unlike that of many gay and lesbian people, as Butler points out: their homosexuality is considered monstrous in the larger society, and they face punishment if they fail to correctly "perform" a (heterosexual) gender.

The narrator also learns that mass-market images of women represent impossible ideals. As a shapeshifter, she can imitate ideals better than real women can, and thereby learns that such images are not meant to be imitated perfectly. For example, she realizes that people wear different clothing to sleep in from what they wear during the day. When her landlady knocks on her door in the morning, she realizes she will raise questions if she appears in the same clothing she wore the previous day, so she changes her appearance to imitate a billboard advertisement. However, when her landlady gets "her first look at me in my new negligee ... [she gasps], and her eyebrows [arch] suddenly into two inverted V's. At first, I thought I'd done something wrong. But I could see myself in a long mirror in the hall, it looked just like the illustration on the billboard. Then I realized what a sap I'd been. [...] I wasn't dressed for sleeping, but for modeling an advertisement" (137–38). When the narrator complains to Mike Bonito about all the rain, he seems perplexed: "Some girls come all apart at the seams the minute they get a drop of water on 'em. I guess your hair is natural" (138–39). Fortunately, the narrator knows by now that she can disarm this type of probing observation with a coy smile.

Throughout the story, the narrator's efforts to disguise herself as a "real" woman repeatedly confront Merril's women readers with their own performances, thereby calling into question essentialist thinking about gender identity. Ingeniously, however, Merril deploys the shapeshifter trope to represent gender performance in terms of embodiment rather than as a purely discursive or symbolic practice. Her alien fashions the accessories of femininity — blonde hair, a comb, lipstick, a raincoat — out of her very body; indeed, her accessories cannot be completely separated from her body: when a man tugs at her raincoat, she feels pain. This image differentiates the narrator from "real" women who wear their clothing. However, is the narrator's situation really all that different from that of Merril's 1950s readers, whose identities are almost as deeply invested in the symbols and accessories with which they adorn their own bodies?

## *"Exile from Space"* (1956)

"Exile from Space" (1956) is also told from the point of view of a woman "alien," an orphaned human born on Earth and raised by aliens identified only as "they." We learn through a series of obscure references that the aliens' laws forbid them from interfering with other worlds, so they have raised the orphan on their spaceship to become a spy for them on Earth — not with malevolent intent, it seems, but out of curiosity. Unlike the narrator in "Rain Check," this "alien" has no shapeshifting tricks up her sleeve, only some rough ideas about how to fit in (behaviorally and physiologically), raise some cash to get by on, and stay out of trouble:

> I found a place to park the car near the drugstore. That was the first thing I was supposed to do. Find a drugstore, where there would be a phone directory, and go in and look up the address of a hock shop. [...] I didn't dare get into any trouble that might end up with a policeman asking to see my license, which always seemed to be the first thing they did on television, when they talked to anybody who had a car ["Exile," 7].

Like the narrator in "Rain Check," the narrator of this story has learned about Earth from the media — television and books — and learns through trial and error on the ground about discrepancies with respect to aspects of earthly life that books and television contradict or seem silent about — especially sex. The narrator, Tina, meets and falls in love with Larry, a human who is revealed to be a pilot working for a nascent space-exploration program. Because representations of heterosexual love on television "stop at kissing," and books are contradictory, the narrator knows little about sex beyond its biology; she is at a loss to understand her feelings toward Larry or what is in store for her when Larry promises to teach her about "a little thing we have around here we call sex" ("Exile," 25). Again, the alien's position is not unlike that of Merril's 1950s women readers, who were taught that "good girls"— before they marry — know nothing of sex beyond the limited sex education they received in school. Merril was, after all, writing this story before the oral contraceptive ("The Pill") era of reliable birth control. Meanwhile, the 27-year-old Larry assumes the role of teacher where sex is concerned, in keeping with double standards of the time that condoned male sexual experimentation before marriage and ascribed to men the role of educating "nice girls" about sex — after marriage, of course.

The wrench that Merril throws into this conventional romance machinery is that her narrator has been raised entirely within the mores of her alien foster culture, and therefore cannot be held responsible for not knowing how to be a "nice girl." Indeed, one of Larry's first clues that the narrator is an imposter is that, during a romantic drive, she asks him to park the car. "Any girl on Earth, no matter how sheltered, how inexperienced, would have known better than that" (29). While Larry begins to doubt the narrator's "innocence," a life-

and-death matter to him because of his top-secret work in the space program, the reader understands that the narrator simply hasn't learned how to be a "nice girl." This twist enables Merril to represent a woman learning about sex for herself rather than from her husband, not only through television and books but also through *practice*: "I found out why the television shows stop with a kiss. The rest is very private and personal" (33). In contemplating sex with Larry, the narrator also wrestles with the prospect of a child and how that would complicate her current situation: where would she raise it? On Earth, with the threat of pursuit and capture? On the alien ship? "Getting born is complicated. Oxygen, gravity, things like that. You can't raise a *human* baby on a spaceship.... Human? What's *human*?" (27). Should she end the pregnancy if there is one? All of these questions were barred from open discussion in 1950s American culture. Yet Merril, a woman who was no stranger to the punitive aspects of transgressive behavior and no doubt familiar with the Kinsey Reports — those infamous, pioneering American surveys on human sexual behavior in males, published in 1948, and females, published in 1953 — finds a way to articulate taboo questions through her manipulation of the conventions of science fiction.

Almost immediately upon their arrival on Earth, the protagonists of both "Rain Check" and "Exile from Space" are, like single women on the frontier, beset by predatory men who see unchaperoned young women as fair game. Merril's women readers would be familiar with this experience, raising the disturbing possibility that they were also captives within their own culture: like Merril's aliens, their movement on Earth was restricted at every turn, and they might have perceived a gap between largely male-authored mass-cultural representations of women and their own experiences that could very well make them feel like alien visitors. Perhaps Merril's readers deciphered American patriarchy in tandem with her alien narrators.

Like Merril's alien narrators, Native American characters in nineteenth-century frontier narratives frequently function as social critics of the dominant culture. In Cooper's *Last of the Mohicans*, the villainous Magua voices the crimes his tribe has suffered at the hands of the colonists. Although he is not a sympathetic character, other Native American social critics in frontier texts are: In *Hope Leslie*, Sedgwick's novel of the Puritan colonies, the heroine Magawisca constantly challenges the Puritans' conviction that their colony is divinely ordained (Kelley 1987, xxvii). Like Magawisca, Merril's aliens are, from their position of difference, able to recognize the hypocrisies and contradictions that go unnoticed or disavowed by the dominant culture. If Sedgwick's nineteenth-century Anglo-American readers were confronted with their position as colonists, Merril's 1950s women readers were alienated from the seemingly trivial practices that constituted and naturalized their everyday social reality as women.

## Giant Bugs and the Monstrous Feminine: "Homecalling" (1956)

A third story, published in 1956 and further discussed in Chapter 5, links aliens to the feminine in a different way, focusing on the figure of the monstrous feminine. Merril had begun writing the novella in 1952, but due to the upheaval in her personal life at the time, it got pushed to the side of her agenda until she hit a writing streak in 1955. "Homecalling" (1956) plays on the B-movie "giant insect" films of the 1950s that, according to Noonan, often feature women scientists and displace tensions between their professional and feminine roles onto monstrous, feminized insects that must be contained to save the world (74). This overlapping discourse of alienness, femininity, and the monstrous can be traced to representations of women and Native Americans before 1900. Native Americans were depicted as both feminized and demonic in Puritan captivity narratives, in classic texts such as Cooper's *Last of the Mohicans*, and in countless dime novels in the vein of Edward S. Ellis's *Seth Jones* (1860) — feminized in the sense that Indians in *Seth Jones*, for example, are represented as more animal than human, controlled by instincts and impulses just as women's subjectivity was commonly thought to be determined by biology rather than reason. If the monstrous can be understood as that which violates natural law, women who claimed power and authority and were depicted as unnaturally "mannish" in nineteenth-century caricatures of suffragettes (Sheppard 1994, 88–89), for example, can be linked to Noonan's feminized giant bugs.

"Homecalling" intercedes in this discourse of female power as monstrous. This story features a powerful, giant female termite-like insect called Daydanda, the benevolent queen-mother of the colony who adopts a scientist couple's children after their spaceship crashes and the parents are killed. In the eight-and-a-half-year-old Deborah's first encounter with the alien lifeform in the forest, she mistakes it for "a fairy-delicate translucent spiral thing and then a large mauve mushroom in the center" (22). Although only a child, Deborah tries to make sense of it, for "things don't just happen this way, somebody planted it" (22). Then she realizes that the "it" *is* a "somebody": "The thing was lying on its side, sucking a lower follicle of the arch, its livid belly working as convulsively as its segmented mouth, its many limbs sprawled out in all directions" (22). Deborah counts six legs and six lips and also notices the absence of eyes. Only the lips are frightening to her, "all thick and round-looking, not like people's lips" (23).

At first repulsed by the hideous appearance of the bloated queen termite, Daydanda, the orphaned girl gradually learns to trust and communicate with her, which enables Deborah and her baby brother Petey to survive on the alien planet. But it is very much a two-way street; Deborah's narrative moves in tandem with Daydanda's, as the latter tries to figure out what and who the strangers are, and if they pose a threat to her colony. That the strangers are children is not readily apparent, except for the single fact that one of the strangers is larger than the other. The children are roughly the scale of the insects, but what are they to each other: "lady and consort," or perhaps "mother and baby" (34)? By intercepting their thoughts and observing their behavior, Daydanda concludes correctly that not only are they children, they are also motherless (35).

When "Homecalling" was published in the mid–1950s, Merril was approaching the pinnacle of her success at writing and editing in American science fiction. Perhaps she needed to be riding high and confident in order to grapple with depicting a grotesque "alien" like Daydanda. Merril had discovered (through therapy) her own long-standing self-identification as a monster. It was an idea developed early on when, as a small child, she was made to feel responsible for her older brother's accidental death and then lived alone with her mother after her father's suicide a few years later. Her widowed mother had to make a livelihood and home for the two of them. Merril's mother raised her to be a man, in the sense of encouraging her to express her opinions and to not hide her intelligence, and she also encouraged her to be a writer like her father had been (Merrill and Pohl-Weary 2002, 32–33).

Children often appeared in B-movie giant-insect films to reinforce the threat constituted by the professional woman: they were the victims of the unleashed, monstrous femininity represented by the giant insect on the loose (Noonan 2005, 80). Thus, in "Homecalling," young Deborah is the protector of her baby brother Petey, a sort of stand-in mother who, in the short term, copes with the essential chores, everything from creating makeshift diapers to amusing Petey with little games and preparing food suitable for a human baby to eat. Deborah and Petey are saved not through the containment or conquest of the giant insect, a standard science fiction film plot, but by learning to trust Daydanda to look after and care for them despite her alien appearance and ways. It is as though Merril is asking her readers to overcome, like Deborah and Petey, their own knee-jerk revulsion to the monstrosity of empowered femininity that Daydanda represents.

## Misrecognition of the "Other"

The child focalizer of "Homecalling" is an improvisation on another convention of science fiction: its reification and revision of the colonial gaze. As John Rieder demonstrates, early encounters with aliens in science fiction were a close relative of the western European anthropological narrative, thick with the Eurocentric assumptions of colonialism. The classic anthropological observer of the nineteenth and early twentieth centuries was the product of centuries of technological achievement centered in Europe, which enabled "him" (the gaze was overwhelmingly constructed as masculine) to observe the so-called primitive world with an enlightened, rational, and objective gaze. The objects of this gaze were indigenous as well as non–European peoples, fixed in an earlier time historically, more subject to natural forces and instincts, and without a critical consciousness of their own. Rieder points out, however, that the structure of the gaze holds within it the source of its own undoing — that is, the potential for the positions to *reverse*, for the observed to become observer.

Science fiction realized this potential early in its history with narratives of alien attack such as H. G. Wells's classic story *The War of the Worlds* and stories of alien abduction (Rieder 2008, 6–12). In her child focalizer in "Homecalling," whose point of view is repeatedly contrasted with that of the indigenous aliens, Merril deploys a colonizing subject — significantly, the young daughter of a geologist-mother. She is used to encountering aliens on family visits to outer space and is not fully habituated to the colonial gaze, and therefore more predisposed to reevaluate her relationship to the alien. As we have seen, Deborah is therefore able to overcome her fears and prejudices and accept protection from the insect-queen Daydanda. This is one of several stories in which Merril foregrounds the limitations of the colonial gaze.

## *Outpost Mars (1952) and "Daughters of Earth" (1952)*

In *Outpost Mars*, the novel she co-authored with Cyril M. Kornbluth under the joint pseudonym Cyril Judd, a mysterious presence threatens a fledgling colony on the planet Mars — or so some of the colonists believe (*Outpost Mars* 1952). The main character and protagonist, Dr. Tony Hellman, is adamant that there is no native animal life on Mars, no aliens; however, the earliest of the colonists tell stories about sightings of a race of "dwarfs" that inhabit the planet. The stories are puzzling because Mars had been scientifically checked over for alien life and none were detected. But the rumors persist. One colonist, a new mother on Mars and a patient of Tony's, is convinced that a dwarf-like figure came to her bedroom window with the intention of taking her newborn baby. Equally convinced that his patient, Polly, is fantasizing, Tony quiets her with sedatives. This scene was another move on Merril's part to reflect on the complexity of gender identity as an effect of discourse and an embodied experience. The 1950s witnessed a "tranquilizer boom" to reduce nervous tension and anxiety, mostly for regulating the out-of-control body of the female patient, typically a middle-class housewife (McCracken 2002, 61; Hughes and Brewin 1979). Leona Crabb in "Mother's Little Helper" (1992) links the mass popularity of tranquilizers with the 1950s-era obsession anxiety and gender-role conformity.

As the plot unfolds in *Outpost Mars*, however, Polly's point of view is validated, to a point: we learn eventually that there are dwarfs—they are indigenous and humanoid, the biologically adapted offspring of members of a (now extinct) early human colony on Mars that, for genetic reasons (the presence of a lethal gene), could not conceive on Earth but could do so on Mars. The dwarfs are hiding out in caves and indeed taking the colonists' babies, but for benevolent reasons—to aid the babies' survival on the planet. The babies are able to breathe in the Martian atmosphere—they do not require oxygen—but can survive only on a diet of marcaine, a substance mined in the colony for sale on Earth as a narcotic. For the sake of the future of their colonization project, the colonists decide to accept and protect the dwarfs, including their own mutant babies born on Mars, as their own people. This ending to the novel led the critic Brian Stableford to highlight *Outpost Mars* as a type of romantic colonization story, one that emphasizes the "quasimystical process of adaptation to the alien environment: a reharmonization of mankind and nature that often echoes the Eden Myth" (Stableford 1993, 245). The novel's male authority figure, a medical doctor and representative of privileged, colonial subjectivity, cannot make the discovery without his lab assistant Anna's help, because she proves to be receptive to telepathic communication from the aliens. This collaboration between Anna and Tony mirrors the very production of the novel, itself the result of male-female collaboration.

The more sophisticated, sole-authored novella "Daughters of Earth," to which we return once more, is also critical of the colonial enterprise and, in particular, stresses the limits of the colonists' ability to comprehend alien beings. The main storyline of "Daughters of Earth" pertains to the character Emma's depiction of life with fellow human colonists on a distant planet, Uller. The colonization phase of the expedition deals with themes familiar to American frontier literature, especially encounters with an unfamiliar landscape populated with alien and threatening inhabitants, which is part of a larger western European tradition of colonial narrative that pits a Eurocentric "civilization" against an exoticized, orientalized "other" (Said 1978, 1–31). As Susan A. George (2000) observes of certain 1950s science fiction films, "Daughters" is critical of the colonial enterprise and in particular resists orientalizing its aliens. The several generations of "Daughters" who collectively participate in Merril's epic story of space colonization include the adventurous Emma, medic for the colonizing ship *Newhope*. Shortly after arriving on the planet Uller, twenty-one light years from home, Emma becomes disillusioned when she watches her husband and fellow traveler, Ken, killed without fanfare by an Ullern: "It might have been a segment of petrified log.... But it had *six* legs, and the head was too shapeless; there was no visible mouth and there were no ears at all" ("Daughters" 1952, 231).

Subsequent developments, however, are quite different from traditional narratives of colonization and conquest insofar as the colonists are forced to redefine their own understanding of what constitutes an advanced civilization. For example, there is in the end no retribution for the killing of Ken, although there are those in the colony, including Emma, who hate the aliens for their actions. Nevertheless, they try to learn more about them to the point that Emma, her young daughter Leah, and a few others leave the first colony and establish a second one to study the Ullerns in peace.

The initial scientific observations of the planet by Emma and others had revealed no life in human terms — only flora and fauna of silicon, very brittle and therefore adapted to noiseless conditions. They eventually conclude that the Ullerns attacked the colonists and killed Ken out of fear, because of the noise and vibrations they made with their machinery, guns, and tools. This discovery sparks a heated epistemological debate over the measures involved in determining the presence of nonhuman intelligent life. Most of the colonists simply refuse to believe that intelligence is possible without sound. Nor is there any way for most of the space colonists to imagine mediating the ensuing encounter with the Ullerns other than with loud noises and deadly weapons, so completely unprepared are they for the presence of aliens in their midst. The colonists' assumption that intelligence cannot evolve without sound — a precondition for language — is reminiscent of European colonists' assumption that Native American languages — and therefore their level of intelligence and civilization — were inferior to that of Europeans because they did not use a written alphabet. Merril's colonists eventually learn that the Ullerns communicate by means of radio waves undetectable as sound by the human ear. Rethinking their definition of intelligence, Merrill's colonists learn to communicate with and win the trust of the Ullerns, whose cooperation and silicon bodies prove crucial to the success of the colony. In this aspect Merril's narratives of space colonization are in keeping with a pervasive trajectory of American frontier mythology — famous examples of which include the Pocahontas legend and Natty Bumppo's famous partnership with Chingachgook in Cooper's *Leatherstocking Tales* (1823–1841)—which, rather than questioning the colonial enterprise, inscribes a version of it in which the colonized willingly cooperate.

### *"Shrine of Temptation" (1962) and "The Lonely" (1963)*

Spaceships and the laws of biology and physics play almost no role in Merril's back-to-back stories of misrecognition of the "other": "Shrine of Temptation" (1962, written for a cover painting by George Barr) and "The Lonely" (1963, written for a cover painting by Virgil Finlay). Instead, first contact with alien worlds raises questions about the limits of both the dominant epistemologies undergirding the authority of science and a future Earth modeled after the Euro-American philosophical tradition to "know" cultures and peoples whose traditions differ radically from that of so-called "Western civilization." Ethnography, relying on participant observation in the field and systematic comparison of different cultures, and an important branch of social science by the 1950s, is the methodology Merril explores. Becoming ever more experimental with her writing in the early 1960s, Merril foregrounds the subjectivity of the space explorer through alternative narrative forms such as diaries, letters, anthropological field notes, and memos, rather than third-person narration; events in her stories are described obliquely, mediated through narrating subjects whose vision is highly provisional and uncertain. Merril's two stories absorb and discuss anthropology and the study of humankind in addition to questioning anthropological authority.

In "Shrine of Temptation," a member of an anthropological team from Earth narrates a first-person account of their study of an indigenous island people on a planet that we only know as alien through brief references to another human "ship" that "came down" ("Shrine," 22). Aside from that, there is very little to distinguish the story of these "brown-skinned and dark-eyed, black haired" (11) people from a stereotypical colonial encounter on Earth familiar in popular colonial narratives. The protagonist of the story is an eight-year-old island boy called Lallayall, nicknamed "Lucky" by the anthropologists. Presenting their "findings" in a scholarly article, the self-reflexive narrator refers with embarrassment to her field notes, which describe Lallayall as "a stolid impassive indigene" (13), as well as to a series of incorrect assumptions that expose the deepest ideological assumptions of the narrator and her colleagues. Here is one example:

> When we asked if [Lallayall had] prepared the food himself, he laughed uproariously and then said, with ostentatious patience, "*Mothers* cook food." Whether he meant mothers as a class (and in this case *his* mother), or several women of the class, mother, we did not know. Both assumptions were wrong, as it happened. He meant *his mothers* [14].

Because the anthropologists cannot conceive of mothering as work that can be carried out collectively, they completely misinterpret Lallayall's culture.

The narrator is especially preoccupied with the island people's terms *hallall* and *oklall*, which she interprets as meaning "in the fullness of time" and "unripe, green, out of place and time," respectively (18, 22). The elder islanders use these terms to answer many questions, especially from the children and the anthropologists, indicating an epistemology that differs from colonial epistemology in its view of knowledge as something that organically unfolds ("in the fullness of time") rather than something that is actively pursued. The

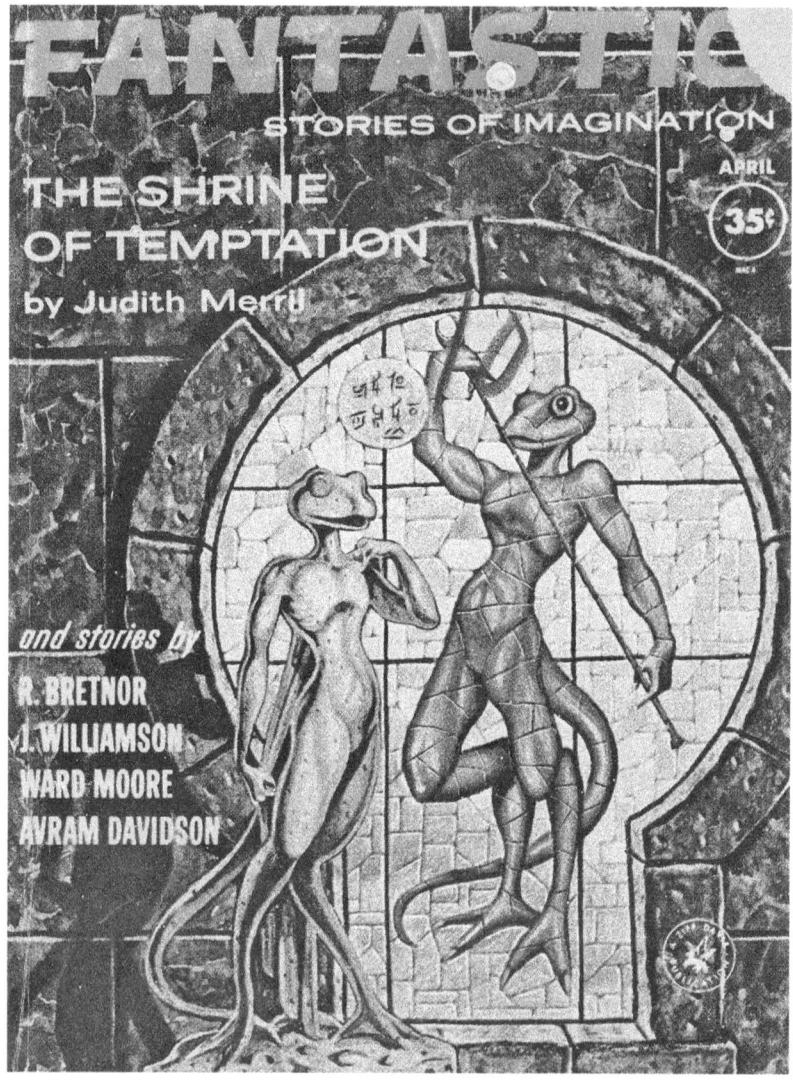

Merril's "Shrine of Temptation" was the cover story for *Fantastic Stories of Imagination*, April 1962. Illustration by George Barr.

anthropologists are also particularly interested in gaining knowledge about the islander's Shrine, which seems to be the source of their sacred knowledge, guarded by a mysterious statue. Brown-robed priestly figures called Shrinemen "had daily rituals to say; they performed certain calculations" (17). Throughout the story, the team of anthropologists works to gain the trust of the islanders in order to learn more about the mysterious Shrine, the gateway to which is represented in the cover art for the magazine. Instead of being laid bare by scientific inquiry, the Shrine becomes increasingly more mysterious as the story — or report — progresses. Merril does not describe the Shrine's appearance in full, orderly detail, but only suggestively, in stages: it is comprised of a structure fronted by a "Window of Light," guarded by two statues — one is a "blue Guardian" carrying a blue mace, and the other is an "amber Lifegiver" on a pedestal (17). Tended by the Shrinemen, the Shrine's significance to the community has to do with their memory of "the Life of the Shrine," an event or phenomenon that existed long ago but no longer, but that they expect to return in the future, which they call "the Recurrence" (16–17). At this time, the islanders believe that new wisdom will be given to them. This is about as much as we ever learn about the Shrine and its surrounding practices.

What the narrator finally does witness at the Shrine confounds her: three humans with malevolent but unexplained intentions arrive on a ship from Earth, and are met by Lucky, who just happens to be around when their ship lands. They tell Lucky that they have come to visit the famous Shrine, and they ask disturbing questions about the other humans they learn about on the island. Sensing something *oklall* about the new arrivals, Lucky takes them directly to the Shrine's Window, a violation of his people's etiquette that turns out to be fortunate, for when the invading humans attempt to violate the Shrine, its Window opens, and all three of them dash into the Shrine, taking Lucky with them; they are never seen again. An even more bizarre series of events ensues that includes mysterious blue men ("demons," 26) emerging "crouching and perilous" (24) from the Shrine only to be shot dead with darts, followed by two equally mysterious brown-gold creatures ("angels," 26), who are welcomed with joy by the Shrinemen and appear to have come as a reward for Lucky's sacrifice, perhaps even as a twin reincarnation of Lucky.

The narrator alone witnesses the emergence of these entities from the Shrine. The meaning of these events is as opaque to the narrator as it is to the reader, so much so that she concedes her colleagues' conclusion that "I had been the victim of some extraordinarily powerful hypnotic illusion" (25). This is the official, scientific explanation and record of what she saw, but the narrator is privately unconvinced. "My own tendency ... is to believe that the Shrine is a sort of outpost of some other planet — but why this should feel any more 'scientific' to me than the Shrinemen's belief in an ancient lost magic, I don't know" (26). The whole adventure has engendered in the narrator a new respect for the "stolid impassive indigene[s]" of the island, whose quick action protected her from the malevolent intentions of the three human invaders, and a sense of ambivalence about the ability of science as she knows it to explain Lucky or his world.

In her 1963 story "The Lonely," which we first introduced in Chapter 3,

Merril again invokes alien intelligence to defamiliarize assumptions about the transparency of language that undergirds the authority of Euro-American claims to superior knowledge; this time, however, she extends this critique to consider different modes of perception and interpretation among men and women as well as among different species. As a "future history" story type, "The Lonely" is also a type of historical ethnography, or "ethnohistory," a field of knowledge that was itself a direct product of the anthropological research in the 1950s for the U.S. Indian Claims Commission, when the United States had to grapple in government hearings with the legacy of its nineteenth-century acts of territorial expansion and co-option of Native Americans. As with "Shrine of Temptation" (1973, "Author's note," 100), "The Lonely" (1973, "Author's note," 228) was one of Merril's cover art stories — she was given a description of a cover illustration by her editor (in this case, her former husband Frederik Pohl) and asked to write a story that made some reference to the art: "I have a Finlay cover and need something to go with it," Pohl wrote to Merril (June 22, 1963, 40.20, MP). The image by illustrator Virgil Finlay, who was one of science fiction's most prolific and honored artists, was of a giant statue of a woman holding a rocket, phallus-like, in her lap, seated on an alien landscape: "Could be anywhere. Statue seated, is maybe 15 feet high. [...] But you can kiss off the cover story with 'shortly after they landed, they saw a statue,'" Pohl wrote to Merril, making it clear that he mostly just wanted a story from her for that particular issue of the magazine (June 22). Illustrations of giant alien women looming over tiny human men were a mainstay of pulp science fiction at the time, as Roberts has shown (1993, 40–64). Whereas Roberts interprets the phallic objects these statues wield as a sign of feminine power (49–50), Laura Mulvey argues that such images of women holding or wearing phallic or fetish objects function to both titillate the male viewer and assuage his anxiety by simultaneously revealing and concealing female difference — that is, her lack of a penis and the threat of castration it represents (Mulvey 1975, 13–14). Merril, however, writes a story that makes clever use of the cover image, managing to subvert completely the authority of the male gaze for which such spectacles are usually performed. Further, Merril rejects the standard plot that typically accompanied such covers, which undermined the female power depicted on the cover by having the woman-alien sacrifice her power, or even her life, for the sake of a human male lover (Roberts 45). Instead, Merril leaves uncertain the fate of the men who discover the statue of the giant alien woman.

Merril's narration of "The Lonely" is particularly sophisticated: the entire story is focalized through a complex layering of narrative frames — an exchange of memos between officials of Earth's Spaserve (Space Service) and a senior anthropologist describes an alien transmission that they have intercepted, translated, annotated, and encoded for top-secret access. The transmission is of a lecturer, a "sort of electric eel type," who is describing a mishap on the planet Aldebaran IV as part of what the senior anthropologist believes to be a broader lecture series of the Galactic University about the "development of communicating intelligence" among different planetary races ("Lonely," 126). The mishap involves the demise of an all-female crew of space colonists who perish in a failed attempt to colonize the planet. The transcription informs

Merril wrote "The Lonely" to accompany this illustration by Virgil Finlay, which appeared on the cover of *Worlds of Tomorrow*, October 1963.

us that the female colonists' ships were launched during a "brief Matriarchy" on Terra, which has since given way to a return to the patriarchal status quo, represented by the memos that frame the narrative as a whole. However, the authority of this restored patriarchy is challenged by the intercepted alien transmission attached to the memo, which reveals that Earth is itself an object of scrutiny by older, more advanced beings — namely, an intergalactic empire of alien races advanced enough to communicate across species, not only through language but also through psychic transmissions of sensations and feelings. The alien lecturer describes the Terrans as a "newly emerged race from Sol III [Earth]" who are only just beginning to communicate with other species, but not very successfully, as the Aldebaran IV incident demonstrates. Interestingly, in an age in which women were taught that embracing their femininity was both natural and their contribution toward American progress (Yaszek 2008, 8–15; see also May 1988), Merril imagines a species for which sex difference represents a primitive state of life: the alien communication thus notes that the Terrans are a sexual race, a relatively "rare phenomenon among civilized species" ("Lonely," 127), and that the causes and effects of sexuality are worthy of investigation. The main event described in the story, the mishap on Aldebaran IV, is mediated by this complex frame, preventing any of its multiple layers of discourse from achieving a position of absolute authority or transparency.

The main incident of the story is as follows: When the survivors of an all-female colony of humans land on the planet Aldebaran IV, having scientifically detected virtual evidence of intelligent life, they are surprised to find no immediate evidence of this life. The Terrans, however, are "psi-blind"— that is, incapable of psychic communication. As a result, they fail to recognize the indigenous intelligent life on the planet, which consists of Arlemites, who originated as a social-colonizing lichen, then developed as a highly psioid culture, and thus communicate only telepathically (132). The psychologists who had prepared the voyage "ingeniously bypassed their most acute psychosocial problem" for the mother ship by sending an all-female crew — because women are better suited to the confinement of intergalactic space travel — equipped with a supply of sperm so that they can reproduce when they arrive (130). Unable to successfully reproduce in space, and unable to recognize the Arlemites as a benevolent and intelligent life-form, however, the Terran colonists perish. Because of their inability to recognize the Arlemites as beings at all, let alone intelligent ones, they do not benefit from the wisdom of "one of the oldest and most psioid of peoples ... [with] virtually all the accumulated knowledge of the Galaxy at their disposal" (131).

In a humorous twist, no doubt influenced by the fact that the story was written as a cover assignment, which Merril, it seems, took more seriously than the editor expected, the Arlemites decide to prevent future human colonists from experiencing a similar fate by constructing a monumental statue to warn off others of their kind. As a single-sex species, the Arlemites do not understand the notion of two-sex creatures, and so construct, by reading the brain of one of the dead Terran children, a warning beacon "to the shape of the strongest fear-and-hate symbols of—a female" (132): the image of the spaceship-wielding woman. Different, gendered interpretations of this image draw a parallel between the failure to communicate between species and between men and women: the phallic spaceship, resting "obscenely" (133) in a woman's lap, strikes "fear and hate" in the minds of females, possibly because it represents the ship and space travel as a phallic enterprise in which women can play only a passive role. Male viewers, however, read it as a sign of welcome: "The Woman waits, as she has waited ... always? ... to greet her sons, welcomes us ... home? ... She sits in beauty, in peacefulness, perfect, complete, clean and fresh-colored. [...] Allmother, Woman of Earth, enveloped ... enveloping, in warmth and peace" (133). Unfortunately, this interpretation leads to disaster—the so-called Aldebaran IV mishap—for the next Terran ship to arrive in the vicinity of Aldebaran IV has an all-male crew who are lured to the deadly planet instead of warned away from it. The breakdown of communication that has led to this tragedy is twofold: First, overemphasis on gender difference has impaired the psychic ability of the Terrans, who cannot fully comprehend "the principal of unity underlying all successful communication" (129). Second, the rift between the sexes causes men and women to interpret the Arlemites' idealized female image in completely opposing ways that lead to disaster for both: the women who flee Earth to escape it perish, as will the men who are lured by it to Aldebaran IV.

A particularly puzzling aspect of "The Lonely" is that it depicts tragic events, yet the masculine figures within the story react with laughter and jokes. The eel-like, alien lecturer periodically emits sparks, particularly when discussing Terran sexuality, which the Terran observers interpret, for no apparent reason, as something he does when he is "being funny" (126). The male colonists who arrive an Aldebaran IV "are deeply moved" by the statue "and they make jokes. 'Allmother,' one hears them say sarcastically, 'Old White Goddess, whaddya know?'" (133). In psychoanalytic theory, jokes and anxiety are closely linked. Is misplaced laughter in "The Lonely" provoked by male anxieties about female difference, on the one hand, and the threat of their own objectification by aliens, on the other? Do they find threatening the possibility that sex difference, and therefore their own masculinity, is a backward mode of existence in galactic terms? Is the implied author referencing her own joke, played upon the editor who assigned her the phallocentric cover story?

## Reading Merril's Alien Figures

In many ways, Merril's science fiction conforms to its time in depicting whiteness as the norm (Lavender 2009, 185). There is nothing in her fiction to suggest that her explorers, however futuristic, are other than middle-class, white Americans. She also did not imagine indigenous people or people of color as *participants* in the scientific adventure, which, as Sierra S. Adare (2005) astutely points out in the case of indigenous people in the United States, would constitute a profound shift away from the assumption that they "have a future that has not been assimilated into the dominant society" (6). Merril did, however, radically critique the colonial position taken for granted in mainstream science fiction of the time through her experimentation with narrative form as a vehicle for foregrounding the subjective and the provisional, and also her storylines in which explorers learn from and are changed by the aliens they encounter or that question the colonial project in space altogether. Her alien figures also engaged the classic frontier linkage between the foreign and the feminine to defamiliarize and critique patriarchal gender ideology and epistemology. In these and other ways, Merril's science fiction was as deeply situated in the social present as it was in the future, resulting in some of the most complex, radical, and innovative narratives of alienness in the postwar period.

CHAPTER 5

# Psychology and "Primary Communication"

> I came to science fiction with a very specific agenda which had to do with ending war, and particularly making sure that as many people as possible understood what the consequences of war would be. Then I became interested in the whole area of what I like to call primary communication [Merril, interview in Jirgens and Francis 1991, 11].

Just as Judith Merril's fiction explored the topic of alien encounters, it also experimented in the realms of psychology and the paranormal, including extrasensory perception (ESP). Human encounters with aliens and alien worlds demanded imaginative techniques for coping with the challenges of space travel and communicating across species. Psychology and the paranormal were of interest to Merril because of her commitment to advancing "soft," as opposed to "hard," science approaches in speculating about the future. She took a particular research interest in the full spectrum of "psi" phenomenon, from ESP to ghosts and magic.

Merril also had a very personal stake in the field of psychology: After she and Frederik Pohl separated in 1951, she became a patient of the New York psychotherapist and science fiction fan Joe Winter, underwent Gestalt therapy, and in 1952 began practicing ESP alone and with others. Writing to Fritz Leiber in 1952, Merril told of how Winter "got his therapeutic fingers under my skin" by reading her published work and then offering her psychotherapy based on it. The experience produced an epiphany: "And the nice thing that hit home was: 'You're a *nice* girl'" (April 11, 1952, 39.3, MP; see also Weiss 1997). To be in science fiction was to be a bit of a freak, a sentiment shared among those with Futurian roots. When interviewed for Damon Knight's history of the Futurians, Merril was asked what she thought of the group. Knight himself recalled that he had once referred to the Futurians as a "gallery of grotesques." Merril agreed: "Callow, or extremely unattractive, or both [...] I felt I belonged very much to that group, and I think this was characteristic of everyone there, that each of us regarded ourselves as grotesque, and felt comfortable in a gathering of grotesques" (Knight 1977, 149).

Her time with Pohl had proven to be a terrifically challenging period in her life: there was the elation of the initial success of her first atomic frontier story and novel that led to her decision to write full-time, the excitement of co-founding and co-hosting with Pohl the Hydra Club for science fiction, and the birth of their baby, Ann, all in 1947–1950. Then, in 1951, came the completion of a collaborative novel with C. M. Kornbluth and the move from a small New York City apartment to a thirteen-room old house in the little town of Red Bank, New Jersey; the pain of her first serious writer's block; her decision to have an abortion; the completion of a second novel with Kornbluth; and, in the fall, the breakdown of her marriage. By the fall of 1952, Merril had fallen deeply in love with the writer Walter Miller, Jr., and in 1953 spent six months traveling with him, borrowing heavily financially from friends and family, and cutting herself off from, and being shunned by, her science fiction friends because Miller was married. Merril was involved in a child custody battle with her first husband, which she lost in the fall of 1953, at which point her plans with Miller also fell through.

Surrounded by personal and domestic conflict, Merril became increasingly interested in psychology and in alternative forms of communication. Much of Merril's science fiction writing after 1952 had to do with what she liked to call "primary communication":

> In the mid-fifties particularly, many of us [in science fiction] were concentrating on an aspect of human existence which was then considered mostly "outside science." Some people called it "ESP," some called it "psionics," some called it "spiritualism." My own preference is for the more recent phrase, "primary communication" [Merril 1973, Author's note to "Exile from Space," 70].

Although Merril's output of science fiction would decline after 1956, and end altogether in 1963, what she did write became increasingly experimental and complex. At the core of her experimentation during this period lay an intense engagement with psychology and primary communication. As we shall see, although seemingly remote from popular Westerns or other frontier narratives, the 1950s popular psychology on which Merril based her narratives of telepathy was deeply rooted in frontier mythology.

## Psychology and Frontier Mythology

Merril's interest in links between psychological inquiry and the concept of telepathic, "primary" forms of communication brought her into a conversation that had been ongoing since the colonial period and taken quite seriously by at least some psychoanalysts, including Sigmund Freud himself. At first, Freud attributed the belief in telepathy to "primitive" peoples. In *Totem and Taboo*, originally published in 1912–1913, he articulated his theory of the Oedipus complex, engaging discourses of subjectivity that were already firmly entrenched in colonial discourse. Freud likened the stages of development of the civilized ego to those of human civilization writ large: "primitive" people, like children, were narcissists, unable to distinguish between themselves and an external world. Civilized peoples were noteworthy for their possession of an individuated ego, a concept of the self as a distinct, bounded subject in relation to an external, objectified reality. Primitive peoples had not yet developed this characteristic, according to Freud, leading to the irrational belief in such phenomena as telepathy, prophecy, and magic: Since primitive subjects do not distinguish between their own thoughts and a reality external to them, they logically believe in the power of thought to both perceive and affect events across space and time. They also invest more importance in ideas — in spirits, omens, and magic — than in objects. The civilized ego, by contrast, understands the difference between self and other and the limitations of "his" own mental powers, and has "adjusted himself to reality and turned to the external world for the object of his desires" (Freud 1912–1913, 90).

Freud was drawing on a pattern of representing the unbounded indigenous subject that had been emergent for at least two hundred years in narratives about encounters between Europeans and indigenous people. American Puritan captivity narratives such as Mary Rowlandson's depicted indigenous people en masse, not as individuals, and referred to them animalistically, as "wolves," "cursed Blood-Hounds," or "Dragons" (Vaughan and Clark 1981, 21). These accounts recorded little ethnographic information because indigenous people were not believed to have any "culture" (17). Tribal attacks on Puritan settlements were depicted as acts of barbarism unmotivated except by God's will, enacted through Indians, rather than in their political and historical context (1). James Fenimore Cooper refined these patterns of representation in *The Last of the Mohicans* and other novels in which stereotyped Indians act in one chaotic mass of unchecked appetite, as demonstrated by this scene in which a stereotypical Indian tribe responds to a speech delivered by Magua, the novel's antagonist:

> His voice was no longer audible in the burst of rage which now broke into the air, as if the wood, instead of containing so small a band, was filled with the nation. [...] They had answered his melancholy and mourning by sympathy and sorrow; his assertions, by gestures of confirmation; and his boastings, with the exultation of savages. [...] With the first intimation that [vengeance] was within their reach, the whole band sprang upon their feet *as one man*; giving utterance to their rage in the most frantic cries, they rushed upon their prisoners *in a body*, with drawn knives and uplifted tomahawks [107, emphasis added].

As in much of Cooper's fiction, indigenous figures who possess individual identities and civilized traits, such as Magua's abilities as an orator, are either antagonists like Magua or noble savages who side with the white men. All other indigenous figures are represented as hoards entirely at the mercy of passions and impulses rather than thought and reason.

In the twentieth century, countless Western films such as John Ford's *The Searchers* (1956) would make familiar such scenes of Indians swarming en masse, in contrast with the highly individualized and self-controlled hero. The Indians' mass behavior did not signify any sophistication of organization, but rather the lack of individual consciousness, the complete melding of the self into the group consciousness characteristic of insects, birds, and herding animals. The collective emphasis of tribal societies supposedly reflected an inferior stage of development rather than cultural difference.

By way of Freudian theory, this discourse that defined the bounded, contained individual in opposition to the primitive hoard persisted into the Cold War period. The growing authority of psychology in this period coincided with a broader surge in the popularity and authority of the psychological "expert," whose role was to help subjects achieve a well-adjusted psychological state (May 1988, 178). Such "experts" particularly stressed the importance of maintaining a "normal" psychological "balance." The emphasis on normalcy through the 1950s (discussed at length in Chapter 2) was steeped in the Freudian tradition: for Freud, psychological health is achieved by balancing the pressures that the irrational, passionate, and inchoate id (a remnant of our savage origins) exerts on the censoring ego, the function of which is to enforce social taboos and strictures. Psychoanalysis enables the subject to release this pressure by verbalizing the id's unconscious, antisocial desires, allowing the id to express its primitive demands in a controlled and rational form that the fragile ego can withstand. In this way, therapy maintains, or restores, the balance between id and ego. A simplified version of Freud's model of the psyche was easily amenable to the "containment culture" of the Cold War period, which emphasized containment of potentially unruly forces in virtually all aspects of American life, including politics (communism), sex (licentiousness), gender identity (abnormality), and nuclear energy (atomic Armageddon) (Nadel 1995, 5). The psychological narrative of the ego's ongoing efforts to contain the id neatly fit this paradigm.

Just as Merril's fiction about aliens calls deeply entrenched colonial discourses of alienness into question, so, too, does her fiction about psychology and primary communication probe the deep assumptions underlying popular psychological theory of the 1950s, which was closely linked to Merril's conceptualization of primary communication.

## Psychology and the Psychological Expert

### *"A Little Knowledge" (1953)*

During the 1950s, the concept of the bounded, individual self propped up the authority of the psychological expert. In Merril's space-travel narratives, the task of psychologists and other such experts is usually to maintain a "balanced" community of space workers, following the Freudian model of the balanced psyche. In "Project Nursemaid," for example, a psychologist describes his ideal space-nanny candidate as "wonderful. [...] When it came to psych tests [...] he knew she'd come up with every imaginable symptom and psychic disorder ... in small, safe quantities. A little of this, and a little of that, and the whole adding up to the rare and 'balanced' personality" ("Nursemaid," 31). And in her novella "Daughters of Earth," the role of "psych testing" becomes critical to the success of the faster-than-light space journey in which married couples are frozen until it is their turn, with another couple, carefully chosen for psychological and skill compatibility, to operate the ship.

While psychological experts often occupy positions of authority in Merril's writing, in "A Little Knowledge," published in *Science Fiction Quarterly* in 1953, Merril satirizes this figure. The story is about a former psychology student so brilliant that he was rejected as too threatening by mainstream experts in the field. Believing that life is a game, Harry goes freelance, using his skills as a psychologist to win at poker and seduce a much younger woman, Irene: "[He] won her away from younger, handsomer, and wealthier men, by exercising every psychological skill at his command" (88). He invents and markets, through advertisements and lectures to local self-help groups, a technique called "Self Synthesis," which involves a guidebook by the same name and blueprints that clients can use to build their own therapeutic device called a "Sure Self Cell." A product of Harry's unofficial company, "Help Yourself Inc.," this device enables the subject to self-direct the Freudian process of relaxation, confession, and integration of repressed thoughts into the conscious psyche:

> The flashing lamp [...] induced light auto-hypnosis. The recorder [...] played back questions previously set by the user, as soon as the relaxed trance position caused a limp finger to fall on a sensitive pushbutton. The ingenious mechanism [...] switched the machine from play-back to recording as soon as the patient's voice hit the sounding board. The lie detector circuit [...] cut off the recorder again, shortly after the patient's pulse-beat indicated a peak of excitement. The electric massage [...] stimulated circulation and consciousness simultaneously, inducing a rare sense of well-being as the user came out of trance and heard his confessions played back to him [89].

Whereas Freud is known for especially pathologizing his female patients, perpetuating stereotypes of women as hysterical, neurotic, and in particular need of psychological intervention, Merril deliberately undermines assumptions that women are more malleable psychologically than men. In "A Little Knowledge," she does so by revealing that Harry, not Irene, is the victim of psychological manipulation. Throughout the story, it becomes clear that Harry himself is the ideal candidate for his invention — he is getting older, balding, and feels like a fraud, particularly in his relationship with Irene: "[Harry] began to despise himself— for the first time consciously — as a charlatan, a fraud. He had nothing to offer but deceptions; and Irene was the one living person he did not want to deceive" (88). He does not believe that his Cell will work and tries to persuade Irene not to try it because he fears she will discover that it (and, by implication, he) is a sham. However, by the end of the story, Harry learns that Irene has successfully built a Cell from his blueprints and has been using it in secret with great success: her influence over Harry has been increasing while his self-confidence has been eroding. All the time Harry has been feeling guilty for manipulating Irene, he has actually been the victim of her growing influence over him. Merril thus exposes the self-contained ego as itself a fragile state of delusion rather than an advanced, "civilized" form of subjectivity.

## *"The Deep Down Dragon" (1961)*

Sometimes the balance between primitive and civilized components of the psyche must be manipulated because of the abnormal demands of space exploration, as is the case in the short story "The Deep Down Dragon," written for *Galaxy* in 1961, in which members of a human couple being screened for a colonizing mission to Mars undergo a *simulation* of a primitive scenario of female captivity and male rescue. In their simulation, the male partner, a "pale-skinned, ninety-five-pound, five-foot product of slum-crowded Earth" (153) — in other words, an average, normal guy — successfully rescues his wife from a *simulated* alien monster — a projected image — thereby discovering the power of his own inner savage, while his wife learns to trust that he *can* protect her. "Dragon" was a "cover" story for Merril, with the cover painting executed by the legendary "EMSH" (Ed Emshwiller): according to Merril, "The idea of using a projected image as a sort of super–Rorschach basis for the colonists' tests stemmed directly from the event that I myself was doing just that, writing the story around the cover-painting which depicted the opening scene of the 'test'" (Merril 1973, author's note to "Dragon," 178). Both husband and wife witness the other's simulation. The examiner explains the importance of this aspect of the test to a junior associate: "Ever think how much more therapy there might be for him in knowing she *knows* he can handle a dragon? Or for her, knowing that he really *can*?" ("Dragon," 153). In other words, the test is meant both to demonstrate that this civilized, normal couple has the primitive traits — respectively, the instincts to protect and to be protected — necessary to adapt to conditions on Mars, and to serve as therapy that will help them cope with these conditions. Without the security of civilization, she will need to rely on her husband's protection, he will need to guard her, and both will need to embrace their newly discovered primitive selves.

## The Tomorrow People *(1960)*

Merril's novel *The Tomorrow People* (1960) looks at the psychological effects of exploration and long-term residency on Mars, ultimately calling into question the ability of the psychological enterprise to fully master the human psyche. The novel concerns the aftermath of a trip to Mars gone wrong when only one of the two top spacemen sent there, Johnny Wendt, returns. The main narrator is Lisa Trovi, a dancer and the live-in lover of Johnny. In addition to the formal investigations under way to find out what went amiss with the excursion, Lisa is on a more subjective and intuitive quest of her own to find out what happened and to help Johnny to overcome the obvious trauma he suffered. So severe is his trauma that Lisa decides to hide from him the fact that she is pregnant with his child, something that even readers of the novel learn only slowly. The reasons why Johnny's partner Doug Laughlin wandered off and disappeared elude the mission's psychiatrist, Phil Kutler, who is convinced that psychological screening techniques would have detected any unsuitability in these two spacemen: "Here are two guys who got psych tested inside and out and upside down before they left." The psychs had even screened for homosexuality, "an eventuality the training program had prepared them to cope with. Plus neither one of them showed any appreciable tendency to panic over anything like that, if it *did* happen" (71). Perhaps, muses the director of the Moon lab, Peter Christiansen, the problem was something unanticipated: "something in the psychological — I don't know — atmosphere?" (71–72). Johnny's deteriorating mental health threatens the masculine image of the entire project. He has returned to Earth "out of commission" — a space hero turned alcoholic recluse, a changed, depressed personality. He refuses to submit to further psych testing and has to be fully sedated just to travel to the space dome on the Moon, "flipping his lid if anyone even talked about space" (71). In this story, the male hero is the hysterical one, and the mystery of what happened to Johnny's partner is eventually solved, not by Johnny, the psychiatrist, or the psych testers, but by the telepathic powers of Johnny's calm, artistic girlfriend Lisa, as we shall explain later in this chapter. Scientific discourses can categorize the psyche but not necessarily heal it; ultimately it is a "primitive," nonsymbolic form of communication — primary communication — that uncovers the reality of Johnny's trauma.

## Primary Communication

As was the case for Freud and other early-twentieth-century psychoanalysts, speculation about human psychology in much popular American science fiction includes exploration of the "paranormal" concept of ESP, an umbrella category for forms of perception that transcend the normal five senses. ESP and its variants existed within the purview of psychological inquiry as early as the early-nineteenth-century mesmerist movement, when the boundaries of legitimate scientific inquiry included many topics now considered beyond its pale. Franz Mesmer was a visionary eighteenth-century German physician whose system of therapeutics (mesmerism) was based on a belief in magnetic forces that animated all life (a phenomenon Mesmer called *magnétism animal*, or "animal magnetism," a forerunner of the modern practice of hypnotism). Mesmer and his followers claimed that it was possible for trained mesmerists to treat physical and mental ailments in subjects by taking command of and manipulating the magnetic forces that both animated the subject and connected him or her to the environment (M. Willis 2006, 47–48). Mesmerists thought of themselves as scientists and defined and defended their activities in terms of the scientific debates of their day. They were aided in their claims by the discovery of the force of electricity, widely speculated to be the animating force that differentiated animate, conscious beings from the matter of which they were made (70). The most famous example of electricity serving as an animating force is Mary Shelley's *Frankenstein; or, The Modern Prometheus,* published in London in 1818, in which electricity is the key ingredient needed to animate the consciousness of the human body that Dr. Frankenstein creates from the remains of corpses. It is this type of substance, this energy, that mesmerists claimed to control in others, a practice that gave mesmerism the veneer of a foundation in observable natural phenomena. To this day, spiritualists still claim to be able to perceive the spirit that exists in the form of energy that both precedes and transcends our existence in the human body.

Even after the emergence of psychology as a formal academic discipline in the early twentieth century, psychologists argued for the plausibility of telepathy. This ability to send and receive thoughts from one mind to another without employing the recognized physical senses (thus representing, along with clairvoyance and precognition, a form of ESP) had to be reckoned with, given (a) the frequency with which their patients reported telepathic experiences and (b) the potential for new technologies based upon invisible matter and forces to explain the transmission of thought between subjects. Freud himself at first dismissed telepathy as a belief of the primitive part of the human mind, unable to distinguish between its own thought and an external, material reality. Yet he later conceded that telepathy may be possible and explainable in terms of the same principles that governed the invention of the telephone (Freud 1953, 108). Even as the study of ESP was relegated to the margins of scientific inquiry as parapsychology — a term popularized in the 1930s for the study of paranormal psychic phenomena — it continued to have its defenders within the scientific community. In 1935, the Parapsychology Laboratory was formed at Duke University to conduct experiments in that field, separating from Duke in 1965 but continuing its work using scientific methodology. More recently, Fred M. Frohock has argued in an academic study, *Lives of the Psychics: The Shared Worlds of Science and Mysticism* (2000), that ESP deserves a legitimate place in the study of human psychology.

Merril developed her professional interest in perception and communication very early in her science fiction writing career, leading her to publish a pioneering anthology, *Beyond the Barriers of Space and Time*, on the theme of what she called "the curious and controversial phenomena known as the '*psi* powers'" (Merril 1954, "Editor's Preface," xiii) — the full spectrum of mental powers examined by the pseudoscience of parapsychology, from mass hypnosis, telepathy, séances, clairvoyance, precognition, levitation, shapeshifting, and predestination to ghosts and magic. Merril soon became a close, lifelong friend of Katherine MacLean, one of the contributors to the volume. MacLean had postgraduate training in psychology and, like Merril, a keen interest in telepathy.

Merril and MacLean started a series of long-distance ESP tests and Gestalt therapy sessions after Merril separated from Pohl in 1951 (see Merril and Pohl-Weary 2002, "Katherine MacLean and the ESP Letters," 116–28). MacLean stayed with Merril at the big house in Red Bank for a few months in 1952, and for several years afterward the two writers kept up a steady correspondence with each other about their ESP trials: "Here's a picture of a room — Any relation to yr. or a memory room?" Merril wrote to MacLean (April 19, 1952, 10.24, MP). "Anything happen to anyone Saturday night?" asked MacLean (May 1, 1952), and elaborated, "I felt a jolt of low-sorrow around 10:15 P.M. and an impression of fright through to 10:30." They also conducted edgier discussions around their adventures in ESP: Merril once wrote that, while trying to visualize McLean in her mind, she had received such a scalp-prickling feeling that she "consciously tried to empty conscious thought from mind" (April 22, 1952). MacLean, in response on April 27, said she had felt a definite contact but was horrified at Merril's "technique": "holy smokes if you empty your mind you're emptying my thoughts out with yours. How can you tell one from the other off hand?" Despite all efforts, Merril had to concede that the two of them had failed to accomplish any real breakthroughs with this ESP enterprise, unless one counts Merril's rather amusing claims that she believed she had at least been able to make her own hair curlier and appear black (Merril and Pohl-Weary 2002, 116) and to improve the focus of her left eye (Merril to Les Cole, February 28, 1952, 37.1, MP) with ESP techniques.

## Psi and the Primitive/Feminine

Psi, the twenty-third letter of the Greek alphabet — which, for Merril, writing in the early 1950s, "name[d] a field of little knowledge and much emotional conviction, covering a multitude of myths, uncertainties and possible great discoveries" (Merril 1954, "Editor's Preface," xiii) — was just the sort of combination of ambiguity and potential that suited her approach to speculating about the future. In science fiction, the psi-individual represents a superior being, and elements of psi powers are necessary for communication between humans and aliens (xiv). Peter Nicholls refers to a "psi boom" in American science fiction coinciding with the American Cold War that the influential science fiction editor, John W. Campbell, Jr., promoted in *Astounding Science Fiction* in the early 1950s. Campbell upheld psi in the belief that psi powers were "the next step" in human evolution (Nicholls 1993b, 971–72). But with the waning of the Cold War in the second half of the decade, psi-based science fiction is thought to have quickly lost its "impetus" to ESP, and in particular to the aspect of telepathy.

This shift in emphasis to telepathy over time is reflected in the evolution of Merril's writings on mental powers and "primary communication." From the mid–1950s onward, Merril was explicitly moving her explorations in primary communication in ever more "complex directions" as she probed more deeply its underlying psychological theory (Merril 1973, author's note to "Connection Completed," 81–82; see also Merril and Pohl-Weary 2002, 157). Merril saw primary communication as an implication of Freudian theory because the alternative to the bounded subject was the unbounded one, and primary communication was a possibility enabled through access to this more "primitive" stage of subjectivity. But primary communication was also a scientific advance in the sense that the insights of the science of psychology made it possible, in fiction at least, to master the processes behind telepathy, ESP, and so on. In her explorations of primary communication, Merril encounters this contradiction, unsettling the very basis of science fiction in a dominant frontier discourse predicated on the metanarrative of civilization's steady expansion and progress and a clear definition of what "progress" means. The idea of a primitive attribute as an *agent* of progress made women, perennially identified with the primitive, central agents of scientific progress in Merril's fiction about primary communication.

Although the study and practice of psi was regarded by some as an evolutionary improvement, a more deeply entrenched counter-discourse of psi links it with the overlapping concepts of the primitive and the feminine. In many frontier narratives, women and "primitive" people are both depicted as primarily irrational beings with underdeveloped egos, more subject to the impulses of the emotions and the body than the rational will, the latter being a trait identified with "civilized" subjects. Hence in *Last of the Mohicans*, a novel that set the standard for the frontier narratives and Westerns that followed it, the white female characters are as hysterical and emotional as the Indians themselves during Indian attacks, whereas the white men, Hayward and Leatherstocking, are always in control of their actions. The discourse of mesmerism, current when James Fenimore Cooper was writing the novel, echoes frontier mythology and anticipates Freud in its model of subjectivity: the ability to mesmerize was linked to an active and masterful personality, or strong ego boundaries, in the mesmerizer, while those subjects most susceptible to mesmerism were characterized as passive, permeable, and suggestible — that is, lacking strong ego boundaries (M. Willis 2006, 48). In 1921, the Viennese psychoanalyst Dr. Wilhelm Stekel would assert that "strong emotion, particularly love, jealousy and anxiety [...] predispos[ed] the agent and percipient to the telepathic event, and that women in love could sense when they were betrayed by their partner" (Eisenbud 1970, 7).

When Freud in his later years began to take telepathy seriously, he wrote that "it is usually mediocre and even inferior people" who practice as professional fortunetellers (1953, 98), again linking telepathy implicitly to an underdeveloped capacity to reason. In the 1960s, Phyllis Gotlieb's novel *Sunburst* (1964) invoked this discourse more explicitly. Her novel depicts an outbreak of psi youths who carouse in savage hordes, committing collective acts of vandalism. She contrasts this primitive form of psi with that of a new, highly evolved species of human that Gotlieb calls "supernormal." Their powers include the ability to read and manipulate — even destroy — minds, temporarily conceal their presence from others ("shielding"), teleport objects, and communicate with each other telepathically. The supernormal heroine of the novel is able to resist the will of the horde — her mind cannot be penetrated by the psis — and act as an individual despite her psychic powers; she realizes that although the psis appear to be "superhuman," they are nothing of the sort. Their psychic power is actually a primitive form of communication, she concludes, one relied upon by children, herding animals, ants, and other beings that "can't quite express themselves very well by talking" (Gotlieb 118). That a female can be "supernormal" is a challenge to the gender configuration articulated by Freud; however, Gotlieb ultimately preserves the boundary between primitive and civilized by privileging the concept of normality, whereas Merril hybridizes the savage/civilized binary in several stories and a novel from the 1950s and early 1960s.

### "Peeping Tom" (1954), "Whoever You Are" (1952), "Homecalling" (1956), and The Tomorrow People (1960)

In "Peeping Tom," published in *Startling Stories* (1954), Tommy, a wounded American soldier in Korea, learns the art of telepathy from a local villager, whose abode is described as "a curious mixture of East and West":

> The furnishing consisted primarily of low stools and tables, with a few shelves somehow set into the clay wall. There was one large, magnificently carved mahogany chest, which might have contained Ali Baba's fortune; and on a teakwood table in the corner, with a pad on the floor for a seat, stood a large and shiny late-model American standard typewriter. [...]
> 
> On the wall over the bookshelf hung two strips of parchment, such as may be seen in many eastern homes, covered with ideograph characters brilliantly illuminated. Between them was a glass-faced black frame containing the certification of Armod's license to practice medicine in the state of Idaho, U.S.A. [108].

While this passage invokes links between primary communication and primitivity, elsewhere Merril calls into question the premise that the bounded, individual, impermeable Western subject represents the pinnacle of advancement.

In "Whoever You Are" (1952), also discussed in Chapter 4, telepathic aliens are discovered on a scout ship returning to the Earth-governed Solar System. Their telepathy is construed and debated by the humans as one of two possible extremes: it is either a malevolent form of mesmerism that has enabled the aliens to telepathically penetrate and control their human subjects, commandeer the ship, and invade the Solar System, or it is an advanced form of communication that transcends the boundaries of difference and offers an opportunity for the mutual enlightenment of both aliens and humans. For the public relations chief of the base, Lucy Ardin, the aliens had the "unbeatable weapon — the psychological weapon. '"You can't fight 'em because you don't want to. People call modern P.R. mass hypnotism. [...] They've got the real thing'" (74). Psychofficer Bob Swartz has the final call about terminating the aliens but is deeply conflicted on the matter:

> I think the human race is too damned scared and too damn hungry to be able to face this thing. Hungry for security, for reassurance, for comfort — for love. And scared! Scared of anything different, anything Outside, anything one degree more than the rules allow. [...] The very fact — that we sit and stew over it, I mean — makes them dangerous [75–76].

He concludes that, under the circumstances, the aliens will have to be eliminated.

Merril's human characters opt to destroy the aliens, along with their human escort, rather than risk mesmerism by them for the sake of possible enlightenment of the sort referred to by Psychofficer Swartz. This outcome does not resolve the quandary of what kind of telepathy the aliens possess, but it does make a clear statement about the lengths to which the human ego is prepared to go to maintain the integrity of its borders. Similarly, in "The Lonely" (1963; also discussed in Chapters 3 and 4), human space explorers perish on an alien planet because they are unable to recognize or communicate with its advanced inhabitants, who take the physical form of lichen but are in fact a highly advanced, psioid race able to both communicate and manipulate their environment telepathically. Here, Merril invites her readers to question some of their most basic assumptions about what constitutes both "primitive" and "advanced" forms of civilization.

In the novella "Homecalling" (1956; also discussed in Chapter 4), the opposite plot unfolds when a spaceship crash-lands on an alien planet, killing the parents of two children. The children survive because telepathic communication with the native inhabitants enables the older child, Deborah, whose ego is more fully developed, to overcome the natives' horrific appearance (they are giant termites) and recognize and accept the benevolent assistance of the queen of the alien planet, Daydanda:

> The bugs were really pretty nice people [Deborah] thought, and giggled at the silly way that sounded ... calling bugs *people* [...] [but] once you got used to how they looked, (And how they looked at you too: it still felt funny having them turn their backs on you when you talked to them, so they could see you.) it was just natural to think of them that way [71–72].

Although the physical differences also mark a communications gap, the mother-daughter relationship that develops between Daydanda and Deborah transcends these differences:

> When the Mother-bug laughed, it tickled in her mind; when the Mother was angry, it prickled. When the Mother called to her, it was a feeling that came creeping; when she didn't want to hear, it came seeping anyhow [59].

Returning briefly to Merril's novel *The Tomorrow People* (1960), telepathy is the key to solving both the mental illness of Johnny Wendt and the disappearance of his partner. "Mars bugs," brought back by Johnny and sequestered in a vat at the "All America Laboratory on the Moon," prove to be telepathic, as Johnny's girlfriend Lisa secretly discovers. Skeptical about the existence of ESP, Lisa nevertheless receives thoughts when she is around the Mars bugs, leading her to undertake covert experiments on her own, tape-recording herself with the bugs by speaking out loud the thoughts she hears in her head. Lisa discovers she is strongly telepathic around the bugs and believes that her pregnancy has heightened her awareness and "feminine intuition." She also uses her recordings of these ESP sessions to introduce Johnny to the idea of telepathic messages. With the aid of the telepathic bugs, Lisa is able to clear Johnny's mind of the haunting memories of his dead space partner. The bubbling vat of Mars bugs is, in fact, "a sort of brain center" networking with other colonies of bugs. Johnny learns from the bugs that his lost partner Doug had been mesmerized into following the waves of calls, "love-thoughts, greetings, warm yearnings and welcomes" (187) of the Mars beings all the way to what turned out to be an old Martian information bank. The bank had been created when the Martian atmosphere disappeared, forcing the original Martians to take on a new form. The bug colonies formed

> to guard, preserve, tend, grow, the brain-center of the planet-wide "body" of the last Martian — the brain into which was poured the memory and knowledge [...] and yearnings and ideals of a race which could not in its original form survive the stripping of the atmosphere from the old planet [188].

Doug communicated all the knowledge necessary for the Martians of the bug colony to learn to pass on to the next Earthmen who visited; then, because the Martians (through ignorance about human bodies) had kept his brain alive but had not provided him with food or water, he died.

In this novel, Merril is examining an idea about "primary communication" that would continue to engage her for many years:

> that "primary communication" on a cellular level might be responsible for many instances of "miracle cures," "stigmata," "psychogenic" disease, etc.— and might, under full conscious control, allow a sentient organism to make much larger changes in morphology — which might permit anything from the legendary transformations of witches and werewolves to the idea of a single widely diffused individual existing on an airless planet, or even in empty space, its scattered cells surviving on radiant energy, plus perhaps the odd hydrogen atom [Merril 1973, author's note to "Connection Completed," 82].

In spite of Merril's ambitious approach, which garnered praise from a number of reviewers for being important and fresh (Miller 1961; Pohl 1960), not all of her contemporaries in science fiction appreciated the implications of the science, communications, and psychology in the novel, or the complexity of its structure, opting instead — as Damon Knight did in a chapter in his book of critical essays on modern science fiction titled "More Chuckleheads"— to ridicule Merril's work on the basis of a masculinist standard of literary value, especially regarding her lapses in hard science and the sentimentality in her tone and dialogue (Knight 1967, 104–5).

Merril's narratives about psi, ESP, and telepathy reflect her characteristic concern with the distinct experiences of women, engendering novel twists on popular conventions of frontier and science fiction writing. In several of her stories, she explicitly explores the topic of the experiences of women and telepathy in the context of romantic, heterosexual relationships between men and women.

## "Connection Completed" (1954), "Stormy Weather" (1954), and "Peeping Tom" (1954)

In putting telepathy in the context of romantic relationships, and as a specifically "feminine" form of advanced communication, Merril envisioned it as alternately a means of circumventing the social barriers that inhibit truthful communication between the sexes and as a form of power in the context of the gendered politics of romance. In this way, she used science fiction as a vehicle for exploring and critiquing of the conventions, rituals, assumptions, and double standards that structured romantic and sexual relationships between men and women.

If her alien heroine in "Rain Check" (1954) is flummoxed by seemingly nonsensical behaviors of human men in search of no-strings-attached sex, the partners in a telepathic courtship in "Connection Completed" (1954) try to bypass the uncertainties of normal courtship rituals and find their perfect partner. When Merril wrote this story, she had already been through two divorces; the fantasy of there being a means of avoiding such pitfalls of romance must have been as attractive to her as to her implied reader. The more specific context in which it was written, however, had to do with her romantic relations with Walter Miller in 1952–1953, and thus with romance in her own life: Merril claimed that she wrote the short story "more or less to and about Walt." It was, she writes, "about what was going on between us, how two people can find each other and no longer feel alone" (Merril and Pohl-Weary 2002, 131). However, in "Connection Completed," telepathy creates as many complexities as it resolves as the two characters balance telepathic and normal communication: after a lengthy telepathic courtship, the "lovers" arrange to meet in person at a cafe, but when they do, neither is sure of the other's identity or of the reality of their telepathic communication:

> "Pardon me, miss," he asked courteously, "I wonder if you happen to know whether there's a post office open anywhere near here? At this hour, I mean?" *Pretty feeble, I know, babe, but you're rushing me.*
> "I don't think ... there's one that *might* be open, but I'm not sure. It's just about five blocks. You turn to the left at the corner, and...."
> He didn't listen to the rest. He didn't need a post office for anything.
> *Oh my God!* her voice screamed inside his head. *What am I doing now? I've never seen this man before. I don't, I don't, I don't know who he is or anything about him! He looks like ... like like somebody I invented. But that's an accident. It has to be! Daydreaming isn't so bad. Anybody who's lonely daydreams. But when you get it mixed up with reality....*
> *Yeah, I know. It's time to go look up a good old-fashioned psychiatrist and confess all your guilts. I know. Don't think you're the only one, kid* ["Connection," 45].

As the story's title suggests, the lovers do eventually "complete" their "connection," but one wonders if telepathy has made their courtship any easier than conventional methods.

In another story published that year, "Stormy Weather" (1954), a female "psichosomanticist" is the lone crew member of a minute space station — "her own hollow cylinder of metal" (78) — that detects and disarms potentially dangerous "traffic" in space. In an unusual move for Merril, the story unfolds almost entirely though Cathy's internal monologue. Cathy's special psi training enables her to communicate with "Control" when normal communication is impossible in the far reaches of space. She also uses telepathy to sustain her extra-long-distance romantic relationship while she completes her thirty-days-on, thirty-days-off tour of duty: "Seven more tours to retirement — and they'd both agreed it was foolish for her to quit. They could spend almost half the time together anyhow; and with both of them p-s-trained, no more was necessary. They could always keep in message-touch" (79). This scenario is a departure from stories such as "Daughters of Earth" that depict professional marriage as the primary social unit in the context of space exploration. In "Stormy Weather," Merril contemplates the implication of professional contexts that separate heterosexual women from their partners — in this sense, a more accurate prediction on Merril's part of the future of romance and marriage with the rise of professional women. Merril was also forward-looking in her depiction of the ways in which advances in communication could alter both public and private relationships, except that cell phones and the Internet, not ESP, have realized some of her speculations.

When Cathy loses telepathic contact with her romantic partner, Mike, her anxieties start to get the best of her: "she could find excuses, invent reasons.... *Drunk? ... doped? ... dead?* ... she asked herself brutally, marveling that she found these answers easier to contemplate than anger or indifference" (79). Her usual avenues for chasing away the blues — eating, smoking, drinking, even trying to contact Mike — would in effect constitute an act of suicide, for they would result in the elimination of her limited supplies of oxygen and heat, the dwindling levels of which she is constantly and automatically reminded about by the ship's glowing bulbs, clacking tapes, spinning dials, and computer voice messages. While she contemplates all that, she mentally taunts herself with the "thread of lonely melody" of a popular American torch song from the 1930s, "Stormy Weather": "*Gloom an' misery everywhere.... Since my man an' I....*" (80). As anxieties about her relationship multiply, she also has to contend with a dangerous "particloud" — a body of rocky debris suspended in space. The remainder of the story depicts her negotiating these two different forms of "stormy weather" in her life, another of Merril's innovative blendings of the conventions of women's magazine fiction with those of science fiction. Although Merril was often criticized for depicting women so stereotypically preoccupied with romance, both by her contemporaries who believed romance had no place in science fiction and by later feminists who found her female characters too conventional, such 1950s romances of professional, adventurous women both cleared ground for later feminist science fiction writers and addressed the growing numbers of professional women in the postwar era who were soon to make their presence felt in mainstream North American society.

While telepathy enables men and women in some of Merril's stories to bypass both the psychic barriers of social conventions and the physical barriers created by conflicting professional demands, in other stories Merril depicts the need for telepaths to erect various psychic "blocks." In the resolution of "Stormy Weather," we learn that Cathy lost communication with her partner because he had broken his leg in an accident and "blocked" her from experiencing his pain. Cathy also admits to having blocked Mike so that he would not know how afraid she had been of losing him. Telepathy, it turns out, is not such a guarantee of honest communication after all; rather, it adds yet another layer of complexity to the already fraught scene of romance.

If we return for a moment to another 1954 story, "Peeping Tom," we discover that Merril depicts telepathy as an advancement with special appeal for women because it enables them to influence others without "seeming" to, a form of power American women have been writing about since the sentimental movement of the mid-nineteenth century. Although "Peeping Tom" is told from the point of view of Tommy Bender, an American soldier in Korea who learns something of the art of telepathy from a local villager, a surprise ending reveals that it is he who has been the subject of telepathic manipulation all along. Bender uses his telepathy to learn more about women and is unpleasantly surprised to learn "the kind of language some of those girls knew. [...] The ones who talked the most refined were almost always the worst offenders in their minds ... the kind of feminine innocence he'd grown up believing in just didn't seem to exist" (112). Candace, an American nurse at the army hospital, is the exception to the rule:

> Candace really lived up to his ideal of the American girl. Her mind was a lovely, orderly place, full of softness and a sort of generalized liking for almost everybody. Her thoughts on the subject of most interest to him [sex] were also in order: She was apparently well-informed in an impersonal sort of way; ignorant of any personal experience and rather hazily, pleasurably, anticipating the acquisition of that experience in some dim future when she pictured herself as happily in love and married [112].

Tommy proposes marriage to Candace, who promptly refuses him, leaving him disillusioned. Tommy also stops his telepathic training despite his teacher's warning that it is incomplete, that he will need to return for further study, because Tommy hasn't learned "to build a barrier against intrusion" and his "mind is open to all who come and know how to look—" (113). As in "Connection Completed," we see the need for telepaths to erect various psychic blocks. Some years later, Tommy and Candace are reunited in the United States, and Tommy proposes a second time, this time successfully; however, Tommy worries that he won't be able to show Candace "the fulfillment she had hoped for" in marriage (116). He realizes that "he had use for the further talents the old man had promised him.... *Maybe I should have gone back for a while, after all,* he thought idly" (116). Reminiscent of Irene, the wife in Merril's "A Little Knowledge," Candace replies to this thought: "Perhaps you should have, dear [...] I did" (116). In this last line of the story, Tommy and the reader learn that he is the one who has been telepathically manipulated—by Candace. Everything that Tommy and the reader have assumed about Candace—her purity and docility—is called into question by this revelation that Candace has been performing telepathically the psyche of the kind of woman Tommy desires.

In her constructions of telepathic women, Merril presents telepathy as both a potential advance in the ability of humans to communicate and a primitive trait against which the civilized, Freudian subject constructs itself. In "Homecalling," the orphaned boy and girl survive because telepathic communication with the queen of the alien planet enables the young girl to overcome her revulsion of the aliens' appearance. In *The Tomorrow People,* the protagonist's pregnant girlfriend uses her telepathic powers to solve the mystery that is destroying him. In "Connection Completed," telepathy enables kindred spirits to find each other, bypassing social custom. In "Stormy Weather," telepathy means that women can pilot rocket ships beyond the reach of conventional communication systems, but it also creates a whole new layer of social complications as lovers block, or otherwise manipulate, telepathic communication. "Peeping Tom" ultimately dismantles the superiority of the privileged, white male subject by exposing it as the victim of a higher level of feminine telepathic manipulation. In all of these stories, telepathy is a form of progress in which women play a central role.

## Psi and Narrative Innovation

Merril makes deft choices of narrative form in her representations of primary communication, crossing boundaries between thought and speech, self and other, that underwrite conventional narrative form. In her earlier stories about ESP and psi, Merril depicts secondary communication from the point of view of a single internal focalizer who is manipulated telepathically. As Mieke Bal (1997) explains, the focalizer in a narrative, or "the one who sees" (as distinct from the narrator, "who tells"), plays a crucial rhetorical role in the narrative because it is the focalizer's interpretation of events that readers are most likely to accept as true (146). Merril uses this strategy to satirize characters who assume their own dominance and control over their environment. Such is the case with a number of stories discussed in this chapter—for example, "A Little Knowledge" and "Peeping Tom," in which the male characters learn that they have been the subjects of telepathic manipulation by the women they thought they were influencing. Readers likewise experience a moment of defamiliarization as the male focalizers turn out to be the subjects of psychic manipulation, and seemingly passive female characters are suddenly revealed to be the agents behind the male characters' thoughts and actions.

In "A Little Knowledge," Harry's young wife, Irene, at first appears naïve, shallow, and blind to Harry's shortcomings. The reader is privy to Harry's private worries that it is only a matter of time before Irene realizes that he is in fact an aging, balding, has-been of a man. Although Harry's lack of self-confidence seems somewhat pathetic, his assumption about Irene's naiveté does her no credit. However, when we learn that during Irene's many "shopping trips," she has been secretly building Harry's self-help device and learning how to psychologically control others, especially Harry, our opinion of Irene changes completely. The same is true of Candace in "Peeping Tom." Throughout the story, the reader is privy to Tommy Bender's use of ESP and psi to read Candace's mind in order to make sure she is the pure, virginal, American girl of his dreams. When Candace reveals, shortly after their marriage, that she, too, has been practicing the art of psi, Tommy's sense of mastery is revealed to be an illusion of Candace's creation so that he will marry her. Again, the stereotypically placid, conforming woman is revealed to be the one in control of the egocentric male focalizer. In both cases, telepathy is depicted through its disruptive effects on the subject's perception of reality and its place within that reality. Both Harry and Tommy assume that they are the all-powerful subjects in relation to their objectified wives, but the latter's telepathic penetration and manipulation of their psyches leave their very identities in question.

In "Homecalling," Merril deploys a more experimental narrative device to speculate on how telepathic communication might engender very different perceptions of reality. In her fiction about alien encounters, such differences, and not the primitivity and savagery of the alien other, are at the root of misunderstandings between humans and aliens. As is conventional in science fiction, the ability to communicate telepathically goes hand-in-hand with an apparently more primitive body; thus Daydanda, the giant insect queen, is barely mobile but keeps watch over her domain through telepathic communication with her winged offspring. She tries to communicate with Deborah, the orphaned child, in the same way and does not understand why Deborah insists on *seeing* Daydanda: "The thought was so far-removed from precedent and past experience, it would not have occurred to her at all to have the girl come to her chamber. [...] The girl seemed to *assume* that an exchange of information would occur only when an exchange of visimages was also possible!" (55–56).

Whereas "A Little Knowledge" and "Peeping Tom" depict the fallibility of the ego through a single focalizer, "Homecalling" uses two focalizers, Daydanda and Deborah, to depict the profound differences between the ways the two perceive the same reality. To further emphasize these differences, Merril at one point uses a parallel column layout:

| DAYDANDA | DEBORAH |
|---|---|
| And now the child was standing in the entrance to the new chamber, and the background patter of her mind was a complaint about the difficulty of seeing clearly. [...] Nobody had ever thought her anything but beautiful before. The Stranger child, at the first clear look, thought she was ... *Ugly and awful and frightening and fat!* | Deborah stood in the open archway between the two big rooms, and peered intently at the great bulk of the Mother-bug on the couch of mats against the far wall. [...] It was a good thing, Dee thought, that she hadn't seen the Mother-bug this close the day before. She never could have made herself believe that anything that looked ... that looked like *that* ... could possibly be friendly. |

Over the course of this section of the story (56–57), Daydanda and Deborah's thoughts and feelings about each other are both exchanged and altered. Confused by the conflict between Daydanda's appearance, which horrifies her, and her telepathic presence, which is soothing and comforting, Deborah begins to rethink her assumptions about the relationship between Daydanda's alien appearance and her character: "The big old bug was ugly, all right, Dee thought, but so were a lot of *people* she'd seen ... and the bug was really pretty nice" (58). Daydanda is at first irritated that another being could think her ugly, but learns to overcome her vanity for the sake of improved communications with Deborah. Both learn that communication is work entailing self-reflexive critique and acceptance of difference. Readers are also prompted to read more actively; they must make choices about how to read the unfamiliar narrative layout, and they are encouraged to adopt critical reading practices such as multiple readings and comparison. Far from transforming communication into an exchange of transparent meanings, telepathy in Merril's fiction highlights the ways in which communication is mediated by complex relations among subjects, and by egocentrism, emotion, and culturally specific values and assumptions.

## Exploring the "Civilized" Subject

Merril's narratives about psychology and psi, and telepathy in particular, are yet another way in which her writing can be distinguished from the dominant trends of the 1950s, when "hard" sciences were an important focus. Recognizing the psychological demands that would come with new technologies of travel and communication, Merril emphasized the importance of mental and emotional, as well as physical, adaptation to ways of living, not only in the context of space adventure but also in everyday human relationships, particularly romantic ones. This interest in the psychological sciences brought Merril into critical conversation with deeply entrenched assumptions about the agent of progress featured in both frontier mythology and much popular science fiction — that is, the "civilized" subject. In frontier mythology, the conquest of indigenous people was rationalized as a natural by-product of human progress from the inchoate, animalistic consciousness of primitive peoples to the coherent, individuated, and, above all, rational civilized man. Popular twentieth-century science fiction would project the progress of this civilized subject into the future, envisioning an empire encompassing the whole of the planet Earth and beyond, supported by ever-advancing technological achievement. In stories such as "A Little Knowledge" and "Peeping Tom," Merril complicates this picture, depicting the civilized ego's sense of its own individuality and mastery over its environment as a fantasy-construction. In narratives about psi, ESP, and communication between humans and aliens, Merril deliberately resists oppositions between civilization and savagery by focusing on communication itself as the real site of human progress. Those who fail to critically examine their own identities, assumptions, and communicative practices do so at their peril, as is the case in "Daughters of Earth," when humans inadvertently provoke an Ullern into a deadly act of self-defense, and "The Lonely," when colonists misread an alien civilization's attempt to warn them away from their planet. On the other hand, those who scrutinize their own assumptions when confronted with difference, like Daydanda and Deborah in "Homecalling," prove in Merril's fiction to be the most effective agents of discovery.

PART TWO

# Shifting the Dimensions of Speculative Fiction

CHAPTER 6

# Merril in Dialogue

At the core of Judith Merril's identity as a science fiction practitioner, mentorship and collaboration — being in dialogue — were integral to her experimentation and joy as a writer and editor in the postwar era. What Merril brought to her collaborations and her taste-making work as an editor and workshop leader was an emphasis on speculation and experimentation, and an insistence on the importance of women and women's work. Sharing new story ideas or reworking old ones (both formally and informally), co-authoring works for publication, and publishing and anthologizing each other's work were the essence of Futurian life. Science fiction writers "seem more prone" to engage in collaboration than other types of fiction writers, perhaps due to the phenomenon of fandom (James 1994, 141). The Futurians, writes Frederik Pohl, "collaborated madly." In his memoir *The Way the Future Was* (1978), Pohl, as one of the founding Futurians of New York, talks about "the reciprocal goading-on that we all supplied each other. We were almost all, from time to time, each other's crutch" (58). Yet Merril was not one of the original Futurians; her first stories as a Futurian were not even science fiction, and once she began publishing science fiction, some of her closest science fiction friends, editors, collaborators, and mentors in the 1950s — Anthony Boucher, Algis Budrys, Les Cole, Arthur Hano, Fritz Leiber, Katherine MacLean, and Theodore Sturgeon, for example — were not part of the Futurian Society of New York. Her fiction writing and anthologizing was generated, published, and marketed in the larger give-and-take environment of what Elizabeth Cummins (1999) calls the "New York Nexus," a larger ongoing network that instilled collaboration and extensive critical feedback and (usually) support.

Cummins was the first to explore Merril's deep engagement and experience in publishing in New York during the period 1945–1950, when the city was the center of American science fiction production, conventions, fan clubs, and fanzines. Looking at science fiction's New York Nexus, the "[richly complex] interactions among writers, editors, fans, readers, and publishers" (Cummins 1999, 314; see also James 1994), Cummins highlights Merril's early, critical education in research techniques, blurb writing, genre editing, page layout, marketing, and fiction and fact writing—seven overlapping roles in the 1940s that generated the firm foundation for Merril's becoming the outstanding writer and editor she was by the mid–1950s (316). Merril also learned how to approach influential individuals in the field: for example, she sought tips from one of the preeminent editors and reviewers, the California-based Tony Boucher, for help with preparing her first anthology (*Shot in the Dark*, 1950), and he remained her mentor for the rest of his life. She also had Arthur Hano recommend her earliest science fiction stories and her theme anthologies to publishers, first when he was a reader for Merril's literary agency, Scott Meredith, and later when he was an editor at Bantam (Cummins 1999, 316–17). In 1948, she married the foremost science fiction agent, Frederik Pohl, and became his client.

Mentoring was essential to Merril right into the late 1960s, when she left the United States and the American science fiction field. She had always had a passion for writing and could not remember a time when she had not written, but until she ran into the Futurians in the mid–1940s, she had not written fiction, had not *crafted* stories. She did not want to write Westerns, so she tried a detective story. Fellow Futurians mentored her through her that first fiction piece in 1945:

> I told [Johnnie Michel and Robert ("Doc") Lowndes] I didn't know how to write a story. They said write one and we'll tell you what's wrong with it. [...] I did. They tore it apart. I rewrote it. They suggested a few more changes. I did them and Doc bought it for *Crack Detective Magazine* [Merril and Pohl-Weary 2002, 45].

It was Sturgeon who convinced Merril she was a writer, got her to adopt "Merril" as her literary pen name, and in 1947, when she was ready to give up writing, effectively encouraged her first, and perhaps most famous science fiction story: "That Only a Mother." He told her how "to get this effect and that reaction, how to see a story, how to feel one, how to plan one, how to make a reader see and feel it" (Merril to Sturgeon, "Tuesday evening" [1947], 41.7, MP). "I learned a lot from everything he told me, and every criticism he made, and far more important I knocked myself out trying" (Merril to Les Cole, February 14, 1952, 37.1, MP). This was no beginner's enthusiasm—Merril remained a lifelong, keen, and willing learner who aimed for excellence and sought creative, collaborative environments in which to work.

The Futurian Society had broke up at the end of World War II. Merril, Pohl, and a few other Futurians provided leadership in founding the Hydra Club in New York in 1947 (not exactly a fan club or a writers' circle, just a large get-together); in establishing the annual Milford, Pennsylvania, workshops for professional writers in 1956 run by Merril, James Blish, and Damon Knight; and in the publication of Merril's path-breaking science fiction anthologies and Year's Best series. The field was thereby energized and challenged, with standards instituted, in ways that would only become fully apparent in the subsequent decade.

Being "in dialogue" was critical for Merril, especially during her periods of inertia as a writer and at times of complications in her domestic life, and she was exceptionally adept and successful at it. Although she didn't collaborate on writing projects often, these cooperative efforts had their practical side as well. In the uncertain profession of science fiction writing, collaboration could enable writers to see a project through to completion (and payment) more quickly than they could do on their own. For example, Merril and collaborator Cyril ("C. M.") Kornbluth shared domestic duties so that each had equal time to concentrate on writing their co-authored novel *Gunner Cade* (1952). (Ironically, Merril was unable to forge such a productive writing partnership with her husband at the time, Frederick Pohl.) Just as Merril used the new frontiers of the space race and the atomic age in the 1950s as backdrops for thinking about certain sets of issues in her independent writing, she was also a kind of literary pioneer on the new frontier of science fiction writing and anthologizing. Collaborative writing, which, as Edward James points out, has generated "some classic sf" (1994, 141), is not often investigated. This is likely because of the persistent belief that the best writing is single-authored, and that creativity is best fostered in solitude. What emerges from an examination of Merril's collaborative writings is the consistency of what Merril brought to them.

## The Big Year of Collaboration, 1950–1951: Cyril Judd

Interaction with ideas and people had already become vital to Merril's intellectual practice as a writer and anthologist in the late 1940s, but it was only in her formal collaborations with one of the original Futurian writers, C. M. Kornbluth, from the fall of 1950 to the fall of 1951, that she discovered the process of building a concept and ideas in interchange with another person. Operating under the joint pseudonym Cyril Judd, theirs was a completely integrated collaboration due to their special approaches to the enterprise. Together they developed distinct and significant stylistic and creative characteristics for their publications that were consistent across their joint output: adventure stories generated from the important social questions of the Cold War era.

Merril's first anthology, *A Shot in the Dark*, was an acclaimed mix of science fiction and mystery stories, reproduced with permission of the Merril Estate.

Although still a novice to science fiction writing when she met Kornbluth in 1950, Merril's first science fiction story "That Only a Mother" (1948), her novel *Shadow on the Hearth* (1950), and her anthology *Shot in the Dark* (1950) had already won critical acclaim and earned for Merril a reputation as one of the most promising new writers in the American field — a prodigy. Kornbluth was himself a highly reputable young writer, a prolific talent who, although the same age as Merril, had been publishing science fiction short stories on the side for a decade, beginning when he was about fifteen. Most of his work was co-authored with one or more writers using a pen name. Given his previous experience with collaboration, creating the fictional entity "Cyril Judd" was most likely Kornbluth's idea. This particular pen name was created for convenience, according to Kornbluth's biographer, Mark Rich, "with transparency in mind" (Rich 2010, 169). Forged from the authors' first names, publishers and reviewers could always identify the writers behind "Cyril Judd." The collaboration seemed like a good fit for Merril and Kornbluth: The two of them had similar mind-sets and shared Futurian backgrounds. Both were thinkers who, according to Merril, "could be quite detached, analytical, and frequently cynical" (Merril and Pohl-Weary 2002, 113). Both were authors whose work was unsentimental and who were known for their elegant prose. Unlike Merril, however, Kornbluth could be bitter and at times quite nasty. Merril recalled Kornbluth's physical appearance: "Cyril was a very small man, just a little taller than five-foot-three. He was short and stocky, not in a cartoon style, but in a typically New York, Jewish-looking style. He was dark-haired, had not quite olive skin. He wore thick glasses" (Rich 2010, 155). Kornbluth, for his part, was impressed by Merril's intelligence; according to Rich, "it struck sparks with Kornbluth — sparks not, apparently, of physical attraction, but of literary friendship" (155).

## *From "Mars Child" (1951) to* Outpost Mars *(1952)*

For their first project, "Mars Child" — which was completed in January–March 1951, serialized in three installments in *Galaxy Science Fiction* (May–July 1951), and sold to Abelard in December 1951 for hardback publication in 1952 under the title *Outpost Mars*—Merril and Kornbluth reworked a 20,000-word manuscript she had already drafted. Merril had originally intended to collaborate with Pohl, who had the original idea for the story but was not writing at the time. She shelved her draft and all other writing projects when she became pregnant in early 1950 and found herself "totally submerged in biology," as she put it (Merril and Pohl-Weary 2002, 102). When interviewed by Rich in 1994, Merril explained that she really liked the story idea "of children born to human settlers on Mars becoming Mars natives. They mutated in certain ways. They have different characteristics. It depended on a whole 'lethal gene' concept, which was new to me and interesting" (Rich 2010, 156). Pohl agreed with Merril that he had written only a little bit for the story, then it sat around for a long time, so he let Merril play with it (Pohl 1978, 147).

The Cyril Judd collaboration on "Mars Child"/*Outpost Mars* began in a simple way. Pohl and Kornbluth were close friends from the early days in the Futurians, before they joined the armed services during World War II, and they had published the occasional story together. Merril and Kornbluth knew of each other through Pohl and also, of course, through each other's work. Kornbluth, who had settled in Chicago after the war, paid Pohl and Merril a visit right after the birth of their baby, Ann, in September 1950. The Pohls still lived in Manhattan, in a basement apartment on East Fourth Street. It is not certain whether Kornbluth discovered the partial draft of Merril's manuscript, as she claims in her memoir (Merril and Pohl Weary 2002, 102), or she simply showed it to him and asked for an opinion, as she told Rich when interviewed in 1994 (Rich 2010, 156). But either way, Kornbluth apparently read it, got excited about it, and asked if he could take a stab at extending the story. He "holed himself up" for several days at the Pohls' home and wrote, essentially doubling the length of Merril's original draft to produce a version that Merril truly liked: "It was considerably changed, but not in such a way that I felt violated" (Merril and Pohl-Weary 2002, 102). The two writers agreed to collaborate on a serialized novel, with both of them quickly establishing an easy rhythm in their work together.

The "Cyril Judd" enterprise proceeded by mail. Merril rewrote Cyril's new section from his visit and mailed it to him in Chicago. He re-wrote her contribution and then added a new section to the story, mailing it back to her. She edited his new section and added a new section of her own, and so it went for three or four passes during the months of November through January until they had produced about half a novel. Half a novel was enough to make a pitch to Horace L. Gold, who was a protégé of the legendary science fiction editor, John W. Campbell, Jr., and now headed up a new magazine: *Galaxy Science Fiction*. Gold launched *Galaxy* in 1950 to compete with Campbell's *Astounding Science Fiction*; he wanted to pick up the best of the established writers from *Astounding* and recruit bright new writers such as Merril and Kornbluth (Silverberg 2010, 168), and he also wanted to publish stories that treated science fiction "with intelligence" and were "the best" (Rich 2010, 159–60). Gold agreed to publish the Cyril Judd manuscript as a three-installment novel, for which the authors showed their appreciation by dedicating the book version to him. Because Pohl was agent for Kornbluth and Merril as well as Cyril Judd, he did the pitching. By this time, Pohl represented thirty-five (approximately seventy percent) of the serious American science fiction writers of the day and was highly successful at selling their work to top magazines, some of which he also edited (Pohl 1978, 130).

While Merril and Kornbluth quickly turned what they had into the first two of the three installments for publication, the relatively smooth procedure they had developed stalled when they tackled the third, and final, installment in the spring of 1951. The collaboration on the first half had required Merril to travel to Chicago in early January to give that part of the novel "intensive treatment." Kornbluth met with her in New York later in January to give the second part of the book the same treatment. She emerged from these January meetings "chastened but encouraged" by her progress in collaborative writing (Merril to Leiber, January 26 and 31, 1951, 38.8, MP). But now, with the deadline for the complete set of installments looming, they received news that their publisher might fold, meaning they would not get paid. As Justine Larbalestier reminds us in her discussion of the Kornbluth-Merril letters, market worries and "lack of ready cash" were occupational hazards in the science fiction field in the 1950s (Larbalestier 2002b, 281–82). Discouraged about the future of the book project, Merril began meeting a few other writing deadlines on the side, while Kornbluth worked on several short stories and finished his first (and eventually most famous) sole-authored book, a suspense science fiction novel titled *Takeoff* (Rich 2010, 168). Meanwhile, neither of them could find a way to end their serialized novel, which, with all the passing to and fro, had also grown far too long. After missing several deadlines to return the third installment to Kornbluth, it took another visit to Chicago by Merril to finish it. That they were able to complete it in a few days was due to the practice they devised on-the-spot. After a full day's initial "conference" on the weekend of her arrival, they completed a semi-final draft, then on the next day cut and proofread (Merril to Pohl, March [n.d.] 1951, 40.15, MP). The rest of the time, Merril worked in her hotel room on the story during the day, while Kornbluth was working at his day job as a Chicago wire-service operator. He wrote and revised "more or less all night" (Merril and Pohl-Weary 2002, 102). In the Kornbluths' tiny place — a storefront apartment converted into an artist's studio for his wife Mary (105) — he and Merril held a few evening conferences. Merril later recalled that a key to finishing "Mars Child" in Chicago was eliminating a particular character that "had crept in, in the second installment. And we were able to lift him out of the book. [...] He was a character we both loved when he showed up and when we'd written him" (Rich 2010, 167).

The serial was published in book form as *Outpost Mars* (Merril and Kornbluth 1952). The story details the struggle of a cooperative colony on Mars, Sun Lake, to establish itself as a bona fide home for its members. The colony's newborn babies are disappearing, and some blame the disappearances on mysterious dwarf-like creatures that are reputed to live in caves in the Martian desert. In Chapter 4, we discussed the colonists' changing perceptions of these thought-to-be aliens over the course of the story. Here, we focus on the thorny question of how to situate Merril's collaborative writing with Kornbluth in relation to her sole-authored work, and the role that this fiction played in the early phase of Merril's career as a writer. Merril's correspondence suggests that she brought to the work its emphasis on the colony, rather than the conventional male adventurer, as "the hero of the book" (Merril to Leiber, June 7,

1951, 38.9, MP). This focus brought the family into the center of the story: the ability of the colony to sustain human females through pregnancy — the book opens with a human birth — and to raise viable offspring is pivotal to its survival. Merril had already made a name for herself through her story "That Only a Mother" and her novel *Shadow on the Hearth*, both of which unabashedly represented futuristic scenarios through the perspectives and experiences of mothers. *Outpost Mars* integrates this perspective with the male-oriented science fiction adventure story through its protagonist Dr. Tony Hellman, who, as a doctor and community leader, has access to both the domestic and public spheres that comprise the colony as a whole. The adventure component of the novel concerns the disappearance of a large quantity of marcaine, an addictive drug produced from the ore extracted at a nearby mine owned by a large, avaricious corporation and exported to Earth for both medical and illicit purposes.

Kornbluth and Merril's collaboration thus represents a merging of the well-established genre of male-oriented colonization stories with the new, domestically oriented science fiction that Judith Merril was introducing to the field. The drug theme addressed pressing social issues of the early 1950s — the increasing prominence (and abuse) of pharmaceuticals in American medicine and society, the growing illicit drug trade, and the increasing influence of corporate interests in American society. Such social engagement was an element of science fiction that Merril was to insist upon throughout her career.

*Outpost Mars* draws contrasts between the noble aspirations of the colony — to "a better, saner way of life, to retrieve some of the dignity of men, to escape from the complexities and inequities and fear pressures of Earth. [...] Building a new life, with hard work and suffering, on the precise pattern of the old" (*Outpost Mars*, 67) — and those of the mine — "There was no thought of the future on the other side of the hill, no worry about permanence, no eye to consequence" (69). Whereas the colony is comprised of simple family dwellings, a hospital and laboratory, and experimental farms attempting to develop Mars-hardy crops, the mine consists of temporary structures, bachelor-workers, and prostitutes. Again, Tony Hellman has access to both of these facets of Martian society because of his role as a doctor. Through his perspective, the reader observes anxious couples awaiting the births of their children, as well as, in one of the more graphic sections of the novel, the body of a prostitute mysteriously beaten to death in the process of attempting a self-abortion. In her correspondence, Merril attributed such graphic mining-camp scenes to Kornbluth (Merril to Leiber, June 7, 1951, 38.9, MP). In contrast to Hellman's conscientious care of the colony, medical care at the mining camp is described in terms that could well apply to the World War II battlefield that Kornbluth, a decorated soldier (see Rich 2010, 111–25), had experienced first-hand:

First thing they think of whenever anybody gets smashed up is he don't look neat enough, so they yank him around to lie nice and straight and they yank him up so they can get a pillow under his head and then they haul him like a sack of meal to a bed [*Outpost Mars*, 103].

The colony and the mine represent two competing visions of future development on Mars, as well as commentary on the poor state of American development in the 1950s. The Earth that the colonists are leaving is the future that Merril and Kornbluth predict if current trends are not held in check — an overpopulated, filthy place where people have starved and poisoned the atmosphere. Merril and Kornbluth brought to the work complementary perspectives on these social problems: Merril infuses the novel with a sense of hopefulness in the future that she represents as implicit in the role of the mother who opens the novel by giving birth. Kornbluth, meanwhile, brings to the text the unflinching gaze of the realist upon scenes of human greed and degradation. They were alike in their interest in extrapolating future scenarios from social and environmental problems they observed in the present.

While finishing "Mars Child" that spring, Merril was hit by a severe writer's block of the sort that made collaborations and serializations such as this one with Kornbluth agonizing, especially with the concomitant pressure to meet tight deadlines. In a separate writing project that she attempted between book ventures with Kornbluth, the novella "Survival Ship" (1951), Merril associated the writer's block with her need for a "room of one's own," in Virginia Woolf's sense of the phrase. In her extended essay of the same name published in 1929, Woolf famously explores women as both writers and characters in fiction and argues for a literal and figurative space for women writers within a literary tradition dominated by men. This was not the first time Merril insisted on a room of her own: she had also done so in the summer of 1949 in order to finish her first book, *Shadow on the Hearth*, which she had begun writing "furiously" in February of that year, then shelved for lack of time and opportunity to complete it (Merril to Les Cole, December 15, 1951, 37.2, MP). With an advance acceptance from Doubleday for *Shadow* in hand, thanks to her Hydra Club connections, she escaped from the city in August to write, settling into a motel cabin she rented for a month and wrote at a fever pitch (Merril to Pohl, November 5, 1949, 40.15, MP), leaving Pohl unhappy and resentful that she would up and leave him and her daughter Merril alone in order to write (Pohl, interviewed by Dianne Newell, January, 2004 Palatine, Illinois).

It was after submitting *Shadow* in late 1949 that what Merril called the "fever-and-inertia cycle" first set in, in this case compounded by finding herself pregnant for a second time (Merril to Leiber, September 24, 1950, 38.8, MP), and having to cope with all the unexpected media attention lavished on her when *Shadow* appeared that spring. To Tony Boucher, she wrote in the summer of 1950 of the state of creative paralysis she faced over events of the past year and the pending war between North and South Korea, and asked him to talk to her, to

> help me in digesting this goulash of ideas [for a new story] which is currently clogging my so-called brain. The book [*Shadow*], get-out-of-town, ba[b]y coming, slick stories, the book, Me As A Writer, style and technique, war and peace, the book, the baby, science fiction boom ... maybe you know a nice peaceful 20-dollar-a-month hole in a warm climate, away from newspapers, bombs, critics, editors, publicity depts., relatives, and editors, where I can live for nothing while having my baby and thinking out the things I want to write about when I want to write? [June 18, 2.42, MP].

In the spring of 1951, after submitting "Mars Child" and needing to meet other publishing deadlines, Merril once again set up a temporary writing space of her own, this time in a small apartment on Christopher Street, in New York City's West Village, which she rented for a few months from a science fiction friend. Despite access to the new retreat, Merril truly struggled with the writing. To Fritz Leiber she wrote several *cris de coeur* "from a room on Christopher Street." First, she revealed that she had needed to escape from the collaboration in order to write something on her own, but it was not working: "I've got a good story (the novelette I told you about — on board the ship SURVIVAL), and I know what I want to say, I know my characters, I want to do it, and it won't write." Worse still, she lamented, "what does come reluctantly out is so far inferior to what wants to be said that it hurts" (May 1, 1951, 38.8, MP). Her productivity improved over the next few weeks, but only marginally: "I did finally get a couple of thousand satisfactory words past the title. [...] Still, one page is my self-imposed limit until I am further along" (May 11, 1951, 38.8, MP). Meanwhile, the Pohls had bought an old thirteen-room Victorian house across the river from the small town of Red Bank, New Jersey, at 386 West Front Street, which they moved into with their growing family in mid–May. Once settled in the house, Merril immediately refurbished a secluded top-floor office, set up daytime office hours, and installed a makeshift intercom system, all in the hopes of generating uninterrupted creative and productive writing time.

During the weeks leading up to the move to Red Bank, Leiber subtly mentored Merril from his home in Chicago: offering her encouraging words and talking about his own past battles with unproductive periods, of his tendency to "hold back and quit too soon in the good stretches" (May 14, 1951, 38.8, MP). Leiber also raved to Merril about "Mars Child." He wrote that he was jealous — but in a good way — of the first two installments and thought that Merril and Kornbluth had produced "a landmark of American SF," one that likely would win the title of the year's best novel. Leiber loved the idea of the "cooperators" and enjoyed all the characters, he said, and "those constant behind-the-scenes peeks at family life that having Tony a doctor makes possible;" he also praised the "raw realism of abortions, brothels, and suckling problems" that contributed to the novel's landmark status (May 24, 1951, 38.8, MP). Soon, Merril was back on track with her writing and ready to tackle a second novel with Kornbluth. Having a room of her own had helped, but so, it seems, did being in constant and intimate dialogue with Leiber: what Merril would in later years refer to as the "loving contact with my special friends" that could pull her through "almost anything" (Merril to Boucher, April 26, 1958, 2.41, MP). So the 1950s was a period of both professional *and* emotional collaborations for Merril.

## *Cyril Judd at Red Bank*

With the successful publication of "Mars Child," and with dreams of its sale as a hardback novel and of other novels to come, Kornbluth quit his day job and dove into science fiction writing full-time. His launch as a full-time writer began with a second collaboration with Merril. No sooner had they submitted "Mars Child" than Merril began scheduling their "joint output" for the remainder of the year:

> I think the best procedure might be to do an outline and first 20 thou of a new "major" novel, maybe another Mars piece (which I find myself sort of eager about), during the six-week-or-so period till mid–Aug. Then within a month's time, we'd probably have a commitment either for book or magazine [...] with six-weeks-or-so left, again, before the end of the year to plot out something new and do a submission sample [Merril to Kornbluth, April 23, 1951, 9.28, MP].

Merril's formula anticipated the routine of frequent intervals of working individually, interspersed with face-to-face collaborations every few months, that had worked for the "Mars Child" collaboration, and in that same letter to Kornbluth she calculated that they could produce two hardcovers and three magazine stories a year, from which they could each earn a respectable income. After moving to Red Bank in May, Merril and Pohl invited the Kornbluths to come live there. Merril figured them to be "handy" people who could pitch in with the repairs and renovations that the old place needed and Pohl was incapable of tackling: "the very thought" of having to do it scared Pohl "out of his wits" (Merril to Cyril, Mary, and Princess [the dog], May 24 [1951], 9.28, MP). After a few false starts, the Kornbluths joined Pohl and Merril in the big house in Red Bank at the end of July 1951.

The timing of the Kornbluths' arrival was not exactly opportune. Mary was now pregnant, in poor health and in danger of losing the baby, so she was confined to bed. Merril, whose marriage was now in serious difficulty, had just undergone a secret abortion and was hemorrhaging, so she, too, was confined to bed for a time. The Pohls' live-in babysitter, Lois Miles, married to Futurian Jack Gillespie, was also pregnant and confined to bed. Pohl spent most of his time in New York City, in part because he was running a literary agency called the Dirk Wylie Agency, and in part because he was having an affair, or affairs (Rich 2010, 176). With her one-year-old, her nine-year-old, and her mother in tow, visitors to host, and a marriage that was seriously unraveling, Merril, who was still in her twenties, was under considerable strain. It had turned out to be a miserable summer, she confided to a friend: "Three cheerful young couples with all these intense troubles of different kinds. Jeese!" (Merril to Les Cole, December 15, 195[1], 37.2, MP).

Merril and Kornbluth were left to run the big house at Red Bank pretty much on their own All the duties got divided: "I tended the baby, [Cyril] tended Mary, I marketed and laundered, he burned the trash and washed the dishes" (December 15). In spite of the hurdles, Merril and Kornbluth were determined to capitalize on their time together to collaborate on a second novel, *Gunner Cade*, vowing to finish it for publication as a serialized book within three weeks. It took six or seven, filled with "blood, sweat, and misery" (December 15). Complicating the need to write *Gunner Cade* quickly was the authors' determination to publish the serialized version in yet another top magazine, *Astounding Science Fiction* — hence the need to write to the specific tastes of editor John Campbell. Merril considered the speed of completion to be "pretty phenomenal," all things considered (Rich 2010, 185). But then, she recalled, "we were all desperately broke" (Merril and Pohl-Weary 2002, 111).

## *Gunner Cade* (1952)

*Gunner Cade* moved with lightning speed from draft to published book. Written over the period of late July and August 1951, it appeared in *Astounding* in three installments from March through May 1952 and was quickly published under the same title in hardback with a major publishing house, Simon and Schuster, also in 1952. This time, the story idea was entirely Kornbluth's. He brought to the collaboration on *Gunner Cade* a complete, seventeen-page synopsis he had for a book, tentatively titled *Time of Troubles* (Rich 2010, 171).

Together the two of them laid the groundwork — creating a new mode of collaboration — for the book project they renamed "The Gauntlet" and "Armsmen of the Klin" (Merril to Pohl, September 25, 1951, 40.16, MP; Rich 2010, 175–76) before finally settling on *Gunner Cade*, jointly breaking down the synopsis, building up the parts, and adding to the story. Rich has closely examined the synopsis and the authors' notations to it, remarking on Merril's impressive editing talents (Rich 2010, 175–81) and noting the easygoing, back-and-forth banter this writing partnership enjoyed. The revised, expanded synopsis was then broken into roughly equal sections that would eventually become several thousand-word installments for serialization.

Merril did not like working from an outline (although an outline was exactly what she had proposed to Kornbluth in April when she detailed a plan for their future collaborations): "*Gunner Cade* was," Merril would later recall, "the only time I have ever worked from a fairly rigid outline, or from any kind of outline. Any other time when I've been working on my own when I've tried to outline something, I didn't write it afterward" (179). She did not even like writing a synopsis of a story in advance: "once it's on paper, it's on paper," she wrote to Tony Boucher (March 12, 1959, 2.42, MP). What Merril strove for in her writing was, as she explained to Leiber once the first installments of *Gunner Cade* came out, the "Gestalt approach [...] to the story as a whole. I've always worked from characters, letting them have their heads as the story progressed," something she says she learned from Sturgeon (April 11, 1952, 39.3, MP). As a result of the collaborative process that produced *Outpost Mars* and *Gunner Cade*, however, the characters developed as the books got written (Rich 1999, 4; Rich 2010, 177).

While sharing major responsibility for household chores and Merril's children by day, Merril and Kornbluth worked at the story on alternate nights, with one of them adding a segment of new text at a time, but each in their own way, ways that Merril describes as "exactly opposite" (Rich 2010, 185): Kornbluth would cut and rewrite the text she had left the previous night and add about 3,000 words of what needed to be a beefed-up 5,000-word section. The next night, she would edit and flesh out his contribution, and then add an 8,000-word section that needed to be shortened to 5,000 words, then "[h]e would rewrite my section to shorten it, and so on, and so forth" (Merril and Pohl-Weary 2002, 111; and see also Rich 1996, 409–10). The result was relatively seamless, according to Merril: "So when [*Gunner Cade*] was finished it was very hard for either of us, except for specific things, to know who had written what" (Rich 1999, 6). The few "specific things" she could identify as written by Kornbluth were, in a sense, stereotypically gendered perspectives — the barracks and battle scenes ("I hardly changed anything in those") — whereas the love sections we her own("he hardly touched those") (Merril and Pohl-Weary 2002, 111; Rich 2010, 185). At the same time, she also immersed herself in writing what was, on the whole, a male-centered adventure story.

*Gunner Cade* is not much like anything Merril ever wrote on her own; however, it shares with other Cyril Judd works its future–Earth setting in which the potential effects of such developments as unchecked industrial growth, nuclear proliferation, and resource scarcity are explored. This was the kind of social science fiction that many other Futurians, like Pohl and Knight, were writing as well. *Gunner Cade* imagines a post–Armageddon Earth of 2600 A.D., the center of a galactic empire, known as the Realm of Man, that also comprises Mars, Jupiter's moons, and some man-made planets. While popular memory of the Armageddon has faded, taboos that came into existence to prevent another such war are still in place: war has been relegated to a tightly controlled set of rituals practiced by a special military class called the Armsmen. Raised in a radically patriarchal belief system based on regimen, obedience, and sacrifice, Armsmen put their training into practice in ritualized battles that have little real military significance. Among their most sacred taboos is to never fire a weapon from the air; all combat is hand-to-hand or with guns, and carried out on foot. While the Armsmen are trained to blindly accept such rules without understanding why, the reader, living in the beginning of the nuclear age, would recognize that nuclear bombs dropped from the air must have brought about the Armageddon that is not even a distant memory except for one person in the text's diegetic universe.

With *Gunner Cade*, Merril was willing to work within the outline initially prepared by Kornbluth, which centers on the most masculine protagonist of the three Cyril Judd writing projects: Gunner Cade is a devout Armsman looking forward to another predictable, ritual-filled day when the novel begins. Instead, he finds himself caught up in a web of rebellion and conspiracy that lies beneath the surface of the apparently stable, autocratic political system governing the Realm of Man. Female figures in the text are more objectified than in other Merril and Cyril Judd works: they are spies, rebel-aristocrats posing as prostitutes, or conniving aristocrats — all of which are disguises that represent women as exotic, mysterious, and (for the most part) beautiful, and all are employed by the Lady Jocelyn, the feisty niece of the emperor, who secretly shares her knowledge of history with Cade and convinces him to rebel.

Even within this male-centered paradigm, patriarchal ideology is represented in a complex fashion. Kornbluth's experiences as a soldier on the front in World War II, where he observed atrocities committed in the name of masculine, military obedience and resistance to unnecessary sentiment, played a key role in the conceptualization of Gunner Cade's susceptibility to, and rebellion against, indoctrination in Klin philosophy, a patriarchal, military doctrine predicated on blind obedience to the existing hierarchy and the repression of all pleasure and sentiment as, at best, frivolous, and at worst a threat to order in the empire. When Cade finds himself, after a series of plot twists, a fugitive on the run from his own people, he is forced to think critically about this doctrine. At first, he longs for a return to the comfort of ideology and routine. But, gradually, Cade learns that Klin is merely a tool of dominance and control, and that what he has been taught are the weaknesses of commoners — desire, pleasure, and sentiment — are actually the essence of humanity.

Merril claims in her memoir that they plotted *Gunner Cade* by departing from Kornbluth's original outline, intentionally modeling their story after a prototypical Campbell story, Leiber's recent hit *Gather, Darkness!* (Merril and Pohl-Weary 2002, 111), but going too far. This sort of heavy borrowing was purely pragmatic: they were determined to have Campbell buy their novel, and he did. When the deal was complete, Merril claims that they sent Leiber a telegram: "Congratulations. *Gather, Darkness!* has sold again!" (111). She suggests that although in other literary fields using the ideas of other writers would be considered "plagiarism," this was not so in science fiction, especially among the Futurians (46). Yet she also confessed that the heavy borrowing from Leiber's work in this instance turned out to be extremely problematic for her:

> As far as I know, with all the authors Cyril and I talked to, we never met any other writer of quality who ever recognized that they had done something like that. No one has had our level of awareness about the extent to which writers plagiarize, model themselves after, or derive inspiration from other writers' work [111–12].

How did she feel about that? "I could only morally justify doing something like this because it was collaboration. Somehow that made it totally different for me — it was just a cheap evasion for me. I assumed that by putting another name to it, I could do something I wouldn't normally do," but she did not think the sort of moral issues that bothered her troubled Kornbluth, who was an excellent writer but, in her view, "lacked integrity about being an author" (112).

Here we see Merril's awareness of the effectiveness — for better or for worse — of masquerading under a pseudonym: in writing novels with Kornbluth as Cyril Judd, even though the true identities of the authors were transparent, she could behave differently. Merril raised this idea again when she wrote "The Lady Was a Tramp" (1957) as Rose Sharon. "Rosie" was, in addition to being created out of necessity at a time when Merril's personal life was under close scrutiny, a type of second self for Merril, a persona that, as she explained to Boucher, could take over the typewriter and bring a different set of experiences and feelings to the writing, "a wealth of background information that Judy could never have used at all" (October 24, 1956, 2.41, MP). Like collaboration, writing under a pseudonym enabled Merril to experiment with her very identity as a writer, though the decision to use a pseudonym to say something she could not under her own name seemed "extraordinary" to her, "the *idea*, even, of using any other name" (Merril to Boucher, March 10, 1956, "Merril 3/4," White Mss).

If the *Gunner Cade* collaboration began on an ethically questionable note, it proceeded as an intellectually rich collaboration, for a time. Despite the chaos of Merril's Red Bank household that summer, *Gunner Cade* was written in a particularly productive space: the third-floor office that Merril had created for her writing. She and Kornbluth could talk and argue about anything in that small space, she recalls: "We were exploring our feelings and exploring the world through the book we were writing [...] we were also intensely involved with our characters" (Merril and Pohl-Weary 2002, 113). On the other hand, their writerly friendship did not run very deep, for, as she also notes, it was entirely confined to her office, despite the fact that they were also collaborating on the domestic front. She realized much later that she did not really get to know Kornbluth in any meaningful way and that he was socially and politically very conservative and reluctant to discuss personal issues, especially when it came to his childhood or to sex.

Merril had much to deal with once Pohl left in October 1951. Merril began coming and going to New York for a few days two or three times a month, where she had access to a room in MacLean's basement apartment. Merril's mother babysat while Merril wrote in solitude and saw her friends at the Hydra Club (Merril to Leiber, December 18, 1951, 38.9, MP). The emotional risks for Merril were considerable: New York was "full of old friends and ex-husbands and ex-boyfriends and distasteful gossips" (Merril to Frederik Brown, January 4, 195[2], 3.16, MP), so there was also a downside to the chumminess of the New York Nexus. At Red Bank, the Kornbluths stayed on until March 1952. Merril had trouble sorting out the Kornbluths' share of expenses; negotiating an increase from the couple was stressful to relations (see Merril's letters to Kornbluth, November 1951 to February 1952, 9.28, MP). Adding to the tension in the Merril-Kornbluth household, the Kornbluths' baby was four weeks overdue. Merril was at the time trying, with no success, to extricate herself (as an author) from Pohl's control as her agent regarding her published and unsold stories, including her collaborations with Kornbluth, but Kornbluth, for various reasons, was unwilling to cooperate with Merril in her struggle. By February, Merril was also in therapy and riding an emotional roller-coaster, which further hurt her relations with Kornbluth: "I have taken to talking back to people when they are rude to me. This has thrown C. Kornbluth for several loops" (Merril to Les Cole, February 28, 1952, 37.1, MP). The Kornbluths moved out on March 1, "stewing about something," and leaving Merril both anxious for an explanation and hoping, unsuccessfully, to remain friends (Merril to Mary Kornbluth, March 15, 1952, 9.28, MP).

## "Sea-Change" (1953)

The Cyril Judd collaboration produced one more work, and it is worth noticing, although it has received little or no attention in science fiction circles: the 12,000-word novelette titled "Sea-Change" (Merril and Kornbluth 1953). This story, which appeared in "Doc" Lowndes's *Dynamic Science Fiction* in March 1953 was written in September 1951, immediately after the serialized novel *Gunner Cade* was finished (Merril Memo [reflections], April 1950 [updated in late fall of 1951], 40.17, MP). The Kornbluths still lived in the Red Bank house at this time, and Merril and Pohl had not yet separated. "Sea-Change" was potentially the beginning of a new serialized novel by Cyril Judd, for in October, Merril outlined for Kornbluth the procedure for the next Cyril Judd book (October 6, 1951, 9.28, MP). But things went no further than this single story. Merril seems not to have thought highly of it, recalling that "neither of us regarded ['Sea-Change'] as worth thinking about particularly" (Rich 2010, 189), and that it was of "no great significance" (Rich 1999, 4). In a letter to Kornbluth, she refers to "Sea-Change" as "mostly yours" (Merril to Kornbluth [filed with the Frederik Pohl correspondence], January 11, 1952, 40.16, MP). Like *Gunner Cade*, "Sea-Change" is largely unrecognizable as a Judith Merril story, but bears many of the hallmarks of a Cyril Judd story.

"Sea-Change" is noteworthy as an early departure from the Anglo-American ideological hegemony in American science fiction, as well as for its somewhat prescient commentary on global politics. At a time when much American science fiction projected the process of Manifest Destiny into the future, envisioning a virtually Americanized Earth, "Sea-Change" identifies the ideological blind spot in such scenarios by representing Africa and the Muslim world as major players in the consolidated superpowers of Earth's future, along with Latin America ("Latimer"), Europe, China and Russia ("Sino-Russia"), and America. At the crux of the global politics of the future is the technology for salvaging metals from the sea, a promising new source of the scarce metals needed to manufacture weapons, to which America seemingly holds the key. The story echoes the early Cyril Judd novel *Outpost Mars* in its emphasis on the implications of unbridled industrial development.

In the beginning of the story, the central character, engineer Lev Sloane, sees a security guard on the hunt for a youth who has stolen some salvaged copper to sell on the street. When the youth is hit by a brick thrown by the guard, Sloane can't help but feel "distaste" for the guard and a "worrisome feeling" for the youth ("Sea-Change," 14). This beginning economically introduces the social themes that are characteristic of *Outpost Mars*: industrial expansion, scarcity, and the social unrest that these developments engender.

When he arrives home in his apartment, Sloane is greeted, Raymond Chandler style, by an armed man who turns out to be a Latin American spy, offering to buy technological secrets from Sloane. When the man leaves empty-handed, Sloane calls the police and has the man arrested. This proves to be a setup: in custody, the man "confesses" that Sloane has been selling information to him, and Sloane is accused of treachery by his own people.

Sloane is helped out of his predicament by a female African scientist, Dr. Vanderpoel, visiting the plant where Sloane works, and where metal is harvested from beneath the ocean. Dr. Vanderpoel embodies a future, consolidated Africa comprised of its antecedent Dutch, indigenous, and Arab influences: she speaks with a Dutch accent and has a Dutch name, is "dark-skinned," and has "rather everted lips" and the "classic nose and brow of an Arab" (18). She practices a religion reminiscent of Islam, called Ma'di, named for its prophet who, 100 years earlier, brought industrialization and unification to Africa. Dr. Vanderpoel reminds Sloane and the reader that, contrary to Euro-centric versions of progress, her ancestors, the ancient Egyptians, were its earliest originators, despite Western attempts to appropriate Egypt's legacy by erasing its African identity: "You call them 'Egyptian,' pretending that Egypt was not a part of Africa and did not continuously exchange, culturally and genetically, with all its peoples" (21). Together, Sloane and Vanderpoel expose and defeat an international conspiracy involving espionage and assassination, designed to shift the global balance of power in favor of the aggressive Sino-Russia. Unique to this story is its prescient attention to Africa and Islam, global players usually aligned with the so-called vanishing civilizations so often left out of near-future science fiction narratives.

## *Post–Cyril Judd: The Refashioning of "Mars Child" as* Sin in Space *(1961)*

While the departure of Pohl from Red Bank in the fall of 1951 ended a promising collaboration between Merril and Kornbluth, it prompted a successful one for Kornbluth and Pohl, who quickly entered into a series of collaborative novels and stories until Kornbluth's untimely death in 1958 at the age of 35. Collaborating with Kornbluth, Pohl regained his stride as a writer, beginning with the science fiction classic by Kornbluth and Pohl under their joint byline, titled *The Space Merchants* (1953). According to Rich, Pohl occasionally revised Kornbluth's work after the author's death by "adding decidedly cheapening elements" (Rich 2010, 352). *Sin in Space*, a "version" of the Cyril Judd serialized book for *Galaxy Science Fiction*, "Mars Child," is a prime example. As the new editor of *Galaxy* and an author with a quarter royalty in "Mars Child" (because the original story idea was his), Pohl revised the book for publication as a Galaxy Beacon paperback in 1961, under the title *Sin in Space: An Expose of the Scarlet Planet*, by Cyril Judd. The novel's content is sensationalized not only in Pohl's choice of a new title but also in the jacket blurbs and the notoriously sexualized cover art depicting a shapely blond female human who is raising her sweater over her bare breasts for the benefit of a leering spaceman. According to Rich's findings, "Judy Merril 'refused to add a paragraph to justify the cover painting' and the new title," and only after its publication did she learn that Pohl himself undertook that task (Rich 2010, 352). Comparing the original *Outpost Mars* to *Sin in Space*, one finds that there are at least three points in the latter novel where sexual scenes have either been added or embellished. Meanwhile, in the end, it is the Pohl-Kornbluth collaboration *The Space Merchants* that is remembered and admired, not Cyril Judd.

## *The Reception of Cyril Judd*

Despite the excellent professional reputation of each of the collaborators at the time, both *Outpost Mars* and *Gunner Cade* received fairly mixed reviews when they first appeared, with the reviewers sharing in a general disappointment with the collaboration itself: they expected something exceptional from two such promising and talented authors. Of the collaborative punch of *Outpost Mars*, the joint editors of *Magazine of Fantasy and Science Fiction*, Anthony Boucher and J. Francis McComas, had this to say, not all of it bad:

> Collaboration is (as who knows better than we?) a very serious relationship, offering many of the problems and few of the rewards of marriage; it is difficult to analyze why the Kornbluth-Merril product adds up to a little less than either author is capable of separately [...] [it] is a trifle slow, a bit unsubtle in its characterizations and plotting; but despite these flaws it does proffer virtues worthy of its authors: a detailed convincing study of the problems of a cooperative colony on Mars; a startling genetic theory, planted with the possibility and cumulative surprise of a good detective story; and above all, the intimacy of impact which comes from placing small-scale personal problems of the near future ahead of the mind-whirling vastness of the Hypergalactic Tenth Millennium [Boucher and McComas 1952, 114–15].

Boucher's review of the book in the *New York Herald-Tribune* as H. H. Holmes is less tempered, noting that the collaboration was "slightly less sharply economical than the writing of either author alone" (July 20, 1952, quoted in Rich 2010, 209). P. Schuyler Miller in *Astounding Science Fiction* wondered "why Cyril Kornbluth — who gave us 'Takeoff' last spring — and Judith Merril — who has had two intelligent anthologies to her credit during the year — need to combine forces as 'Cyril Judd' is anyone's guess." *Outpost Mars* was "a sound and relatively simple story" (Miller 1953a, 81).

These reviewers failed to see in the novel what Leiber had when he wrote to Merril of the wonderful characters, "raw realism," and inside look into family and routine life on Mars. Perhaps *Outpost Mars* was ahead of its time, a possibility suggested by Kim Stanley Robinson's selection in 1999 of it as one of his favorite Mars novels of all time (2009, "My 10 Favorite Mars Novels"). Robinson, author of the award-winning Mars trilogy, compares *Outpost Mars* favorably to Arthur C. Clarke's classic *The Sands of Mars* (1951), calls it "a hidden gem among Mars novels," and suggests that it offers a "feminist perspective that brings a new emphasis on family and relationships" (Robinson 2009, 3). Leiber notwithstanding, a feminist reading of *Outpost Mars* such as Robinson's was not in the cards in the early 1950s, when the book first appeared.

When it first appeared, *Gunner Cade* fared no better in the hands of reviewers than *Outpost Mars* did, despite the favorable private comments from other writers such as Robert Heinlein, whose reaction to the first installment of the serialized version was all kudos: "New stuff it is and most intriguing stuff, wonderfully worked out. I do love the new cultural pattern, logically developed," he wrote Merril (February 18, 1952, 7.55, MP). The authors' old Futurian friend Fletcher Pratt, writing for the *Saturday Review* called it "a knock-out thriller," and Basil Davenport's review for the *New York Times* hailed *Gunner Cade* as a superior melodrama: "For both action and fiction, this is a long way ahead of its time" (both quoted in Rich 2010, 209). Boucher and McComas, however, had nothing good at all to say about *Gunner Cade* "either as story-telling or thinking," calling it, perhaps in recognition of the silent debt it owed to a Leiber story and the commonplace nature of the plot, "a competent but not particularly palatable rehash of standard ideas" (1953, 90). Reviewing it for the *New York Herald-Tribune* as H. H. Holmes, Boucher leaves no doubt as to the novel's hackneyed storyline, referring to *Gunner Cade* as "supposedly a brand-new 1952 novel without one element of novelty in plot, characters, or 'science,'" adding that it was "[p]rofessional, readable, and completely uncreative [...] though perhaps new readers, unfamiliar with the countless stories from which it stems, may find it enjoyable enough" (quoted in Rich 2010, 209, 405n48). P. Schuyler Miller concludes of the collaborative effort, "Cyril Judd can do better. I know they can" (1953b, 160–61).

While reviewers generally expected Cyril Judd to transcend the genius of its parts, Merril and Kornbluth collaborated for far more practical reasons: they both had reputations they could capitalize on for quick publication, they worked productively together, and they needed the cash. Yet, read as a collaborative production in its own right, without expectations of transcendent genius, Cyril Judd's work demonstrates distinct and important stylistic and creative characteristics: in different ways, the authors pushed the boundaries of the science fiction genre with respect to conventions of both gender and race. They are stylistically consistent, engaging a realist narrative style reminiscent of hard-boiled fiction to create adventure stories about complex and imaginative future Earths and Mars, which they extrapolated from social questions that preoccupied Americans in the early 1950s. These qualities make Cyril Judd worthy of critical attention, not as a transcendent synthesis of two of science fiction's most promising writers of the early 1950s, but as an authorial entity quite distinct from either Merril or Kornbluth alone.

## Collaborating with Fredrik Pohl

*"A Big Man with the Girls" (1953)*

Other than their work together on Robert Heinlein's anthology, *Tomorrow the Stars* (Heinlein 1952), which Pohl claims he and Merril ghost-edited although Heinlein's correspondence with them (Heinlein to Pohl and Merril, June 26, 1951, 7.55, MP) and his preface to the anthology suggest that Heinlein and several others also played an editorial role, Merril's only collaboration with Pohl was on a short story, "A Big Man with the Girls," published in *Future Science Fiction* (Merril and Pohl [as James MacCreigh] 1953). No details have come to light about the workings of this collaboration, other than that it was a fully collaborative story for which they shared royalties fifty-fifty, and that it was finished before their breakup, but not yet sold, in the fall of 1951 (Merril to Pohl, November 19, 1951, 40.16, MP). A witty satire on consumerism, which was a trademark of Pohl's writing in the 1950s, it also features a desirable female character who outfoxes the male central protagonist with her cleverness, a plot twist that would appear again in Merril's fiction, in "A Little Knowledge" (1953), "Peeping Tom" (1954), and "Rain Check" (1954). Thus, Merril brought to this collaboration, as she had to Cyril Judd, a woman's perspective.

"A Big Man with the Girls" is set in a generic American town just after an approaching alien rocket has been detected. Its protagonist, Bart Mandell, a military man, is among those searching for possible alien invaders, which leaves him little time to date Sally, "a party girl, always on the move, fast on her feet and quick with a quip. Not the sitting-home type at all" ("Big Man," 45–46). On the way to see her, Bart purchases a model of a rocket from one of the many souvenir stands that have popped up to capitalize on the event, a gift for Sally. But when he arrives at her house for dinner, he notices another rocket on her hearth, "almost twice as big as his — and a really beautiful job.

Shiny, silver-colored metal, not cast but seamed along the sides ... even a miniature air-lock standing open." It is even "scarred and dented in spots" (46), as if it had recently been launched. Concluding that he has a rival — one with a much larger and more authentic "rocket" to offer — Bart works hard to stifle his jealousy. And he also immediately starts to think of marrying Sally. As the plot unfolds, we learn that the rocket is in fact a real one, belonging to a "one-inch high Martian" who had asked Sally for protection after landing on Earth without realizing that its inhabitants were hundreds of times larger than he was — not to mention the "fierce" giant squirrels (51). This plot twist pokes fun at the machismo that spurs both Bart's jealousy and the military search for a possible Martian monster. It had, it seems, never occurred to Bart and the others that the alien's first contact might be with a woman. It is an old story-type that the Merril-Pohl collaboration updated by playing with issues of gender and perspective, both of which, as noted elsewhere, are hallmarks of Merril's work.

## Pseudo-Collaborations
*With Les Cole, "A Woman of the World" (1957) as Rose Sharon, and with A. J. Budrys, "Death Cannot Wither" (1959)*

Merril quickly lost interest in formal collaborations. From the outset of her co-authorship with Kornbluth, Merril felt compelled to write her own stories, which she considered a superior literary contribution to that of collaborative writing. When she began work on "Mars Child," she wrote to Boucher drawing a distinction between that type of writing and her "real" writing (November 16, 1950, 2.42, MP). After completing that project she wrote of it again, this time to Leiber: "I've *got* to write something of my own, not collaboration" (May 1 [1951], 38.8, MP). To Les Cole she related her split with Pohl in the fall of 1951 and acknowledged, with joy, "I have been writing ever since. Not just collaboration — writing" (December 15, 1951, 37.2, MP). A year later, she wrote to Cole about getting a story into print: "My own under my own name" (October 4, 1952, 37.6, MP).

Writing under her own name entailed certain practical realizations, including the efficacy and freedom of the short story. In 1956 she admitted to Cole, "Best thing I ever did educationally, committing myself to writing something *short*" (August 23, 37.6, MP). Like the Cyril Judd collaboration, however, Merril's stories often became much longer than intended and needed cutting, causing delays in meeting publishers' deadlines; after she discovered the novella form in the early 1950s, writing short stories no longer came easily to her.

Although her letters to Cole profess her desire to publish her own fiction under her own name, Merril stumbled into a collaboration of sorts with Les Cole himself, for which she used the pseudonym Rose Sharon. While the result was two parallel stories—"A Man of the World," by Cole, and Merril's "A Woman of the World," published together in the first issue of a new magazine, *Venture Science Fiction* (1957)—the process was not unlike that of her past collaborations with Kornbluth. In Chapter 2, we briefly discussed "Woman of the World" for its alignment of nuclear and patriarchal societies. Here, we consider the story in the context of Merril as a collaborator. In this publisher-driven collaboration, Merril was assigned the task of supplying the woman's point of view.

*Venture*, a short-lived companion to *Magazine of Fantasy and Science Fiction* that started up in 1956, was dedicated to stories of action and adventure, and so placed a greater emphasis on sex and violence than was usual for science fiction magazines of the day. The publisher, Bob Mills, sent Merril a copy of Cole's manuscript for a story titled "Morale." Cole was a West Coast engineer, science fiction fan, and aspiring writer with whom Merril had been corresponding for many years. As Merril explained to Cole, Mills was willing to publish Cole's story if it was revised to half the length, paired with a 2,000-word story by Merril "telling how the other half lives" (in other words, depicting a woman's point of view), and ready for publication in three weeks. The "other half" consisted of a young heterosexual couple assaulted by a lone male. Cole's story depicted the events from the lone male's point of view, and Merril was to write a companion story telling the story from the perspective of the young couple. Nonetheless, Cole's story inspired her and the prospect of parallel story-making and focusing on the female character's viewpoint delighted her (Merril to Cole, July 27, 1956, 37.7, MP).

Within days, Merril knew exactly how to proceed; she had a clear idea for her story—what to keep, what to cut, what to add to Cole's, and what hook was needed to link the two stories. She presented Cole with a synopsis with the exact details of the story she eventually submitted for publication (August 15, 1956, 37.7, MP). Cole agreed to the idea of parallel stories: "you know goddamn good and well that I would not turn down the opportunity of working with (and/or on) you in just plain selfish terms of reputation." But he also cautions that this is likely to be their one and only collaboration together: "too much of a personality clash" (Cole to Merril, July 29, 1956, 37.7, MP). Given that the advantage of this scheme to Cole was appearing alongside a big-name writer such as Merril, he must have been disappointed to discover that she would publish her story under a pseudonym. But Merril's story was her most sexually explicit to date; on a practical level, writing as Rose Sharon shielded her from prying eyes in this period of ongoing disputes over custody of one of her daughters. On a more positive note, it also meant that Cole's efforts as a novice would not be overshadowed by being linked with Merril's name.

The two stories are so intertwined that they should both be described together: both stories narrate a confrontation and struggle between survivors of a nuclear holocaust. Cole's "A Man of the World" was meant to be read first: Its main character, John Reeves, has been surviving on his own for a year. His last remaining tie to civilization is hygiene, and his supplies of toothpaste, razors, and so on are wearing thin. He stumbles upon a deserted farm and is about to claim it when he spies a young man and woman. He quietly stalks them, knocks the woman unconscious, and attacks and kills the young man. As he rifles through the other man's things, he is delighted to find a razor, strop, and unbroken mirror. "John, John, you can shave again. John, you will be clean-shaven! You will be civilized again, John" (Cole 1957, 74–75). But when John remembers the woman, "[t]ears ran from his eyes as the tension began again. With dirty, red-stained fists he wiped them away until he was no longer aware of them." Then, "[h]ypnotically, unaware [...] he strode toward the supine form of the woman" (75). John's fragile, civilized self is no defense against the primal urges unleashed in the aftermath of nuclear war.

Merril's "A Woman of the World" explains the identity and backstory of the young couple: Tommy and Ellen are escapees from a small, tightly controlled community that had formed shortly before the bombing. Tommy is naïve and cloying; Ellen soon tires of him, and wishes for a man with more control of the situation. After Reeves's attack, in which Ellen is knocked unconscious, she awakens to Tommy and Reeves fighting. Aware that they are fighting over her, Ellen remains still, waiting for the men to determine her fate. This is how Merril describes the ending in the outline she sent to Les Cole: "Hypnotized immobility as he approaches her with razor in hand, relaxing into awareness of his intention with resultant pleasure-plus-tension, and final satisfying thought, 'If I fight, he'll kill me.' So she don't" (August 15, 1956, 37.7, MP). In the published version, Ellen ultimately welcomes Reeves's domination of her. While certainly inscribing a construction of masochistic female desire that feminists would labor for decades to discredit, Merril constructs a history and destiny for the "girl" of Cole's story beyond his own imagining, something that Cole acknowledges from the outset: "Your story, as outlined, sounds pretty good. In fact, it sounds damned good, damn your eyes (jealousy)" (July 29, 1956, 37.7, MP).

A second type of pseudo-collaboration stemmed from the frequent informal sharing of ideas and editorial suggestions and work that happened outside of formally acknowledged collaborations — more along the lines of "participating in an author's fictional creation," in the words of Edward James (1994, 141). There are instances when this practice created confusion over attribution of authorship. Such was the case with Merril's 1959 story "Death Cannot Wither," which, although originally published under her name alone, when reprinted bore acknowledgment of the contribution of a science fiction author, editor, and critic who was part of Merril's circle, Algis ("A. J.") Budrys.

After several years of trying, Merril had been unable to publish the story in her preferred magazine, *Fantasy and Science Fiction*. She first submitted it to the editor, her mentor Tony Boucher, in the summer of 1956 and rewrote it for him numerous times over the next few years. The story is identified in her letters as her "Edna" story, after the name of the story's protagonist. Exasperated, resistant to many of Boucher's editorial suggestions, and needing time for meeting her family responsibilities (such as proving to the court her fitness as a mother), as well as other writing deadlines, Merril asked him to take over the revisions and offered to call it a "collaboration," publishing it under a joint byline, or a pen name, or even in *Venture* using the name Rose Sharon (October 17 [1957], 2.41, MP). She truly liked the feel of the story and the quality of the writing, though she admitted it needed shortening (Merril to Boucher, June 10 and August 5, 1956, 2.46, and July 18, 1956, 2.41, MP). Boucher, even after two rounds of Merril's revisions, found it emotionless, "uncertain in tone" and lacking in "warmth," "irony," "humor" or "grimness" (Boucher to Merril, October 13, 1957, 2.41, MP) and so eventually rejected it. Merrill, apparently with the editorial assistance of Budrys, sold it as "Death Cannot Wither" to *Fantasy and Science Fiction* for publication in February 1959.

The genres of science fiction and ghost story merge in "Death Cannot Wither." Reprinted in Merril's collection *Out of Bounds* in 1960, this story goes "out of bounds" not only in its exploration of psychosomatic phenomena and the mind-body relationship, but also in its frank treatment of the themes of marriage, sex, infidelity, pregnancy, and birth control — issues of which Merril was all too aware in her personal life. Edna Colby, Merril's main character in "Death Cannot Wither," is Merril's polar opposite: repulsed by sex, married purely for status, and powerless to address her husband's thinly veiled lies about his overnight absences from home. Edna married Jack with designs of molding this wayward heir to a landed family "into everything he should be, and to provide the proper mode of life to set him off, like a perfect work of art in a perfect frame" ("Death" 1960, 141). Accordingly, Edna, as a perfect homemaker, transforms the ancestral home "into a condition appropriate to genteel country living" (139). This penchant for higher modes of life causes Edna to view sex and pregnancy together as a "dirty, humiliating mess that was, in fact, a blind animal response to the indiscriminate need of the brute organism indiscriminately to reproduce itself" (145).

This domestic drama turns into a ghost story when Jack disappears while on a local hunting expedition in winter and is presumed dead. After several months, Jack reappears to Edna, and we learn that he is indeed dead, that his body lies undiscovered at the bottom of a quarry, and that he is caught in a kind of limbo between life and death, bound to the farm and unable to explore the afterlife unless Edna will release him. Lonely and unfulfilled after months of widowhood, the middle-aged Edna refuses to let Jack go, and uses sex to win him over to this arrangement. Pleasantly surprised by this change in his wife's attitude toward sex, the ghost of Jack returns to Edna every night. Now that there is "No Danger" of pregnancy, as Merril euphemistically writes, Edna quite enjoys her new sex life with her husband's ghost (152). But Edna's period of carefree sex comes to an end when she develops a psychosomatic pregnancy, suggesting allegorically that it will be some time before new reproductive technologies will displace deeply entrenched ideas about women's relation to sex. Edna takes revenge for her pregnancy by secretly giving birth at the quarry, then "giving" the baby to Jack: "'Take him — take him, Jack, quickly,' she moaned. 'Take him where he'll be warm, and safe'" (159). She had planned "to saddle Jack with the brat forever" but then, as she attempts to leave the quarry, her body breaks through the ice "to sink into company with that other abandoned shell" (159–60). The chilling realization for Merril's readers comes here, at the end of the story: Edna may have simply been talking to herself all along. It is an ambiguity that Merril's many letters to Boucher suggest she had introduced early on and managed to preserve across all drafts of this piece.

While nothing seems to be known about the details of Budrys's editorial assistance with this story, or what, if anything, Merril promised him for his assistance (she had, after all, told Boucher that if he edited it, she would call it a collaboration), Merril said she later regretted that she had not acknowledged Budrys, so she recognized his contribution when she reprinted "Death" (though still under her own name) in the first of her own story collections, *Out of Bounds*, in 1960, adding an introductory note: "[T]he revision and condensation [A. J. Budrys] did on my own rambling earlier draft was so extensive that the story should properly carry a joint byline" (Merril 1960, author's note to "Death Cannot Wither," 137). Merril offered a more formal acknowledgment (though not a joint byline) when the story was anthologized in *The Ninth Fontana Book of Great Ghost Stories*, which lists the story in the table of contents under Merril's name alone but the byline for the story itself is "Judith Merril with A. J. Budrys" (Merril with Budrys 1973, 11), as is the bibliography entry for "Death Cannot Wither" in Merril's memoir (Merril and Pohl-Weary 2002, 268). Whether she was being overly conscientious or simply sheepishly admitting an oversight is unclear. What is clear, however, is that this was not a formal collaboration: Budrys's input was in the late stages and purely editorial. It is also clear that at the point at which she published the story in 1959, she was publishing less and anthologizing more, producing anthologies that were both heavily collaborative and stimulating within a field that had begun to decline.

## The Merril Anthologies of the 1950s

[In a big house in Red Bank, New Jersey] I slowly understood that [Judy] was doing something I had never heard of, arranging the anthology like a banquet — flavors in sequence, biting and tangy, sweet and sour, rich and salty and strong and needing thoughtful chewing over, so don't cut the flavor with a sharp change of mood. [...] I was awed by the volume of paperwork, letters, permissions, copyright releases from publishers, contracts....
And listening to her phone calls I was fascinated by the interesting people she got on the phone and the letters she wrote to the more original and brilliant of the contributors of the finished anthology, discussing their ideas and the way she could turn them into friends and sometimes brief glorious love affairs [MacLean 1996, 15].

Regardless of her other writing plans, collaborative projects, and the peaks and troughs in her personal and professional life in the 1950s, Merril had always had an anthology in the works: first-rate, innovative projects that connected her to the entire science fiction and fantasy community, plus other outstanding fiction and nonfiction writers around the world. To begin with, she published five theme anthologies of reprinted stories — mostly science fiction and fantasy, but the first book, *Shot in the Dark* (1950), was a mix of science fiction and mystery stories and the last, *Galaxy of Ghouls* (1955), was an anthology of ghost, vampire, and witch stories. While all the books were innovative, perhaps none was more impressive at that time than her second one, on the theme of other possible forms of intelligent life: *Beyond Human Ken* (1952). For one thing, Merril completed this work in June 1952 amid the shambles — though with a happy sense of release from domestic problems — at Red Bank after the Kornbluths had left. MacLean was with her that summer, and the two of them were writing as fast as they could, not collaborating in a formal sense but discussing ideas and sharing household duties and childcare in a communal way (Merril to Cole, July 1, 1952, 37.2, MP) reminiscent of her living arrangements with Virginia Kidd in New York during the mid–1940s and, on the domestic front, evocative of her working relationship with Kornbluth at Red Bank. Merril was still broke due to the split with Pohl and was shouldering the burden of an anthology to finish and a house full of half-finished stories, including a "big stumbling block story [Daughters of Earth], the one that finished me last winter," she wrote to Cole (June 17, 1952, 37.4, MP). On behalf of the anthology, she was editing, as MacLean observes in the opening quote of this section, ten to twenty letters a day, reading volumes of interesting writing, looking for material to fill holes, and responding to tight publisher's deadlines for the preface and bibliography. For another thing, *Beyond Human Ken* not only mobilized the top writers among her distinguished network of new colleagues, including Boucher, del Rey, Clifton, Leiber, MacLean, Lewis Padgett (joint pseudonym of Henry Kuttner and C. L. Moore), and Ted Sturgeon and former Futurians, such as James Bliss with Fletcher Pratt providing the introduction, but it also carried what would become one of Merril's signature contributions as an anthologist and mentor-collaborator: a bibliographical essay and lengthy, detailed editor's notes commenting on each story and author.

Subsequent anthologies by Merril become ever more editorially elaborate. Her third anthology, *Human?* (1954), finds Merril exploring the basis on which one might define "human." The book, assembled while she had dropped out of sight in 1953 to live and travel with Walter Miller, is dedicated to Miller's parents for sustaining her, support that she clearly valued as she tried to moved forward with her life. In the fourth anthology, *Beyond the Barriers of Space and Time* (1954), Merril addressed the highly complex and controversial world of "curious and controversial phenomena known as 'psi powers'" in which she had become so immersed after her break-up with Pohl. In the "Bibliography," Merril talks about the stories that "got away" and describes for readers the list of titles of fiction and nonfiction books that she had solicited from the contributors to this book. This anthology earned for Merril the high accolades of the sort bestowed upon her by Sturgeon in his introduction: "Miss Merril's extraordinary taste and erudition assure us beforehand of a notable helping of sheer entertainment; any book with her name on it, whether as author or editor, is guaranteed good reading" (xii).

In *Beyond the Barriers*, Merril was in full collaborative mode. Extensive collaboration was the secret of her success as an anthologist. The acknowledgments sections of her anthologies confirm that she tapped many individuals for assistance in obtaining stories and suggesting reading materials, and many others for access to their personal libraries and files, advance copies of magazines, and so on. Then, with the publication of *Galaxy of Ghouls* in 1955, Merril was primed to launch a major anthology series that would bring to science fiction, in the words of Connie Willis, a member of a later generation of science fiction writers, "a clear and passionate vision of what it was and what it could be, with extraordinary results. [Merril], quite literally, reinvented the field" (C. Willis 2003, 138). What Willis noted about Merril's anthologies could also be said of the sort of shift in vision that Merril was modeling in her independent and collaborative fiction writing.

## The Milford Mecca: Launching the Year's Best Series and the Writers' Workshops

> I visited Judy in a small town in the woods [Milford] and she was again surrounded by stacked magazines and books with slips of paper sticking out of them, but this time she was selecting science fiction stories from magazines and collections that were not science fiction specialty magazines.
> When she asked me to read the preliminary stack she had chosen I dove in eagerly and after six stories became aware of a kind of indefiniteness and freedom of form where the plot should be, an unusually detailed ordinary life, a description of feeling. And on the average the characters were not aliens and the first pages did not leap into action with a planet-wide crisi. [...] "Science fiction fans are getting too specialized. It's turning into a ghetto," [Merril] said. "We should bring in the general readers, give them something they can understand" [MacLean 1996, 15].

Merril's Year's Best anthologies took up where the less ambitious but useful E. F. Bleiler and T. E. Dikty annual *Best Science Fiction Stories* that ran from 1949 to 1955 (and continued for a few years more by Dikty) left off. The Year's Best series ran from 1956 until 1968 and played an integral role in shaping the direction of American science fiction as a genre. As Pierre Bourdieu has shown, when emergent cultural fields coalesce, they become subject to more explicit standards of value (Bourdieu 1996, 226). Often, this transition is articulated in the form of anxiety that the field has become overcrowded by works of inferior quality and is in need of critical oversight, as was the case in the early-twentieth-century popular literary field when tools such the bestseller list and the Book-of-the-Month Club were devised to help American readers navigate the proliferation of affordable books (Radway 1991, 170).

Merril stepped into her annual anthology role at just such a juncture in the literary history of American science fiction. Rich notes the "feeling of doom and gloom [that] was unexpectedly descending over the field of science fiction by the fall of 1955" and was a topic of concern at conventions and in book columns (Rich 2010, 289). In his introduction to the first Year's Best anthology, published in 1956, Orson Welles declared, "One thing's sure about science-fiction: there's too much of it" (8), and advised the novice reader that "an anthology is probably best for a beginning" (8–9) in the genre because its contents had been screened for quality. Even so, Merril, in her preface to the same edition, asked for forgiveness from "the serious-minded reader" for "the frivolities of space-ships and flying bath-mats," explaining that the science fiction writer's "first big job is entertainment ... and *that* hasn't changed since Aesop's time at all" (10). Merril's light-hearted apology and reference to a classic storyteller register the tenuous state of science fiction's legitimacy at the time. In her summation at the end of the anthology, Merril focused on what she and most other critics perceived as a decline in the quality of modern

American science fiction, and the first order of business for the 1956 Year's Best anthology was to address that head-on: "This was the year the house collapsed. The house of cards, I mean, otherwise known as the Science Fiction Boom [...] since five years ago, when the structure first began to climb precariously higher than its foundations could support" (Merril 1956, "Summation," 343). She proceeded to discuss what the literary critics were writing and to analyze the history and contribution of each of the American and British science fiction and fantasy magazines, plus mainstream magazines that carried science fantasy stories, providing readers, writers, editors, and anthologists with a much-needed sense of the field.

Although the reviewers of her Year's Best series in the 1950s often disagreed with the contents of the volumes she edited (especially concerning the inclusion of nonfiction essays), and not everyone valued the annual summation, the English ground-breaking author J. G. Ballard would later claim in a tribute to Merril that science fiction was indeed in trouble in the second half of the 1950s and that Judith Merril's annual anthology stood out as practically the single beacon of knowledge and taste (Ballard 1992, 12). Reviewers of the first volume corroborate this claim that the anthology was needed "to lift the public concept of science fiction to a higher plane" (*Authentic Science Fiction* 1956, 152). "Something of this kind has been badly needed: an authoritative, perceptive, organized collection of the year's best, at a price everyone can afford," wrote Damon Knight (1956, 67). Tony Boucher and John Carnell, respectively, praised Merril's wide-ranging coverage of the whole field, assuring readers that they were indeed getting the year's best (Boucher 1956, 107; Carnell 1956, 2–3).

The Year's Best anthology series raised the bar for what constituted the best science fiction and science fiction writers; the series both challenged and broadened the definition of science fiction by selecting previously published evocative short stories from American and foreign authors, as well as poetry (which she had been including in her theme anthologies) and nonfiction. Aside from the literary content, however, the science fiction dialogue these volumes created — through Merril's introductions, editorial comments (which, according to Ballard, seemed to place each story on a pedestal of its own [1992, 12]), honorable mentions, and, above all, the editor's summation of the year's "S-F"— became her unique contribution to promoting and shaping the field. Her acknowledgments each year signaled the impressive scope and intensity with which she collaborated with fans, publishers, editors, and writers — hunting down copies of magazines, finding advance copies of future issues, obtaining tips on who and what was hot, and getting help with locating and contacting authors.

Strengthening Merril's ability to produce path-breaking annual anthologies was her simultaneous leadership in another arena for taste-making work: the annual Milford Science Fiction Writers' Conference, with its collaborative mix of professional writers. Merril's work for these gatherings was part and parcel of her growing reputation as a science fiction connoisseur. Having relinquished the Red Bank house to Pohl late in 1952, she moved to, and fell in love with, the small town of Milford, Pennsylvania, in late 1953, shortly after she had lost custody of her oldest daughter and was forced to give up on her plans to marry Walter Miller due to the sheer force of social and financial barriers. She had briefly returned to New York in the fall of 1953 from that one-year affair with no money, in debt, and facing uncertain prospects both as a writer and as custodian of her younger daughter. For most of 1953, she had been "out of touch" with her science fiction circles, with almost all correspondence and manuscripts being filtered through her lawyer and friend, Milt Amgott. She ended up in Milford and, for her first year there, she wrote almost no new fiction and had difficulty publishing any of her unpublished stories. Nevertheless, she wrote approximately fifty profiles, stories, and editorials for the local newspaper, the *Milford Dispatch*, and waitressed in a local hotel. The small but steady income she earned made things easier for her to begin paying off her pile of debts. She also did a great deal of fence-mending

Merril founded the Milford Science Fiction Conference in 1956. Pictured at the conference are (left to right) Theodore Cogswell, James Blish, Damon Knight, Anthony Boucher and Judith Merril." Reproduced from *Aloud Magazine*, (Judith Merril issue), October 1992, page 12, with permission of the Merril Estate.

to repair her many neglected relationships with writers, editors, and publishers in the field. And from this small village she launched her annual anthology series and the famous annual Milford workshop.

Remarkably, given the state of her personal life and finances in the mid-1950s, by 1956 she had become a leading figure in the burgeoning science fiction writers' community started in Milford, when, together with her Futurian colleagues (and Milford neighbors) Blish and Knight, she co-founded, and until 1960 directed, the annual Milford workshop to create a critical dialogue around science fiction for professional writers. The institution lives on to this day in the Clarion Science Fiction and Fantasy Writers' Workshop, founded by Knight and his wife, the writer Kate Wilhelm, in 1968 to provide a proving and training ground for aspiring writers and an arena for professional discussion. (Blish, who emigrated to England in 1968, founded the international Milford UK Workshop in 1972, and Merril, who in the same year emigrated to Canada, started the Hydra Club North in 1985 as a type of Milford workshop for Canadian science fiction writers.) One critical spin-off of the Milford workshops was a publication started in 1959 and edited by Theodore Cogswell called, irreverently, *Proceedings of the Institute for Twenty-first Century Studies*, a fanzine for the pros that published letters and essays by science fiction professionals.

Established writers of science fiction and fantasy, and most of the up-and-comers, participated in the annual Milford gatherings; the lists of participants over the years read like a *Who's Who* of the genre. Merril seems to have put the same thought and collaborative energy into selecting the annual mix of participants that she did for her Year's Best series. At these meetings, a day was set aside for a more general, Hydra Club–type open house and state-of-the-market discussion with writers, publishers, editors, and others, and then invited professional writers stayed on for several days; each one of them had to share unpublished work and receive comments from other writers. This regime became known among science fiction writers as the "Milford System" (Sterling 2001). The first workshop drew thirty professionals, mostly established authors but also new, younger writers such as Robert Silverberg, Harlan Ellison, and Jane Roberts. For Merril and most of the participants, the experience was uplifting, but for a few, such as the established writer Mildred Clingerman (Clingerman to Merril, September 14, 1956, 4.14, MP), who left early, and Ellison, who left in a storm of anger (Weil and Wolfe 2002, 37), it was a humiliating experience. Small, intense, boundary-pushing sessions aimed at critiquing each other's work were a novel phenomenon and clearly not for everyone.

As with Merril's Year's Best series, the Milford gatherings, under her direction, were structured to encourage dialogue and debate and to legitimize and raise standards in the field. These lofty aspirations for the Milford workshops surpassed anything expected of, or delivered by, the Hydra Club of New York, which in any event had by this time lost its edge for serious practitioners in the field. Merril had stopped attending Hydra meetings and abandoned the New York scene, largely because of the gossip and ill will surrounding her split with Pohl and affair with Miller: "I most particularly know that I did *not* want to become re-entangled with the 'science fiction crowd' here in New York, the people whose good opinion I once worked very hard to earn, whose admiration, envy, tongue-cluckings, hatred, pity, and/or sympathy I had when I left," she wrote to Les Cole (April 25, 1954, 37.5, MP). With the exception of a few months here and there, never again would she live in New York or even enjoy visiting there.

## Reflections on Merril's Collaborative Practices

Judith Merril's activities in the 1950s as a collaborative writer, editor, and facilitator of science fiction reveal a dimension of the science fiction writing process — its community aspect — that is far less familiar than traditional visions of the author as thinker, loner, and creator. Merril coveted what little solitude and time she could steal away for her writing and always desired a private writing space of her own. When Merril and Kidd were apartment-hunting together in 1945, Merril already had a strong opinion on the matter: "The only thing I ask for is a room of my own. [...] I don't mind noise of any kind — apartments overhead, typewriters, loud voices, or symphonies. The only time I do is when I am writing, and then it's ok if the noise is on the other side of the door" (Merril to Kidd, February 7, 1945, 38.1, MP). Nonetheless, she corresponded extensively about her writing process and most of her writing, collaborative or not, was produced in the context of the highly social, and often tumultuous, science fiction community of Futurians and the Hydra Club, whose members constantly debated, supported, argued, feuded, lived, visited, corresponded, read, published, got drunk with, and even slept with, married, and divorced each other. In such an environment, indeed, collaboration was virtually unavoidable.

Merril's particular collaborations were intertwined with facets of life often excluded from accounts of great authors: her work with Kornbluth, for instance, arose from his fortuitous social visit, and was fostered in the context of domestic arrangements that made it easier for Merril to write while having and raising children. During periods of domestic upheaval, financial strain, or inertia as a writer, when the solitude for steady, "real" writing was hard to come by, Merril could still work on her editorial and collaborative writing projects. Practicalities aside, Merril's collaborations with Kornbluth created a distinctive and significant "Cyril Judd" story type that is worthy of critical attention. It seems that what she brought to those collaborations was the same thing she brought to her science fiction: a realistic woman-centered emphasis on the mundane and the domestic in the future imaginary. By the same token, she also used these collaborations and the occasional use of pseudonyms to explore the male point of view.

Most importantly, though, Merril was a collaborator by nature: as a young fan of science fiction in the 1940s, she had sought out the company of the Futurians and many others in the field and written her first stories with their mentorship and support. Later, she facilitated similar mentoring relationships for young writers at the highly interactive workshops she helped establish and the collaborative Year's Best anthologies she created. Deeply interested in what other writers were doing, Merril not only read voraciously but also would often look for and strike up a lifelong dialogue with writers she particularly admired. As an anthologist, she happily immersed herself in the extensive correspondence and networking required to keep abreast of and broaden the field. She would in the next decade push her science fiction agenda entirely through editorial work and criticism, using the incredible range of skills she developed in the 1940s and 1950s. No account of Merril's career would be complete without addressing her collaborative practices, to which we have endeavored to do justice in this chapter.

CHAPTER 7

# New Waves and New Communities

Judith Merril moved around a lot in the 1960s and 1970s — curious, energized, optimistic, if also apprehensive and usually scrambling to meet deadlines. In the 1960s, Merril shifted and thereby expanded her range of interests and accomplishments, in addition to her anthology work, to become a major critic-reviewer, an essayist, and an anti-war activist. She increasingly called for a more political, speculative, and stylistically adventuresome approach to writing — an approach present in her own postwar science fiction — which she promoted as speculative fiction, or "SF," a term she preferred over "avant-garde" or "New Wave." Merril debated revitalizing and revolutionizing science fiction across all twelve volumes of her Year's Best anthology series, in her special anthologies, and in her remarkable "Books" review column in the *Magazine of Fantasy and Science Fiction*. Then, in the fall of 1968, after spending some time in England and witnessing the suppression of anti–Vietnam War protesters in Chicago, she gave up on American science fiction altogether. Moving to Toronto, where she lived for the rest of her life, Merril embraced new experimental and intellectual outlets: she lived for a year in a counter-culture experimental college as a writer in residence and spent time in the 1970s with the science fiction community of writers and translators in Japan. In Toronto, she also plunged into the city's vibrant social and political scene as a catalyst for change, a creator of an internationally renowned public library of science fiction and fantasy, an educator, a radio and TV documentarist and presenter, and, in the 1980s, a founder of the Canadian science fiction community. Although Merril effectively stopped writing science fiction in the early 1960s (but for another few decades worked intermittently on a science fiction book and published a few science fiction poems), she looked to achieve through her promotional work the impact and growth in the field that characterized her own science fiction at its best.

## Anthologist-Editor in the 1960s

Reflecting on the state of the genre in the late 1950s, J. G. Ballard remarked that "already science fiction was beginning to formulise itself and strengthen the ghetto walls that screened it from what was going on in the real world." But, he suggested, "[o]ne American editor stood alone against this deliberate narrowing of science fiction's imaginative possibilities, and that editor was Judith Merril" (Ballard 1992, 12). For Ballard, while Merril's Year's Best collections of the 1950s coincided with his time as an apprentice writer, "I would have devoured those precious volumes even if she had never glanced at me" (12). By the 1960s, Merril's annual anthologies promoted new and more serious forms of science fiction that adopted a broad definition of science, and they took on a more urgent and didactic tone than can be found in her earlier ones. In her "summation and honorable mentions" section each year, she observed that science fiction was entering the mainstream: in her summation for the sixth annual, which carried stories originally published in 1960, for example, she observed that, within the specialty field, fact articles and critical essays were becoming much more common (Merril 1962 [1961], "Summation," 376); and in the seventh edition, she described science fiction as having a "floating island nature" that was being absorbed into the main body of literature from whence, she argues, it came (Merril 1963 [1962], "Summation," 391). At the same time, she was also alarmed at the reluctance of publishers and literary reviewers to acknowledge science fiction novels *as* science fiction, however broadly or narrowly defined. Merril lamented the situation wherein the best science fiction was published "under wrappers and headings that either angrily disclaim the 'science fiction' label, or ignore it completely" (Merril 1963 [1962], "Summation," 392).

Triggering Merril's exposé of the publishing industry's erasure of the science fiction category was the critical, first-ever survey of science fiction, *New Maps of Hell* (1960), by the English novelist, poet, and critic Kingsley Amis, based on his lecture series at Princeton University. A famous conflict, more apparent than real, developed between Merril and Amis over the state of science fiction in the early 1960s. Merril had, in the cloth edition of her fifth annual (1960), criticized *New Maps of Hell* for its arrogance, poor research, patronizing list of science fiction's faults, and description of science fiction as a lost age (MacLeod 2003). Her "violent disagreement" with Amis dismayed most of her friends in the field, including Boucher, who distanced himself from her stance in his belated review column in Merril's sixth volume, "SF Books: 1960" (Boucher 1962, 380). In a humorous letter to Amis in the summer of 1961, Merril diffused the situation: requesting forgiveness for her bad manners, she explained that her real frustration lay with the general literary reviewers (and some "science fiction names") who were so readily impressed when an outsider like Amis actually paid attention to science fiction (August 12, 1961, 1.32, MP). What had begun as a feud transformed into a friendly exchange of letters between the two in which Merril invited Amis to submit to future anthologies, which he did, and to attend the Milford workshop (Amis to Merril, February 23 and May 8, 1961; Merril to Amis, August 12, 1961, 1.32, MP). Merril worshiped talent. It was clear that she would forgive, or at least tolerate, any behavior on the part of writers she thought gifted.

As a leading anthologist internationally in 1965, Merril was riding high. Initially published by a small specialty press, the annuals had received a more lucrative contract with Delacorte. Merril had also signed up for a British edition of the entire Year's Best series with Mayflower-Dell in 1963, which, together with the cloth and paper editions, meant she now had three editions on the go. With the new contract with Delacorte and for the British edition, full royalties on all three editions were going completely to the editor and authors. This new arrangement doubled her income from the anthologies and made her — for a few years, at least — financially independent. She could hire an assistant (Virginia Kidd) and could at last purchase all the books and magazines she needed for researching her anthologies, forgoing the time-wasting work, as she explained to Boucher, of "haunting libraries and second hand stores endlessly." Of equal importance, under the new contract she now had greater control: "I got my book, at last my way" (Merril to Boucher, January 26, 1956, "Merril 3/4," White Mss.). She wanted to address the problems in the American field, which, while continuing to expand, commercialize, and become respectable (a new phenomenon), had, in her eyes, lost both focus and ground.

By mid-decade, her anthologies started to register shifts in the field: as the output of the traditional science fiction community impressed Merril less and less, the mainstream fiction market co-opted the science fiction genre — and, according to her, did a better job of it. As if to indicate that there were not enough new developments in the science fiction field proper to warrant discussion, Boucher stopped supplying the review section for Merril's annuals, starting with the tenth edition (Merril 1966 [1965]), and was not replaced. By the next edition, Merril had dropped her honorable mentions section for the same reason that she no longer carried a review section: it had simply become too difficult to draw the line between science fiction "and anything else" (Merril 1967 [1966], "Summation," 380): "[t]he important things happening in American s-f are not happening *in* it at all. We have writers comparable to

Ballard in stature but not in current achievement," Merril notes (382). She produced no annual volume in 1967, and in 1968 produced what turned out to be her final volume, *SF12* (Merril 1969 [1968]). In *SF12*, Merril dropped her summation essay and, most significantly, eliminated the words "year's best" from the title, opting instead for *New Dimensions in Science Fiction, Fantasy, and Imaginative Writing*. Merril now mourned the loss of the specialty field in the United States. American science fiction writers, in her view, had lost sight of their obligation to "be aware of, and [work] with, revolutionary (technological, political, artistic, scientific, philosophic) concepts of 1968" (1969 [January], "Books," 37). Apparently, her annual anthologies had not influenced the American science fiction field as much as Merril had hoped.

## *The Special Anthologies*

Merril, like most science fiction writers, editors, and anthologists, usually had several different projects going at any one time. In the early 1960s, "The Thin Edge" project was planned as an anthology of unusual stories, previously unpublished. Although the book was not completed, the few details known about the project demonstrate Merril's willingness in the 1960s to experiment, to shake up science fiction and take on new roles within it, exactly as she had as a fiction writer, editor, and collaborator in the 1950s. In her call for submissions in 1961, she described it as "a collection that is neither science fiction nor fantasy, neither psychological suspense stories nor terror yarns, but a melding of all four: stories that literally defy categorization. [...] They can be rugged politically, sexually, violently, emotionally, or theologically" ("Invitation" [1961], "Merril 4/4," White Mss.). Wanting to hit the quality market with "offtrail-mainstream" rather than "category" fiction, the new publisher Regency approached the adventurous Merril, as the leading anthologist of the day, to take on the project. In a letter to Boucher, she explains, "I am dancing with sugarplum visions of a book of violent, quiet, sober, funny, serious, satiric, stories, covering any aspects of every[thing], as it were" (August 23, 1961, "Merril 4/4," White Mss.). She goes on to say that this sort of undertaking was novel for her. As an anthologist of previously published stories, she was new to the more active editorial role she would be playing as an anthologist of new stories, which, unlike those in the Year's Best volumes, would involve significant editorial input. Now she was offering to read anything the writers on her list had at hand: "notes, outline, unfinished typescript, draft, or yellowed reject" ("Invitation" [1961]). Her editor on the project, Harlan Ellison, the talented "enfant terrible" whom Regency had just brought in to edit their whole line of paperbacks, was soon off to Hollywood — and so out of the picture (Weil and Wolfe 2002, 41).

Merril for some reason had eventually to abandon the book but did not officially inform her authors; a letter from Kidd to Rosel George Brown written in 1965, four years after Merril started the project, suggests why. Kidd describes herself as Judith's friend of twenty years who is "assisting, secretarying, meeting crises, and catching up on [Merril's] back filing and correspondence" while Merril is away in England. Kidd refuses to offer authors such as Brown polite excuses. Instead, she hints at a terrible history of publisher and co-author "trouble" and "sabotage," along with Merril's own inability to handle the "frustration, fury, trauma and fugue ever since" (October 7, 1965, 37.19, MP). Ellison would later describe this episode in his *Dangerous Visions* anthology as a failed project on the part of the "well-known anthologist" (Merril) he hired; the stories she produced were "either silly or pointless or crude or dull," he announced to his readers (Ellison 1967a, xxv). Merril countered with an admission of her own: she remembered the project as a "painfully abortive effort" (1967 [December], "Books," 28). This whole fiasco was perhaps the basis for Merril's later reputation for abandoning projects and letting others "sweep up" the mess, as Brian Aldiss puts it in *Billion Year Spree* (1973, 303); it surfaces again in Robert Sawyer's 1997 obituary for Merril and Spider Robinson's review of Merril's memoir in 2002 (Sawyer 1997; Robinson 2002).

The first of Merril's two capstone anthologies in the 1960s, *SF: The Best of the Best*, published with Delacorte in 1967 (and the paperback with Dell in 1968), contained twenty-nine of the "best" stories from the first five years of the annual anthology series, so stories originally published in 1955–1959. Its goal was to bring the late 1950s writing to the attention of mid–1960s readers and reinforce her opinion that science fiction was now in a period of "adjustments, culmination, transitions, announcements, rather than new achievements" (Merril 1968 [1967], "Introduction," 5). Merril produced this stand-alone anthology in lieu of an annual volume that year, a first step in phasing out the label of "year's best" or "greatest" from the title of her annual anthology, which, as we know, she did in 1968. In *Best of the Best*, she warns that, unfortunately, science fiction no longer usefully describes a type of story or category of publishing; it means so many different things to so many people that she prefers not to use the label at all (2). As part of her ongoing claim that science fiction was merging with mainstream literature, her introduction provides a quick summary of the recent historical developments in the science fiction field to explain, in context, why the stories selected are so special. She focuses on stories from the 1950s on the grounds that the later stories did not by and large achieve the mark established earlier:

> The beginning of the industrial, political, and technological space age meant the beginning of a new period of exploration in "the human factor," as opposed to the "hardware," for both science and science fiction. The interesting new work tended

to emphasize literary qualities rather than philosophical ones. And by 1955, the field had achieved just enough literary respectability to be able to serve a vital function: during the entire period covered by this anthology, it was the science-fiction magazines that provided the only widely read medium for protest and dissent in a witch-haunted country [5].

In *Best of the Best*, Merril repeated what had become her mantra: "Science fiction is not fiction about science but fiction which endeavors to find the meaning in science and the scientific-technological society we are constructing" (3). Its role was to critique the contemporary scientific-technological society and speculate about its future. Reviewers of the anthology, however, considered it largely outdated. Joyce Churchill in *New Worlds* regarded it as "a sad old work, tarted up" (Churchill 1969, 62); Algis Budrys called it "a bag of lusty prototypes, peaks of evolution, and flies in amber" (Budrys 1968, 123); and for Joanna Russ, reviewing the book in *Fantasy and Science Fiction*, it was, typical of Merril, a "reaction against too much hardware in the science fiction field (both now and back then)" (Russ 1968a, 54), a criticism to which we will return.

Merril's other special anthology, *England Swings SF: Stories of Speculative Fiction*, published by Doubleday in 1968, in paperback by Ace in 1970, and in the British paperback (abridged) as *The Space-Time Journal* by Panther in 1972, is altogether different from *Best of the Best*. Yet it was tied to the same intellectual project: revitalizing and revolutionizing science fiction. The Doubleday edition contained twenty-five stories and two poems with the deliberate intention of introducing American audiences to new forms of writing science speculative fiction in Britain. Drawing parallels with the "British invasion" in music under way at the same time, the newly released *Sgt. Pepper's Lonely Hearts Club Band* (The Beatles, 1967) is quoted throughout Merril's introduction (these quotations were, for technical reasons, dropped from the Ace and Panther editions). Hartwell and Wolf write of Merril's novel introduction, which they reproduced in their 1996 anthology *Visions of Wonder*, that "it is a fine example of the stylistic exuberance of the time" and called *England Swings SF* a "groundbreaking" work that "introduced the emerging generation of ambitious young SF writers (the British New Wave) of the 1960s to the American SF audience" (Hartwell and Wolf 1996, 250). Given that Ellison's *Dangerous Visions* eclipsed *England Swings SF* in popularity, Hartwell and Wolf's recognition of the latter as innovative, which occured at the end of Merril's life, must have been deeply gratifying to her.

*England Swings SF* was inspired by Merril's time in London—first at the Worldcon in 1965 (Loncon II), then when she lived in London for a year in the period 1966–1967, hanging out at *New Worlds* magazine with its editor, Michael Moorcock, and his wife at the time, science fiction writer Hilary Bailey, as well as with J. G. Ballard, Brian Aldiss, and others. She was incredibly happy in England, surrounded by a blaze of talent. She and Moorcock influenced each other's experimental approach to writing, though it is difficult to assess to what extent. In London, she brought British science fiction writers together and introduced them to academics, actors, film stars and directors, folk singers, painters, philosophers, poets, pop artists, publishers, scientists, and the like at the soirées she organized and Moorcock held (Moorcock 1998, 5). Moorcock called *England Swings SF* "her monument to that wonderfully pixilated period when everything seemed possible and it was your duty to try everything at least once" (4). Beyond partying and "try[ing] everything at least once," however, we know from the extensive correspondence between Moorcock and Merril housed in the Merril papers in Ottawa that when *New Worlds* was going broke in the late 1960s, she not only contributed her personal funds but also raised money within the American science fiction community to help save the magazine.

*England Swings SF* included stories by both established authors such as Aldiss, Moorcock, and the American Thomas M. Disch, and new authors, many of whom went on to have substantial writing careers: Hilary Bailey, Daphne Castell, Charles Platt, Chris Priest, Keith Roberts, and Josephine Saxton. The anthology also reflected the different relation in Britain of science fiction to the broader literary community: as Merril would later discover in Canada as well, the United States was relatively unique in segregating its science fiction community from the literary mainstream. Such was not the case in Britain, where Merril's contributors included the likes of John Calder, the English publisher of Beckett and Ionesco, and Ballard, who would go on to write works such as *Crash* (1973) and *Empire of the Sun* (1984), both made into major films by David Cronenberg and Steven Spielberg, respectively.

Thematically and stylistically, the anthology represents Merril's view that speculative fiction, to use the term she now preferred, can and should transcend narrow generic categories. Thus the anthology represents a wide range of topics, themes, and settings: a woman space explorer finds herself trapped in the limbo between the positive and negative universes (Saxton); an attempt to break into the Tomb of the Unknown Soldier is linked to extraterrestrial visitations (Ballard); an amnesiac writer wonders who is keeping him in a white, cubic cell where his only diversions are a typewriter and regular delivery of *The Times* (Disch); a housewife in California experiences entropy in her kitchen (Pamela Zoline); European culture in the far future is transformed by the cult of speed and the automobile (Aldiss). Implicit in Merril's selection of stories is the principle that the term "speculative" encompasses far more than science and technology in the narrow sense: social, cultural, and psychological (what Ballard regarded as "inner space") realities are equally emphasized throughout the anthology, as is formal experimentation. Stories by Aldiss, Ballard, Disch, and Zoline, among others, engage techniques that would eventually be dubbed "postmodern": nonlinear and fragmented narrative, stream-of-consciousness monologue, free-indirect discourse, metafiction, satire, and lack of closure.

The opening story, "The Island" by Roger Jones, transitions the reader into the new mode of speculative fiction that Merril was trying to capture in *England Swings SF*. On the one hand, it begins in familiar science fiction territory as the reader is dropped into an alien environment and situation and must piece together the background as the story unfolds. Thematically, "The Island" recalls Beckett's legendary *Waiting for Godot*, with military hierarchy replacing Godot as the placeholder for structures of authority that have lost their meaning. The story appears to be set on a former military base, situated on an island, whose occupants have all been killed in some sudden unnamed disaster, except for the story's three characters, who cling to military hierarchy and routines as they await rescue. The leader of the group holds on to power by withholding from his underlings the fact that their superiors are dead, but his plan unravels as one of his men becomes suspicious, ultimately leading to tragic consequences. Reflecting Merril's view that speculative fiction should concern itself with much more than just the "hardware" of science and technology, thus raising sociological and political awareness, "The Island" explores what happens to sociological technologies of human organization in the absence of the institutional settings in which they are formed.

Reviews of *England Swings SF* demonstrate the fault lines of the debate over New Wave science fiction. As an experimental anthology, *England Swings SF* departed from the strict selection criteria Merril had become known for, precisely because Merril was attempting to call into question narrow generic definitions. Barry Gillam was disappointed that Merril had not engaged the high standards she used for her Year's Best anthologies (Gillam 1970, 11). Robert Hughes, on the other hand, recognized that the experimental nature of the collection called for an open-minded editorial practice: "If what you want is a cracking good yarn, with a conventional hero solving an objective problem with a plausible stratagem, you will find few examples of this [in *England Swings SF*]. If, on the other hand, you respond to the sometimes muddy, sometimes brilliant work of [...] J. G. Ballard, [this book is a treasure]" (Hughes 1968, 23).

While some reviewers took a "live and let live" approach to the New Wave debate, others challenged outright the legitimacy of New Wave science fiction. Writing in *Analog*, the champion of traditional science fiction, P. Schuyler Miller, questioned the tendency of New Wave science fiction to reject the traditional science fiction understanding of "reality" as ultimately knowable: "It seems to me that an axiom of the 'new' SF [...] is that the universe does *not* make sense" (Miller 1969, 166, emphasis in original). Reviews of *England Swings SF* mark a turning point in Merril's career: the science fiction field she had helped shape in the Cold War 1950s had, in her view, been largely co-opted by the establishment. Hence she gravitated toward, and eagerly promoted, the British New Wave movement in hopes of recovering the critical edge that mainstream American science fiction had lost. Regardless of debates over their merits, Merril's fondness for the New Wave as expressed through the special anthologies makes sense when we consider them in the light of her larger career. After all, much of what she valued about the New Wave was precisely what she had been struggling with in her own fiction a decade earlier.

## Critic-Reviewer: The "Books" Column (1965–1968)

Merril's position as review editor for *Magazine of Fantasy and Science Fiction* gave her further opportunities to assess and influence the future direction of science fiction. Founded in 1949, *Fantasy and Science Fiction* gained renown for the literary quality of its stories and was in the 1960s the leading magazine in the field. She began as books editor on a trial basis beginning with the March 1965 issue of the magazine that her mentor Anthony Boucher had co-founded and retired from in 1958, and she stayed with it for four critical years during the beginnings of the larger social and political revolutionary era known as "the Sixties." Given the growing difficulties she experienced trying to distinguish science fiction writing from general fiction, taking on the top review column in the field was a perfect chance for her to do in this forum what she could not do as easily in her annual anthology. Merril thought the world of Boucher and was aware that she had big shoes to fill, as evidenced by the August 1968 column, which begins with a memoir-like obituary of Boucher. She frames his death in April of that year as shocking news, deplorable even in the turbulent social and political context of 1968, and compares its effect on the science fiction community to that of the assassination of Martin Luther King, Jr., only a few weeks earlier on the progress of civil rights. Boucher had showed the way forward in science fiction but his voice was now stilled, "his plans and passions were now and evermore *stopped*" (1968 [August], "Books," 16). She still thought of Tony as her mentor and "Books" as "Tony's column":

> For almost twenty years, every word I have written for publication has been addressed at least in part to Anthony Boucher. These columns, above all, have

been done with an awareness of audience so acute he might have been looking over my shoulder as I wrote. [...] I think most writers have some such single-person audience, one ideally-understanding-and-ultimately-critical-reader — a teacher, fellow writer, editor, and friend, to whom specifically they address themselves [16–17].

Merril proceeds to "collaborate" with the absent Boucher by documenting his earlier writings on the nature and promise of "creative originality," something that he had always argued, even in the book review section of Merril's annual anthologies, was an essential ingredient of science fiction. In this way, Merril frames her own column as a continuation of Boucher's past "tirade[s]" (18). Her tribute to Boucher is in marked contrast to the more typical accolades found in the editorial pages of this issue of the magazine, where other writers offer testimonials to Boucher's genius as a writer and his kindness and fairness as a reviewer, anthologist, and editor. Merril, on the other hand, explores his mentorship in terms of its effect on all of her work.

While holding the influential position of books editor from 1965 until she resigned in late 1968 (her last column appeared in the February 1969 issue), Merril's columns displayed a great deal of novelty, with learned discussions of hot topics of the day — everything from LSD and the rest of the drug scene to SDS (Students for a Democratic Society, the anti–Vietnam War group). As elsewhere, she engaged readers in a dialogue on the newest developments in science fiction, not only promoting the idea of speculative fiction but also raising awareness of speculative nonfiction by leading scientists, including the I. S. Shklovskii and Carl Sagan co-authored classic *Intelligent Life in the Universe* (1966) (see 1967 [June], "Books," 37–43). Merril paid particular attention to fiction by the American writer Samuel R. Delany, whom she considered a particularly important innovator in the field, as well as British writers (Ballard in particular) and the growing experimental science fiction scene in Britain (see 1966 [January], "Books," 39–45).

## *Themes: Delany, New Wave, and the Merril-Russ Intersection*

Three themes in Merril's review column are useful to discuss in some detail: her continual championing of the talent of Delany, her contributions to the New Wave debate (including promoting *New Worlds* and British writers), and her troubled dialogue with Joanna Russ, the emergent feminist writer. With respect to the first, Merril reviewed every science fiction novel that Delaney published during her "Books" editorship with *Fantasy and Science Fiction*, including some of the best work ever produced in the field by any writer: *The Ballad of Beta-2* (1965 [November], 16–22), *Empire Star* and *Babel-17* (1966 [December], 30–37), *The Einstein Intersection* (1967 [November], 28–36), and *Nova* (1968 [November], 42–49). Delany, like Ballard, created stories that were difficult to pin down as one style or another, a trait that Merril admired. Merril was especially captivated by Delany's challenging novel *The Einstein Intersection*: "I read the book at a gulp, delighted page by page, and disappointed at the end, without quite knowing why" (1967 [November], 34–35). "When I went back to skim through and refresh myself before writing about it, I found myself re-reading instead: and found out that it was the gulping that gave me that faint indigestion the first time" (35). Acting as a guide to Delaney's often challenging prose, Merril shares with readers her practice of reading the new mode of science fiction, which involves open-mindedness, flexible expectations with respect to generic conventions, and acceptance of open-ended or polysemic meaning. We know discussions such as these had an impact. In particular, Japanese translators applied Merril's reflexive close-reading methods to the American science fiction they translated. This was especially so in the case of Norio Ito's translation of *Nova* and *The Einstein Intersection*. Ito notes in his tribute to Merril in 1997:

> The reason [I consulted Judy] was that I could understand that mysterious novel to some degree only after my second try, in 1971, a year after Judy returned to Canada [from Japan]. I did not realize it at the time, but perhaps something had greatly changed inside me after I attended the SF symposium and encountered Judy. Whatever that change was, I used her influence to approach Delany's writing [Ito, "Regret"].

For Merril, the new direction of science fiction engaged a shift not only in the literary practice of its authors but also in the reading practice of its critics, fans, and translators, a practice that she modeled in her reviews.

A second significant theme that played out in Merril's books column was the one for which she is best remembered — the so-called New Wave controversy, or, as Merril playfully called it in her review column, "The New Thing" ("TNT" and "NT"). Elizabeth Cummins (1995) has done an admirable job of untangling the controversy and offering a realistic appraisal of Merril's actual role in it, as has Rob Latham (2006), who has explored the struggle that took place in face-to-face encounters at conventions and in letters columns, first in Britain in the 1960s, and then migrating to North America in 1965 after that year's Loncon II. Nevertheless, it is worth revisiting the discussion in Merril's review columns of this topic.

Her column for November 1967 — sometimes cited as Merril's "New Wave" essay — began as follows: "They call it The New Thing. The people that call it that mostly don't like it, and the only agreements they seem to have are that Ballard is its Demon and I am its prophetess — and that it is what is wrong with Tom Disch, and with British s-f in general" (28). Merril demystified new trends in science fiction and diffused the polarization that was clearly developing over the issues by pointing out that American science fiction, while less organized than the British variety, had a strong claim to writing in the "NT" vein. By naming the work of American writers such as Samuel Delany, Philip K. Dick, Carol Emshwiller, Kit Reed, Cordwinder Smith, and Jack Vance, and the best work of Ted Sturgeon and Fritz Leiber, as well as some of the work of James Blish, Damon Knight, and C. M. Kornbluth, she concluded that "the Thing isn't so New: it is nothing more than the application of contemporary and sometimes (though not very) experimental literary techniques to the kind of contemporary/experimental speculation which is the essence of science fiction" (29). She could, of course, have added her own name to the list of American experimentalists.

Merril's defense of "TNT" does not mean she no longer applied standards of excellence to science fiction; she was still critical of much of the purported "NT" American science fiction, giving unfavorable reviews to Knight's anthology of original short stories, *Orbit 2: The Best New Science Fiction Stories of the Year* (1967), and, in the next column, Ellison's award-winning anthology *Dangerous Visions* (1967). Merril was not buying either Knight's or Ellison's claims to avant-garde status. Only two of the stories in *Orbit 2* (Kate Wilhelm's "Baby, You Were Great" and Brian Aldiss's "Full Sun") would, just barely, she suggested, "satisfy any reasonable, traditional definition of science-fiction-proper" and only one, Kit Reed's "The Food Farm," could unarguably be considered TNT (30–31).

Merril was even harder on Ellison. In *Dangerous Visions*, Ellison collected previously unpublished stories (unpublished because, according to Ellison, of the taboo subjects they addressed), and was at pains to distance his "new thing" from that promoted by Moorcock and Merril (Ellison 1967, xxv). In her review, Merril found Ellison a "bold" visionary but "lacking in taste" (1967 [December], "Books," 30). His volume was "all pyrotechnics," nothing dangerous about the stories, she wrote, except the "dangerously familiar" (29), and certainly nothing "'unpublishable' about them" (28). More importantly, many of the stories were missed opportunities. Carol Emshwiller's "female-viewpoint examination of the ambiguities of sex in 'Sex and/or Mr. Morrison,'" for example, might "disturb" readers, "but where are the extrapolations and projections of legalized homosexuality and abortion? female sexuality in the era of the Pill and antibiotics? rioting and assassination as political-action patterns in the U.S.? ... the Rand Corporation, and your daily newspaper, both make predictions freely" (29–30).

At the time of these reviews, Merril believed that American science fiction field was not adequately responding to the new political and social climate of the late 1960s, whereas British authors were. Even Americans such as Knight and Ellison were, in Merril's view, playing it safe politically. Latham summarizes the divide between the American and British approaches to the "New Thing" in this way: whereas Ellison wanted to reform the science fiction field "by expanding its range of content," Moorcock and Merril advocated "revolutionary new forms of expression" (Latham 2006, 313–14). Merril's pronouncements carried weight with fans and writers, but also generated resentment from established writers such as Pohl and Asimov, and even British writers such as Moorcock and Aldiss, who, to a certain extent, felt blamed for causing divisions in the United States between the experimentalists and the more conventional writers (and between British and American writers).

The New Wave in science fiction was accompanied by the emergence of a self-identified feminist movement in science fiction, closely identified with the work of Joanna Russ. Merril's review column provided a platform for what Dianne Newell and Jenéa Tallentire (2009, 64–80) refer to as the Merril-Russ intersection, in which Merril found herself at odds with the newcomer Russ despite the many interests, convictions, and friends the two women held in common — a third important theme to emerge, if only briefly, in Merril's column. In 1968, Merril was an accomplished author-anthologist at the peak of her power and influence in Anglo-American science fiction circles. Russ published her first novel, *Picnic on Paradise*, that year; it featured a smart, tough, autonomous female hero, Alyx, and hinted at her emerging feminist stance. She had become an occasional substitute in Merril's "Books" column for the increasingly experimental and tardy Merril — sure signs of a rising star. She was, like Merril, both a woman who stood out and a reviewer who was a "booster for the true spirit of SF," as Edward James puts it (James 2009, 30). Merril, by contrast, was that year seriously reconsidering the worth of her own leadership within the American science fiction community.

At this pivotal moment — a point when a torch could be passed, from established authority to rising star–a failure to connect occurred that would resonate in Russ's own scholarship and conceptions of women's literary contributions to science fiction. Despite Russ's later reputation as *the* innovative and first truly feminist science fiction author and critic, in 1968 she was still a proponent of traditional, "hard" science fiction. In fact, as a guest reviewer in Merril's columns, she publicly opposed Merril's established position as the foremost editor of superlative new science fiction authors in the United States and Britain — those who distanced themselves from traditional science fiction by exploring the radical potential for social change inherent in the genre. Given Russ's reputation just a few short years later for her commitment to women's writing, the transformative nature of science fiction, and feminist practices of solidarity and inclusion, the clash between Russ and Merril seems strange. Not only were these two women rare examples of respected female reviewers and critics in the field, but they also shared a circle of top professional male colleagues. People such as Delany, Leiber, and Silverberg, who respected and admired Russ, as a rule respected and admired Merril too. The failure in the meeting of minds between Russ and Merril tells us something of the largely unexplored generational and intellectual tensions within science fiction in the late 1960s, a turning point for radicalism in the West (Kurlansky 2004).

Although Merril was understood to be a "gender-bender in a man's world" and was certainly non-orthodox in her attitudes and practices of sexuality, authority, experimentation, and ideas about women's capacities, as revealed both in her life and her fiction writing (Merril and Pohl-Weary 2002, 11), she disavowed the term "feminist" and did not connect her own individualist, feminist principles of personal equality and competence to a wider movement of women's liberation. David Laskin argues that this position was not uncommon among intellectual radicals of Merril's generation: feminism was a problematic "brand of radicalism" that also eluded the famous group of left-of-center writers and critics known as the New York Intellectuals in the 1960s (Laskin 2001, 246). The women in this group and others they knew "didn't notice, weren't interested, or actively opposed 'women's lib' until it was a fait accompli. In fact, the whole business irritated the hell out of them" (247). Indifference, rather than outright opposition, appears to have been Merril's reaction to feminist discourses. But certainly Merril was promoting the subversive tendency of the genre, to stir up questions on all kinds of social issues, including (but not exclusive to) gender. One of those authors operating in the new mode was surely Russ, whose writing was undergoing a crucial transitional period from that of a "hard" science fiction advocate and up-and-comer in the mid–1960s to feminist forerunner and lesbian activist a decade later.

In her review, as a guest contributor to Merril's "Books" column, of *SF: The Best of the Best* anthology, Russ criticized the "Merrilian bent" of the collection for being "human," "poignant," and caught up (through "retrospective interest") in "New Thing" writers (Russ 1968a, "Books," 54). In Russ's view, the conspicuous absence of the hard sciences made for a "surprisingly monotonous book" (55), which she was careful to lay not at the feet of the authors, whose stories she individually lauded, but at the editing hand of Merril, who here was clearly not fulfilling her reputation as a science fiction connoisseur. Russ's target was not only Merril's reputation as a foremost editor-critic but also her credentials as an intellectual leader and connoisseur who was pushing science fiction in the new, experimental directions to which Russ also seemed committed.

Merril reciprocated Russ's criticism. Reviewing *Picnic on Paradise* (1968), Merril found that Russ had all the necessary potential but was missing the key element, the "binding energy that holds a novel of ideas [science fiction] together": that is, "Prophetic Power" (Merril 1968 [September], "Books," 35).

As a first novel it was "startlingly superior," Merril conceded; "I cannot think when I last enjoyed so much reading anything so unconvincing" (36). "The girl can *write*," she said (37). "Joanna Russ *writes* so well, it doesn't really matter if she makes sense" (36). However, Merril did not find the characters, events, or world Russ created credible. And not too long after her *Picnic on Paradise* review, Merril vanished from the scene, an anticlimactic transition of leadership. Merril gave up the review column and Russ declined to take it over, a double loss for the science fiction field.

## Essayist

### *"Fritz Leiber" (1969) and* *"What Do You Mean: Science? Fiction?" (1966)*

While a champion of the New Wave in the late 1960s, Merril by no means disavowed science fiction's past; as was the case in her *Best of the Best* anthology and summation sections in her Year's Best annual series, her essays of the late 1960s put to productive use her expertise as a historian widely read in the field and her stature as a living witness to science fiction's rich history. Edward F. Ferman's edited volume *The Best from Fantasy and Science Fiction: A Special 25th Anniversary Anthology* (1975) is a collection of six extraordinary stories by major science fiction writers and a commissioned "entertaining biography" of each author by one of their "famous peers" (Ferman 1975, flyleaf). The stories and biographical essays were originally written for the special one-author issues of *Fantasy and Science Fiction*. Of the six biographies, two were written by Judith Merril. One was on Theodore Sturgeon, whom she adored, for the September 1962 issue (Merril 1962, "Theodore Sturgeon"), and it informs the chapter on Sturgeon in Merril's memoir. The subject of her other biographical essay, which was published in the July 1969 issue, was Fritz Leiber (Merril 1969, "Fritz Leiber").

In her essay on Leiber, Merril recites the author's complex credentials and career, calls him a "writer's writer," an inveterate letter writer, and omnivorous reader ("Fritz Lieber," 44). Shifting into a more personal narrative mode, she assumes the role of reader to evoke Leiber's unmistakable impact on her: "There are authors one admires, authors one agrees with, and authors one loves. The first two sorts are taught in schools, displayed on coffee tables and book shelves, discussed at cocktail parties, bought as gifts, and generously lent out. Leiber gets borrowed, tattered and read" (44–45). She then reveals his direct connection with her: "Fritz is my good friend, and has been for nearly twenty years, but the fact is I fell in love with him half a decade before we met. This is not to say my passion is a purely literary one: simply that the man and his work are not separable" (45). His public and private communications were also not separable, according to Merril: "The rhythms of his prose are those of his speech; his letters and conversations seem to pick up where the last story stopped and run into the start of the next, if not in topic, then in theme and style. Writing about him, I find it difficult to remember whether this phrase or that image was from the public or private communications" (45). To call Merril's essay on Leiber a "biography" is woefully inadequate. Whereas the other profiles of top writers collected and reprinted in Ferman's anthology fit the term, filled as they are with the raw facts and anecdotes associated with the lives of their subjects, Merril offers insights into her understanding of Leiber that foretell the approach she will take to her own memoir: to reveal "a life in which almost all relationships and objectives have combined literary, political, personal intensities, inextricably woven" (Merril and Pohl-Weary 2002, 9).

Another highlight of Merril's essay-writing endeavors is "What Do You Mean: Science? Fiction?," which first appeared as two installments in the academic journal *Extrapolation* in 1966, was later reprinted in Thomas Clareson's influential collection of science fiction criticism, *The Other Side of Realism* (1971), and is perhaps her most significant and sustained statement on the shifts she saw in science fiction in the 1960s. Taking the broad historical view that both modern literature and modern science have common Enlightenment origins (Merril 1971, 56), this essay traces the fraught relationship between science fiction as a distinct sub-genre and "literature" more generally, as well as connecting the history of science fiction to broader social and cultural developments in the Western world. Defining "literature" in its most artistic sense as "rooted in the accumulated human experience of its day" (54), Merril predicts that, as the achievements of science and technology in twentieth-century society play an increasingly more profound role in human experience, the concerns of science fiction will eventually merge with the concerns of contemporary literature: "[As science fiction] achieves that [special literary] validity, it ceases to be 'science fiction' and becomes simply contemporary literature instead" (54). The current state of science fiction, she argues from a mid–1960s standpoint, is that of transition from sub-genre to "literary" status.

Merril locates science fiction in the context of broader developments in the history of modern thought in order to make the case that what she calls "speculative fiction" is not a new deviation from science fiction's roots, but rather the truest expression of those roots. All great works of fiction both engage speculation and seek "knowledge of the universe, the nature of man, and the nature of 'reality'" (Merril 1971, 61). On the other hand, science fiction's forerunner, "'realistic' fiction [...] was the transient oddity—[a] grotesque a product of nineteenth-century super-rationalism and mechanistic philosophy" (61–62). This "mechanism," Merril argues, was an attempt to cope with the exponential expansion of knowledge in the late nineteenth century: "the twentieth century opened to a compartmentation [*sic*] and fragmentation of knowledge unprecedented in scope" (58). Merril links this compartmentalization of knowledge into separate fields with the development of realism in fiction: both phenomena attempt to painstakingly describe and categorize reality (58). She argues that the mechanistic penchant in the past to categorize and compartmentalize influenced the division of literature into increasingly distinct and firmly defined genres (62–63). It was also in this context that the exploration of science in fiction became a sub-genre dominated by hard science.

The shift away from hard science fiction in favor of "speculative" fiction, then, marked the return of science fiction to its literary roots. Merril, who led the way with her own writing and promotional work in the 1950s, saw the 1960s as a historical moment when the aims and interests of "literature" and those of "science" were converging once more:

> In our culture, within the last quarter century, purely technological accomplishments have radically altered (though not *quite* erased) the meaning of a phrase like "American literature." [...] [Our] increasingly global culture is inescapably involved with the implications of modern scientific thought [Merril 1971, 87].

Therefore, to speak for the culture as a whole, "literature" must become science fiction.

We still use the term "science fiction." We still struggle to define it, travel to conventions to discuss it, and write essays and books about it. In this sense, Merril's prediction of the end of science fiction, of its re-absorption into "literature," has not been borne out. However, Merril was insightful in locating the boundaries between science fiction and literature, not in objective generic definitions, but in contingent and shifting historical processes. She was also prescient in foreseeing the blurring of boundaries between genre fiction and literature that characterizes the literary landscape of the twenty-first century. Consequently, her essay on science fiction in the 1960s deserves a place as one of the most important statements on the New Wave movement.

## Activist: From Chicago to Toronto, 1968

Between the year 1965, when she wrote "What Do You Mean," and 1968, when she dropped the term "year's best" from her annual anthology, Merril became disillusioned with the conservative direction of American science fiction relative to that in Britain, and disillusioned with American politics more generally. According to a story collected by the American-Canadian science fiction writer Spider Robinson, Merril had apologized for the American involvement in Vietnam at an invited talk at Loncon II, something that at the time deeply embarrassed and angered several of those who remembered the event: "The war hadn't embarrassed them; only a sincere apology for it" (1998, 6). In America, however, all the writers, like the rest of the country, were divided over the war. Merril and Kate Wilhelm Knight raised funds for an ad with the signatures of dozens of writers who opposed "the participation of the U.S. in the War in Vietnam" that ran in the March 1968 issue of *Magazine of Fantasy and Science Fiction*; an equally long list of writers signed an ad supporting the war that ran in the same issue. Both ads also appeared in the June 1968 issue of *Galaxy* magazine. Merril once told her friend and confidante Lorna Toolis that she became convinced her stance on Vietnam had cost her any chance of having her anthologies reprinted by the U.S. publishers (Toolis, email message to Dianne Newell, June 9, 2011).

When in the spring of 1967 Merril returned home to the United States from her extended working trip to London in 1966–1967, she walked into a scene of growing social and political unrest, finding herself unable either to defend the U.S. government's involvement or to do anything to stop it. Her sense of hopelessness triggered a severe bout of emotional paralysis, a cyclical phenomenon typically associated with her own struggles as a fiction writer to communicate alternative ideas. She described this spell of acute paralysis to others variously as "waver[ing] in sort of immobilized anxiety for months" (Merril to Aldiss, [n.d.] August 1968, 1.15, MP) and "a terrible depressive lethargy" (Merril to Dennis Lee, September 25, 1968, 9.50, MP). She also found herself in an impossible position of power — a "boss," rather than collaborator — within the science fiction field, an issue highlighted in Merril's infamous and very public lawsuit against Harlan Ellison.

Briefly, Merril had not included an award-winning 1965 story of Ellison's in her eleventh annual volume (1966), a story that he had aggressively promoted to her: "'Repent, Harlequin!' Said the Ticktockman" (Merril, "For the SFWA Bulletin," March 1, 1968, 1.6, MP). She did not like the story and she told him so. Ellison then parodied Merril cruelly and openly in an episode he wrote for the popular television series *The Man from U.N.C.L.E.* (Ellison 1967b). In this episode, "The Pieces of Fate," Ellison gave the name Judith Merel to the character of a literary critic whose mission from THRUSH was to crush the spirits and ruin the writing careers of promising young writers. According to Merril, this was Ellison's reaction when she rejected his story ("For the SFWA Bulletin"). Merril sued him for $1 million for defamation of character, which, despite the reputation Ellison had for suing others at the slightest provocation, led to much tension and anger against Merril within the science fiction community. The out-of-court settlement was for a mere fraction of the original amount, and Merril's lawyer, who operated on a contingency basis, got most of that, but the point is that she won. She told Toolis that as a result of the lawsuit, Ellison was banned by the studio from submitting any scripts for a year, which probably hurt him more than the cost of the settlement (Toolis, email message to Newell, June 9, 2011).

A tipping point for Merril was when she witnessed the police violence at the infamous Democratic National Convention in downtown Chicago in August 1968 (see McCann 2006; Farber 1998). Much has been written on the phenomenon of "1968" as an international turning point for revolutionary action (see Kurlansky 2004). Merril's Chicago convention review column, published in her second to last "Books" column, skillfully conjoins her despair over what she saw as the lack of political freedom in her home country and the impoverished state of American science fiction as a medium for protest and ideas:

> *The SDS is waiting on the corners, and the police make the Yippies look better all the time. Black Chicago growls and glowers and grins in the ghettos (except for the watchers patrolling the Loop: "Go home, sister—no black blood spilled here tonight."), but what happens if the next reporter the cops club down and Macespray on the ground is black?*
> *From here and now, the batch of books I brought out to review seem remote and pallid...* [Merril 1969 (January), "Books," 34, italics in original].

After this bleak introduction to her column, Merril describes the growing tension between her politics and her role as science fiction editor. She prefaces her reviews with an anecdote about her experiences at the Chicago convention, where she interviewed medical staff and patients, intending to write about the event from the perspective of a witness to the violence. But publishers rebuffed her: "[No] one who wasn't there wants to believe it the way it was; some of the publishers I approached made it clear they'd be glad to discuss a new science fiction anthology" (35). She then historicizes the current political indifference in science fiction, comparing it to an earlier time when Merril was a budding writer and science fiction writers were intellectually engaged:

> For fifteen years, through and around the forties, the science fiction magazines maintained an open, continuous, and almost exclusive forum for speculation, debate, and poetic vision stemming from such self-evident phenomena as: the dynamics of Big-Business-and-Bureaucracy [...] the economic and anthropological implications of an accelerating technology on the verge of atomic power, robotics, space flight, and computerized high-speed decision making; the incipient conflict between nationalist, racist, cultural, and religious patriotisms and the ecumenical imperative implicit in the developing technologies of communication, transportation, and warfare [35–36].

Of the several books that Merril then reviews, only two receive more than faint praise; the rest she describes as formulaic, imitative, and conservative. She concludes with a mixed review of Alexei Pashin's *Star Well*: "A good read: a fun book: it goes quickly enough to take to bed with you at night, and you can be sure it won't keep you awake *thinking*. Well, that's science fiction, I guess: great escape literature" (43). By the time this piece appeared in the magazine, Merril had made her exit from the United States and had found a welcoming, experimental niche in Canada.

## Rochdale College and the Spaced Out Library

It was Merril's subsequent quest for a radically different landscape — a new country and novel modes of communication — that led to her relocation in November 1968 to Toronto as a political and intellectual refugee. A "radically different landscape" had been a reason for getting into science fiction in the first place, and also for spending an extended period in London in the 1960s. Her immediate destination was a revolutionary "free university," an eighteen-story concrete high-rise apartment building that housed a radical experiment in co-operative education called Rochdale College (Merril and Pohl-Weary 2002, 173; see also Sharpe 1987). Rochdale afforded her a recuperative environment in what was both the heart of the city and the radical edge of the University of Toronto student district. In Toronto, where she identified as a political refugee, the forty-five-year-old Merril helped to organize the Committee to Aid Refugees from Militarism (CARM). She also co-founded "Red, White, and Black," a counseling group for American draft dodgers and deserters, and worked with the Rochdale Medical Clinic started by her teenage daughter Ann, who had followed her mother north (Lee 1998, 115).

Merril found in Toronto what she had been looking for: a new voice and personal space as the Resource Person on Writing and Publishing at Rochdale. Her fellow American science fiction writer from the 1950s, a blacklisted university mathematician now teaching university in Toronto, Chandler Davis, introduced Merril to Dennis Lee, a founder of Rochdale College in 1967. Lee would become a well-known Canadian poet and children's writer. He also founded a small Canadian press, House of Anansi. In January 1968, the newly minted Anansi famously published *Manual for Draft-Age Immigrants to Canada*, the "underground" guide on how to survive as a draft dodger in Canada that Merril had picked up in Chicago and that set her on the trail to Toronto.

Rochdale was the important catalyst for Merril's extraordinary Spaced Out Library (SOL) of science fiction and fantasy. Not only did she establish this informal lending library at the college but she also raised funds to organize and maintain the library throughout the two-week Rochdale Summer '69 Festival of science fiction and fantasy (and art and drugs), July 12–27, billed as an "Inner Space Odyssey" (Sharpe 1987, 64–65). Merril timed the festival to coincide with the first walk on the Moon on July 20, 1969, and gathered together friends who were speculative thinkers, including Delany, Pohl, Leiber, and Ed and Carol Emshwiller. The backbone of the library was the massive collection of books that had accompanied Merril to Toronto in the fall of 1968 in a rented trailer with "eight thousand books and magazines" and "fifteen file drawers of jumbled junk and value" (Merril and Pohl-Weary 2002, 191, 173). But the sheer volume and disorganized state of the materials made their transfer to Toronto an emotionally daunting prospect. To a friend she confessed, "My accumulated books and files occupy so much space that I periodically have to flee" (Merril to Lee, quoted in Merril to Aldiss, September [n.d.], 1968, 1.13, MP). As if to reinforce the permanence of her move, she had purged herself of almost all her possessions. All Merril asked of Rochdale was a small private room in which she could sleep and write and a separate, accessible storage space for the special possessions she had kept: her library of books and boxes of personal papers. She lived there for only one year but remained involved with the college for most of its short existence.

When Merril moved out of Rochdale into a co-op house in Toronto's downtown co-op and commune residential area known as the Annex, she took the books and papers with her. Having her library and personal papers filling the wall of her tiny bedroom, however, proved an unnerving coexistence. The solution, at least for her book collection, lay in the connections she had forged at Rochdale College and, via Rochdale, with the Toronto Public Library system. In the summer of 1970, the Toronto library took over the Spaced Out Library as an official collection, and — in exchange and at her request for access to her books and her personal papers that she stored there — hired Merril as the resident consultant with an office for life. Her office became a delightful home base for all her activities, and the small monthly salary she received permitted her a valuable core of subsistence and eventually a small pension. She outlines this arrangement in an exuberant letter to a friend, Harvey Jacobs. She can barely contain her joy:

> There's a little six-room house with an acquisitions budget, a seminar budget, two library staff people, room for ALL my papers and books (those I've given the library and those I haven't) and an office for the Consultant — namely me — I get $200 a month [...] for telling them what books I think they should buy and what seminars I think we should hold and having my name connected with the place [October 11, 1970, 8.30, MP].

Lorna Toolis recalls that in the 1990s, Merril's office at the permanent home for the library on College Street "always had the density of a small black hole, she kept enormously detailed files pertaining to her own writing interests as well as items she passed on to the Merril Collection" (email to Newell, June 9, 2011).

Toronto (and by implication, Canada) was now Merril's base for experimental and creative work and for activism. From the day of her arrival in the city, she had celebrated its creativity, experimentation, and "communications ferment" and relished its "psychic freedom, communications and contact" (Merril and Pohl-Weary 2002, 182, 188). In *Travels by Night* (1994), Douglas Fetherling maps in words many nodes of creativity, experimentation, and radicalism in the downtown streets and districts of Toronto in the late 1960s. Doug Owram identifies Toronto, and in particular Yorkville Village and the neighboring Rochdale College and the University of Toronto's downtown campus, as the center of a developing counterculture and youth movement in Canada at that time (1997, 211, 294–95). And John Hagan recalls that Toronto's "atmosphere was electric" and the era was one of "urban protest and uncertainty" (2001, x, 69). The downtown was highly livable when Merril arrived, a place to which the celebrated American urbanist, writer, and activist Jane Jacobs had also moved that year. But the city had, by the mid–1970s, become much more than that. It was the place Merril had been looking for: a culture, a "feel," and a language beyond anything she had ever encountered. In Toronto she had rediscovered "why cities were invented" (Merril and Pohl-Weary 2002, 182).

Judith, after moving to Toronto. Reproduced from Judith Merril and Emily Pohl-Weary, ***Better to Have Loved: The Life of Judith Merril*** (Toronto: Between the Lines, 2002), page 174, courtesy of the Merril Estate.

## Translator-Editor: Japan in the Early 1970s

If it was in Toronto that Merril rediscovered why cities were invented, it was in Japan that, stimulated by the language, culture, and dynamic circle of top Japanese translators of science fiction and fantasy, she discovered her fascination with translation as a key to language, communication, and collaboration (Merril, "Essay on Translation," 1972 [typescript], 32: "Science Fiction Correspondence,

1972–1980," MP). In a pattern almost identical to her earlier engagement with London writers' circles in the mid–1960s, an international science fiction conference brought Merril, the only female foreign invitee, to Tokyo and Kyoto, but the people, ideas, and culture there encouraged her to stay on past the meeting and to plan for a return visit for a longer period. The initial visit opened up a "storehouse" of experience and memory that seemed to transform her outlook completely (Merril to Tetsu Yano, December 29, 1970, 20.19, MP). Writing afterward to Katherine MacLean, she said she was only "sort of" back: "because I found an awful lot I didn't want to leave so soon in Japan. Like a language with no way of making a categorical statement about the future (can only express intention, wish, probability, etc.) ... It all adds up to a relativistic culture: lacking in both absolute and dualism in its basics" (October 12, 1970, 10.26, MP). This interest in the Japanese language had drawn Merril to the Japanese translators at the international conference and moved her to develop a book project with herself as editor, involving the improvisation of an entirely new translation method.

Merril began her involvement with translation by assisting a colleague, as she explained when interviewed in Japan by a Japanese translator by the last name of Muto. She helped one of the Japanese delegates, a translator by the last name of Saito, review the editorial work of an English speaker he had hired to polish his very literal English translation of a Japanese science fiction story by Shinichi Hoshi. Typically, the translators worked on Japanese versions of writings in English, not the other way around. Merril regarded the English translation as adequate, but a poor version of the original, noting, "She'd done a beautiful job, and I could see why she had done it, because she was trying to make sure that everything that was there to start with was clearly there in the story, and of course unless you can do it by evocation and suggestion, you're not translating Hoshi" ("Merril Interview with Muto," section 6, 1, 1972, 30: "Language," MP). In polishing the English of the rough translation, the young Englishwoman in question — the budding fantasy writer Angela Carter, as it happened — had produced "a sort of Wellsian story," quite "Victorian in style," Merril explained in the same interview with Muto. So, in search of that ephemeral "evocation and suggestion," she and Saito recruited a second translator and started again from the original Japanese version of the story, searching collaboratively for the right meaning and voice of Shinichi Hoshi. Merril would identify each phrase that seemed wrong: "And I would just say what else, you know, give me some other meanings for this, and then they would give me some, and I would eventually come up with an English phrase which they both would like and say 'yes, that's right'" (section 6, 1–2). From this seemingly insignificant episode as she was leaving Japan in 1970, Merril became interested in the specifics of translation, getting at the nucleus of the author's intent, rather than just the surface language; for Merril the joy was in the language — and, of course, being in dialogue.

As a result of this chance event, Merril planned a return visit to Japan to work on "The Book," an English-language collection of the best original Japanese science fiction stories that Merril, together with her translator colleagues and the members of the Japanese Science Fiction Writers' Club, led by Tetsu Yano, would edit and translate, using the novel translation method that felt right to her. As she explains,

> It's a matter of the Japanese translators working with me until they feel reasonably sure that I know, not just what is said, but what was meant. And what the character or the personality of the story or the writer is and so forth. And then I write it in English, not polishing something but writing it, and then they reread it and where they are dissatisfied I try to find something else. And it keeps going until they're satisfied and I am, so it's very slow, but we think we're actually getting translation. Not just information translation, but the best quality and style and cultural translation as well ["Merril Interview with Muto," section 7, MP].

The Japanese counted on Merril's skill and reputation as a superb anthologist of advanced writing; they believed the book project would be epochmaking for Japan (Aritsune Toyota to Merril [c. 1971], 29: "Correspondence and Reference Materials, 1970–1972," MP). To help develop their English-language and collaborative skills, Merril worked with translators to found Honyaku Benkyo-kai, the "Translation Study Meeting" (Asakura 2007, 263), which Grania Davis and Dana Lewis, American writers and translators who occasionally participated, claim was a major force in advancing the art of translating English-language science fiction into Japanese (Davis 2007, 2; Lewis, interviewed by Dianne Newell in Tokyo, December 2004). These meetings of Japanese translators were informal drinking parties that always included one or more native English speakers; it was a tradition that lasted for over twenty years.

Despite continuing to plan and correspond with colleagues about future working visits to Japan and even telling her American science fiction friends that she planned in the future to travel back and forth between Canada and Japan (see Merril to Knight, February 16, 1976, 9.20, MP; Kidd 1976, 13), Merril's second visit to the country proved to be her last. Newell and Tallentire (2005b) note that, for Merril, this intense and unique collaboration project with the Japanese translators of English-language science fiction was an opportunity to experiment with an entirely new mode of communication and to forge connections with a new circle of colleagues. Personal interaction and dialogue offered her rich emotional rewards, but also created difficulties after she returned to Toronto; without consistent, ongoing pressure, she found it impossible to follow through on the project.

Once the emotional and physical proximity to her Japanese circle was stretched and eventually broken, guilt became associated with the project for

Merril, who, after nine years of taking stabs at the English end of the team translation, was never able to complete more than a handful of individual stories (Komatsu Sakyo, "The Savage Mouth," translated by Merril; Morio Kita, "The Empty Field," translated by Merril and Kinya Tsuruta; and Ryu Mitsuse, "The Sunset, 2217 AD," Takashi Ishikawa, "Road to the Sea," and Masami Fukushima, "The Flower's Life Is Short," all translated by Merril and Tetsu Yano). With the exception of "The Flower's Life Is Short," Merril published the translated stories individually in various American and Australian magazines and collections, but that was not at all in the spirit of the arrangement: to showcase outstanding, original Japanese stories to American readers. Similarly, though Merril is credited with assisting in an eventual English-language collection published in 1989 by editors John L. Apostolou and Martin H. Greenberg and titled *The Best Japanese Science Fiction Stories*, this collection was nothing like the book of select, high-quality stories by members of the Japanese Science Fiction Writers Club envisioned by Merril and Tetsu Yano almost two decades earlier (Lewis, interviewed by Newell, December 2004). Ballantine tore up Merril's contract for "The Book" in 1979, which brought a final end to the original project. Yet warm memories remained of Merril as a mentor, teacher, and wonderful and inspiring friend who caused much trouble but was also much loved among translators and science fiction writers in Japan. In their tributes to Merril when she died, the three key translators emphasized the contributions she made to their work and their lives, along with her affection for Japanese language and culture, not her failure to produce the book (see Newell and Tallentire 2005b, 9–10).

Merril had cherished her time in Japan as much as she had her year in London, and she developed a deep personal identification with translation of Japanese stories as part of her life's work. The excitement of crossing cultural boundaries and being exposed to a whole new way of "nonlinear" thinking via the Japanese language had drawn Merril to reconstruct translation theory and practice as an experimental and collaborative, multi-stage enterprise of the kind that her earlier work as a writer, anthologist, and workshop leader had prepared her to do. However painful it was to fail at this project, Merril believed that these very qualities of Japanese language would revive the "far out" mode of expressing what was in her head — a task she struggled with at this stage in her career.

## Documentarist and Broadcaster in Toronto: Developing Her Voice and Ear

What eventually revived Merril's spirits and productivity level was her simultaneous work in the 1970s on radio documentaries, which in turn brought her into the orbit of the Canadian Broadcasting Corporation (CBC) in Toronto. Her new work as a freelance writer, interviewer, narrator, and producer of radio documentaries of a speculative nature helped bring structure back to her work and remade her connections within Toronto. Armed with her new awareness of the magic of language and a sense of herself as a translator, Merril honed this ability as a radio documentarist. As Newell and McCann (2009) discuss, when Merril returned from her first visit to Japan, she threw herself into producing a series of Canadian radio documentaries, struggling with the process of learning new communication techniques — working with reel-to-reel tape recording and editing machines — even changing the quality of her physical voice and improving her "ear" to accommodate radio documentary work:

> The human voice has always been My Thing. As a prose-writer, my greatest asset was my "ear." The style I worked toward eventually was one of deceptive "talk" feel.... Working on tapes, I have discovered a particular talent in myself: I seem to understand, when I listen hard, what people are trying to say.... And then [I use] the voices in painstaking juxtapositions to add up to what I want to say [Merril to Walter Miller, November 3, 1974, 40.23, MP].

On both trips to Japan, Merril taped interviews for CBC Radio and began as a freelance producer with CBC Radio's *Ideas* series in 1971. From her first trip, she produced "Women of Japan" (a one-hour segment for *Ideas*, 1971), and from her second, "Growing Up in Japan," for CBC's Radio Schools Kaleidoscope (five half-hour segments, 1973), followed by an even larger *Ideas* series: "Japan Future Probable" (aired in ten hours, 1975). Other radio documentaries by Merril focused on ecological and speculative topics that often drew material from science fiction conferences held in Toronto that she helped to organize. These included a panel discussion with Merril and other broadcasters, "The Egg of Time," as a segment of the *Ideas* series: "Man and Cosmos" (aired January 15, 1971); "Power and Science Fiction" (1975), her recording of a discussion at the 1971 Secondary Universe Conference between Merril, Pohl, and Delany; the *Ideas* documentary "How to Face Doomsday without Really Dying," from Merril's tapes of the Toronto Worldcon 1973 (aired in five hours, March 18–24, 1974); and, for Radio Schools Kaleidoscope, "How to Think Science Fiction" (aired in four half-hour segments, 1971–1972), and "Science Fiction Special" for CBC Radio International (aired in two hours, 1975).

Not surprisingly, there was a time in the mid–1970s when the CBC studios became a central, exciting feature in Merril's life that rivaled the Spaced Out Library as the place she wanted to be. The CBC studios proved to be an extraordinarily stimulating environment that operated much like a cooperative in which producers and writers pitched program ideas. Merril likened the place to "a twenty-four-hours-a-day seminar," or "a jam session"

(Merril and Pohl-Weary 2002, 185; see also Fetherling 1994, 112–13). She made many lifelong friends there, including the venerable producer Max Allen. It was another "flowering of the creative spirit," according to Lorna Toolis (email to Newell, June 9, 2011).

With the phasing out of her radio work in the late 1970s, Merril moved into television broadcasting. For three years (1978–1980) as a television writer and performer, she edited over one hundred episodes of the British television program *Dr. Who* for TV Ontario. It was a remarkable achievement: "[G]iven the importance of what she said, and the weight of the huge audience, it might have been her greatest accomplishment" explains Stafford Beer, founder of management cybernetics and one of the many friends Merril acquired through her radio interviewing with CBC *Ideas* (Beer 1992, 11). Her job was to closely read and identify a critical point in each of the episodes and work it up into "extros," three- to seven-minute filmed segments with which Merril concluded each program as "The Undoctor." Joyce Marshall, a Toronto novelist and friend of Merril's, remembers that in this role Merril became a bit of a celebrity with teenagers: "It was impossible to go with her into a restaurant or other public place without being approached by an eager group of young fans. Nothing makes a person seem so real, [Merril] remarked philosophically, as being seen on the tube" (Marshall 1992, 7).

## Collecting Merril's Writing Retrospectively

### The Print Collections

Over the years, Merril generated four collections of her short stories and one collection of her novellas, starting with the first, *Out of Bounds*, in 1960 and ending with *Daughters of Earth and Other Stories* in 1985. *Out of Bounds* was special. With seven of her favorite stories introduced by one of her closest friends, Theodore Sturgeon, the book appeared at the peak of her powers as a science fiction writer. In 1968, around the time she was leaving the United States, she published her three novellas under the title of the most famous, *Daughters of Earth* with Gollancz (London), and then as *Daughters of Earth: Three Novels* with Doubleday (1969) and Dell (1970). The book was received as a clear reminder that Merril, by now a famous anthologist, had in fact been, as reviewer P. Schuyler Miller explained, "one of the best science-fiction writers we have had" (Miller 1970, 165). Fritz Leiber, reviewing the book in *Fantastic Stories*, shares this view, using the opportunity to introduce Merril's unique talents to readers new to her work (Leiber 1970, 106–8). Unfortunately, such enthusiasm for Merril's early stories would change once she settled in

Canada.

Published in 1973, *Survival Ship and Other Stories* collected twelve Merril stories and one poem, with Merril's internotes providing historical background and transitions from one story to the next. Appearing only in Canada, the book can be seen as a celebration of Merril's arrival in the country and, as the introduction by Donald Theall, a McGill University specialist in English and communications, suggests, a reminder to Canadian readers of the speculative value of Merril's writing: "These stories have a special relevance to Canada and Canadians at this time, since they are extrapolated from the experience of the probabilistic worlds which could come to be as a result of the wrong-directedness of the North American dream as conceived by the official portions of the present rulers of the United States" (Theall 1973, 2–3). D. Reid Powell, in his review of *Survival Ship* in *Luna Monthly*, found the quality of Merril's writing so impressive for its time that the stories "must have shone as a light in the literary darkness of most pulp sf of the fifties and early sixties" (1975, 25).

Later collections, aimed at promoting a science fiction community in Canada and reaching new readers, were not so well received. Because she had not published any new fiction for over a decade, the stories were no longer considered innovative by the time they were reprinted, and the audience had no way of assessing their original impact. *The Best of Judith Merril*, published by Warner in 1976, with an introduction and headnotes by her longtime friend and literary agent, Virginia Kidd, was pitched at American readers who might need to catch up with Merril's move to Canada. Despite containing ten of her classic stories, however, most reviewers felt that the selections simply did not hold up. R. Laurraine Tutihasi, who had no previous exposure to Merril's work, thought them "monotonous, monotonously bad," ranging from "sentimental" and "overwritten" to "touching," and wondered if Merril had ever been very good (1976, 13). Merril's final collection was *Daughters of Earth and Other Stories: A Judith Merril Omnibus*, published by McClelland & Stewart in 1985. Perhaps anticipating criticism for publishing 30-year-old stories without any updates or revisions, Merril suggests that "errors in prediction have not quite blunted the prophetic content." Prophets face, she adds, "unique ambivalence" about becoming "dated" (Merril 1985, *Daughters*, 10).

With the lessons of earlier "prophecies" doubtlessly in mind, the one new science fiction story Merril published during this period, "The Future of Happiness" (1979), originally in the Canadian women's magazine *Chatelaine* and reprinted in *Daughters of Earth and Other Stories*, is far more tentative about the future than any of Merril's early stories, depicting five different future scenarios ranging from industrial collapse to "total automated affluence"

(Merril 1985, *Daughters*, 335), all of which are deemed equally possible.

## *The Japanese Translations*

Although much of Merril's fiction was translated over the years, including several stories for the Japanese *SF Magazine* (see Cummins 2006), Japanese translators did something unusual by compiling and translating her critical nonfiction. They had made a point of translating Merril's anthologies, starting in the 1950s with *Galaxy of Ghouls* (1955) and published as *Uchu no Yakaitachi* (1958). Translations of the entire run of Merril's Year's Best were published in seven volumes between 1967 and 1976 (as *Nenkan SF Kessakusen*), and her *SF: The Best of the Best* anthology (as *SF besuto obu za besuto*) was published in two volumes (1976, 1977). To honor Merril and celebrate her 1970 visit to Japan, Hisashi Asakura selected, translated (assisted by Merril), and published a book-length compilation of her critical writings, *What Do You Mean, Science? Fiction?*, as *SF-ni naniga dekiruka* (1972), a volume that included all of her "Books" columns from *Magazine of Fantasy and Science Fiction* and her major critical essay from 1966, "What Do You Mean: Science? Fiction?"

In an interview in Tokyo conducted by Newell in 2004, Takayuki Tatsumi, a professor of literature at Keio University in Tokyo, and Asakura agreed that these translations of Merril's work have been very influential in Japan (see also Asakura 1992, 3): Asakura's book on Merril's critical writing continues to be read by the Japanese avant-garde, and the volumes of translated Year's Best anthologies are read as primers for introducing Japanese readers and writers to science fiction.

## *The Dramatizations and Recordings*

Given Merril's forays into radio and TV broadcasting in the 1970s and early 1980s, it is fitting that Merril's own fiction was dramatized on radio. "Whoever You Are" was adapted with Charles Dewar for CBC *Ideas* and aired March 19, 1974, as a radio dramatization. The same story was also adapted by Ronald Weihs for an Artword Theatre Production that ran November 11–30, 1997, only weeks after Merril's death. "Headspace," a script adapted with Paul Kelman and performed by the experimental, co-operative Theatre Passe Muraille in 1978, was a stage play based on two of Merril's stories, "Connection Completed" and "The Lady Was a Tramp," and one of her science fiction poems, "In the Land of the Unblind" (1974). Merril also made an LP recording (1979) of two of her stories, "Survival Ship" and "The Shrine of Temptation," that she narrated and for which Frederik Pohl wrote the jacket notes.

Merril was also the central figure and performer in an award-winning video made of her life in speculative fiction, *What If...? A Film About Judith Merril*, which was shot in 1997 and directed by Helene Klodawsky (1999). The film first aired on Canada's Space Channel in 1999, and then on Bravo!, Télé-Québec, and the Dutch Arts Channel. Merril's friends consider it a hagiography, reverential to Merril with all of her zest and flavor bleached out.

## Facilitating the Canadian SF Community in the 1980s

In an interesting symmetry, Merril published in 1985 both her final collection of her old science fiction stories, *Daughters of Earth and Other Stories*, and the first volume in an anthology series of contemporary Canadian short fiction in the field, *Tesseracts*. Merril's ambitious afterword to *Tesseracts*, "We Have Met the Alien (And It Is Us)," summarizes the growth of what was then a very young field in Canada. When Merril arrived in the country in 1968, there was, she reckoned, no one other than Phyllis Gotlieb and H. A. Hargreaves (adding to that Chandler Davis, very occasionally, and herself, at that time) writing "recognizable science fiction seriously" (Merril 1985, "Afterword," 276), and certainly there were no journals, anthologies, libraries, awards, or national organizations dedicated to science fiction. John Clute recalls that until the 1980s, there was simply no family of science fiction writers in Canada, and that made a difference. The field and the "flavor," heroism, and frontier-busting was American, its glory days were 1925 to 1965 or 1970, "and those Canadians who wrote SF for Americans in (say) 1940, like A. E. van Vogt, did not do so as members of a family. They wrote alone" (Clute 1995, 22). Judith Merril helped to change all that. She soon discovered "in the odd corners and coach houses (especially the Coach House Press) that Canadians of rare talent and sensibility were writing truly fabulous funny-serious social-commentary SF" (Merril 1985, "Afterword," 276), as were writers who had moved to Canada from the United States (such as Spider Robinson and, later, William Gibson), Britain (Michael Coney and Andrew Weiner), and France (Élisabeth Vonarburg) (278). In "French" Canada, *Solaris* was founded in 1974; it claims to be the oldest French-language science fiction and fantasy magazine in the world. Merril believed that in "English" Canada in the 1970s, many publishers were publishing, and authors were writing, science fiction but did not know it (278), which is why she rejoiced in the daring of John Robert Colombo's 1979 publication project, *Other Canadas*, that located and collected what Colombo broadly defined as indigenous Canadian science fiction and fantasy written over approximately 200 years (279).

Merril recognized a strong academic, literary side to science fiction in

Canada (which may be why she had a McGill University professor of literature introduce the first collection of her stories to be published in Canada, *Survival Ship and Other Stories*). Canadian critics and teachers were heavily into science fiction by late 1960s and early 1970s. Darko Suvin taught a course at McGill and wrote a definitive monograph on science fiction theory, and there were science fiction classes at the University of Toronto and York University; Susan Woods, perhaps the most famous science fiction fandom persona, lived and taught in Canada; and the journal *Science Fiction Studies* began at McGill University in 1973 (Merril 1985, "Afterword," 278). And, following the intellectual lead of Northrop Frye and Margaret Atwood, Merril discovered in Canadian literature a "certain way of thinking about the environment" and the importance of the theme of survival; for Merril this was a revelation: "Of course! Just like SF" (277).

Like *Tesseracts*, the Spaced Out Library, founded and guided by Merril, contributed to community building among science fiction readers and writers in Canada. It became a gathering place for writers, booksellers, artists, and fans. From that operational base, Merril herself became a leading science fiction consultant, organizing science fiction conferences, writing feature articles for Canadian newspapers and magazines, working with school curriculum projects, and spending time as a writer in residence and lecturer at community colleges and universities. She was also a powerhouse in Toronto's celebrated literary festival at Harbourfront, organizing, for example, the "Out of This World Reading Series on Science Fiction" in 1980. In 1985, in addition to starting the *Tesseracts* anthology series, she founded Hydra North, a writers' workshop along the lines of the Milford workshop. She also organized the First Annual Canadian Science Fiction Writers' Workshop in 1986 and was a founding member of both Science Fiction Canada and the Canadian Science Fiction and Fantasy Association, receiving the Association's 1982 Aurora Award for Lifetime Contribution.

Merril's *Tesseracts* volume attested to, and celebrated, the recent and remarkable progress of science fiction in Canada. The volume reflects no particular theme, only what Merril liked: "What I like is getting my head turned around. I get off on fresh perceptions, widening horizons, new thoughts" ("Afterword," 275). Little wonder she chose the name "tesseract" for the series; it means a four-dimensional cube, though "the eye and the brain detect only three" (Merril 1985, "Foreword," 1). Merril and her colleagues reviewed 400 works by a total of 140 authors before settling on thirty-two selections, an eclectic mix of formats, reprints and (a few) originals, short stories and poems. The strongest stories were reprints by "pros" such as Gibson, Gotlieb, and Robinson. Among the original stories included are works by a dozen or so relative newcomers to the genre, such as Candace Jane Dorsey, who would go on to achieve international recognition. There were three stories translated from French, including one by Vonarburg, who later became an award-winning author.

These contributions of Merril to the Canadian science fiction community were those of innovator and catalyst, not necessarily dedicated participant. She tended to set her progeny free, to sink or swim. Lorna Toolis points out that in the case of *Tesseracts*, Merril insisted that there be a different editor or editors for each volume, and that the anthology series has flourished under this practice (email message to Newell, June 9, 2011). A number of contributors to Merril's volume went on to become editors in the series, and most of the budding writers she critiqued as part of her 1986 writer in residence program at the Spaced Out Library/Merril Collection were later contributors to *Tesseracts*.

## Summing Up Merril's Later Career

In his well-known autobiography *In Joy Still Felt*, all that Isaac Asimov had to say about meeting Judith Merril in Toronto in the early 1970s was that she was "a grandmother now" (1980, 537). After Merril left the United States and her position of power as premiere anthologist and critic, there were those who assumed that she did what aging women, according to stereotype, do: fade into the woodwork and dote on their grandchildren. Merril continued, however, to exercise her passion for science fiction until the day she died, leaving an indelible imprint on Canadian and Japanese science fiction through her criticism, translations and anthologies, radio and television broadcasts, work as a library curator and event organizer, and mentoring role in numerous writers' workshops and organizations. She did most of these things for the sheer joy of it, showing little concern for reputation or prestige, satisfied with the modest income her activities generated. Wintering in Jamaica in the 1980s provided cultural and political interest as well as relief from Canadian winters. Having experienced the downside of power in the United States, she does not appear to have missed her former stature as a central figure in science fiction. However, Merril realized that, while her own visibility had declined, her peers from the early days were publishing their memoirs of science fiction's "golden age," and she did not like what she saw: a "golden age" dominated by male activities and achievements, cleansed of the professional, emotional, and sexual entanglements that were so central to her own recollections of the early days. Thus began her final project as a writer, her final collaboration: her memoir, co-authored with her granddaughter.

CHAPTER 8

# The Memoir

Merril's final years before her death in 1997 were spent researching and remembering her life's journey for a memoir that had been "taking shape, slowly, through many transformations" (Merril 2002, "Transformations," 10). The outcome was her controversial and unusual book *Better to Have Loved: The Life of Judith Merril*, written in collaboration with Emily Pohl-Weary, her young granddaughter who is listed as co-author, and published posthumously with a Toronto-based alternative press in 2002. When it appeared, Merril's long-awaited memoir was generally misunderstood, a phenomenon recently explored by Dianne Newell and Jenéa Tallentire (2007). The critical response of most reviewers was guarded disappointment: a general sense that the memoir was frustratingly incomplete, fragmentary, disorganized, and not a "real" autobiography at all. Admiration for the memoir focused chiefly on its very existence and its promise as a frontline perspective from a female practitioner. For the science fiction writer Spider Robinson, reviewing for the Toronto *Globe and Mail*, the book, despite its flaws, was "a fascinating and invaluable historical resource and literary treasure trove" (Robinson 2002). But he, like the majority of reviewers, gives credit for the book to Merril's co-author, who is venerated as a salvage artist who inherited a mess. Judging Merril's memoir in the context of a traditional autobiography, the ultimate goal of which should have been her eyewitness account of the history of science fiction, and interpreting Pohl-Weary's role as that of editorial assistant who rescued the book project, is to miss the point, for it is precisely its collaborative form, authorship, nonlinear content, and careful planning that gives Merril's memoir its force.

Our approach is otherwise. In this account we consider the ways in which Merril's memoir was just as experimental as any of her previous works, testing and crossing the boundaries of traditional biography, as Merril had intended

"When I think of Judy, I see stars." Cover of Judith Merril and Emily Pohl Weary, *Better to Have Loved: The Life of Judith Merril* (Toronto: Between the Lines, 2002), courtesy of Between the Lines.

from the start of the memoir project. We expand upon what Newell and Tallentire (2005a) have argued — that is, how the clear path of Merril's conceptual process, her play with generic elements and autobiographical practices, and the impact of collaboration (from the idea stage dominated by Merril all the way through to the completion and final publication at the hands of Pohl-Weary) facilitated Merril's agenda: to produce late in her life an honest memoir about science fiction in the 1940s, 1950s and 1960s that departed from the sanitized works of the Futurians, and that was about her loves, and loves lost, *combined* with the "excitement of ideas."

Merril's memoir combines the traditional desire of an autobiographer to testify as to the truths of her life with the same keen experimentation with narrative and other conventions of the genre that she had undertaken throughout her career as a writer, editor, anthologist, critic, translator, and broadcaster. It is crafted with an idiosyncratic, nonlinear form, combining original writing for the memoir with fragments and information from tape-recorded informal conversations with her co-author; essays fashioned from author's notes pulled from Merril's own story collections, various introductions to anthologies, and book review columns; published interviews she had given to reporters and researchers over the years, and especially in her later years to science fiction writers and fans such as Mark Rich, Alan Weiss, Ron Weihs, and the filmmaker Helene Klodawsky; and letters she retrieved from her old correspondence files.

Contrary to claims that Pohl-Weary inherited a "mess," Merril had prepared a detailed outline for her granddaughter to follow should she not be able to finish the memoir (Pohl-Weary 2002, 4). Overall, the narration jumps back and forth through time, from the "autobiographer's" voice introducing the memoir before her death in the mid–1990s (and the co-author's voice introducing the finished product in the early 2000s) to chapters Merril prepared in the 1990s on her early years, essays and fragments written in the 1960s through 1990s, correspondence from the 1940s through 1960s and early 1990s, and the end-of-life interviews. This experimentation ultimately produced a text that counters many conventions readers have come to expect from autobiographies. It is also a text that ultimately reverses some of the previous erasure of Merril as a fiction writer and leader in the early history of American science fiction.

## Rereading the Mark Clifton Letters

Unlike other autobiographies by science fiction authors, Merril is painstakingly open about the process involved in her creative intellectual engagement in "life writing," a recent term that encompasses all forms of writing about a life, and about its halting evolution over the course of a decade before she began writing the actual memoir in the early 1990s. In her separate introduction, "Transformations," Merril explains that her first thought about her own life-writing project in the late 1970s was not of an autobiography, but of a published volume of a slightly annotated selection of correspondence with science fiction friends. The thought of publishing a "selected letters" volume originated with Merril's agreement in 1979 to prepare a memorial essay for Barry Malzberg and Martin H. Greenberg's much-belated collection of science fiction stories by Mark Clifton (1980). This assignment, she writes, sent her searching into boxes of old letters she had kept but had not consulted for decades ("Transformations," 10). Once immersed in those letters, she was hooked on the idea of a new writing project.

Merril's correspondence with Clifton went back to the early 1950s, when she had selected his first published story "What Have I Done?" for her 1952 anthology *Beyond Human Ken*. Clifton was an innovative, Hugo-winning writer in the 1950s who died in 1963. With a background in industrial psychology, his science fiction stories quickly stood out for their psychological insight; as a writer, he led the 1950s trend in social scientific speculation. Because of his background training and their mutual interest in ESP, their exchange of letters — what she calls their "long-distance mutual exploration" (Merril 1980, "A Memoir and Appreciation," viii) — helped to shape Merril's thinking about parapsychology and influence the content of her fiction (xiii); the exchange was intimate, though they had almost no face-to-face contact:

> I was twenty-nine years old and a fledgling writer. [Clifton] was "established." A vividly meaningful relationship of personal, literary, and ideological valences exploded to fill some seven hundred pages of typed, single-spaced letters — nearly five hundred of them in the first three years [Merril and Pohl-Weary 2002, 143].

The 700 pages of letters exchanged with Clifton over the decade were emblematic of the intellectually engaged, voluminous correspondence Merril maintained with dozens of other science fiction colleagues over a much longer period, even when they lived in the same city or even the same house; most notable for the volume of their letters are Brian Aldiss, Milton Amgott (her lawyer and friend), Tony Boucher, Ted Cogswell, Les Cole, Virginia Kidd, Fritz Leiber, Katherine MacLean, James V. McConnell, Walter Miller, Jr., Robert Mills, Frederik Pohl, and Ted Sturgeon.

Merril believed that Clifton was a gifted writer and regretted that his work was mostly forgotten. She wrote the Clifton piece as an annotated collection of excerpts from a selection of the first year of their correspondence (1952), calling her unusual essay "A Memoir and Appreciation." The title was perhaps a reference to the way the exchange with Clifton had influenced her stories of the day, and to the way research for the piece on Clifton had inspired her to write a book of her own about the people and places she had encountered over the years, a book based on letters: "I began to feel that some of the best writing I had ever done was in personal letters, rather than the carefully crafted prose of my public work" ("Transformations," 10). The idea would thereafter grow over the next decade from a vague idea for a possible set of published letters to a more formal autobiographical endeavor.

## Learning about Autobiography

True to form, Merril began seriously thinking about and researching what she was about to tackle. There have been very few biographies or autobiographies ever produced on or by science fiction writers, a topic taken up in a rare discussion by the veteran science fiction fanzine editor Bruce Gillespie (2000), and more recently by John Rieder's special issue of *Biography* on life writing and science fiction (2007). Damon Knight had written his own story (1976) in the Aldiss and Harrison essay collection *Hell's Cartographers* and the story of himself and other Futurians in his collective memoir of the group, *The Futurians* (1977). Frederik Pohl put out a lighthearted autobiography in 1978, *The Way the Future Was*, which was followed by Isaac Asimov's two-volume autobiography: *In Memory Yet Green* (1979) and *In Joy Still Felt* (1980). Merril did not care for the autobiographies of the Futurians. Her memory insisted that things were different: "most of us were young, passionate, frail, tough, loving, quarreling, horny human beings testing ourselves against each other and the world" (Merril 2002, "Transformations," 10). It was time for this messier, more sexually charged dimension of the early science fiction community to be revealed.

In her *Globe and Mail* review (Merril 1979) of Asimov's *In Memory Yet Green*, Merril foregrounds the sexuality, passion, and emotion within the early science fiction community as she witnessed and understood it; through this approach, she critiques Asimov's very "logical" and linear text. His memory is about his success in selling books to publishers and winning awards at conventions. His autobiographies were, he admits in his memoir *I, Asimov* (1995, xi), obsessively linear: "I recounted events in precise order to the calendar (thanks to a diary I've kept since I turned eighteen)." There is a lack of "how it was" in Asimov's story, Merril says, which perhaps reflects certain qualities, like ambition and "squareness," that had always kept Asimov somewhat apart from the other Futurians and the regulars at gatherings of the Hydra Club: "when Ike showed up at one of our conferences or parties, he was loveable, and he was sweet, but ... well...." (Merril 1979, 45). Her gentle caveats aside, it seems that in this review of Asimov's autobiography, Merril is attempting to show what an autobiography from the Futurian community could be like, and preparing for her own "stab" at producing one: "somebody, I thought, should tell it like it was" (Merril 2002, "Transformations," 10).

While she was giving thought to writing about her life, two sources of inspiration captured Merril's imagination: the 1980s autobiographical writings of her American science fiction friends Samuel R. Delany and Fritz Leiber. In contrast to Asimov and others, these two writers struck Merril as doing "honest work" in what she regarded as their daring form of autobiography

("Transformations," 10–11). Merril had always rated Delany and Leiber as among the most brilliant, inventive, and respected of the science fiction authors in her circle, and neither of them had roots in the Futurian Society. She had read Delany's 1979 book *Heavenly Breakfast: An Essay on the Winter of Love*, a semi-autobiographical, nonfiction account of life in the Heavenly Breakfast commune in the 1970s, and she also studied his only formal memoir, *The Motion of Light in Water: Sex and Science Fiction Writing in the East Village, 1957–1965*, published in 1988. In *Motion of Light in Water*, Delany is transparent about how his autobiography grew and developed; he openly disavows the autobiographical writings of the established science fiction writers in favor of a more avant-garde, memoir-like approach evident in his favorite works of this genre, all of them written outside the science fiction field: Maxine Hong Kingston's *The Woman Warrior: Memoirs of a Girlhood Among Ghosts*, Paul Goodman's *Five Years: Thoughts During a Useless Time*, Frederick Douglass's *Narrative of the Life of Frederick Douglass, an American Slave*, and sections of Walter Benjamin's *One Way Street*. With these types of "brief and intense models shamelessly in mind," Delany hoped to "sketch, as honestly and effectively as I can," what he could recognize as his own story, knowing that despite his efforts to be honest and accurate, "memory will make this only one possible fiction among the myriad — many in open conflict" (Delaney 1988, xviii ). As if to reflect his doubt about the memoir exercise, his story, which concerns his own sexual coming of age as a young, black, homosexual science fiction writer from Harlem living in the very heart of Bohemian New York, is written in a detached style. The loosely connected paragraphs are numbered, divided, and subdivided to create story fragments. The odd snippet about his science fiction writing is interwoven with the rest of the text.

Leiber is much less deliberate about writing his autobiography than Delany, but daring nevertheless. Leiber writes that in the process of preparing a standard author's note for his new story collection *The Ghost Light*, he simply found himself loosening up: "Reminiscence flooded me in quick pleasurable gushes, like those of story inspiration, but smaller, sharper, though not as strong" (Leiber 1984a, 8). The result of letting himself go was a 113-page autobiography of his youth. In "Not Much Disorder and Not So Early Sex: An Autobiographic Essay" (1984b), Leiber explains that he found sex "the most difficult aspect of my life to write about, but by all odds the most revealing and certainly the funniest" (254). Like Delany, Leiber was a science fiction writer who was prepared to tackle taboo subjects — to do what was not being done in the small amount of autobiographical writing produced in science fiction to that point.

Merril not only read the autobiographical works of Delany and Leiber but she also deliberately visited the two of them individually in January 1990 to discuss their experiences with autobiography: Delany in New York and

Leiber at a science fiction convention in San Francisco, where he and Merril were, she recalls in her memoir, "videotaped in a memoir-esque discussion of extraordinary candour" (Merril 2002, "Transformations," 10; Merril, "Open Letter," March 12, 1991, quoted in Merril and Pohl-Weary 2002, 247). Merril stayed on for a visit with Leiber, who was by now one of the few old, loving friends who were still alive. She remembered Leiber as being very ill at the time, "half-blind, bent over from spine-shortening, and moderately racked with emphysema," and soon afterward he had a stroke (Merril to MacLean, May 21, 1992, quoted in Merril and Pohl-Weary, 250). Leiber died a few years later at the age of 81. The visits to Delany and Leiber got her thinking about life writing and, by now, her own mortality: "When I came home I was planning, rather than thinking, about memoirs" ("Transformations," 11). The choice of memoir was one that her friend, the Canadian science fiction writer Candas Jane Dorsey, would endorse: "memoirs, that much more literary, literate and non-linear term. Judy was never linear" (Dorsey 1997, 31).

## Settling on Memoir

Thus, the memoir as an idea for her project began after those visits to Delany and Leiber in 1990. Merril discovered, as she wrote in an open letter to her friends and well-wishers, that what she wanted to write about was her life, and in a revealing way: "Not an autobio. Just the interesting parts" (March 12, 1991, quoted in Merril and Pohl-Weary 2002, 247). A traumatic brush with mortality—a heart attack and major heart surgery over the winter of 1990–1991—got the memoir project going. Like Leiber, she got the autobiography bug, but also like him, she was in poor health—"disintegrating," as she puts it: "Eyes and ears slowly fading; acute arthritic flare-up in one knee a few years ago; needing to be more careful about diet, blah blah, otherwise known as getting old" (246). She got a battery-powered go-cart to get around in, a situation that really irritated her, and deeply regretted no longer being able to go dancing, according to her friend Lorna Toolis (email communication with Dianne Newell, June 10, 2011). Merril found after her heart surgery that "the shape of the thing was changing again"; from a book about others in her life, it had become something more personal, for she began discovering how rich and unusual her own life had been ("Transformations," 11). The influences of Delany and Leiber are evident in Merril's project, in her very characterization of her project as "memoir," as opposed to "autobiography"; in her fragmented form; in her unabashed attention to love, sex, and emotion, rather than her achievements in science fiction; and, in the case of Delany, in her conscious exploration of the meanings and trickiness of memory.

## *Merril's Gradual Erasure*

Merril's correspondence files from the 1950s and 1960s indicate her importance as a writer and anthologist, as a shoulder to lean on, and as an advisor both for new writers, such as Samuel Delany, Kate Wilhelm, and Anne McCaffrey, and also for foreign writers such as Aldiss and Ballard, who wanted to enter the U.S. market and who quickly rose to the top of the field there and in the United Kingdom. Yet the autobiographical writings and early histories of science fiction produced by her close contemporaries in science fiction — most notably Isaac Asimov and Brian Aldiss — serve to erase Merril's professional standing in the field. The purpose of Merril's memoir was not to tout her own accomplishments; indeed, her focus on lovers and ideas in point of fact de-emphasized her professional role in science fiction. Nevertheless, publishing a memoir of her own that would tell it like it was would inevitably help to restore her reputation and rightful stature in the history of the field.

Isaac Asimov had been a Futurian but dropped out of the group. He lived in Boston and came to the occasional meeting of the Hydra Club and attended a few Milford workshops. The most prolific of the former Futurians (he published hundreds of books and edited collections over the five decades of his career), it was always easy to find an Asimov story to anthologize, especially since Asimov himself was always pitching them to editors such as Merril. She included one of Asimov's stories in her third anthology, *Human?* (1954), and in most of her anthologies thereafter, until he stopped writing science fiction in the early 1960s.

Their letters to each other in the 1950s mix business with pleasantries and promises to try to meet up with each other, plans that usually did not materialize; there was plenty of banter back and forth. He wrote probing requests to her for information on what was happening in publishing, who was selling what stories and who was buying, and what new opportunities were coming up. In 1955, he was particularly keen about the Year's Best series he had heard rumors about; he figured that Merril would be the "perennial" editor, and he volunteered a story of his that might be good for the first volume; to be included, he wrote her, would be "a source of considerable pride" for him (September 30, 1955, 1.39, MP). Asimov liked to recite his story titles, hoping Merril would promote and purchase them. One year, he brought to her attention no fewer than eight titles of his for her Year's Best, just in case she had not come across them, assuring her he would be honored to be "anthologized by you" (June 25, 1956). No letter from him, no matter the main topic, failed to search out professional opportunities, even if only as a postscript: "P.S. What is this about a writers' conference, you guys are setting up?" he added to his December 14, 1955, letter about his vague plans to visit her sometime in New York or Milford. Their two families knew each other well; one of Merril's daughters fondly called him "Icicle" (May 5, 1954). Merril always addressed him as "Ike" and sometimes signed her letters to him as "mit smootchee" or "xxxxxxx's (smoochywet type)" (December 21, 28, 1955), and he signed his to her as "your fan" and "with love, Isaac."

Despite these close personal and professional relations, Merril is all but erased from Asimov's autobiographies. In his linear record of events in the first two books, amid the sightings of pretty girls at conferences and tales of personal successes, he writes that he first met Merril in 1947, at a get-together of the Hydra Club at her place in Greenwich Village. She was twenty-four years old, "a striking-looking girl, and a quick-witted one who was into women's lib decades ahead of her time" (Asimov 1979, 510). Otherwise, the only mentions of Merril in this, his 700-page *In Memory Yet Green* volume, are about her showing up in this or that place as the wife of Frederik Pohl. In the second volume of his autobiography, *In Joy Still Felt* (1980), his references to Merril are usually about the controversies. For instance, he relates the story of an infamous joke on Merril at the 1955 World Science Fiction Convention in Cleveland. Asimov was a guest of honor at the convention, and Merril had agreed to accept a Hugo Award on behalf of the absent winner, the man from whom she had recently separated, Walter Miller, Jr. It was a brave thing for her to do, given the scandal that resulted from her sojourn with him. In announcing the award, the toastmaster noted that Miller had been often anthologized by Merril. Asimov quipped in front of what happened to be a live mike: "anthologized?— always euphemisms" (*Joy*, 40). In the boyish mood of a science fiction convention and for many years afterward, laughter and jokes that played on the sexual innuendo behind Asimov's quip abounded at Merril's expense. At another point in his book, he alludes to the famous feud between Merril and Harlan Ellison in the mid–1960s, describing what Asimov regarded as the trouble Merril created at the World Science Fiction Convention in New York in 1967, when she was in the process of suing Ellison for defamation of character (437).

The only other mention of Merril in *Joy* has to do with yet another World Science Fiction Convention, this time a secondary event that was being held in Toronto in 1971; he writes in a single sentence that he met Merril there for the first time in ten years (which contradicts his story about seeing her at the 1967 convention) and comments only that she was "a grandmother now" (Asimov 1980, 537). The meeting in question was the international Secondary Universe Conference (Secon IV), co-sponsored by the Spaced Out Library and McGill University, and assisted by Merril as program coordinator. Asimov includes nothing about her key role in the conference or her activities in Toronto: her role as a freelance radio producer, in which capacity she interviewed him for a CBC *Ideas* program, or of her role as curator of the Spaced Out Library, about all of which Asimov would have been aware.

In his memoir *I, Asimov*, he makes a point of saying his book presents his "*whole*" life in sections dealing with either aspects of his life or vignettes of people who had influenced him (Asimov 1994, xii), thus attempting to be less linear, more "with it." He includes cameos on those "who strongly influenced my later career or whose lives intertwined with mine in certain ways" (62). And while he profiles Pohl, Sturgeon, and most of the other male writers and editors who were also part of Merril's circle, Merril is not even mentioned.

Then there is Brian Aldiss, who began writing to Merril from England in the late 1950s, when she started including him in her Year's Best anthologies. One of his earliest letters to her praises *Shadow on the Hearth*, which he calls "one of my ten 'best ever': it's a splendid novel by any standards" (February 26, 1959, 1.14, MP). He confesses at the outset that he is not much of a correspondent, and sure enough, his letters are on the short side, but as a collection they are voluminous and extremely chatty and intimate. Over the next several years, he and Merril would exchange gossip: She made inquiries about his new stories; he told her how "highly honored" he was to be included in her latest anthologies (April 19, 1961) and said he would "love" her to look at a story of his that no one else would touch (November 22, 1961). She arranged to visit him and his wife for a day in Oxford in 1963 (Merril to Aldiss, September 19, 1963) and again in 1965 (Aldiss to Merril, September 21). In 1966, Aldiss invited her up from London to "sit in the garden and drink and chat" (February 24). Aldiss welcomed her back to England that year with a laudatory poem he wrote about her that began, "England and her sf lay hid in night; / God said, 'Let Merril be!' and all was light" (n.d. 1966). Aldiss wrote in 1966 of his forthcoming visit to the United States and to Milford (February 24); he writes a month later with warm thanks for showing him and his wife around New York: "we do thank you for the time we spent with you, and the lick of American myth we saw through your eyes. [...] Love from us both, come stay and enchant us soon" (March 28, 1966). He confided in Merril that he had written nothing for two years while he got divorced, remarried, and changed houses, but he was now re-energized, "primed for action again," largely because of his trip to the United States (March 28, 1966). There were running, heated discussions about her important critical essay (1966, "What Do You Mean") for *Extrapolation* and about the basic premise of her controversial anthology project that would be published as *England Swings* (Merril to Aldiss, October 6 and 10, 1966, respectively).

Fifty pages of letters were exchanged between Merril and Aldiss during the period 1967–1968 that create a picture of two old friends and professional colleagues joking, gossiping, disagreeing, confiding, and doing business; she was one of his main contacts in the United States, and he was an important, if not main, contact for her in England. Yet when Aldiss published the first "true" history of science fiction, *Billion Year Spree*, only a few years later, he barely mentioned Merril, and his few references are not about her fiction writing or her as a colleague; they reflect nothing of the flattery and intellectual seriousness that fill his letters to her. The best he has to say about Merril is including her name in a list of "connoisseur" editors (Aldiss 1973, 264) and quoting from her 1966 *Extrapolation* article to valorize the role that *Magazine of Fantasy and Science Fiction* had played in raising literary standards in the genre (279). Otherwise, the only reference to her is in connection with the British New Wave science fiction in the mid–1960s, a mention that serves to trivialize her time with, and positive influence on, the science fiction field in England. For example, he dismisses *England Swings — SF* (1968), in which he was one of the contributors, for its "horrendous" title and for being passé in content (302); he calls Merril a "startling immigrant" who was already "well known as a writer and anthologist, producing a *Year's Best SF*, which grew more autobiographical — and confusing — as the years passed," and whose "madness and excitement" as "the priestess" of New Wave science fiction (302) was disruptive for British science fiction writers. This line of discussion echoes his remark in a footnote that she was a "female incendiary" whose "great gift is her enthusiasm" (284/n/27). He accuses her of stirring things up in England, then walking away in 1967, leaving others to clean up the mess (303).

Merril as a writer is conspicuous by her absence in Aldiss's 1973 history of science fiction: there is no mention of the Merril novel he apparently admired, *Shadow on the Hearth*, even in his section on atomic bomb science fiction; no mention of her even appears in the (almost) one page he devotes to mentioning "the ladies" who wrote American science fiction in the 1950s (263). Turning to Aldiss's 1998 autobiography, *The Twinkling of an Eye: Or, My Life as an Englishman*, only a single reference to Merril is made: her name in a list of fellow guests at the international meeting in Tokyo in 1970 (Aldiss 1998, 284). At the "tribute" to Merril for lifetime achievement made at the Harbourfront Festival in 1992, Aldiss focused on humorous stories about himself, to the exclusion of any tribute to the familiarity, friendship, or professional collegiality of the sort present in letters they exchanged and visits they paid each other over a ten-year period (Aldiss 1992, 1–2). And in a conversation with Dianne Newell about Merril at the March 1998 International Association for the Fantastic in the Arts at Fort Lauderdale, Florida, Aldiss denied really knowing much about Merril, except that she had bit of a reputation for "sleeping around."

Merril's reputation fares no better at the hands of Damon Knight and

Frederik Pohl, who were perhaps the two Futurians who were most knowledgeable about Merril's key role in science fiction. Knight interviewed Merril in the early 1970s for his historical book, *The Futurians* (1977), observing in it that Merril had grown dowdy in appearance and seemed bored and distracted, paying more attention to Knight's recording equipment than to his questions about science fiction in the old days. He also expresses amusement at her choice to call herself a documentarist. Pohl, in *The Way the Future Was* (1978), offers great details about his fellow Futurians but is almost silent regarding Merril's involvement as a writer (or anthologist-critic-reviewer), other than pointing out that she had just written "That Only a Mother" when he met her in the 1940s, a story that made her "a writer to be respected" (140). Yet there is nothing in *The Way the Future Was* to suggest Merril ever advanced beyond that early achievement. True, their divorce in the early 1950s had been acrimonious, something Pohl touches upon (167–68), which could explain his reticence, except for the fact that the two of them had reconciled by the late 1950s and been friends for over two decades before Pohl's autobiography appeared.

## Merril's Memoir Project

At the end of her introduction, in a "note to the reader," Merril states, "This is not an autobiography; these are memoirs of my loves, and my most ardent loves have always been entwined with the excitement of ideas" (Merril 2002, "Transformations," 12). Though she wants to write of her life, she still tries to separate her book from some traditional vision of an autobiography. So the book comes with Merril's warning to her readers: "those who feel the need to know what-happened-next? might find it uncomfortable to follow my obsessive path. [...] I can only move through my life following my own (however idiosyncratic) trail of memory, thought, and speculation" (12). A key element that enabled Merril's reflexive style and facilitated the excavation of her many stories illustrated in her memoir was the careful archiving and consultation of her own voluminous correspondence and other written materials, collected and preserved over many decades and throughout frequent relocations in her life.

### The Correspondence Files

Merril introduces her memoir as "a collection of memoirs and mementos," and the keepsakes to which she refers are snapshots, cover art, and, above all, letters. Merril had been a fastidious and prolific letter-writer. As a matter of course, she typed and kept carbon copies of her outgoing letters, which she then filed with the incoming letters under the names of her correspondents. She kept these files to facilitate the various complex narratives she wrote across rivers of letters over time, and also to use as reference files for her editorial and anthology work. This practice was something that friends such as MacLean remembered and were personally most grateful for: "Remember how you used to show me your letter files and carbons to get me hip on what was going on among your friends?" (MacLean to Merril, 1967, 10.26, MP). When she sold Red Bank to Pohl in the winter of 1952–1953 in order to establish a life with Miller, Merril stored her records with Sturgeon for safekeeping. Highly mobile in the 1960s, she often kept her old files in Milford, usually at Virginia Kidd's house. In a letter to Aldiss, for example, she speaks of making one of her "rapid descents upon Milford, Virginia, the files, and all" (February 12, 1966, 1.14, MP). Her personal papers were extracted from storage in Milford and accompanied her books and magazines when she left the United States for Canada.

In Canada, her letters were key personal objects, salvaged from her former life, a life she gave up. When she donated her Spaced Out Library to the Toronto Public Library in 1970, she simply stored the letters at the library for safekeeping. Although they were cherished as representing the entirety of her life and work, she came to see the letter files as protective barriers that would eventually need to be shed. In the 1980s, when she was thinking about compiling a book of annotated letters, she donated the collection — dozens of large boxes — of her old correspondence and research files to Library and Archives Canada in Ottawa. (The donation was made after a screaming match with the then-head of the Spaced Out Library, with whom Merril did not get along.) In Ottawa, the collection was organized, cataloged, preserved, and (for the most part) open to the public. Only the small amount of correspondence with members of her immediate family (one box) and a larger volume of key letters that were needed for preparing the memoir required the permission of either Merril or her estate to be accessed by the public. After her death, the restrictions on access to the memoir-related letters were removed.

In the sensitive hands of a skilled writer and editor like Merril, a collection of personal papers becomes a map with which to navigate one's history, and if the papers are left with a public repository, as in Merril's case, they are a record or extension of these personal identities for others to share. Their public accessibility also creates future possibilities for writings and reinterpretations by others.

Merril consulted the old letter files in Ottawa time and time again for her memoir project, a process she refers to variously as consulting "my younger self" or "my former self" (Merril to MacLean, May 21 and June 18, 1992, quoted in Merril and Pohl-Weary 2002, 250 and 252). This demonstrates a conscious process of memoir-writing as a desire to get at her personal history through means beyond memory, and beyond the "daily diary" or journal-type memory prompts that inform and texture many of the flat, litany-like autobiographies (such as Asimov's) that she knew she did not want to imitate. It was too easy, she thought, to let one's memory reinvent one's life and history. She told Mark Rich in an interview that, as a memoirist, consulting her letters would give her an advantage over the other Futurian writers, who relied too much on their own memories:

> So I really think to some extent I know where I'm right and wrong, because I've been a pack rat about pieces of paper, and because I've been working on my own rather different type of memoirs, I've done a lot of research into old correspondences. So some of the things I feel quite certain of — *This* was done in this year, and this happened at *this* point. But for other things, where I haven't been able to find reference in the correspondence — there's no reason for me to trust my memory any more than I can trust [Fred Pohl's]. I *know* I can't trust Fred's. I think all of us are self-serving in the way we remember things. We like to have been in the right [Rich 1999, 5].

Even Knight's strategy of taping sessions with the writers he profiled in *The Futurians* did not, she felt, get around the problem of selective memory. She found that all Futurians had different memories of the same events and people, "and Damon, since he was the author, superimposed his memories, so if people had said something different, he stopped quoting them and put it the way he remembered it" (Rich 1999, 1). That she had never been able to dislodge Knight's mistaken certainty that her original birth name was Juliet, not even for *The Futurians*, was a case in point. It frustrated her, because that particular error became entrenched in the literature, but there was no resentment on Merril's part, only an interesting insight about the fallibility of memories, including her own: "So, I think with any of us who were part of that particular tight circle in which we all invested a lot of emotion and in which there were tremendous stresses — not necessarily in a bad sense: but strong personalities pulling on each other in different ways — that you must not trust any of our memories, including mine" (1).

Merril had begun consulting her old letter files in 1990 in Ottawa right after her visit with Leiber. In her March 1991 open letter to friends and well-wishers, she talks about her papers in Ottawa and their importance to the memoir project: "I went up and sorted out a bunch of stuff; began reading, remembering, writing connective stuff" (March 12, 1991, quoted in Merril and Pohl-Weary 2002, 247). She changed her mind about the project many times, knowing always that she wanted to write "individual pieces equivalent to short stories [...] start[ing] with Theodore Sturgeon" (Jirgens and Francis 1991, 9). Then, in September 1990, she squeezed in more days in Ottawa, sleeping only a few hours a night before returning to Toronto, whereupon she suffered a massive heart attack in October of that year. Several attacks later, Merril underwent a bypass operation in May 1991 that left her in extremely poor health but more determined than ever to write her memoir.

By 1992, Merril was back in the archives and doing "some actual writing, and a bit of editing of old letters" for the memoir project, she told MacLean (May 21, 1992, quoted in Merril and Pohl-Weary 2002, 250), adding that she was focused on writing a sixty-page section in order to apply for a government works-in-progress grant for support. To write the piece, she "shunted aside almost everything else." But once that piece of writing was out of the way, she vowed, the memoir would no longer take precedence over getting her health and living space in order. That meant exercising and making her apartment more comfortable, less cluttered, and suitable for visitors such as MacLean. Merril had been living since about 1990 in a tiny apartment in the Performing Arts Lodge, a lively cooperative housing community in the St. Lawrence Market area of downtown Toronto for retired, but active, members of ACTRA (Alliance of Canadian Cinema, Television and Radio Artists). She qualified as a resident because of her television work in the 1970s.

Merril became fascinated with her old correspondence files — not just with the content but also with the engagement, the exchange, represented by the letters, telling MacLean:

> I have become very envious of my former self, doing all this reading of old correspondence, and of course part of it is because I knew so many great people and DID so much all the time, but a good part as well has been just that the letters themselves — in both directions — were so great, and I got out of the habit [of letter-writing] years ago [June 18, 1992, quoted in Merril and Pohl-Weary 2002, 252].

She wanted MacLean to visit her in Toronto as soon as possible, ostensibly to go over her grant submission for the memoir project. That was in June 1992. The caption for a photo of Merril and MacLean taken at a dinner in Toronto one month later, identified as "during a rare visit" from MacLean (261), demonstrates that she did respond to Merril's (and perhaps her own) need to see an old, dear friend when most of her oldest and dearest friends in the United States and Canada had already died.

Once Merril got started with writing the memoir and began to sense the potential importance of the project, she discovered, not surprisingly, that it would be impossible to generate the memoir on her own. In writing to Kidd, she argued that what she needed now that she was aging, becoming immobilized, and in poor health was a savvy editor — a collaborator — for her memoir: "I want/need an editor/reader on this book who can juggle all the perspectives and keep reminding me of them" (July 24 [in section dated July 26], 1992, quoted in Merril and Pohl-Weary 2002, 259). Kidd, her old roommate and fellow Futurian from the 1940s, editorial assistant in the early 1960s, and literary agent for many decades, who understood "the magical world we lived in forty or fifty years ago, when ideas were as important as dinner, and love could not be readily sliced up into sexual or social" (259), was a perfect match for Merril's needs. And in the old days in New York or Milford, she might have volunteered. But those days were long over. The collaborator Merril got in the end was quite different from what she had imagined, but involving her young granddaughter in the project turned out to be critical, for without Emily Pohl-Weary to pick up where Merril had left off, the project would never have been completed. Before Emily Pohl-Weary, Merril had many helpers who assisted her in sorting out her papers and preparing her curriculum vitae. But Pohl-Weary was the only one who got to have any input regarding the book (Toolis, email message, June 10, 2011).

## *The Many Roles of Emily Pohl-Weary*

The various hats that Pohl-Weary wore throughout the memoir project make any simple definition of her role difficult. Spider Robinson characterizes Pohl-Weary's role as Merril's "unpaid secretary-researcher-ghostwriter-editor" (Robinson 2002, "Review"). "Unpaid secretary" would have been a fair characterization of her role on the project *prior* to Merril's death, though even then Pohl-Weary's position went beyond that because of the indispensable companionship she provided. And certainly her role changed dramatically after 1997, when she had to compile, complete, and publish her grandmother's memoir alone.

While she lived, Merril was in charge of the memoir project. The collaboration with her granddaughter, of whom Merril was proud, for approximately the last four years of Merril's life was both a necessary and a natural approach for an author fascinated with collaboration, the interplay of ideas, and mentorship. Pohl-Weary has openly discussed the intense and prolonged experience of engaging with the book in Merril's final years. She was only twenty years old when she began working with Merril. From interviews with Pohl-Weary, we learn of the changing nature of their relationship: "We were very close during her last four or five years. [...] At the end of her life, when she was unable to get around much, I became her main caregiver, and brought her news of things going on outside her apartment" (Bryson c. 2002, para. 7). Yet, in her separate introduction to Merril's memoir, "Writing My Grandmother's Autobiography," she also hints at dissonance between an idealized grandmother–granddaughter relationship and the reality of their close collaboration: "She wasn't exactly the kind of grandmother every granddaughter dreams of" (Pohl-Weary 2002, 7). Merril lacked restraint in her personal habits, argued, swore, smoked pot, and was mischievous. Yet there was acceptance of this behavior on Pohl-Weary's part — more than acceptance: there was respect. As Pohl-Weary stated in an interview, "She was a crazy old broad. She loved to argue and shock [...] I wouldn't say our relationship was easy — she challenged me at all times — but it was filled with love and she encouraged me to follow my inspirations" (Bryson c. 2002, para. 7).

Although the foundation of the memoir is the letter collection in Ottawa, the tape recordings made by Pohl-Weary were also vital to the process. She says she recorded a dozen tapes of Merril's stories and two additional tapes filled with descriptions of the content that she wanted included in the book (Pohl-Weary 2002, 4). Not surprisingly, Merril proved to be a generous storyteller who talked about her loves as she remembered them, sparing no details (7). But not all stories, and certainly not the most painful ones, were available to Pohl-Weary: the stories of the loves that died in the later part of Merril's life caused feelings that were still too fresh for her to talk about (5). And at least one story was not suitable, in Merril's view, for her granddaughter's ears. The story of her relationship with Miller, which is a heartbreaking chronicle of sexual passion and love lost in the early 1950s, was dictated to a third party at the last possible moment. Pohl-Weary tells us that Merril had been unable to share much of the story of Miller with her, other than bits and pieces, now and then, over dinner or late at night as they sifted through the boxes of old photographs (4). She talked about it to her friend Lorna Toolis only on one occasion. As Toolis recalls, "It was painful even to listen. The very short period of total happiness, followed by an ongoing nightmare. When she lived with Miller, they both wrote — it was love and pure creative endeavor" (email message to Newell, June 10, 2011). It seems that the censorship brought to this potential exposé of Merril's life was in the hands of not only the granddaughter who completed the book but also the grandmother who laid it out, with clear instructions.

## *Public Readings*

As she wrote her connective pieces and sections for submission for a writer's grant, Merril found she now had some stories to read at public events. The actual process of writing the memoir changed her writing practice that of seeking and incorporating potential readers' perceptions of it. Thus, although it was a novel experience for her, she found herself showing pieces of the memoir-in-progress to people, and giving readings to large groups of science fiction fans and writers, as well as others with no connection to science fiction. As tributes and awards began to stack up for Merril after her near-fatal heart attack in 1990—at the Eaton Conference in 1991, where Merril received the annual Milford Award for lifetime achievement in science fiction publishing and editing; at Toronto's Harbourfront International Festival of Authors in 1992, where she received a prestigious "tribute" from a host of international science fiction stars; at Readercon 6, Worcester, Massachusetts, in 1994, where she was the guest of honor; at the Vancouver Writers' Festival, 1995; and at WisCon 20 (the 20th-anniversary meeting of this leading feminist-oriented science fiction convention) at Madison, Wisconsin, in 1996, where she was a special guest and the subject of a panel session, "Judith Merril: Her Impact on Feminist Speculative Fiction"—Merril had numerous opportunities to read parts of her memoir-in-progress. She also received the Author Emeritus Award in recognition of her contributions to science fiction from the Science Fiction and Fantasy Writers of America in 1997, the first female to be so honored, but was too ill to take up her invitation to speak at the Nebula Awards weekend (Bailey 2003, 13). She found that young people in her audiences were discovering through her work that what the Futurians did in the science fiction "ghetto" was significant, and they viewed Merril as an important resource in achieving that understanding. There was audience interest in the social movements in which Merril had been involved, which served to put her in touch with her activist side.

At the public readings, Merril also discovered that women wanted to know what it was like being a "gender-bender" in "a man's world" (2002, "Transformations," 11). She had already been alerted to the gender-role element of her life around 1993, when she wrote to Kidd that she was getting interest in her memoir from publishers and from readings she gave, the tributes she attended, and the "non–SF" women she talked to; in fact, she had begun to believe, encouraged by her audiences, that she had been a feminist role model in science fiction after all, after years of denial (July 26, 1993, quoted in Merril and Pohl-Weary 2002, 259). A draft of the chapter of her memoir on Sturgeon was also read by Merril at WisCon 20 and reprinted posthumously in the Helen Merrick and Tess Williams edited collection, *Women of Other Worlds: Excursions through Science Fiction and Feminism* (Merril 1999). She loved being around the WisCon crowd and she even reestablished relations with Joanna Russ (Toolis, email message to Newell, June 10, 2011).

It is difficult to know how much of the subsequent content of Merril's memoir was shaped by the deliberate dialogue she struck up with her audiences. The fact that she sought and discussed that interaction and criticism from her target readership before her work was complete is an important facet of her autobiographical practice. She had been, after all, one of the early promoters and directors of science fiction writers' workshops, which were all about exposing one's unpublished work to close scrutiny. In England, Japan, and Canada, Merril had embraced the role of catalyst, so it only makes sense that the memoir-in-progress was proving to be inspirational for her audiences and critical to her own understanding of her life and the impact of her earlier writing.

## "Writing My Grandmother's Autobiography"

Merril notes in her introduction to *Better to Have Loved*: "Editors are paid (however poorly) to deal with writers' obsessions" ("Transformations," 12). Although she would be speaking from her vast editorial experience, she might as well have been addressing Pohl-Weary's job in compiling, completing, and publishing the memoir, working off and on for three years after Merril's death in the fall of 1997. Merril was a hugely gifted editor, but by this time her strength had run very low. In practical terms, as Pohl-Weary stresses in her introduction to the book, Merril had left a detailed outline, a partially completed manuscript, and thorough instructions, including the two full tapes of directions, about the way the memoir should be built, and all the materials she wanted to be included. Pohl-Weary also had, of course, dozens of her own taped interviews with Merril from which to draw details and narrative. She was now a true collaborator, as Newell and Tallentire have explored in detail (2005a), having to make important choices, including finding a publisher. And she was also a (modestly) paid collaborator, for Merril had left her a small sum to carry on the work (Pohl-Weary, interviewed by Newell, January 2004).

Clearly, Pohl-Weary struggled to include what she could of Merril — to be, in essence, a portal or window into Merril's consciousness — within her compilation of the text; it was a process that was emotionally charged and highly personal: "At first, it was difficult to be surrounded by her voice and thoughts, because I missed and also had some mixed feelings toward her, due to unresolved family dynamics, but it got easier as time passed" (Bryson c. 2002, para. 4). Pohl-Weary also took personal responsibility for inclusions and omissions in the text. She acknowledges her concern about omissions by adding a chapter, "Growing Old in the 1990s: Dear Friends," that reprinted a selection of recent letters "to [Merril's] best loved and not-yet-lost friends" (MacLean, Kidd, and Valerie Alia) and open letters to friends and well-wishers, in order to cover the last years of Merril's life (Pohl-Weary 2002, 6). Pohl-Weary told Newell in an interview in 2004 that she also hoped that by appending to the memoir dozens of mini-biographies she researched and wrote, titling the piece "Some of the People in Judith Merril's Life," she had helped to address the remaining omissions. Nevertheless, her introduction includes a general apology to those she left out (7).

Pohl-Weary worked from the materials selected by Merril: she told Newell in 2004 that she did not visit, nor was she familiar with the contents of, the Merril papers in Ottawa. And, according to her introduction to the memoir, she tried to plug into her subject and thereby avoid inserting herself in the text. Pohl-Weary's separate introduction is the only place where she speaks in her own voice. Nevertheless, as revealed in an interview with Justine Larbalestier, Pohl-Weary clearly had serious editorial and moral decisions to wrestle with, including the need to preserve her own identity:

> My role of the sewer-together and filler-inner of text was like walking a tightrope. I had to make decisions that balanced being true to Judy and feeling comfortable with the fact that many people will believe that I agree with her version of events [Larbalestier 2003, 122].

But she also wanted to protect the people she loved and respected:

> After she died I found myself making tough choices about whether to censor her stories, however slightly, for the sake of people I love and respect dearly. At a certain point I realized that Judy's ghost would not strike me dead, and I chose to walk the diplomatic line of middle ground [Pohl-Weary 2002, 7].

Apparently, achieving this middle ground involved the cutting of portions of some essays and letters from the text rather than editing the narratives Merril had already written or commissioning biographical essays from Merril's friends, the latter idea being something she toyed with and rejected in favor of sticking to Merril's blueprint for the book (Pohl-Weary, interviewed by Newell, January 2004). She was a strong-minded person in her own right but well aware that her task was to deliver approximately what Merril wanted and what other members of the family would tolerate rather than using her own creative authority in the final product.

## *Better to Have Loved*

Upon publication, the memoir was negatively criticized because of its fragmented, untraditional format. We argue that this criticism, which we shall map out in greater detail, is based on expectations of canonical autobiographies that marginalize women's life writing, as has been well documented by Sidonie Smith and Julia Watson, among others. For example, canonical biographies in Western culture tend to follow a teleological narrative of self-realization consistent with the ideology of individualism (Friedman 1998, 72); by this measure, Merril's memoir certainly is, as one critic puts it, a "mess." Using the more flexible term "memoir" did not spare Merril and Pohl-Weary criticism of the memoir as being "frustrating" and "fragmented." However, in light of feminist theories about life writing arguing that normative definitions of the autobiography privilege a male-centered model of subjectivity and narrative form, this "mess" can be read quite differently, and more positively, as an alternative form built on a different model of subjectivity than that of the traditional autobiography.

Whereas traditional autobiographical narrative represents the gradual unfolding of a fully realized, independent self (something not available to women in the West until very recently) (Benstock 1998, 152), scholars of women's life writing point out that women writers privilege a relational and communal self, resist seamless narrative cohesion, and foreground such problematics of life writing as memory and ideology. "The whole point of such works [as *The Autobiography of Thomas Jefferson* and *The Education of Henry Adams*] is to seal up and cover over gaps in memory, dislocations in time and space, insecurities, hesitations, and blind spots," Shari Benstock writes (1998, 152), whereas "[t]he self that would reside at the center of the text is decentered — and often is absent altogether — in women's autobiographical texts" (151). However difficult it may be to posit a separate, feminine category of subjectivity and autobiographical form (Stanton 1998, 137), the critical reception of Merril's memoir clearly would have benefited from reviewers better versed in, and open to, alternative forms of life writing. Reading the memoir in light of theoretical work by the likes of Smith and Watson, Benstock, and Stanton reveals a carefully mapped out and highly sophisticated example of alternative autobiographical form. Assembled from prose written especially for the memoir, as well as letters, transcriptions of interviews, and previous writings (fiction and nonfiction, published and unpublished), this "mess" of different forms and discourses is no less representative of the reality of Merril's "life" than the most seamless and coherent of autobiographical narratives.

As Susan Stanford Friedman (1998) points out, the highly individuated self characteristic of traditional autobiography is itself an ideologically charged form that tends to exclude the relational models of self associated with women in their roles as mothers and wives. Although by no means a stereotypical domestic woman, Merril saw herself as profoundly relational, and Pohl-Weary was careful to follow this model of selfhood as she completed the memoir after her grandmother's death. Merril's very title for the memoir, *Better to Have Loved*, stresses interdependence of self and other, a model she applied to all of her significant relationships, sexual or otherwise.

As Pohl-Weary completed the memoir, she followed an explicit and detailed outline left by Merril, in which the chronological narration of her life story is interwoven with chapters that focus on significant friends, fellow writers, and lovers in Merril's life. To inscribe these relationships, Pohl-Weary used Merril's selections from her own correspondence files — not simply as a measure of last resort after Merril's death but also as a means of carrying out Merril's plan to structure the autobiography according to her conviction that the memory of the retrospective, or "writing," self could not be trusted to truthfully remember events "as they were":

> Going through these old letters, I was first startled, then bemused, to discover time and again how my memory corrects my life — not substantively, not in major ways, but almost exactly as one revises a carefully crafted piece of fiction — adding telling detail, pinpointing motivations, adjusting the view and the time flow to enhance emotional rhythms — making it all more believable [Merril and Pohl-Weary 2002, 69].

By allowing Merril's existing correspondence and previously written nonfiction to tell significant parts of the story, Merril and Pohl-Weary represent a multidimensional self that cannot be understood in isolation from the many interlocutors and discourses that enable the self to come into existence. Rather than partitioning Merril's writing self from other facets of her life, as Merril had observed in autobiographies by male Futurians, Merril and Pohl-Weary construct Merril's multidimensional self as wife, mother, writer, lover, friend, activist — even cat-sitter — and demonstrate how inextricably intertwined were these different modalities of self. Doing so represents an aspect of Futurian history excluded from other autobiographies that isolate the professional writing self from the body, the domestic sphere, and mundane and practical matters of everyday life.

## *Memoir of Letters*

As an example of this multidimensionality, Merril's correspondence with Virginia Kidd sheds a rare light not only on the experience of women in the science fiction field during its "golden age" but also on the crucial role played by Merril and Kidd (and no doubt many more women), who took on roles as both writers and facilitators of the broader science fiction community — in Merril and Kidd's case, this role took shape through the weekly dinners they hosted for the Futurians at the apartment the two women shared toward the end of World War II. Their correspondence conveys an intimacy between the two women, both Futurians and mothers whose husbands were away at war, which developed almost immediately upon their first meeting in October 1944. Kidd's letter of January 30, 1945, reminds Merril of this first meeting and asks "to talk to you alone. That sounds like Secrets, doesn't it? Not though. Bring your offspring, of course. I have enough toys here, I think, to keep him or her happy" (quoted in Merril and Pohl-Weary 2002, 50). Merril's reply of the next day arranges to see Kidd at an upcoming Futurian function: "I'm already beginning to feel a tickling temptation to confuse and confound Futuria by greeting with something sweet and feminine like, 'Darling, did the baby get over that colic you wrote me about?'" (50). This exchange offers a rare glimpse of how Futurian discourse marginalized mothering, creating the basis for the almost-immediate friendship between Merril and Kidd as a space in which both women's identities as mothers and science fiction writers could coexist.

As a young writer, Merril regarded her involvement in a larger community of writers as integral to her own development. When she was not socializing with other writers, she was corresponding with them. The particularly prolific exchange between Merril and Clifton beginning in 1952 is a strong case in point. Merril explains in her memoir that she first wrote to Clifton on June 10 after reading two of his stories and being struck by their quality and overlap with her own preoccupations with psychology and ESP (144). The correspondence excerpted for the memoir is mainly Clifton's, articulating his ideas about ESP and his frustration with the reluctance of science fiction editors to take ESP seriously. A Clifton letter from August 20 states, "[John Campbell] has such a long, LONG way to go before he would consider some of the things you and I say as being more than drivel" (151). Clifton's reference to Merril as a confidante on these matters is repeated throughout the excerpted correspondence and offers a glimpse of the complex, intersubjective relations that structured both Merril's subjectivity and science fiction discourse more broadly. Even in a literary field that regarded itself as the most open and progressive of its time, margins existed that become visible to us through the Merril-Clifton correspondence as they find in each other a sounding board that does not exist in the broader science fiction community. The choice to include this particular correspondence thread in the memoir contributes to a recovery of the complex politics that structured the science fiction field in the 1950s, largely absent from other Futurian memoirs.

Interestingly, the one time Merril and Clifton met in person, at the Thirteenth World Science Fiction Convention in Cleveland (Clevention) in 1955, Merril and Pohl-Weary write retrospectively that "some curious inverse chemistry sent each of us away with a sorely wounded sense of rejection by the other" (148), putting a temporary end to their correspondence. While we can only speculate on why their relationship did not extend beyond its epistolary form, the Merril-Clifton correspondence demonstrates the multidimensional structure of the American science fiction community and the importance of correspondence as a means for writers to discourse on marginalized topics within the field.

## Memoir of Loss

Among the most painful chapters in the memoir is that about Merril's affair with Walter Miller, which played out amid very ugly custody battles with her first two husbands and ultimately ended when Miller's wife wouldn't give him a divorce and threatened suicide if he left. In keeping with her conviction that "almost all [of my] relationships and objectives have combined literary, political, and personal intensities, inextricably interwoven" (Merril 2002, "Transformations," 9), the memoir devotes a chapter to "Walter Miller and the Custody Battles" at what must have been considerable emotional cost: Merril was not able to tell the story until only days before her death, and even then, she could not do the interview with Emily Pohl-Weary, whose mother, Ann, had been a subject of one of the two custody suits. It was for that reason that Merril enlisted a member of the local Toronto theater community to conduct the interview.

The chapter is an example of the lengths Merril was prepared to go to address the erasures that she saw in the autobiographies of her male peers:

> I was snow-blinded by the bleach in the detergent. Here were lists of stories sold, banquets attended, speeches given, editors lunched, even wives married and divorced, with never a shriek or tear or tremor or orgasm, and hardly a belly laugh anywhere [Merril 2002, "Transformations," 10].

The resulting narrative is, however, matter-of-fact in style despite, or perhaps because of, the intense emotion associated with the events. The custody battles began not long after Merril and Miller had moved in together: Dan Zissman and Frederik Pohl colluded to sue for custody of their respective children. First, Zissman hired a detective to gather evidence that Judith was living with Miller as his wife. Shortly thereafter, Zissman and a sheriff seized Dan and Judith's daughter Merril from school without forewarning. A subsequent custody hearing awarded custody of their daughter to Zissman, and Judith then learned of Pohl's plan to capitalize on Zissman's victory and sue for custody of Ann. Her colleague James Blish testified against her, an act she never forgave. And the pain when she talked to Toolis in the 1990s about losing her daughters was "still alive and very sharp" (email message to Newell, June 10, 2011). Meanwhile, Miller returned to his ailing wife, who was having second thoughts about their divorce, a move that would prove to be the end of his relationship with Merril. Throughout, Merril struggled to make financial ends meet with her writing. However dramatically these events may have actually played out (at one point, Miller pointed an unloaded rifle at Pohl), the narrative is relatively restrained, tending to narrate events but only hint at emotional states, as, for example, in the chapter's understated concluding sentences:

Walt died [January 1996] about a year and a half before I sat down to tell this story. It always startled me that there was no longer any chance of seeing him again. However, it may have been even more of a blow to find out that his wife had died six months before he did and he made no attempt to see me [Merril and Pohl-Weary 2002, 142].

As the memoir progresses chronologically through the various phases of Merril's life, from her youth through her writing and editorial career, her emigration to Canada, the relationships she developed in the Canadian arts community, and so on, the theme of loss, alluded to in the title *Better to Have Loved*, becomes more palpable, particularly as the memoir relates the deaths of Merril's close friends, both old (Fritz Leiber) and new (the Canadian writer Marian Engel), and her own worsening health. This, too, is a narrative arc that departs from canonical autobiographical form — specifically, the teleological narrative that culminates in the retrospective narrator's fully realized self (Friedman 1998, 76). By contrast, Merril's memoir emphasizes the accumulation of loss over time.

The very title *Better to Have Loved* also registers loss as an overarching theme, for it is the inevitable cost of loving. In the chapter "The Crazies Are Dying," originally published in Toronto's *Now Books* in 1986, Merril memorializes her late friend, the Canadian poet Milton Acorn, whose recent death had been the latest in a growing list of recent losses Merril was grieving at the time, including Ted Sturgeon and the Canadian writers Robert Zend and Elizabeth Smart: "Well, hell, I know I'm not the only one left, but we seem to be an endangered species [...] and every time another one dies there's that much more crazed the rest of us have to be. And it's really hard to be the right kind of Crazy when you're crying" (Merril and Pohl-Weary 2002, 238). The chapter "Growing Old in the 1990s: Dear Friends" narrates Merril's later years, during which her health declined rapidly, confining her for the most part to her apartment. Letters exchanged with MacLean and Kidd, two of Merril's oldest friends from her early career as a science fiction writer, are permeated by a sense of the impending loss of these surviving intimacies: "I don't know if I will ever actually walk in your woods," Merril wrote to MacLean in 1992 (253). To Kidd, she wrote in 1993 of "[g]rowing old, approaching death, accepting limitations, above all surviving the deaths of friends/lovers/network[s]" (259). The memoir's later chapters simultaneously reminisce about and reassess Merril's early years in the science fiction field and her cumulative impact: "I also hear testimony [...] that it was reading my work/anthologies in the fifties that made [women] realize that they could write/expect to read stuff that included them in sf" (259).

In the chapter "Future Improbable," which Merril had insisted should end the book and Pohl-Weary reluctantly included (Pohl-Weary 2002, 6),

Merril had become pessimistic about Toronto; in the new politically conservative climate of her final year of life, Merril was beginning to feel about the city the way she felt about the United States when she left it in 1968, only this time, "there's no place left for me to go" (264). It is clear, however, that the losses Merril suffered in her later years were commensurate with — and the price that she had to eventually pay for — the incredible richness of the life she had lived.

## Reception of the Work

The reception of Merril's memoir is multivaried and fascinating to observe (Newell and Tallentire 2007, 8–10, and 2005a, 19–20). *Better to Have Loved* was lauded by Carol Cooper (2002) of the *Village Voice* as "a gleefully unsanitized" memoir giving "the trench-level perspective of the artist-practitioner." And the Toronto *National Post*'s reviewer Jeet Heer seems to have understood Merril's point that the memoir was a deliberate departure from the life writing of the New York Futurians:

> Futurian memoirists have almost invariably whitewashed both their politics and sex lives. By writing about their younger selves with breezy irony, they minimize their tangled emotional and intellectual histories. Their autobiographies feel as though they were written in the third person. [Merril] [...] does not engage in this sort of retrospective distancing [Heer 2002].

Asta Sinusas's (2002) review for *SFRevu* finds it "an important record in the history of sf" and hopes that the Merril letters informing the work are eventually published as well.

For reviewers familiar with Merril's previous writing, however, the book was disappointing. Toolis suggests why: "They were hoping not only for Judith's view of the sf community's history, but her unmatched gift for analysis. Because, while it was applied structurally, it wasn't actually on the page [and] everyone wanted more Judy, and Judy not to be gone" (email message to Newell, June 9, 2011). Elisabeth Carey's review (2002) concluded that it was "[a]n interesting but frustrating book" that left out too much about Merril's later life. Spider Robinson (2002) recalled Merril's memoir-in-progress (before Pohl-Weary's editing) as "a jumbled heap of bright shards." Another reviewer called the book "the mess we always thought it would be" (Clute 2003, 372). Terms such as "shards and fragments" (Heer 2002), "mess," and "series of stabs" (Clute, 372) were raised in most of the reviews consulted. According to Robinson (2002), Merril's erratic approach to writing was "perfectly typical" of her: "Her particular genius was coming up with splendid ideas, then finding someone else to do the actual grunt work, and wandering off"—"wandering off" in this case meant dying. Cooper's reading of the memoir, however, found the shards and fragments to be a strength of the work, something particularly fitting for a memoir in science fiction. Unlike other autobiographical writing in science fiction, she writes, Merril's memoir focuses on "the huge amount of paraliterature" (private letters, previously published and unpublished essays, cover art, snapshots, convention speeches, taped interviews) that necessarily flows from a life in science fiction, a genre that is remarkably interactive, generating creative input and feedback (Cooper 2002).

The credit for the narrative coherence sought by all these readers is given to Merril's co-author. According to Robinson (2002), "Like so many of Merril's past victims, Pohl-Weary [...] has responded magnificently, managing to turn the jumble-sale she inherited into a clear, accurate and balanced representation of one of the most remarkable women in Canadian letters." Critics such as Paul Di Filippo (2003) agree: "Emily Pohl-Weary [...] has done a superhuman job and deserves immense credit" for producing a memoir that "ranks with Damon Knight's *The Futurians*." What exactly did the reviewers identify *as* Pohl-Weary's job? Answer: "editor" (Cooper), "chronicler" and "salvage[r]" (Clements 2002), "assembler" (Di Filippo), and "biographer" (Hawkins 2003). Many of them considered her contribution to be somewhat unfortunate, because she produced a memoir that was postmortem and co-authored, and hence assumed to be incomplete.

Some reviewers identified particular drawbacks to Pohl-Weary's involvement. In her review for *Extrapolation*, Hawkins (2003, 126) figures that the combination of Pohl-Weary's devotion to her grandmother and her wish to protect the living members of her family whom she loves and respects from potential hurt ultimately "cast an uncomfortable shadow over the material." Clements (2002) spells out the nature of that "shadow," suggesting that Merril left her granddaughter "to salvage this book from her notes [...] cutting some of her juicier revelations" and leaving "little of the true Merril to work with." Another reviewer assumed that the notes Pohl-Weary worked with would have been Merril's typical "casually slap-dash" jottings, and therefore rather useless to begin with (Webster 2010). One article contrasts the memoir with the "real" autobiographical writing produced by Futurians: "Perhaps if Merril could have lived to complete her memoirs, they could have rivaled Isaac Asimov's *In Memory Yet Green* and *In Joy Still Felt*" (Clements 2002), which misses Merril's point about Futurian autobiographies being something she wanted to counteract. John Clute (2003) laments simply, "I want more. I wish [Judy] had written the real *Better to Have Loved*."

## Gesturing Toward the Recovery of Merril

Following the publication of the memoir, Elizabeth Cummins (2006) compiled a complete, eighty-one-page, annotated bibliography and guide to Merril's work, and Elisabeth Carey published both the complete sole-authored works of Merril (*Homecalling and Other Stories* [2005]) and, in a separate volume, one of Merril's sole-authored novels (*Shadow on the Hearth*), as well as both of her collaborative novels with Cyril Kornbluth, (*Outpost Mars* and *Gunner Cade*) as *Spaced Out: Three Novels of Tomorrow* (Merril and Kornbluth 2008). With the collection of solo short fiction, Carey hoped to shine a spotlight on Merril's innovative contributions to the genre: an old collection of Merril's stories that she possessed as a young person entering her teens had a great impact on Carey, but later she discovered that none of Merril's fiction remained in print and libraries in her city no longer carried it: "That seemed wrong. I wanted those stories to be available to the next book-devouring preteen who's exhausted the resources of the children's room, and has wheedled or conned the librarian into letting them look for something a little more ambitious, or just new and different" (Carey 2005, 5). In a tribute similar to Carey's, Gene van Troyer and Grania Davis recently edited an English-language anthology of Japanese science fiction and fantasy stories and essays, *Speculative Japan* (2007), dedicated in part to Merril for her initiation of the Japanese SF translation project and her influence on the founding of the Japanese translators' group, Honyaku Benkyo-kai. The "speculative" of the title honors Merril's preference for the term speculative fiction over science fiction (Davis 2007, 2). Above all, Merril and her co-author Emily Pohl-Weary received the ultimate tribute from the international science fiction community: the 2003 Hugo Award for Best Related Book.

For Pohl-Weary, both the project and the inspired relationship with her grandmother afforded rewards that extended well beyond the Hugo Award and the personal insights into her family and herself. She notes in an interview conducted after the book came out that Merril had encouraged her to write and the memoir project equipped her to tackle writing a novel of her own; she explains that she came to "love feeling the solitary pull of being completely absorbed in writing" (Larbalestier 2003, 124). Pohl-Weary's own publications and her community-based projects are detailed on her personal website (http://emilypohlweary.com/).

Emily Pohl-Weary published her first novel, a ghost story called *A Girl Like Sugar*, in 2004. She has also edited an anthology, *Girls Who Bite Back: Witches, Mutants, Slayers and Freaks* (2004). A community activist who conducts writers' workshops for schools, libraries, and community agencies and shelters, Pohl-Weary founded in 2008 a street writers' workshop for at-risk youth in the Toronto neighborhood where she grew up. Perhaps the collaboration on the memoir was Merril's final legacy as a writer, editor, catalyst, activist, and immigrant. Possibly Merril knew exactly what she was doing in bringing Emily into this project — encouraging her granddaughter's life as a writer and mentor just as she had encouraged the careers of so many others in the science fiction community and beyond for over half a century.

Merril's memoir is an important contribution to women's life writing generally and science fiction life writing more specifically. As a cross-generational collaboration of sorts between Merril and Pohl-Weary, it productively tests the boundaries between biography and autobiography, opening up new ways of representing self that do not depend on binary distinctions between self and other. Instead, Merril's self is represented as profoundly relational, in keeping with Judith Butler's conception of identity as ever-shifting and in flux.

The memoir is also a crucial addition to the emerging literary history of American science fiction of the 1940s through the 1960s, a period that saw the genre shift from a marginal sub-culture to a more prestigious literary field. Until the appearance of Merril's memoir, Merril and other women were being gradually erased from the emergent history of this period in science fiction. Merril's memoir makes the depth of their lives and contributions difficult to continue to ignore.

# Epilogue

## The Future of Judith Merril

Judith Merril was among the most innovative women writers of science fiction in the 1950s. Throughout the 1960s, her anthologies and book review columns were the gold standard of American science fiction: authors clamored to be included in them, and they were widely read and acclaimed. From the 1970s to her death in 1997, she remained active in Canadian science fiction through the library of science fiction she founded and also through conferences, essay writing, lecturing, anthologizing, and television and radio work, and political activism. Wherever she went, she made her presence felt, sometimes rubbing people the wrong way. Even her own admiring granddaughter, Emily Pohl-Weary, remembered Merril in her last years as being difficult and trying at times (Pohl-Weary 2002, 7). The Japanese translators with whom she worked called her "Kaibutsu Baasan," roughly translated as "monster grandma" (or, as Grania Davis relates in "Judy-san" [2007, 1], "the demon-grandmother of Japanese science fiction"). The label is a sign of respect (grandmothers are highly esteemed in Japanese culture, and the word "monster" can stand in for science fiction), intermixed with the love for and frustration with Merril that Japanese translators and writers experienced while working with her in the 1970s. Tributes to her published shortly after her death describe her, albeit fondly, as pushy, blunt, even uncouth. "She was probably the laziest person I ever encountered," wrote Michael Moorcock. "She trashed hotel rooms, she embarrassed me in public, she had no judgment where a pretty face was concerned and she became half-involved in intrigues she barely understood — in languages she didn't speak" (1998, 4). Both Michael Moorcock and Spider Robinson lauded her as a liberated woman, sexually and professionally, before the term "women's lib" existed. Like many of her male colleagues in science fiction, they talk about her lustfulness, something that does not usually come up in writings about the men.

And yet this woman, who was impossible to ignore in life, is at risk of erasure from literary history. As scholarship on North American science fiction comes to terms with the enormous developments in the field since its first "boom" in the 1930s, and especially with the role of the Futurians, among whom she got her start, Judith Merril's contributions are routinely passed over (exceptions include Cummins, Larbalestier, Seed, Yaszek and Willis), while the work of her contemporaries — Asimov, Pohl, Leiber, Kornbluth, and others — continues to dominate our understanding of the period. Merril's marginal stature in current scholarship does not come close to representing her overwhelming presence in the inner circles of science fiction throughout the 1950s and 1960s. So what has happened to Judith Merril's memory?

Clues are suggested by the tributes to her from Moorcock and Robinson that we have mentioned. As fond and humorous as they are, they focus almost exclusively on Merril's character, personal exploits, and her penchant for initiating things, then leaving; these writers say little about her work (except, perhaps, to highlight missed deadlines and unfinished projects, not the hundreds that she completed — often brilliantly). But surely, Merril was not the only one bucking convention in a literary field on the fringes of American culture and society? And she was by no means the only creative person to contribute something original to a community and then move on, expecting others to clean up. "Perhaps since she was a woman," says her long-time friend and confidante at the Merril Collection, Lorna Toolis, "the men kept expecting her to do the cleaning up" (email message to Newell, June 10, 2011). Why, then, is Merril remembered primarily for her exploits and eccentricities, when she is remembered at all, while equally "colorful" science fiction authors (Harlan Ellison comes to mind) remain well known as authors — eccentricities, controversies, insobriety, and other shortcomings aside? To some extent, this is a classic case of what Joanna Russ was addressing in *How to Supress Women's Writing* (1983). Although Russ outlined the ways in which denying the legacy of earlier women writers makes the women authors and works that we always hear and read about seem anomalous (Ursula K. Le Guin is a prime example), Russ's own critical work in the 1970s vis-à-vis the creation of a distinctly feminist science fiction literary canon played a strong role in erasing Merril and other female science fiction writers of the 1950s, who wrote science fiction set in a place called "galactic suburbia," a concept introduced by Russ (1971a) in the first place (Yaszek 2008, 3–4; 2009).

In this book, we have attempted to undo the process of erasure that has wrongly relegated Judith Merril to near-footnote status in science fiction literature. We do not believe that this erasure is deliberate on the part of any particular person or group. But it demonstrates that the processes that have excluded previous generations of women writers from literary history are ongoing. At the time of this writing, Merril has been dead for less than fifteen years, and already few students and readers new to science fiction know her name, much less the role she played in shaping the genre they now study and read. And this is true even in Canada, where a world-class science fiction library bears her name. Merril's body of fiction is relatively small, but the issue of reputation is not just about quantity. To be remembered, writers need to be reprinted, reread, anthologized, studied; included in encyclopedias, "key figures" volumes, memoirs, and histories; discussed at conferences, and so on. Whether we realize it or not, the role of critics and scholars in the myriad inclusions and exclusions that constitute literary history will bear the influence of our blind spots and assumptions.

Merril herself once told an interviewer that she wanted to be remembered mainly for her fiction, but, she continued, "I have a suspicion that is not the way most people think of me" (Mermelstein 1985, 8). Although this book is intended to be an account of all of Merril's contributions to science fiction, a particular goal is to draw attention to the full body of her fiction, which, we argue, was groundbreaking for its time. Merril treated the psychological and social sciences as sites of futuristic speculation. Well before science fiction came under the purview of second-wave feminism in the early 1970s, she called into question the assumption that gender was eternal, representing it as a technology subject to human intervention and adaptation to new social conditions. Nor did she characterize space exploration in the patriarchal terms that dominated science fiction of the 1950s and 1960s. While the lone male adventurer was ubiquitous in the science fiction of her day, Merril was one of the first writers to routinely place women and their everyday lives at the center of her stories — women who were not exoticized or eroticized, but rather were fully individuated participants in future scenerios. A case in point is her exploration of the subject of sex in her science fiction writing at a time when that was an unorthodox choice. Debate about whether sex belonged in science fiction was active into the early 1960s, when Merril's new story collection *Out of Bounds* and her novel *The Tomorrow People* were singled out by one reviewer as the best examples of how sex could be handled "maturely, casually, and incidentally to a story of the problems of real people in a real science-fictional situation" (P. Schuyler Miller 1961, cited in Larbalestier 2002a, 139). Yet Merril had been addressing this topic since the mid–1950s, looking, for example, at unwed motherhood in the context of colonizating of Mars ("Project Nursemaid"), alien narrators who visit Earth and have to cope with a sexually-charged atmosphere while confronting the sexual double standard and their own sexual feelings ("Rain Check" and "Exile from Space"), and a male character on a cargo spaceship confounded and threatened by the sexual autonomy of the single female on board, a medic who, in attending to the physical and mental needs of the male crew, dishes out medicinal sex ("The Lady Was a Tramp").

Merril was more self-conscious than most of her contemporaries about the relationship between science fiction and American frontier expansion. In works such as "Daughters of Earth," "Shrine of Temptation," and "Homecalling," to name but a few, she delved into the point of view of the colonized subject in order to speculate about potentially different forms of perception and consciousness. To represent space exploration dialogically, from the point of view of both colonizers and colonized, was to question American imperialism in both its past and potential iterations. Merril's complex vision of human-alien relations on the space frontier was deeply connected to her view that science fiction must engage with the social and political present; rather than legitimize American imperialism by projecting its myths of "discovery" and "progress" into the future, she represented space explorers whose perception was limited and fallible, and space aliens whose subjectivity was complex and difficult to categorize. Similarly, her early fiction exploring the topic of the atomic frontier was highly innovative in its departure from male-centric narratives of atomic energy as feminized nature that had to be controlled. Instead, in works such as *Shadow on the Hearth* and "That Only a Mother," Merril imagined how individual women, ordinary families, and everyday life might be affected by the deadly consequences of atomic testing and warfare. Her interest in the cycles of everyday life in these and other stories situates her fiction in the tradition of pioneer women's diary-writing, which offers us a different version of the frontier myth from that of the male-authored tradition.

Experimentation with form and language, she believed, was also integral to the project of speculative fiction. Stories such as "The Lonely," "Daughters of Earth," and "The Shrine of Temptation" engaged a pastiche of narrative forms — diary, memoir, memo, letters, field notes, transcriptions, and even (as in her story "Death Is the Penalty") a guided tour narration — in ways that foregrounded the role of subjectivity and language in shaping consciousness and perception, turning the speculative gaze inward upon itself as often as upon the external world. Experimentation with the narrative point of view was key to her exploration of telepathy and psychology in stories such as "Peeping Tom" and "Connection Completed," in which male and female characters use telepathy to challenge the social barriers that divide them. These and other stories, such as "Homecalling," enact Merril's conviction that good science fiction must scrutinize the very language it uses to structure and describe the reality from which its speculations originate.

In a literary culture that privileges the individual author, Merril's relatively small oeuvre of individually authored fiction might explain why she has been relegated to minor status. However, when her extensive collaborative work, including the anthologies, is taken into account, her contribution to science fiction multiplies exponentially. As Cyril Judd, she and Kornbluth introduced in *Outpost Mars* a domestic orientation to the well-established genre of the male-colonization story, and within the male-centered paradigm of *Gunner Cade*, patriarchal ideology is represented in all its complexity. Her efforts at collaborative and "quasi-collaborative" writing, and occasional writing under a pseudonym, allowed Merril to experiment with her very identity as an author, although she did not consider such work to be "real" writing in the same sense as her solo efforts under her usual name. She was, however, a collaborator by nature as well as a catalyst. This is evidenced not only in her association with the Futurians and life-long interest in other writers and founding associations of writers, but also in her celebrated anthologies — twenty of them published between 1950 and 1985 — and her radio and television work and Japanese translation projects. Her co-authored memoir *Better to Have Loved* was perhaps her most unusual and innovative collaborative venture. Although it was controversial when published posthumously in 2002, it did, among other things, help to recover Merril's reputation, for a while.

While we have spoken here of Merril being at risk of erasure from literary history, it is clear that she has been written about positively at times over the past few decades, especially around the time of her heart attack in the early 1990s and her death in 1997, and also when the memoir was published posthumously in 2002. She is from time to time remembered as having been a central and socially motivating force in modern science fiction, mostly by virtue of her anthologies. New light has also been recently cast on a few of her earliest works of fiction, notably "That Only a Mother" and *Shadow on the Hearth*. By providing this first comprehensive account and critical evaluation of her full body of fiction, in addition to recounting her many achievements — in and out of the United States — as an editor, critic, translator, broadcaster, catalyst, and memoirist (which we argue, are connected to her approach to fiction writing), we hope to ensure that Judith Merril, and her innovation, activism, and the professional standards and literary qualities she promoted, will have a role to play in shaping the future of science fiction.

# Bibliography

## Judith Merril Sources

### 1940s

Merril, Judith. 1948. "That Only a Mother." *Astounding Science Fiction* 41 (4): 88–95.
———. 1949. "Death Is the Penalty." *Astounding Science Fiction* 42 (5): 56–64.

### 1950s

Merril, Judith. 1950. "Barrier of Dread." *Future Combined with Science Fiction Stories* 1 (2): 72–81.
———. 1950. *Shadow on the Hearth*. Garden City, NY: Doubleday.
———, ed. 1950. *Shot in the Dark*. New York: Bantam.
———. 1951. "Survival Ship." *Worlds Beyond* 1 (2): 59–67.
———, ed. 1952. *Beyond Human Ken*. New York: Random House.
———. 1952. "Daughters of Earth." In *The Petrified Planet*. Twayne Science Fiction Triplet No. 1, 198–263. New York: Twayne.
———. 1952. "Hero's Way." *Space Science Fiction* 1 (3): 108–17.
———. 1952. "Whoever You Are." *Startling Stories* 28 (2): 62–78.
———. 1953. "A Little Knowledge." *Science Fiction Quarterly* 1 (2): 83–94.
———. 1953. "So Proudly We Hail." In *Star Science-Fiction Stories*, edited by Frederik Pohl, 117–34. New York: Ballantine.
———, ed. 1954. *Beyond the Barriers of Space and Time*. New York: Random House.
———. 1954. "Connection Completed." In *Universe Science Fiction* 8:41–50.
———. 1954. "Dead Center." *Magazine of Fantasy and Science Fiction* 7 (5): 3–25.
———. 1954. "Editor's Preface." In *Beyond the Barriers of Space and Time*, edited by Judith Merril, xiii–xv. New York: Random House.
———, ed. 1954. *Human?* New York: Lion.
———. 1954. "Peeping Tom." *Startling Stories* 31 (3): 102–16.
———. 1954. "Rain Check." *Science Fiction Adventures* 2 (3): 126–45.
———. 1954. "Stormy Weather." *Startling Stories* 32 (1): 76–88.
———, ed. 1955. *Galaxy of Ghouls*. New York: Lion.
———. 1955. "Pioneer Stock." *Fantastic Universe Science Fiction* 2 (6): 102–12.
———. 1955. "Project Nursemaid." *Magazine of Fantasy and Science Fiction* 9 (4): 3–74.

_____. 1956. "Exile from Space." *Fantastic Universe Science Fiction* 6 (4): 4–34.
_____. 1956. "Homecalling." *Original Science Fiction Stories* 7 (3): 2–88.
_____, ed. 1956. *S-F: The Year's Greatest Science-Fiction and Fantasy.* New York: Dell.
_____. 1956. "The Year's S-F: A Summation by the Editor." In *S-F: The Year's Greatest Science-Fiction and Fantasy*, edited by Judith Merril, 343–49. New York: Dell.
_____. 1957. (Rose Sharon, pseud.). "The Lady Was a Tramp." *Venture Science Fiction* 1 (2): 41–56.
_____. 1957. (Rose Sharon, pseud.). "A Woman of the World." *Venture Science Fiction* 1 (1): 75–82.
_____. 1958. "How Near Is the Moon?" In *SF: The Year's Greatest Science-Fiction and Fantasy, Third Annual Volume*, edited by Judith Merril, 221–26. New York: Dell.
_____. 1958. "Wish Upon a Star." *Magazine of Fantasy and Science Fiction* 15 (6): 87–100.
_____. 1959. "Death Cannot Wither." *Magazine of Fantasy and Science Fiction* 16 (2): 62–80.
_____. 1959. "Introduction." In *SF: The Year's Greatest Science-Fiction and Fantasy, 4th Annual Volume*, edited by Judith Merril, 8. New York: Dell.
_____, ed. 1959. *SF: The Year's Greatest Science-Fiction and Fantasy, 4th Annual Volume.* New York: Dell.

## *1960s*

Merril, Judith. 1960. "Death Cannot Wither." In *Out of Bounds*, by Judith Merril, 137–60. New York: Pyramid.
_____. 1960. Author's note to "Death Cannot Wither." In *Out of Bounds*, by Judith Merril, 137. New York: Pyramid.
_____. 1960. *Out of Bounds.* New York: Pyramid.
_____. 1960. *The Tomorrow People.* New York: Pyramid.
_____. 1961. "The Deep Down Dragon." *Galaxy* 19 (6): 142–53.
_____. 1961. "The Year's S-F: A Summary." In *The Year's Best S-F, 5th Annual Edition*, edited by Judith Merril, 312–17. New York: Dell.
_____, ed. 1961 [1960]. *The Year's Best S-F, 5th Annual Edition.* New York: Dell.
_____. 1962. Editor's headnote for "Hemmingway in Space," by Kingsley Amis. In *The Year's Best S-F, 6th Annual Edition*, edited by Judith Merril, 323. New York: Dell.
_____. 1962. "Shrine of Temptation." *Fantastic Stories of Imagination* 11 (4): 10–26.
_____. 1962. "Theodore Sturgeon." *Magazine of Fantasy and Science Fiction* 23 (3): 46–55.
_____. 1962 [1961]. "Summation: The Year in S-F." In *The Year's Best S-F, 6th Annual Edition*, edited by Judith Merril, 374–78. New York: Dell.
_____, ed. 1962 [1961]. *The Year's Best S-F, 6th Annual Edition.* New York: Dell.
_____. 1963. "The Lonely." *Worlds of Tomorrow* 1 (4): 124–33.
_____. 1963 [1962]. "Summation: S-F, 1961." In *The Year's Best S-F, 7th Annual Edition*, edited by Judith Merril, 391–93. New York: Dell.
_____, ed. 1963 [1962]. *The Year's Best S-F, 7th Annual Edition.* New York: Dell.
_____. 1965 (November). "Books." *Magazine of Fantasy and Science Fiction* 29 (5): 16–22.
_____. 1966. *Shadow on the Hearth* (revised). London: Roberts and Vintner.
_____. 1966. "What Do You Mean—Science? Fiction?" *Extrapolation* 7 (1): 30–36; 8 (1): 2–19.
_____. 1966 [1965]. *The Year's Best S-F, 10th Annual Edition.* New York: Dell.
_____. 1966 (January). "Books." *Magazine of Fantasy and Science Fiction* 30 (1): 39–45.
_____. 1966 (December). "Books." *Magazine of Fantasy and Science Fiction* 31 (6): 30–37.
_____. 1967. "Summation." In *The Year's Best S-F, 11th Annual Edition.* New York: Dell.
_____. 1967. *The Year's Best S-F, 11th Annual Edition.* New York: Dell.

\_\_\_\_\_. 1967 (June). "Books." *Magazine of Fantasy and Science Fiction* 32 (6): 37–43.
\_\_\_\_\_. 1967 (November). "Books." *Magazine of Fantasy and Science Fiction* 33 (5): 28–36.
\_\_\_\_\_. 1967 (December). "Books." *Magazine of Fantasy and Science Fiction* 33 (6): 28–34.
\_\_\_\_\_. 1968. *Daughters of Earth*. London: Gollancz.
\_\_\_\_\_, ed. 1968. *England Swings SF: Stories of Speculative Fiction*. Garden City, NY: Doubleday.
\_\_\_\_\_. 1968. "Introduction." In *Path into the Unknown: The Best Soviet Science Fiction*, 4–7. New York: Delacorte.
\_\_\_\_\_, ed. 1968 [1967]. "Introduction." In *SF: The Best of the Best*, 1–7. New York: Dell.
\_\_\_\_\_, ed. 1968 [1967]. *SF: The Best of the Best*. New York: Dell.
\_\_\_\_\_. 1968 (March). "Books." *Magazine of Fantasy and Science Fiction* 34 (3): 38–44.
\_\_\_\_\_. 1968 (May). "Books." *Magazine of Fantasy and Science Fiction* 34 (5): 48–55.
\_\_\_\_\_. 1968 (August). "Books." *Magazine of Fantasy and Science Fiction* 35 (2): 16–24.
\_\_\_\_\_. 1968 (September). "Books." *Magazine of Fantasy and Science Fiction* 35 (3): 30–37.
\_\_\_\_\_. 1968 (November). "Books." *Magazine of Fantasy and Science Fiction* 35 (5): 42–49.
\_\_\_\_\_. 1969. "Daughters of Earth." In *Daughters of Earth: Three Novels*, 97–165. New York: Doubleday.
\_\_\_\_\_. 1969. "Fritz Leiber." *Magazine of Fantasy and Science Fiction* 37 (1): 44–61.
\_\_\_\_\_, ed. 1969 [1968]. *SF12: New Dimensions in Science Fiction, Fantasy, and Imaginative Writing*. New York: Dell.
\_\_\_\_\_. 1969 (January). "Books." *Magazine of Fantasy and Science Fiction* 36 (1): 34–43.

## *1970s*

Merril, Judith. 1971. "What Do You Mean: Science? Fiction??" In *SF: The Other Side of Realism: Essays on Modern Fantasy and Science Fiction*, edited by Thomas D. Clareson, 53–95. Bowling Green, OH: Bowling Green University Popular Press.
\_\_\_\_\_. 1973. Author's note to "Connection Completed." In *Survival Ship and Other Stories*, 81–82. Toronto: Kakabeka.
\_\_\_\_\_. 1973. Author's note to "Deep Down Dragon." In *Survival Ship and Other Stories*, 178. Toronto: Kakabeka.
\_\_\_\_\_. 1973. Author's note to "Exile from Space." In *Survival Ship and Other Stories*, 33–70. Toronto: Kakabeka.
\_\_\_\_\_. 1973. Author's note to "The Lonely." In *Survival Ship and Other Stories*, 228. Toronto: Kakabeka.
\_\_\_\_\_. 1973. Author's note to "Shrine of Temptation." In *Survival Ship and Other Stories*, 100. Toronto: Kakabeka.
\_\_\_\_\_. 1973. Author's note to "Survival Ship." In *Survival Ship and Other Stories*, 15–16. Toronto: Kakabeka.
\_\_\_\_\_. 1973. "Prologue." In *Survival Ship and Other Stories*, 5–6. Toronto: Kakabeka.
\_\_\_\_\_. 1973. *Survival Ship and Other Stories*. Toronto: Kakabeka.
\_\_\_\_\_. 1974. "In the Land of the Unblind." *Magazine of Fantasy and Science Fiction* 47 (4): 146–48.
\_\_\_\_\_. 1975 [1974]. "Theodore Sturgeon." In *The Best from Fantasy and Science Fiction: A Special Anniversary Anthology*, edited by Edward L. Ferman, 42–50. London: Robson.
\_\_\_\_\_. 1976. *The Best of Judith Merril*. New York: Warner.
\_\_\_\_\_. 1979. "The Future of Happiness." *Chatelaine* 52 (1): 43, 101.
\_\_\_\_\_. 1979. Review of *In Memory Yet Green*, by Isaac Asimov. *Globe and Mail* (Toronto), June 9, sec. 3: 45.

## 1980s

Merril, Judith. 1980. "A Memoir and Appreciation." In *The Science Fiction of Mark Clifton*, edited by Barry N. Malzberg and Martin H. Greenberg, vii–xii. Carbondale, IL: Southern Illinois University Press.

———. 1985. "Afterword: We Have Met the Alien (And It Is Us)." In *Tesseracts*, edited by Judith Merril, 274–84. Victoria, BC: Press Porcépic.

———. 1985. *Daughters of Earth and Other Stories: A Judith Merril Omnibus*. Toronto: McClelland and Stewart.

———. 1985. "Foreword." In *Tesseracts*, edited by Judith Merril, 1–3. Victoria, BC: Press Porcépic.

———. 1985. "The Future of Happiness." In *Daughters of Earth and Other Stories*, edited by Judith Merril, 331–37.

———, ed. 1985. *Tesseracts*. Victoria, BC: Press Porcépic.

———. 1985. "Woman's Work Is *Never* Done!" *Future Combined with Science Fiction Stories* 1 (6): 51, 97–98.

———. 1986. "The Crazies Are Dying." *Now Books* (literary supplement to *Toronto Star*), October: 1–2.

## 1990s

Merril, Judith. 1993. "Better to Have Loved: From a Memoir-in-Progress." *New York Review of Science Fiction* 59 (July): 1, 8–14.

———. 1999. "Better to Have Loved: Excerpts from a Life." In *Women of Other Worlds: Excursions through Science Fiction and Feminism*, edited by Helen Merrick and Tess Williams, 422–42. Nedlands: University of Western Australia Press.

## 2000s

Merril, Judith. 2002. "Transformations." In *Better to Have Loved*, by Judith Merril and Emily Pohl-Weary, 9–12. Toronto: Between the Lines.

———. 2005. *Homecalling and Other Stories: The Complete Solo Short SF of Judith Merril*, edited by Elisabeth Carey. Framingham, MA: NESFA Press.

## Collaborations

Merril, Judith, with A.J. Budrys. 1973. "Death Cannot Wither." In *The Ninth Fontana Book of Great Ghost Stories*, edited by R. Chetwynd-Hayes, 11–31. Glasgow: Collins.

Merril, Judith, and C.M. Kornbluth (Cyril Judd, joint pseud.). 1951 "Mars Child." *Galaxy* 2 (May): 18–76; (June): 94–156; (July): 44–115.

———. 1952. *Outpost Mars*. New York: Dell.

———. 1952. "Gunner Cade." *Astounding Science Fiction* 49 (March): 8–53; (April): 114–60; (May): 108–54.

———. 1952. *Gunner Cade*. New York: Simon and Schuster.

———. 1953. "Sea-Change." *Dynamic Science Fiction* 1 (2): 10–31.

———. 1961. *Sin in Space: An Expose of the Scarlet Planet* (textual changes by Frederik Pohl). New York: Galaxy Beacon.

Merril, Judith, and C.M. Kornbluth. 2008. *Spaced Out: Three Novels of Tomorrow*, edited by Elisabeth Carey and Rick Katze. Framingham, MA: NESFA Press.

Merril, Judith, and Emily Pohl-Weary. 2002. *Better to Have Loved: The Life of Judith Merril*. Toronto: Between the Lines.

Merril, Judith, and Frederik Pohl (pseud. James MacCreigh). 1953. "A Big Man with the Girls." *Future Science Fiction* 3 (6): 45–51.

## Secondary Sources

Abbott, Carl. 2005. "Homesteading on the Extraterrestrial Frontiers." *Science Fiction Studies* 32 (2): 240–64.
Adare, Sierra S. 2005. *"Indian" Stereotypes in TV Science Fiction: First Nations' Voices Speak Out.* Austin: University of Texas Press.
Aldiss, Brian W. 1973. *Billion Year Spree: The History of Science Fiction.* London: Weidenfeld and Nicolson.
———. 1976. "Introduction." In *Hell's Cartographers: Some Personal Histories of Science Fiction Writers*, edited by Brian W. Aldiss and Harry Harrison, 1–5. London: Orbit, Futura.
———. 1992. "When Things Changed — A Little." *Aloud* (Toronto: Judith Merril issue) 2 (7): 1–2.
———. 1998. *The Twinkling of an Eye: Or, My Life as an Englishman.* London: Little, Brown.
Aldiss, Brian W., and Harry Harrison, eds. 1975. *Hell's Cartographers: Some Personal Histories of Science Fiction Writers.* London: Weidenfeld and Nicholson.
Amis, Kingsley. 1960. *New Maps of Hell: A Survey of Science Fiction.* New York: Harcourt, Brace.
Apostolou, John L., and Martin H. Greenberg, eds. 1989. *The Best Japanese Science Fiction Stories*, with a foreword by Grania Davis. New York: Dembner.
Asakura, Hisashi, ed. and trans. 1972 (translated from the Japanese). *What Do You Mean, Science? Fiction?* Tokyo: Shobun-sha.
———. 1992. "Judith Merril in Japan." *Aloud* (Toronto: Judith Merril issue) 2 (7): 3.
———. 2007. "From Vertical to Horizontal." In *Speculative Japan: Outstanding Tales of Japanese Science Fiction and Fantasy*, edited by Gene van Troyer and Grania Davis, 261–64. Fukuoka, Japan: Kurodahan Press.
Asimov, Isaac. 1979. *In Memory Yet Green: The Autobiography of Isaac Asimov, Vol. I: 1920–1954.* New York: Doubleday.
———. 1980. *In Joy Still Felt: The Autobiography of Isaac Asimov, Vol. II: 1954–1978.* New York: Doubleday.
———. 1995 [1994]. *I, Asimov: A Memoir.* New York: Bantam.
Attebery, Brian. 2002. *Decoding Gender in Science Fiction.* New York: Routledge.
*Authentic Science Fiction.* 1956. Review of *S-F: The Year's Greatest Science-Fiction and Fantasy*, edited by Judith Merril. 72 (August): 152.
Bailey, Robin Wayne. 2003. "Introduction." In *Architects of Dreams: SFWA Author Emeritus Anthology*, edited by Robin Wayne Bailey, 11–14. Atlanta: Meisha Merlin.
Bal, Mieke. 1997. *Narratology: Introduction to the Theory of Narrative.* 2nd ed. Toronto: University of Toronto Press.
Ballard, J.G. 1992. "The Wildest Windows onto the New." *Aloud* (Toronto: Judith Merril issue) 2 (7): 12.
Bartter, Martha A. 1988. *The Way to Ground Zero: The Atomic Bomb in American Science Fiction.* Contributions to the Study of Science Fiction and Fantasy 33. New York: Greenwood.
Beer, Stafford. 1992. "Hi-Fi Sci-Fi." *Aloud* (Toronto: Judith Merril issue) 2 (7): 11.
Benjamin, Marina. 2003. *Rocket Dreams: How the Space Age Shaped Our Vision of a World Beyond.* New York: Free Press.
Benstock, Shari. 1998. "Authorizing the Autobiographical." In *Women, Autobiography, Theory: A Reader*, edited by Sidonie Smith and Julia Watson, 145–54. Madison: University of Wisconsin Press.
Booker, Keith M. 2001. *Monsters, Mushroom Clouds, and the Cold War: American Science Fiction and the Roots of Postmodernism, 1946–1964.* Santa Barbara, CA: Praeger.

Boucher, Anthony. 1956. Review of *S-F: The Year's Greatest Science-Fiction and Fantasy*, edited by Judith Merril. *Magazine of Fantasy and Science Fiction* 72 (August): 107.
_____. 1962. "S-F Books: 1960." In *The Year's Best S-F, Sixth Annual Volume*, edited by Judith Merril, 378–81. New York: Dell.
Boucher, Anthony, and J. Francis McComas. 1950. Review of *Shadow on the Hearth*, by Judith Merril and C.M. Kornbluth (Cyril Judd, joint pseud.). *Magazine of Fantasy and Science Fiction* 1 (December): 104.
_____. 1952. Review of *Outpost Mars*, by Judith Merril and C.M. Kornbluth (Cyril Judd, joint pseud.). *Magazine of Fantasy and Science Fiction* 3 (November): 114–15.
_____. 1953. Review of *Gunner Cade*, by Judith Merril and C.M. Kornbluth (Cyril Judd, joint pseud.). *Magazine of Fantasy and Science Fiction* 4 (January): 90–91.
Bourdieu, Pierre. [1991] 1996. *Rules of Art*. Translated by Susan Emanuel. Stanford, CA: Stanford University Press.
Bower, B.M. [1906] 1995. *Chip, of the Flying U*. Lincoln: University of Nebraska Press.
_____. [1912] 1997. *Lonesome Land*. Lincoln: University of Nebraska Press.
Boyer, Paul S. 1985. *By the Bomb's Early Light: American Thought and Culture at the Dawn of the Atomic Age*. New York: Pantheon.
Bradbury, Ray. 1950. *The Martian Chronicles*. Garden City, NY: Doubleday.
Bradley, David. 1948. *No Place to Hide*. Boston: Little, Brown.
Bryson, Michael. c. 2002. "TDR Interview: Emily Pohl-Weary." *Danforth Review* (Toronto), http://www.danforthreview.com/features/interviews/emily_pohl-weary.htm (accessed January 12, 2007).
Budrys, Algis. 1968. Review of *SF Best of the Best*, edited by Judith Merril. *Galaxy* 26 (June): 121–23.
Burroughs, Edgar Rice. 1917. *A Princess of Mars*. New York: Grosset & Dunlap.
Butler, Anne M. 1985. *Daughters of Joy, Sisters of Misery: Prostitutes in the American West*. Urbana: University of Illinois Press.
Butler, Judith. [1990] 1999. *Gender Trouble: Feminism and the Subversion of Identity*. New York: Routledge.
_____. 1993. *Bodies That Matter: On the Discursive Limits of "Sex."* New York: Routledge.
Carey, Elisabeth. 2002. Review of *Better to Have Loved*, by Judith Merril and Emily Pohl-Weary. New England Science Fiction Association, http://www.nesfa.org/reviews/Carey/bettertohaveloved.htm (accessed March 20, 2011).
_____. 2005. "Introduction." In *Homecalling and Other Stories: The Complete Solo Short SF of Judith Merril*. Framingham, MA: NESFA Press, 3–5.
Carnell, John. 1956. Review of *S-F: The Year's Greatest Science-Fiction and Fantasy*, edited by Judith Merril. *New Worlds* 49 (July): 2–3.
Carter, Sarah. 1997. *Capturing Women: The Manipulation of Cultural Imagery in Canada's Prairie West*. Montreal and Kingston: McGill-Queen's University Press.
Child, Lydia Maria. 1824. *Hobomok: A Tale of Early Times*. Boston: Cummings, Hilliard.
Churchill, Joyce. 1969. Review of *SF: The Best of the Best* and *England Swings SF*, edited by Judith Merril. *New Worlds* 186 (January): 62.
Clareson, Thomas D., ed. 1971. *The Other Side of Realism: Essays on Modern Fantasy and Science Fiction*. Bowling Green, OH: Bowling Green University Popular Press.
Clarke, Arthur C. 1951. *The Exploration of Space*. New York: Harper and Brothers.
Clements, J. 2002. "A Mere Shadow on the Hearth." Review of *Better to Have Loved*, by Judith Merril and Emily Pohl-Weary. Amazon.com, http://www.amazon.com/Better-Have-Loved-Judith-Merril/product-reviews/1896357571 (accessed March 20, 2011).
Clute, John. 1995. "Fables of Transcendence." In *Out of This World: Canadian Science Fiction & Fantasy Literature*, edited by Andrea Paradis, 20–27. Ottawa: Quarry Press and National Library of Canada.
_____. 2003. "A Seethe of Stuff: *Better to Have Loved*." Review of *Better to Have Loved*,

by Judith Merril and Emily Pohl-Weary. In *Scores: Reviews 1993–2003*, edited by John Clute 372–74. Harold Wood, Essex: Beccon.
Cole, Les. 1957. "A Man of the World." *Venture Science Fiction* 1 (1): 70–75.
Conklin, Groff. 1950. Review of *Shadow on the Hearth*, by Judith Merril. *Galaxy* 1 (October): 141–42.
Coontz, Stephanie. 1992. *The Way We Never Were: American Families and the Nostalgia Trap*. New York: Basic Books.
Cooper, Carol. 2002. "Spaceballs." Review of *Better to Have Loved*, by Judith Merril and Emily Pohl-Weary, and *The Battle of the Sexes in Science Fiction*, by Justine Larbalestier. *Village Voice*, July 16, http://carolcooper.org/book/spaceballs-02.php (accessed May 12, 2011).
Cooper, James Fenimore. [1826] 1990. *The Last of the Mohicans*. Oxford: Oxford University Press.
Crabb, Leona. 1992. "Mother's Little Helper: Minor Tranquilizers and Women in the 1950s." Master's thesis, Concordia University, Montreal.
Cummins, Elizabeth. 1992. "Short Fiction by Judith Merril." *Extrapolation* 33 (Fall): 202–14.
———. 1995. "Judith Merril: A Link with the New Wave — Then and Now." *Extrapolation* 36 (Fall): 198–209.
———. 1999. "American SF, 1940s–1950s: Where's the Book? The New York Nexus." *Extrapolation* 40 (Winter): 314–19.
———. 2001. "Bibliography of Works by Judith Merril." *Extrapolation* 42 (Fall): 255–87.
———. 2006. *Judith Merril: An Annotated [Online] Bibliography and Guide*. College Station, TX: The Center for the Bibliography of Science Fiction and Fantasy, http://cushing.library.tamu.edu/collections/browse-major-collections/JUDITH%20MERRIL.pdf (accessed May 11, 2011).
Curtis, Emma Ghent. 1889. *The Administratrix*. New York: John B. Alden.
Davidson, David. 1954. *Atomic Attack* (movie). Directed by Ralph Nelson. Motorola TV Playhouse. ABC.
Davin, Eric Leif. 2006. *Partners in Wonder: Women and the Birth of Science Fiction, 1926–1965*. Lanham, MD: Lexington.
Davis, Grania. 2007. "Judy-san: Judith Merril, 1923–1997." In *Speculative Fiction: Outstanding Tales of Japanese Science Fiction and Fantasy*, edited by Gene van Troyer and Grania Davis, 1–3. Fukuoka, Japan: Kurodahan Press.
Davis, Robert Murray. 1985. "The Frontiers of Genre: Science Fiction Westerns." *Science Fiction Studies* 12 (1): 33–41.
DeGraw, Sharon. 2009. *The Subject of Race in American Science Fiction*. Literary Criticism and Cultural Theory Series. New York: Routledge.
Delany, Samuel R. 1979. *Heavenly Breakfast: An Essay on the Winter of Love*. New York: Bantam.
———. 1988. *The Motion of Light in Water: Sex and Science Fiction in the East Village, 1957–1965*. New York: New American Library.
———. 1994. *Silent Interviews: On Language, Race, Sex, Science Fiction, and Some Comics: A Collection of Interviews*. Hanover, NH: Wesleyan University Press.
Derounian-Stodola, Kathryn Zabelle, ed. 1998. *Women's Indian Captivity Novels*. New York: Penguin Classics.
Di Filippo, Paul. 2003. Review of *Better to Have Loved*, by Judith Merril and Emily Pohl-Weary, http://www.asimovs.com/_issue_0304/onbooks.shtml (accessed March 20, 2011).
Disch, Thomas. 1998. *The Dreams Our Stuff Is Made Of: How Science Fiction Conquered the World*. New York: Touchstone.
Donawerth, Jane. 2006. "Illicit Reproduction: Clare Winger Harris's 'The Fate of the

Posedonia.'" In *Daughters of Earth: Feminist Science Fiction in the Twentieth Century*, edited by Justine Larbalestier, 20–35. Middletown, CT: Wesleyan University Press.
Dorsey, Candas Jane. 1997. "Remembering Judy." *Locus* (November): 31.
"Editorial Page." 1919. *Western Story* 8 (2): 128.
Eisenbud, Jule. 1970 [1949]. "Psychiatric Contributions to Parapsychology: A Review." In *Psychoanalysis and the Occult*, edited by George Devereux, 3–15. New York: International Universities Press.
Ellis, Edward S. 1997 [1860]. *Seth Jones, or, The Captives of the Frontier*. In *Reading the West: An Anthology of Dime Westerns*, edited by Bill Brown, 165–268. Boston: Bedford.
Ellison, Harlan. 1967a. "Introduction: Thirty-Two Soothsayers." In *Dangerous Visions: 33 Original Stories*, edited by Harlan Ellison, xix–xxix. Garden City, NY: Doubleday.
———. 1967b. *The Man from U.N.C.L.E.* "The Pieces of Fate Affair." Directed by John Braham. NBC.
———, ed. 1967. *Dangerous Visions: 33 Original Stories*. Garden City, NY: Doubleday.
Farber, David. 1998. *Chicago '68*. Chicago: University of Chicago Press.
Farmer, Philip José. 1952. "The Lovers." *Startling Stories* (August): 12–63.
Ferman, Edward L., ed. 1975 [1974]. *The Best from Fantasy and Science Fiction: A Special 25th Anniversary Anthology*. London: Robson.
Fetherling, Douglas. 1994. *Travels by Night: A Memoir of the Sixties*. Toronto: Lester.
Foley, Martha. 1955. *The Best American Short Stories: 1955*. Boston: Houghton Mifflin.
Ford, John, dir. 1956. *The Searchers*. Screenplay by Frank S. Nugent. Warner Bros.
Franklin, Ursula. 1990. *The Real World of Technology*. CBC Massey Lecture Series. Concord, Ontario: House of Anansi.
———. 2006. *The Ursula Franklin Reader: Pacifism as a Map*. Toronto: Between the Lines.
Freud, Sigmund. [1912–1913] 1950. *Totem and Taboo: Some Points of Agreement between the Mental Lives of Savages and Neurotics*. Translated by James Strachey. London: Routledge and Kegan Paul.
———. 1953. "Dreams and the Occult." In *Psychoanalysis and the Occult*, edited by George Devereux, 91–109. New York: International Universities Press.
Fried, Albert, ed. 1997. *McCarthyism: The Great American Red Scare: A Documentary History*. New York: Oxford University Press.
Friedman, Susan Stanford. 1998. "Women's Autobiographical Selves: Theory and Practice." In *Women, Autobiography, Theory: A Reader*, edited by Sidonie Smith and Julia Watson, 72–82. Madison: University of Wisconsin Press.
Frohock, Fred M. 2000. *Lives of the Psychics: The Shared Worlds of Science and Mysticism*. Chicago: University of Chicago Press.
George, Susan A. 2000. "Space for Resistance: The Disruption of the Frontier Myth in 1950s Science Fiction Films." In *Space and Beyond: The Frontier Theme in Science Fiction*, edited by Gary Westfahl, 77–84. Westport, CT: Greenwood Press.
Georgi-Findlay, Brigitte. 1996. *Frontiers of Women's Writing: Women's Narratives and the Rhetoric of Westward Expansion*. Tucson: University of Arizona Press.
Gillam, Barry. 1970. Review of Judith Merril's *England Swings SF*. *SF Commentary* (Australia) 16 (October): 10–14.
Gillespie, Bruce. 2000. "The Pure Quill: SF Biographies and Autobiographies." *Scratch Pad* 39 (August 2): 2–7, http://www.efanzines.com/SFC/ScratchPad/scrat039.pdf (accessed May 3, 2011).
———. 2003. "Books, Books, Books." Review of *Better to Have Loved*, by Judith Merril and Emily Pohl-Weary. *Scratch Pad* 52 (March 31): 9, http://www.efanzines.com/SFC/ScratchPad/scrat052.pdf (accessed May 3, 2011).
Gotlieb, Phyllis. 1964. *Sunburst*. Greenwich, CT: Fawcett.
Grey, Zane. 1912. *Riders of the Purple Sage*. New York: Harper and Brothers.

Hagan, John. 2001. *Northern Passage: American Vietnam War Resisters in Canada.* Cambridge, MA: Harvard University Press.
Hartwell, David G. 1984. *Age of Wonders: Exploring the World of Science Fiction.* New York: Walker.
Hartwell, David G., and Milton T. Wolf, eds. 1996. *Visions of Wonder: The Science Fiction Research Association Anthology.* New York: TOR.
Hawkins, Cathy. 2003. Review of *Better to Have Loved*, by Judith Merril and Emily Pohl-Weary. *Extrapolation* 44 (1): 125–30.
Heer, Jeet. 2002. "I Was a Teenage Trotskyist: Sci-Fi of the '40s Predicted Space Travel but Assumed That, in the Western Future, Women Would Stay Home While Men Worked. Judith Merril Shook Things Up." *National Post* (Toronto), June 8.
Heinlein, Robert A. 1950. *Farmer in the Sky.* New York: Charles Scribner's Sons.
———, ed. 1952. *Tomorrow the Stars: A Science Fiction Anthology.* Garden City, NY: Doubleday.
Hersey, John. 1946. "Hiroshima." *New Yorker*, August 31, 1946: 20.
Hughes, Richard, and Robert Brewin. 1979. *The Tranquillizing of America: Pill-Popping and the American Way of Life.* New York: Harcourt Brace.
Hughes, Robert. 1968. Review of *England Swings SF*, edited by Judith Merril. *Magazine of Fantasy and Science Fiction* 35 (October): 23–24.
Ito, Norio. 1997. "Regret" (Originally published in *Japanese SF Magazine* [December 1997]: 100–104). Unpublished trans. by Kenichi Matsui with Dianne Newell, 2005, 1–4.
James, Edward, ed. 1994. *Science Fiction in the Twentieth Century.* New York: Oxford University Press.
———. 2009. "Russ on Writing Science Fiction and Reviewing It." In *On Joanna Russ*, edited by Farah Mendlesohn, 19–30. Middletown CT: Wesleyan University Press.
Jirgens, Karl E., and Jim Francis. 1991. "The Answer to Wickedness: Interview with Judith Merril." In *Rampike* (Toronto). 10th Anniversary Issue, Part 2, 7 (2): 8–12.
Kaplan, Amy. 1990. "Romancing the Empire: The Embodiment of American Masculinity in the Popular Historical Novel of the 1890s." *American Literary History* 2 (4): 659–90.
———. 1998. "Manifest Domesticity." *American Literature* 70 (3): 581–606.
Kelley, Mary. 1987. "Introduction." In *Hope Leslie, or, Early Times in the Massachusetts*, edited by Mary Kelley, ix–xxxviii. New Brunswick, NJ: Rutgers University Press.
Kerslake, Patricia. 2007. *Science Fiction and Empire.* Liverpool: Liverpool University Press.
Kidd, Virginia. 1976. "Introduction." *The Best of Judith Merril*, 7–13. New York: Warner.
Klodawsky, Helene. 1999. *What If … ? A Film about Judith Merril.* Directed by Helene Klodawsky. Montreal: Imageries P.B. Ltd.
Knight, Damon. 1956. Review of *S-F: The Year's Greatest Science-Fiction and Fantasy*, edited by Judith Merril. *Infinity Science Fiction* 1 (October): 67–69.
———. 1967. *In Search of Wonder: Essays on Modern Science Fiction.* 2nd ed. Chicago: Advent.
———. 1976. "Knight Piece." In *Hell's Cartographers: Some Personal Histories of Science Fiction Writers*, edited by Brian W. Aldiss and Harry Harrison, 96–143. London: Orbit, Futura.
———. 1977. *The Futurians: The Story of the Science Fiction "Family" of the 30's that Produced Today's Top SF Writers and Editors.* New York: John Day.
Kolodny, Annette. 1975. *Lay of the Land: Metaphor as Experience and History in American Life and Letters.* Chapel Hill: University of North Carolina Press.
———. 1984. *The Land Before Her: Fantasy and Experience of the American Frontiers, 1630–1860.* Chapel Hill: University of North Carolina Press.
Kristeva, Julia. 2000. "Desire and Language: A Semiotic Approach to Literature and Art." In *French Feminism Reader*, edited by Kelly Oliver, 176–81. Lanham, MD: Rowman and Littlefield.

Kubrick, Stanley, and Arthur C. Clarke. 1968. *2001: A Space Odyssey*. Directed by Stanley Kubrick. MGM Studios, distributed by Warner Brothers.
Kurlansky, Mark. 2004. *1968: The Year That Rocked the World*. New York: Ballantine.
Lamont, Victoria. 2005. "Cattle Branding and the Traffic in Women in Early Twentieth-Century Westerns by Women." *Legacy: A Journal of American Women Writers* 22 (1): 30–46.
Lamont, Victoria, and Dianne Newell. 2009. "Daughter of Earth: Judith Merril and the Intersections among Gender, Science Fiction, and Frontier Mythology." *Science Fiction Studies* 36 (1): 48–66.
Larbalestier, Justine. 2002a. *The Battle of the Sexes in Science Fiction*. Middletown, CT: Wesleyan University Press.
———. 2002b. "The New York Nexus and American Science Fiction in the Postwar Period." *Extrapolation* 43 (3): 277–87.
———. 2003. "Interview with Emily Pohl-Weary." *Extrapolation* 44 (1): 122–24.
———, ed. 2006. *Daughters of Earth: Feminist Science Fiction in the Twentieth Century*. Middletown, CT: Wesleyan University Press.
Larbalestier, Justine, and Helen Merrick. 2003. "The Revolting Housewife: Women and Science Fiction in the 1950s." *Paradoxa* 18: 136–56.
Laskin, David. 2001. *Partisans: Marriage, Politics, and Betrayal among the New York Intellectuals*. Chicago: University of Chicago Press.
Latham, Rob. 2006. "*New Worlds* and the New Wave in Fandom: Fan Culture and the Reshaping of Science Fiction in the Sixties." *Extrapolation* 47 (2): 296–315.
Lavender, Isiah. 2009. "Critical Race Theory." In *The Routledge Companion to Science Fiction*, edited by Mark Bould, Andrew M. Butler, Adam Roberts, and Sherryl Vint, 185–93. New York: Routledge.
LeBlanc, Michael. 2002. "Who Watches the Watchers? Science Fiction and Political Criticism in Cold War America." Graduating essay, Department of History, University of British Columbia.
———. 2005. "The Future Isn't Always Science Fiction: Judith Merril and Isaac Asimov's Speculative Nonfiction of the Early 1970s and Their Visions of Tomorrow." Master's thesis, Department of History, University of British Columbia.
———. 2006. "Judith Merril and Isaac Asimov's Quest to Save the Future." *Foundation: The International Review of Science Fiction* 35 (98): 59–73.
Lee, Dennis. 1998. *Body Music: Essays*. Toronto: House of Anansi.
Leiber, Fritz. 1970. "Some of the Ladies." Review of *Daughters of Earth and Other Stories*, by Judith Merril. *Fantastic Stories* 19 (April): 106–8.
———. 1984a. "My Life and Writings, Part 8: Conclusion." *Fantasy Review* (September): 7–8, 42.
———. 1984b. "Not Much Disorder and Not So Early Sex: An Autobiographic Essay." In *The Ghost Light*, edited by Fritz Leiber, 252–365. New York: Berkley.
Ley, Willy, with Chesley Bonestell. 1949. *The Conquest of Space*. New York: Viking Press.
MacLean, Katherine. 1996. "Judith Merril vs. Plotto." *WisCon 20* (souvenir book for Wiscon, May 24–27). Madison, WI: 15.
MacLeod, Ian. 2003. "Old Maps of Hell." *Interzone* 189 (May/June): 39–40.
Malzberg, Barry N., and Martin H. Greenberg, eds. 1980. *The Science Fiction of Mark Clifton*. Carbondale: Southern Illinois University Press.
Marable, Manning. 2007. *Race, Reform, and Rebellion: The Second Reconstruction and Beyond in Black America, 1945–2006*. 3rd ed. Jackson: University Press of Mississippi.
Marshall, Joyce. 1992. "A Romantic Realist." *Aloud* (Toronto: Judith Merril issue) 2 (7): 7.
Masters, Dexter, and Katharine Way, eds. [1946] 2007. *One World or None: A Report to the Public on the Full Meaning of the Atomic Bomb*. New York: New Press, distributed by W.W. Norton. Commissioned by the Federation of American Scientists.

May, Elaine Tyler. 1988. *Homeward Bound: American Families in the Cold War Era.* New York: Basic.
McCann, Jolene. 2006. "The Love Token of a Token Immigrant: Judith Merril's Expatriate Narrative, 1968–1972." Master's thesis, University of British Columbia.
———. 2008. "Judith Merril's Spaced Out Library." *Foundation: The International Review of Science Fiction* 35 (102): 1–15.
McClintock, Anne. 1995. *Imperial Leather: Race, Gender, and Sexuality in the Colonial Conquest.* New York: Routledge.
McCracken, Allison. 2002. "Study of a Mad Housewife: Psychiatric Discourse, the Suburban Home, and the Case of Gracie Allen." In *Small Screens, Big Ideas: Television in the 1950s*, edited by Janet Thurmin, 50–66. New York: IB Tauris.
McElrath, Frances. [1902] 2002. *The Rustler: A Tale of Love and War in Wyoming.* Lincoln: University of Nebraska Press.
McEnaney, Laura. 2000. *Civil Defense Begins at Home: Militarization Meets Everyday Life in the Fifties.* Princeton, NJ: Princeton University Press.
Mead, Margaret. 1970. *Culture and Commitment.* New York: Natural History Press/Doubleday.
Mendlesohn, Farah. 1994. "Gender, Power, and Conflict Resolution: 'Subcommittee,' by Zenna Henderson." *Extrapolation* 35 (Fall): 120–29.
———, ed. 2009. *On Joanna Russ.* Middletown, CT: Wesleyan University Press.
Mermelstein, Lois. 1985. "The Doyenne of Canadian Sci-Fi." *Varsity* (University of Toronto campus newspaper), October 21: 7–8.
Merrick, Helen. 2003. "Gender in Science Fiction." In *The Cambridge Companion to Science Fiction*, edited by Edward James and Farah Mendlesohn, 241–52. Cambridge: Cambridge University Press.
Miller, P. Schuyler. 1953a. Review of *Outpost Mars*, by Judith Merril and C.M. Kornbluth (Cyril Judd, joint pseud.), *Astounding Science Fiction* 51 (4): 81.
———. 1953b. Review of *Gunner Cade*, by Judith Merril and C.M. Kornbluth (Cyril Judd, joint pseud.). *Astounding Science Fiction* 51 (March): 160–61.
———. 1961. Review of *The Tomorrow People*, by Judith Merril. *Analog* 66 (January): 165–67.
———. 1969. Review of *England Swings SF*, edited by Judith Merril. *Analog* 82 (February): 163–66.
———. 1970. Review of *Daughters of Earth: Three Novels*, by Judith Merril. *Analog* 84 (January): 164–65.
Mogen, David. 1982. *Wilderness Visions: Science Fiction Westerns, Vol. 1.* 1st ed. San Bernardino, CA: Borgo Press.
Mogen, David, and Daryl F. Mallett. 1993. *Wilderness Visions: The Western Theme in Science Fiction Literature.* San Bernardino, CA: Borgo Press.
Moorcock, Michael. 1998. "Tribute to Judith Merril." *Sol Rising* (Toronto) 20 (January — Judith Merril Tribute issue): 4–5.
Morrison, Philip. 1946. "If the Bomb Gets Out of Hand." In *One World or None*, edited by Dexter Masters and Katharine Way, 1–6. New York: McGraw-Hill.
Mulvey, Laura. 1975. "Visual Pleasure and Narrative Cinema." *Screen* 16 (3): 6–18.
Nadel, Alan. 1995. *Containment Culture: American Narratives, Postmodernism, and the Atomic Age.* Durham, NC: Duke University Press.
Newell, Dianne. 2003. "Home Truths: Women Writing Science in the Nuclear Dawn." *European Journal of American Culture* 22 (3): 193–203.
Newell, Dianne, and Victoria Lamont. 2005a. "House Opera: Frontier Mythology and Subversion of Domestic Discourse in Mid-Twentieth-Century Women's Space Opera." *Foundation: The International Review of Science Fiction* 34 (95): 71–88.

_____. 2005b. "Rugged Domesticity: Frontier Mythology in Post-Armageddon Science Fiction by Women." *Science Fiction Studies* 97 (32), Part 3: 423–41.
Newell, Dianne, and Jolene McCann. 2009. "Judith Merril Moving In and Out of This World: Urban Landscape Encounters of a Science Fiction Personality in the Sixties and Seventies." In *Emotion, Place and Culture*, edited by Mick Smith, Joyce Davidson, Laura Cameron, and Liz Bondi, 267–82. Farnham, Surrey, U.K.: Ashgate.
Newell, Dianne, and Jenéa Tallentire. 2005a. "Co-Writing a Life in Science Fiction: Judith Merril as a Theorist of Autobiography." In *Further Perspectives on the Canadian Fantastic: Proceedings of the 2003 Conference on Canadian Science Fiction and Fantasy*, edited by Allan Weiss, 19–33. Toronto: ACCSFF.
_____. 2005b. "Translating Science Fiction: Judith Merril in Japan." Paper presented at Worldcon, Glasgow, August 4–8, http://www.sf-foundation.org/sites/default/files/imported/publications/essays/TranslatingSF.pdf (accessed May 12, 2011).
_____. 2007. "'For the Extended Family and the Universe': Judith Merril and Science Fiction Autobiography." *Biography: An Interdisciplinary Quarterly* 30 (1): 1–21.
_____. 2009. "Learning the Prophet Business: The Merril-Russ Intersection." In *On Joanna Russ*, edited by Farah Mendlesohn, 64–80. Middletown, CT: Wesleyan University Press.
Nicholls, Peter. 1993a. "Aliens." In *The Encyclopedia of Science Fiction*, edited by John Clute and Peter Nicholls, 15–19. London: Orbit.
_____. 1993b. "Psi powers." In *The Encyclopedia of Science Fiction*, edited by John Clute and Peter Nicholls, 971–72. London: Orbit.
_____. 1993c. "Sex." In *The Encyclopedia of Science Fiction*, edited by John Clute and Peter Nicholls, 1088–91 London: Orbit.
Nicholls, Peter, and Brian Stableford. 1993. "ESP." In *Encyclopedia of Science Fiction*, edited by John Clute and Peter Nicholls, 390–91. London: Orbit.
Noonan, Bonnie. 2005. *Women Scientists in Fifties Science Fiction Films*. Jefferson, NC: McFarland.
Oppenheimer, J.R. 1946. "Atomic Weapons." *Proceedings of the American Philosophical Society* 90 (January): 7–10.
Orwell, George. 1945. "You and the Atomic Bomb." *Tribune* (London), October 19.
Owram, Doug. 1997. *Born at the Right Time: A History of the Baby Boom Generation*. Toronto: University of Toronto Press.
Pohl, Frederik. 1960. Review of *Tomorrow People*, by Judith Merril. *Worlds of If* 10 (September): 89–90.
_____. 1978. *The Way the Future Was*. 1st ed. New York: Del Ray.
Pohl, Frederik, and C.M. Kornbluth. 1953. *The Space Merchants*. New York: Ballantine.
Pohl-Weary, Emily. 2002. "Writing My Grandmother's Autobiography." In *Better to Have Loved: The Life of Judith Merril*, by Judith Merril and Emily Pohl-Weary, 1–7. Toronto: Between the Lines.
_____. 2004. *A Girl Like Sugar*. Toronto: McGilligan.
_____, ed. 2004. *Girls Who Bite Back: Witches, Mutants, Slayers and Freaks*. Toronto: Sumach Press.
_____. n.d. "Homepage." http://emilypohlweary.com/ (accessed March 20, 2011).
Powell, D. Reid. 1975. Review of *Survival Ship and Other Stories*, by Judith Merril. *Luna Monthly* 60 (December): 25.
Radway, Janice A. 1991. *Reading the Romance: Women, Patriarchy, and Popular Literature*. Chapel Hill: University of North Carolina Press.
_____. 1997. *A Feeling for Books: The Book-of-the-Month Club, Literary Taste, and Middle-Class Desire*. Chapel Hill: University of North Carolina Press.
Rich, Mark. 1996. "Gunner Cade." In *Magill's Guide to Science Fiction and Fantasy Literature, Vol. 2*, 409–10. Pasadena, CA: Salem Press.

_____. 1999. "Remembering Cyril: An Interview with Judith Merril." *New York Review of Science Fiction* 12 (1): 1, 4–6.
_____. 2010. *C.M. Kornbluth: The Life and Works of a Science Fiction Visionary*. Jefferson, NC: McFarland.
Rieder, John. 2007. "Life Writing and Science Fiction: Constructing Identities and Constructing Genres." *Biography* 30 (1): v–xvii.
_____. 2008. *Colonialism and the Emergence of Science Fiction*. The Wesleyan Early Classics of Science Fiction Series, Vol. 183. Middletown, CT: Wesleyan University Press.
Riley, Glenda. 1996. *Building and Breaking Families in the American West*. Albuquerque: University of New Mexico Press.
Roberts, Robin. 1993. *A New Species: Gender and Science in Science Fiction*. Champaign: University of Illinois Press.
Robinson, Kim Stanley. 2009. "My 10 Favorite Mars Novels." http://spectrum.ieee.org/aerospace/space-flight/my-10-favorite-mars-novels (accessed December 31, 2010).
Robinson, Spider. 1998. "Anecdotes from My Own Files, Excerpted from a Speech Given on the Occasion of the Tribute to Judith Merril at Harbourfront in October 1992." *Sol Rising* (Toronto) 20 (January—Judith Merril Tribute issue): 6–7.
_____. 2002. Review of *Better to Have Loved*, by Judith Merril and Emily Pohl-Weary. *Globe and Mail* (Toronto), May 18: D7, D19.
Rowlandson, Mary. 1682. *The Sovereignty and Goodness of God: A Narrative of the Captivity and Restoration of Mrs. Mary Rowlandson*. Cambridge, MA: Samuel Green.
Russ, Joanna. 1968a. "Books." *Magazine of Fantasy and Science Fiction* 35 (1): 53–57.
_____. 1968b. *Picnic on Paradise*. New York: Ace.
_____. [1971a] 1972. "The Image of Women in Science Fiction." Reprinted in *Images of Women in Fiction*, edited by Susan Koppleman Cornillion, 79–94. Bowling Green, OH: Bowling Green Popular University Press.
_____. [1971b] 1995. "What Can a Heroine Do? Or Why Women Can't Write." In *To Write Like a Woman: Essays in Feminism and Science Fiction*, by Joanna Russ, 79–93. Bloomington and Indianapolis: University of Indiana Press.
_____. 1983. *How To Suppress Women's Writing*. Austin: University of Texas Press.
_____. 1995. *To Write Like a Woman: Essays in Feminism and Science Fiction*. Bloomington and Indianapolis: Indiana University Press.
Said, Edward W. [1978] 1979. *Orientalism*. New York: Vintage.
Sargent, Pamela, ed. 1974. *Women of Wonder*. New York: Vintage.
_____, ed. 1995. *Women of Wonder: The Classic Years. Science Fiction by Women from the 1940s to the 1970s*. New York: Harcourt Brace.
Sawyer, Robert J. 1997. "Judith Merril's Presence Commanded Attention." *Globe and Mail* (Toronto), September 16: A13–14.
Schaefer, Jack. [1949] 1984. *Shane: The Critical Edition*, edited by James C. Work. Lincoln: University of Nebraska Press.
Schlissel, Lillian. 1982. *Women's Diaries of the Westward Journey*. New York: Schocken.
Sedgwick, Catharine Maria. [1827] 1987. *Hope Leslie, or, Early Times in the Massachusetts*, edited by Mary Kelley. New Brunswick, NJ: Rutgers University Press.
Seed, David. 1997. "One of Postwar SF's Formative Figures." *Interzone* (U.K.) 126 (December): 13–15, 26.
_____. 1999. *American Science Fiction and the Cold War: Literature and Film*. Edinburgh: Edinburgh University Press.
_____. 2003. "Debate Over Nuclear Refuge." *Cold War History* 4 (1): 117–42.
Sharp, Patrick B. 2007. *Savage Perils: Racial Frontiers and Nuclear Apocalypse in American Culture*. Norman: University of Oklahoma Press.
Sharpe, David. 1987. *Rochdale: The Runaway College*. Toronto: House of Anansi.
Shelley, Mary. 1818. *Frankenstein; or, The Modern Prometheus*. London.

Sheppard, Alice. 1994. *Cartooning for Suffrage*. Albuquerque: University of New Mexico Press.

Silverberg, Robert, ed. 1970. *Science Fiction Hall of Fame, Vol. 1*. New York: Doubleday.

———. 2010. "Science Fiction in the Fifties: The Real Golden Age." In *Nebula Awards Showcase 2010*, edited by Brett Fawcett, 163–72. New York: ROC.

Sinusas, Asta. 2002. Review of *Better to Have Loved*, by Judith Merril and Emily Pohl-Weary. *SFRevu*, http://www.sfrevu.com/ISSUES/2002/0205/Col%20-%20Can%20Books/Can%20Books.htm (accessed March 20, 2011).

Slotkin, Richard. 1998. *Gunfighter Nation: The Myth of the Frontier in Twentieth-Century America*. Norman: University of Oklahoma Press.

Smith, E.E. ("Doc") [and Lee Hawkins Garby, uncredited]. [1928] 1958. *The Skylark of Space*. New York: Pyramid.

Smith, Henry Nash. [1950] 1970. *Virgin Land: The American West as Symbol and Myth*. Cambridge, MA: Harvard University Press.

Smith, Sidonie, and Julie Watson, eds. 1998. *Women, Autobiography, Theory: A Reader*. Madison: University of Wisconsin Press.

Space Frontier Foundation (SFF). www.spacefrontier.org (accessed February 3, 2010).

Stableford, Brian. 1979. "The Short Fiction of Judith Merril." In *Survey of Science Fiction Literature, Vol. 4*, edited by Frank N. Magill, 2014–18. Englewood Cliffs, NJ: Salem Press.

———. 1993. "Colonization of Other Worlds." In *The Encyclopedia of Science Fiction*, edited by John Clute and Peter Nicholls, 244–46. London: Orbit.

Stanton, Domna C. 1998. "Autogynography: Is the Subject Different?" In *Women, Autobiography, Theory: A Reader*, edited by Sidonie Smith and Julia Watson, 131–44. Madison: University of Wisconsin Press.

Stephens, Ann S. [1860] 1997. "Malaeska; The Indian Wife of the White Hunter." In *Reading the West: An Anthology of Dime Westerns*, edited by Bill Brown, 53–164. Boston: Bedford.

Sterling, Bruce. 2001. "The Milford System (or, the Modern Science Fiction Workshop)." November 17, http://everything2.com/title/The+Milford+System+%2528or%252C+the+Modern+Science+Fiction+Workshop%2529 (accessed January 2, 2010).

Streeby, Shelley. 2002. *American Sensations: Class, Empire, and the Production of Popular Culture*. Berkeley: University of California Press.

Theall, Donald F. 1973. "Introduction." In *Survival Ship and Other Stories*, by Judith Merril, 1–3. Toronto: Kakabeka.

Turner, Frederick Jackson. [1893, thesis] 1928. *The Frontier in American History*. New York: Holt.

Tutihasi, R. Laurraine. 1976. Review of *The Best of Judith Merril*, by Judith Merril. *SF Booklog* 9 (May–June): 13.

van Troyer, Gene, and Grania Davis, eds. 2007. *Speculative Japan: Outstanding Tales of Japanese Science Fiction and Fantasy*. Fukuaka, Japan: Kurodahan Press.

Vaughan, Alden T., and Edward W. Clark. 1981. "Cups of Common Calamity: Puritan Captivity Narratives as Literature and History." In *Puritans among the Indians: Accounts of Captivity and Redemption, 1676–1724*, edited by Alden T. Vaughan and Edward W. Clark, 1–28. Cambridge, MA: Harvard University Press.

Weart, Spencer R. 1988. *Nuclear Fear: A History of Images*. Cambridge, MA: Harvard University Press.

Webster, Bud. 2010. "Merrily We Roll Along, or, That's Funny, You Don't Look Judith." *Jim Baen's Universe 23*, vol. 4 (5): http://www.baens-universe.com/articles/Merrily_We_Roll_Along_or__That_s_Funny__You_Don_t (accessed March 20, 2011).

Weil, Ellen, and Gary K. Wolfe. 2002. *Harlan Ellison: The Edge of Forever*. Columbus: Ohio State University Press.

Weiss, Alan. 1997. "Not Only a Mother: An Interview with Judith Merril." *Sol Rising* (Toronto) 18 (April): 1, 6–9.
Welles, Orson. 1956. "Introduction." In *S-F: The Year's Greatest Science-Fiction and Fantasy*, edited by Judith Merril, 8–9. New York: Dell.
Wells, H.G. 1898. *War of the Worlds*. London: Heinemann.
Westfahl, Gary, ed. 2000. *Space and Beyond: The Frontier Theme in Science Fiction*. Westport, CT: Greenwood.
Williams, Paul. 2009. "Nuclear Criticism." In *The Routledge Companion to Science Fiction*, edited by Mark Bould, Andrew M. Butler, Adam Roberts, and Sherryl Vint, 246–55. New York: Routledge.
Willis, Connie. 1992. "The Women SF Doesn't See." Guest Editorial. *Asimov's Science Fiction Magazine* 16 (11): 4–6, 8.
———. 2003. "Judith Merril (with a Capital E)." In *Architects of Dreams: SRWA Author Emeritus Anthology*, edited by Robin Wayne Bailey, 137–39. Atlanta: Meisha Merlin.
Willis, Martin. 2006. *Mesmerists, Monsters, and Machines: Science Fiction and the Cultures of Science in the Nineteenth Century*. Kent, OH: Kent State University Press.
Wister, Owen. 1902. *The Virginian*. New York: Signet.
Wolfe, Gary K. 1989. "Frontiers in Space." In *The Frontier Experience and the American Dream: Essays on American Literature*, edited by David Mogen, Mark Busby, and Paul Bryant, 248–63. College Station: Texas A&M University Press.
Woolf, Virginia. 2008 [1929]. *A Room of One's Own*. Edited by Morag Shiach. Oxford: Oxford University Press.
Wrobel, David M. 1993. *The End of American Exceptionalism: Frontier Anxiety from the Old West to the New Deal*. Lawrence: University of Kansas Press.
Yaszek, Lisa. 2004. "Stories 'That Only a Mother' Could Write: Midcentury Peace Activism, Maternalist Politics, and Judith Merril's Early Fiction." *NWSA Journal* 16 (2): 70–97.
———. 2006. "From *Ladies Home Journal* to *The Magazine of Fantasy and Science Fiction*: 1950s SF, the Offbeat Romance Story, and the Case of Alice Eleanor Jones." In *Daughters of Earth: Feminist Science Fiction in the Twentieth Century*, edited by Justine Larbalestier, 67–96. Middletown, CT: Wesleyan University Press.
———. 2008. *Galactic Suburbia: Recovering Women's Science Fiction*. Columbus: Ohio State University Press.
———. 2009. "A History of One's Own: Joanna Russ and the Creation of a Feminist SF Tradition." In *On Joanna Russ*, edited by Farah Mendlesohn, 31–47. Middletown, CT: Wesleyan University Press.
Zarlengo, Kristina. 1999. "Civilian Threat, the Suburban Citadel, and Atomic Age American Women." *Signs* 24 (4): 925–58.

# Index

Numbers in **bold italics** indicate pages with photographs.

Abbott, Carl 11, 48
ABC television network 39
Abelard 17
Ace Books 17, 152
Acorn, Milton 203
ACTRA (Alliance of Canadian Cinema, Television and Radio Artists) 193
Adare, Sierra S. 22, 88
*The Administratrix* (Curtis) 49
"Afterword: We Have Met the Alien (And It Is Us)" 176-77
Aldiss, Brian D. 16, 18, 151, 153, 154, 158, 159, 183, 188-89; correspondence 164, 167, 182, 186-89, 191; Merril, Judith, tribute 189
Alia, Valerie 197
Alien encounter *see* American alien encounter theme
Allen, Max 173
*Aloud Magazine* iii, 27, 143
*Amazing Stories* 17
American alien encounter theme 5, 23, 65-88, 211; alien attack/threat, linked to Cold War paranoia 66-71, 78, 79; and Anglo-American colonialism (the "colonial gaze"), underpinning ideologies of called into question 5, 65-67, 77-79, 81, 85, 88, 92, 212, 214; the child internal focalizer in 76-77, 89, 98, 107; communication across species in 67, 68, 80, 85, 89, 98, 109; European anthropological narrative tradition, linkages to 77-78, 81-83, 84-85, 88; frontier narratives, linkages to 69, 70, 71, 75, 76, 80, 84-87; giant insects and the monstrous feminine in 70, 71, 76-77; interspecies romance and marriage in 68-70; misrecognition of the "other" in 66, 67-68, 80-87, 107; racist ideology incorporated in 65-66, 77-79; sexuality in 71-73, 74-75, 86-87; white, male identity, shored up in 65-66; woman as the alien "other" in 66, 70-77, 84
American atomic frontier theme 5, 11, 18-19, 29-43; and atomic Armageddon 41-42; and domesticity 25-29, 34, 44; frontier narratives, linkages to 31-32, 33, 40-41, 43; and normalcy, mothers and the home 29-39; *see also* atomic bomb; atomic science; Hiroshima: atomic attack
American frontier mythology 3, 4-5, 11-24, 35, 40, 46-49, 58, 66, 69; American science fiction, linked to 3, 4-5, 12, 26, 29, 31, 41-43, 46-49, 70, 80, 211; frontier captivity narratives in 70, 76, 91; frontier hero, a staple of 46-47; frontier linkages between the foreign and the feminine in 88; frontier linkages between the primitive and the feminine in 98-106; frontier women's diaries in 21, 51, 211; indigenous people, conquest as natural outcome of human progress in 109; Native Americans, as figures in 71, 75, 76; single women on the frontier, popular theme in 75; white, patriarchal underpinnings 43, 65-66; women's contribution to 3, 5, 13, 15-17, 24, 69; and women's skills at translation and communication, assumed to be "innate" in 23; *see also* Turner, Frederick Jackson; Westerns
American psychology and primary communication theme 6,48, 49, 54, 89-109, 140, 182, 211; and ESP 6, 48, 89-90, 96-98, 101-2, 104, 106-7, 109, 182, 207; frontier mythology, linked to 90-92, 98-99, 109; impact on human communication in 6, 86, 211; and narrative innovation 106-9; and parapsychology 97, 182; and psychological expert/tests, role of in 68, 86, 92, 93-96, 100; and romantic relationships 102-5, 106; and telepathic women, role of 6, 79, 89, 95, 98, 101-2, 105-6; telepathy/psi and notions of the primitive/feminine in 91, 96-97, 98-107
American science fiction field: androgynous names, use of by female authors 17; authority (50s) 3, 12, 17, 92; collaboration within

229

113–15, 143–44; edge and focus, decline 139, 140–41 148, 149–50, 151–52, 155, 158, 165; and the "hard" sciences, pre-dominance 48, 89, 102, 109, 151, 152, 154, 159–60, 163; and magazine cover art stories 79, 80, 82, 84–85, 94; as a medium for political criticism, uncensored in Cold War era 2–3, 26, 152, 155, 159, 165; and modern literature, difference between 155, 162, 163; and narrative form and language, innovation in 51, 55, 81, 84–86, 106–9, 211; New York, center of science fiction production 113–14, 145; normalcy in, attitudes toward 5, 26, 28–29, 32–38; plagiarism in 127; and planetary romance stories 45–46; professionalization 141–42, 145; sex, treatment in 34, 50, 53, 59–60, 64, 69, 120–21, 135, 137–38, 158, 211; and the "soft" sciences 48, 54, 89, 120, 151, 152, 154, 160; space flight, synonymous with, in 30s and 40s 45; space opera 12, 17, 24, 46, 60, 65; women's participation in, and arguments explaining away ("myth of exclusion") 16, 24, 27, 34, 207, 209–10; *see also* American frontier mythology; feminist science fiction and criticism; the Futurians; Hydra Club, New York; Milford Science Fiction Writers' Conference; New Wave science fiction; the New York Nexus; speculative science fiction; Westerns

American space frontier theme 5, 11, 19–22, 44–64; the child main character in 49, 62–63, and colonialism 13, 14, 20, 54, 55, 57–58, 62; and domesticity 47–49, 53–54; and female identity and gender relations, ideas about (50s) 11, 46, 48–51, 53–54, 59–60, 210; and galactic empires 46, 47; and professional womanhood 50–51, 54, 56, 59–63, 64, 77; and romance to realism shift, post–World War II 45–47; and sex and reproduction 48, 50, 53, 55–58, 59–60, 64; and space colonization/travel, more suited to women than men 22–23, 49–51, 86; and space exploration 11–12, 19, 195; Westerns, linkages to 58, 60, 61, 63, 64

Amgott, Milton 143, 182
Amis, Kingsley 148–49
*Analog* 154
Anderson, Pohl **29**
anti–Vietnam War movement 25, 156, 164, 166; U.S. draft resisters 2, 25, 166; *see also* Committee to Aid Refugees from Militarism (CARM); *Manual for Draft Age Immigrants to Canada*; Red, White, and Black
Apollo Program 20
Apollo II Moon landing 45, 167
Apostolu, John L. 171
*Architects of Dreams: SFWA Author Emeritus Anthology* (Bailey) 30
Armageddon *see* American atomic frontier theme
Artword Theatre 175

Asakura, Hisashi xiii, 170, 175
Asimov, Isaac 4, 6, 12, 24, **29**, 159, 178, 186–87, 209; and autobiography, approach to 183, 186–88, 192, 205
*Astounding Science Fiction* 17, 30, 40, 45, 98, 118, 124, 131
*Astounding Stories* 17
*Atomic Attack* see *Shadow on the Hearth*
atomic bomb 26, 30–31, 35, 36–38; atomic testing (Bikini Atoll tests) 15; female "bombshell" 15, 27, 38; feminized nature 14–15, 26–29, 38, 43, 211; savage, regenerative power 14–15, 18–19, 30, 33–38, 43; *see also* atomic science; Hiroshima: atomic attack
Atomic Energy Commission 39
Atomic frontier *see* American atomic frontier theme
atomic science 11–13, 26–29, 36–37, 40, 43; *see also* atomic bomb
Attebery, Brian 17, 33
Atwood, Margaret iii–iv, 177
Aurora Award for Lifetime Contribution 177
*Authentic Science Fiction* 142

*Babel-17* (Delany) 156
Bailey, Hilary 152–53
Bailey, Robin Wayne 30
*The Ballad of Beta-2* (Delany) 156
Ballantine Books 17, 171
Ballard, James (J. G.) 142, 150, 153, 154, 156, 157, 186; and Merril, Judith, tribute 142, 148
Bantam Books 1, 29, 34, 114
Barr, George 80, **82**
"Barrier of Dread" 46; contribution 46
*The Battle of the Sexes in Science Fiction* (Larbalestier) 69
The Beatles 152
Beckett, Thomas 153, 154
Beer, Stafford 173
Benjamin, Marina 20
Benstock, Shari 199
*Best American Short Stories: 1955* (Foley) 62
*The Best from Fantasy and Science Fiction: A Special 25th Anniversary Edition* (Ferman) 161
*The Best Japanese Science Fiction Stories* (Apostolou and Greenberg) 171
*The Best of Judith Merril* 174
*Best Science Fiction Stories* series (Bleiler and Dikty) 141
"Better to Have Loved: Excerpts from a Life" 196
*Better to Have Loved: The Life of Judith Merril* (Merril and Pohl-Weary) x, xiv, xv, 2, 29, 40, 56, 138, 161, 162, 168, 178, 179, **180**, 181, 190–207; contribution 179–81, 200–4, 207, 212; and readings of the "memoir-in-progress" 195–97, 204; reception 151, 179, 181, 198–99, 204–7
Between the Lines xiv, xv, 29, 168, 179, 189
*Beyond Human Ken* 139–40, 182

*Beyond the Barriers of Space and Time* 97, 140; contribution 97; reception 140
"A Big Man with the Girls" (Merril and F. Pohl [pseud. James MacCreigh]) 133–34; contribution 134
Bikini Atoll tests *see* atomic bomb
*Billion Year Spree: The History of Science Fiction* (Aldiss) 151, 189
birth control 74, 137–38, 158
Bleiler, Everett F. 141
Blish, James 28, 115, 140, *143*, 144, 158, 202
*Blue Book* 17
*Bodies That Matter: On the Discursive Limits of "Sex"* (Butler) 72
Book-of-the-Month Club 141
the "Books" review column *see The Magazine of Science Fiction and Fantasy*
Boucher, Anthony (William Anthony Patrick White) x, xvii, 34, 39, 58, 113, 114, 122, 123, 125, 127–28, 131, 132, 134, 137–38, 140, 142, *143*, 150, 155–56, 182; as H. H. Holmes [pseud.] xvii, 131, 132; and Year's Best anthology series, reviewer for 148–49
Bourdieu, Pierre 141
Bower, B.M. 15–16, 24, 49, 58, 61
Brackett, Leigh 17, 22, 46, 64
Bradbury, Ray 4, 13–14, 46, 54
Bradley, David 34–35, 36
Bradley, Marion Zimmer 22
British science fiction field 6, 142, 152, 153, 156, 158, 186; *see also* New Wave in science fiction; *New Worlds*
Bronx High School 25
Brown, Rosel George 151
Budrys, A[lgis]. J. 113, 134, 137–38, 152
Burroughs, Edgar Rice 45, 46, 65, 68, 69
Butler, Judith 72, 73, 207

Calder, John 153
Campbell, John W., Jr. 17, 30, 45, 98, 118, 124, 127, 201
Canadian Broadcasting Corporation (CBC) Radio 172–73; CBC Radio *Ideas* series xv, 2, 172–73, 175, 188; CBC Radio International 172; CBC Radio Schools Kaleidoscope 172; CBC studios (Toronto) 172–73
Canadian Science Fiction and Fantasy Association 177
Canadian science fiction field 6, 144, 153, 176–78; and "French" Canada 176, 77; *see also* Merril Collection of Science Fiction, Speculation and Fantasy; *Tesseracts*
Canadian Science Fiction Writers' Workshop 177
Carey, Elizabeth 2–3, 204, 206, 209
Carnell, John (Ted) 142
Carter, Angela 169
Castell, Daphne 153
Chase, Helen Reid 27
*Chatelaine* 174
Chetwynd-Hayes, R. 138

Child, Lydia Maria 69
*Chip, of the Flying U* (Bower) 58, 61
Christian, Linda 15
Churchill, Joyce 152
Ciardi, John 52–53
civil defense 27, 38, 39, 71
Clareson, Thomas D. 106
Clarion Science Fiction and Fantasy Writers' Workshop 144
Clarke, Arthur C. 12, 20, 45, 132
Clements, J. 205
Clifton, Mark 140, 182, 201
Clingerman, Mildred 144
Clute, John 176, 204–5
Coach House Press 176
Cogswell, Ted *143*, 144, 182
Cold War 1, 4, 11–13, 18, 19, 26, 27–29, 31, 37, 45, 66–67, 71, 92, 98, 115, 155
Cole, Les 113, 134–36, 139, 145, 182
*Colliers Magazine* 17, 20
*Colonialism and the Emergence of Science Fiction* (Rieder) 23
Columbo, John Robert 176
Committee to Aid Refugees from Militarism (CARM) 166
Communism *see* McCarthyism
Coney, Michael 176
Conklin, Geoff 39
"Connection Completed" 98, 103–5, 106, 175, 211; contribution 103–4, 106; stage adaptation ("Headspace") 175
*The Conquest of Space* (Ley) 20
Coontz, Stephanie 27
Cooper, Carol 204, 205
Cooper, James Fenimore 19, 31–32, 40, 69, 75, 76, 80, 91–92, 99
Crabb, Leona 78
*Crack Detective Magazine* 26, 114
"The Crazies Are Dying" 203
Cummins, Elizabeth 2, 26, 48, 113–14, 157, 175, 206, 209
Curtis, Emma Ghent 49

*Dangerous Visions: 33 Original Stories* (Ellison) 151, 152, 158
"Daughters of Earth" 47, 52–55, 79, 93, 109, 139; contribution 47, 53, 54–55, 61, 79, 211
*Daughters of Earth* (1968) 173
*Daughters of Earth, and Other Stories: A Judith Merril Omnibus* (1985) 173, 174, 176
*Daughters of Earth: Three Novels* (1969) 169, 173; reception 173
Davenport, Basil 132
Davin, Eric Leif 4, 16–17
Davis, Chandler (Chan) 166, 176
Davis, Grania 170, 206, 208
Davis, Robert Murray 13
"Dead Center" 49, 61, 62–63; contribution 63; reception 62
"Death Cannot Wither" 134, 136–39; Budrys,

A[lgis]. J., assistance with 137, 138–39; contribution 137
"Death Is the Penalty" 40–41; contribution 43, 211
de Camp, L. Sprague **29**
*Decoding Gender in Science Fiction* (Attebery) 17
"The Deep Down Dragon" 94; contribution 109
DeGraw, Sharon 13, 65
Delacorte 149, 151
Delany, Samuel R. 156–57, 158, 160, 167, 172, 209; autobiography, approach to 183–85, 186
Dell Publishing 149, 151, 173
del Rey, Lester **29**, 140
Democratic National Convention, Chicago (1968) 147,165–66
Dewar, Charles 175
Dick, Philip K. x, 158
Di Filippo, Paul 205
Dikty, T.E. 141
Dirk Wylie Agency 124
Disch, Thomas M. 153, 154, 157
*Dr. Who* series (TV Ontario) 2, 173
Donawerth, Jane 16
Dorsey, Candas Jane 177, 185
Doubleday 17, 34, 38, 121, 152, 173
*Dynamic Science Fiction* 129

*The Einstein Intersection* (Delany) 156–57
Ellis, Edward S. 76
Ellison, Harlan 144, 150, 151, 152, 158–59, 164–65, 187, 209
*Empire Star* (Delany) 156
"The Empty Field" (Kita) 171
Emshwiller, Carol 158, 167
Emshwiller, Ed (byline "EMSH") 94, 167
Engel, Marian 203
*England Swings SF: Stories of Speculative Fiction* 6, 152–55, 188; British abridged edition (*Space-Time Journal*) 152; contribution 153–54; reception 152, 153, 154–55, 189
ESP (Extra Sensory Perception) *see* American psychology and primary communication theme
*Esquire Magazine* 17
"Exile from Space" 5, 70, 71, 74–75; contribution 71, 210
*The Exploration of Space* (Clarke) 20
*Extrapolation* 162, 188, 189, 205

Family Book Club 38
*Fantastic Stories* 173
*Fantastic Stories of Imagination* 82
*Fantastic Universe* 17
*Fantasy and Science Fiction* see *The Magazine of Fantasy and Science Fiction*
Farmer, Philip José 69
*Farmer in the Sky* (Heinlein) 54
feminist science fiction and criticism 4, 7, 16, 27, 159–60, 196, 210; and pre-feminist women's writings (40s and 50s), erasure 4, 16–17, 24, 27, 56, 64, 105, 207, 209–10
Ferman, Edward L. 161–62
Fetherling, Douglas 168, 173
Finlay, Virgil 80, 84, **85**
"The Flower's Life Is Short" (Fukushima) 171
Foley, Martha 62
Ford, John 60
*Frankenstein; or, The Modern Prometheus* (Shelly) 96
Franklin, Ursula M. v, xiv-xvi
Freud, Sigmund 91–92, 93, 96, 97–98, 99, 106
Freudian Theory 92, 98
Friedman, Susan Stanford 198–99, 203
"Fritz Leiber" 161–63
Frohock, Fred M. 97
Frontier mythology *see* American frontier mythology
*Frontiers of Women's Writing: Women's Narratives and the Rhetoric of Westward Expansion* (Georgi-Findlay) 21
Frye, Northrop 177
Fukushima, Masami 171
"The Future of Happiness" 174
*Future Science Fiction* 17, 46, 133
The Futurian Society of New York 1, 27, 28, **29**, 49, 113, 114, 117, 184
The Futurians 1, 3, 11, 18, 25, 26, 27, 28, **29**, 89, 113, 114, 115, 124, 126, 127, 132, 140, 144, 145, 146, 181, 183, 186, 190, 192, 194, 196, 200–1, 209, 212; collaborative spirit 113, 114–15; as "grotesques" 89–90; and the Parallax clubhouse 28; *see also* life writing
*The Futurians: The Story of the Science Fiction "Family" of the 30's That Produced Today's Top SF Writers and Editors* (Knight) 89, 183, 190, 192, 205

*Galactic Suburbia: Recovering Women's Science Fiction* (Yaszek) xiii-xiv, 27
Galaxy Beacon 131
*Galaxy of Ghouls* 139, 140; Japanese translation 175
*Galaxy Science Fiction* 39, 94, 117, 118, 130, 164
Garby, Lee Hawkins 45, 46
*Gather, Darkness!* (Leiber) 127
*Gender Trouble: Feminism and the Subversion of Identity* (Butler) 72
George, Susan A. 79
Georgi-Finlay, Brigitte 21
Gestalt therapy 89, 97
*The Ghost Light* (Leiber) 184
Gibson, William 176, 177
Gillam, Barry 154
Gillespie, Bruce 183
Gillespie, Jack 124
Gold, Horace L. 118
Gollancz (Victor Gollancz Ltd.) 173
*Good Housekeeping* 17
Gotleib, Phyllis 99, 176, 177
Greenberg, Martin H. 16, 171, 182

# INDEX 233

Grey, Zane 24, 41
Grossman, Ethyl Hurwitch (mother of Judith Merril) 77, 124
Grossman, Josephine (Judith J.) *see* Merril, Judith
Grossman, Samuel (Shlomo, father of Judith Merril) 77
"Gunner Cade" (Merril and C. M. Kornbluth [Cyril Judd, joint pseud.]) 124–25, 127–28, 129; reception 132
*Gunner Cade* (Merril and C. M. Kornbluth [Cyril Judd, joint pseud.]) 124, 125–27; contribution 126, 212; reception 132–33, 206

Hagan, John 168
Hamilton, Edmund 46, 65
Hano, Arthur 113, 114
Harbourfront *see* International Festival of Authors at Harbourfront; Out of This World Reading Series on Science Fiction at Harbourfront
Hargreaves, H.A. 176
Harrison, Evelyn **29**
Harrison, Harry **29**, 183
Hartwell, David G. 3, 12, 152
Hawkins, Cathy 205
"Head Space" (stage play) 175
*Heavenly Breakfast: An Essay on the Winter of Love* (Delany) 184
Heer, Jeet 204
Heinlein, Robert A. 4, 6, 12, 54, 60, 132, 133
*Hell's Cartographers: Some Personal Histories of Science Fiction Writers* (Aldiss and Harrison) 18, 183
"Hero's Way" 46–47
Hersey, John 34
"Hiroshima" (Hersey) 34
Hiroshima: atomic attack 12, 18, 25, 30, 44; and infanticides 30, 31; and radiation-induced birth defects 29–33
Hiroshima-Nagasaki Relived 25
*Hobomok: A Tale of Early Times* (Child) 69
Holmes, H.H. (pseud.) *see* Boucher, Anthony
"Homecalling" 23, 70–71, 76–78, 100, 101, 106, 107–9; contribution 70, 78, 106, 107, 211
*Homecalling and Other Stories: The Complete Solo Short SF of Judith Merril* 2, 206
*Homeward Bound: American Families in the Cold War Era* (May) 26–27, 28–29
Honyaku Benkyo-kai (the "Translation Study Meeting") *see* Japanese translators of English-language science fiction and fantasy
Hoover, J. Edgar 68
*Hope Leslie, or, Early Times in the Massachusetts* (Sedgwick) 71, 75
Hoshi, Shinichi 169
House of Anansi Press 166
"How Near Is the Moon?" 44
*How to Suppress Women's Writing* (Russ) 24, 209
Hughes, Robert 15
Hugo Awards xi, 2, 182, 187, 206

*Human?* 140, 186
Hydra Club, New York 2, 20, 29, 90, 114–15, 121, 128, 144, 145, 183, 186, 187
Hydra Club North (later Toronto Hydra, Ontario Hydra) 144, 177

*I, Asimov: A Memoir* 183, 188
*Ideas* radio series (see Canadian Broadcasting Corporation)
*If* 17
"If the Bomb Gets Out of Hand" (Morrison) 34
*Imagination* 17
*Imperial Leather: Race, Gender, and Sexuality in the Colonial Conquest* (McClintock) 21
*In Joy Still Felt: The Autobiography of Isaac Asimov, Vol. II: 1954–1974* 183, 187–88, 205
*In Memory Yet Green: The Autobiography of Isaac Asimov, Vol. I: 1920–1954* 183, 187, 205
"In the Land of the Unblind" 175; stage adaptation ("Headspace") 175
*Infinity* 17
*Intelligent Life in the Universe* (Shklovskii and Sagan) 156
International Association for the Fantastic in the Arts xii, 189
International Festival of Authors at Harbourfront 177; and Merril, Judith, tribute (1992) 196
International Milford UK Workshop 144
"Interview with Emily Pohl-Weary" (Larbalestier) 198
Ishikawa, Takashi xiii, 171
"The Island" (Jones) 154
Ito, Norio 157

Jackson, Andrew 66
Jacobs, Harvey 167
Jacobs, Jane 168
James, Edward 115, 145, 159
Japanese English-language translation project 2, 169–71, 178, 206, 212
Japanese International Science Fiction Symposium (1970) 157, 169, 189
Japanese science fiction field 6, 157, 169–71, 178, 208
Japanese Science Fiction Writers Club 170, 171
*Japanese SF Magazine* see *SF Magazine*
Japanese translators of English-language science fiction and fantasy xi, xiii, 6, 157, 168–71, 208; and Honyaku Benkyo-kai ("Translation Study Meeting") xiii, 170, 206
Jones, Alice Eleanor 27
Jones, Roger 154
Judd, Cyril (joint pseud. for C. M. Kornbluth and Judith Merril) 3, 6, 23, 78, 115–33, 134; distinctive creative and stylistic contributions 115, 129, 132–33, 146, 212
"Judith Merril: Her Impact on Feminist Science Fiction" (panel session) 196, 203

Kaplan, Amy 21, 48, 65
Kelman, Paul 175
Kerslake, Patricia 13
Kidd (Emden, Blish), Virginia 28, 49, 139, 145, 149, 151, 174, 182,191; correspondence 170, 182, 193–94, 196, 197, 200–1, 203
*The Kinsey Reports* 75
Kita, Morio 171
Klodawsky, Helen 175 181
Knight, Damon 27, 89–90, 102, 115, 126, 142, *143*, 144, 164, 170; Futurian history project 183, 189–90, 192, 205; and New Wave writing 158
"Knight Piece" (Knight) 183
Kolodny, Annette 14–15, 20–21
Kornbluth, Cyril. M. (C. M.) 3, 6, 23, 47, 56, 78, 90, 115–33, 134, 135, 139, 145, 158, 206, 209, 212; *see also* Judd, Cyril; Pohl, Frederik
Kornbluth (Byers), Mary 119, 123–24, 128
Kristiva, Julia 15
Kubrick, Stanley 45

"The Lady Was a Tramp" (Merril [Rose Sharon, pseud.]) 53, 59–60, 64, 127; contribution 59, 211; reception 60; stage adaptation ("Headspace") 175
*The Land Before Her: Fantasy and Experience of the American Frontiers, 1630–1860* (Kolodny) 15, 21
Larbalestier, Justine 4, 16, 17, 18, 22, 48, 69, 119, 198, 206, 209
Laskin, David 160
*The Last of the Mohicans* (J. F. Cooper) 40, 69, 75, 76, 91–92, 99
Latham, Rob 157, 158–59
*The Lay of the Land: Metaphor as Experience and History in American Life and Letters* (Kolodny) 14–15
*The Leatherstocking Tales* series (J. F. Cooper) 31, 80, 91
Lee, Denis 166
Lefanu, Sarah 16
Le Guin, Ursula K. 209
Leiber, Fritz 35, 39, 53, 58, 89, 113, 119, 120, 121, 122–23, 125, 127, 128, 132, 134, 140, 158, 160, 161–62, 167, 173, 182, 185, 192, 203, 207, 209; and autobiography, approach to 183–85
Lewis, Dana (formerly David) xiii, 170
Ley, Willy 19, 20
Library and Archives Canada ix, xi, xii, 2, 7, 191; Merril Fonds ix, xvii, 153, 186, 190–93, 195, 198
*Life Magazine* 15
life writing 179–207; and autobiography, alternate forms 199–201, 204–5; and autobiography, male-centered model of subjectivity and narrative form, privileged in traditional 178, 199, 202, 203, 205; experimental approaches to 179–81, 183–84, 190–91; and the Futurian community 183, 192, 196, 200, 201, 204, 205, 207; and memoir versus autobiography 183, 185, 190–91; and memory, untrustworthiness 183–85, 190, 191–92, 199, 200; and women's lives, marginalized in canonical autobiographies 179, 198–200
"Life Writing and Science Fiction: Constructing Identities and Constructing Genres" (Rieder) 183
"A Little Knowledge" 93–94, 106–8, 109; contribution 94, 107, 109, 133
*Lives of the Psychics: The Shared Worlds of Science and Mysticism* (Frohock) 97
Lockhart, Caroline 15
"The Lonely" 23, 49, 51–52, 80, 81, 83–84, *85*, 86–87, 101, 109; contribution 51–52, 81, 83, 86, 211
*Lonesome Land* (Bower) 15–16, 49
"The Lovers" (Farmer) 69
Lowndes, Robert A.W. ("Doc") 114, 129
LSD 156
*Luna Monthly* 174

MacCreigh, James (pseud.) *see* Pohl, Frederik
MacLean, Katherine 64, 97, 113, 128, 139, 140, 141, 169, 182, 185, 191, 192, 193, 197, 203; and the ESP trials 97–98
*Maclean's Magazine* 17
*The Magazine of Science Fiction and Fantasy* 17, 39, 51, 56, 131, 137, 152, 164, 189; "Books" review column 2, 6, 147, 149, 155–60, 165–66; *see also* What Do You Mean, Science? Fiction? (*SF-ni naniga dekiruka*)
*Malaeska* (Stephens) 69
Malzberg, Barry N. 182
*The Man from U.N.C.L.E.* 164
"A Man of the World" (Cole) 41, 135–36
*Manual for Draft-Age Immigrants to Canada* 166; *see also* anti–Vietnam war movement
Mars 45, 46, 62, 68–69, 78–80, 94, 95, 96, 132
"Mars Child" (Merril and C. M. Kornbluth [Cyril Judd, joint pseud.]) 117–19, 120–22, 123, 130, 134; reception 122–23; *see also* Outpost Mars; Sin in Space
Marshall, Joyce 173
*The Martian Chronicles* (Bradbury) 13–14, 46, 54
*Marvel Science Stories* 17
Masters, Dexter 47
May, Elaine Tyler 26, 28–29, 31
Mayflower-Dell 149
McCaffrey, Anne 186
McCann, Jolene xi, 165, 172
McCarthyism 18, 66, 68; and Communism 68
McClelland & Stewart 174
McClintock, Anne 21
McComas, J. Francis 39, 131, 132
McConnell, James V. 182
McElrath, Frances 15, 21, 49, 58
"A Memoir and Appreciation" 182

Mendlesohn, Farah xii, 4
Merrick, Helen 4, 14, 18, 196
Merril, Judith: anthologist-editor (50s through 80s) 5, 114, 139–42, *143*, 146, 148–55, 173–74, 177–78, 186, 191, 212; anti-war activist (60s and 70s) xv, 25, 163–*68*; beginnings as an activist and writer (30s and 40s) xv, 1–2, 5, 25, 26, *27*, 29–30, 44, 89, 114; by-lines and pseudonyms 26, 53, 59, 114, 117, 127, 135–36, 137, 138, 146, 211; career summary 1–2, 3–4, 6; catalyst-mentor (60s through 80) 147–61, 166–78, 186; collaborative writer (50s) 113–39, 146, 186, 212; correspondence files 7, 119, 139, 146, 167, 181–93, 200–1; critic-reviewer (60s) 155–61, 165; documentarist-broadcaster (70s) xv, 39, 171–73, 187–88, 190; erasure from sf history 7, 181, 186–90, 209–10, 212; essayist (60s) 161–63; family and friendships, intertwined 5, 27–28, *29*, 53, 56, 58, 70, 76, 89–90, 103, 113–14, 117–19, 121–23, 127, 128, 135–36, 139, 140, *143*–44, 145–46, 151, 161–62, 173, 182, 185, 187, 190–91, 197–98, 200–3; fiction writer (late 40s through early 60s) xv, 26, *29*–43, 44–64, 66–88, 210; health 7, 56, 89–90, 121–22, 124, 164, 185, 193–94, 203; Japan period xiii, 1, 2, 3, 4, 6, 147, 169–71, 172, 175, 189, 197, 206; library curator (70s through 90s) xvi, 166–*68*, 178, 188; London period 1, 2, 3, 6, 147, 151, 152–53, 164, 166, 169, 171, 188, 197; memoirist (80s and 90s) 7, 178–*80*, 181–207, 212; reputation 2, 3–4, 6–7, 24, 52, 120, 134, 140–41, 142–43, 151, 157, 160, 164–65, 174, 181, 182, 186–90, 195–97, 203, 204–7, 208 (Kaibutsu Basasan, or "monster grandma") 212; science fiction consultant (70s and 80s) 177, 187–88; Toronto years xv, xvi, 1, 2, 3, 4, 6, 25, 144, 157, 166–207, 210; translator-editor (70s) *168*–71, 212; tributes and honors xi, xiii, xvi, 2–3, 140, 151, 157, 171, 177, 189, 196, 206, 208–9; "woman's" perspective 17, 22, 49, 54, 74, 133, 135
Merril Collection of Science Fiction, Speculation and Fantasy (formerly Spaced Out Library (SOL)) ix-xi, xiii, xvi, 2, 7, 25, 166–68, 172, 177, 187–88, 191, 209, 210; as center for Canadian science fiction field xvi, 2, 177; and writer in residence program 178
Merril papers ("Judith Merril Fonds") *see* Library and Archives Canada
Mesmer, Franz 96
mesmerism 96, 99, 100–1, 102
Michel, John (Johnnie) 114
Miles, Lois 124
Milford, Pennsylvania 141–45, 186–87, 188, 191, 194
Milford Award for Lifetime Achievement in Science Fiction Editing and Publishing 196
*Milford Dispatch* 145

Milford Science Fiction Writers' Conference (annual Milford workshop) 2, 115, 141–46, 149, 177, 186; and the Milford System 144
Miller, P. Schuyler *29*, 131, 132, 154–55, 173, 210
Miller, Walter, Jr. 90, 103, 140, 143, 144, 172, 182, 187, 195, 202–3
Mills, Robert P. (Bob) 135, 182
Mitsuse, Ryu 171
Mogen, David 11, 12–13
Moon (Earth's) 20, 44, 45, 55, 57, 62–64, 95, 167, 101
Moorcock, Michael 152–53, 158, 159, 208–9
Moore, C[atherine] L[ucille] 17, 22, 64
Morrison, Philip 34
*The Motion Light in Water: Sex and Science Fiction in the East Village* (Delany) 184
Motorola TV Playhouse 39
Mulvey, Laura 84

Nagasaki: atomic attack 12, 30; *see also* Hiroshima: atomic attack
NASA's Women in Space Early (WISE) 49
*New Maps of Hell* (Amis) 148
New wave in science fiction 4, 48, 147, 154–55, 156, 157–60, 161, 163; American 157–59; British 6, 152–55, 156, 157, 158–59, 189; and postmodern techniques 154; *see also Dangerous Visions: 33 Original Stories*; *England Swings SF*; *New Worlds*; *Orbit 2: The Best New Science Fiction Stories of the Year*
*New Worlds* 6, 152, 153, 156
*New York Herald-Tribune* 30, 131, 132
New York Hydra Club *see* Hydra Club, New York
The New York Intellectuals 160
The New York Nexus 113–114, 128, 145
*New York Times* 132
Nicholls, Peter 70, 98
1968 as a socio-political phenomenon 155, 160, 165
*The Ninth Fontana Book of Great Ghost Stories* (Chetwynd-Hayes) 138
*No Place to Hide* (D. Bradley) 34, 36
Noonan, Bonnie 61, 62, 70, 76, 77
Norton, Andre (Alice Mary Norton) 17
"Not Only a Mother: An Interview with Judith Merril" (Weiss) 181
"Not So Much Disorder and Not So Early Sex: An Autobiographic Essay" (Leiber) 184
*Nova* (Delany) 157
*Now Books* 203

*One World or None: A Report to the Public on the Full Meaning of the Atomic Bomb* (Masters and Way) 47
Oppenheimer, J.R. 18
oral contraceptive (the "pill") *see* birth control
*Orbit 2: The Best New Science Fiction Stories of the Year* (Knight) 158
Orwell, George 39

*Other Canadas* (Columbo) 176
*The Other Side of Realism: Essays on Modern Fantasy and Science Fiction* (Clareson) 162
*Other Worlds* 17
*Out of Bounds* 137, 138, 173; reception 210
Out of This World Reading Series on Science Fiction at Harbourfront 177
*Outpost Mars* (Merril and C. M. Kornbluth [Cyril Judd, joint pseud.]) 23, 78–79, 117, 119–21, 125, 129, 130–32, 137, 138; contribution 119–21; reception 131–32, 206, 212; *see also* "Mars Child"; *Sin in Space*
Owram, Douglas 168

Padgett, Lewis (joint pseud. of Henry Kuttner and C. L. Moore) 140
Panther Books 152
The Parapsychology Laboratory (Duke University) 97
*Partners in Wonder: Women and the Birth of Science Fiction, 1926–1965* (Davin) 16–17
Pashin, Alexi 166
"Peeping Tom" 100, 103, 105–6, 107, 108; contribution 106, 107, 109, 133, 211
Performing Arts Lodge 193
*The Petrified Planet* (Pratt, uncredited) 52
*Picnic on Paradise* (Russ) 159, 160–61
"Pioneer Stock" 68–70; contribution 69
*Planet Stories* 17
planetary romance stories *see* science fiction
Platt, Charles 153
*Playboy Magazine* 17
Pluto 52, 55
Pohl, Ann (daughter of Judith Merril) 1, 90, 118, 166, 202
Pohl, Frederik 1, 24, 28, **29**, 30, 47, 52, 58, 84, 90, 115, 117, 121, 123, 128, 140, 143, 145, 150, 166, 172, 175, 182, 188, 191, 202, 209; *Galaxy Science Fiction*, editor 130–31; Kornbluth, C.M., collaborations with 47, 117–18, 130, 131; as literary agent 114, 118, 126, 128; memoir (*The Way the Future Was*) 113, 183, 190; Merril, Judith, collaboration with (as James MacCreigh, pseud.) 133–34
Pohl-Weary, Emily (granddaughter of Judith Merril, daughter of Ann Pohl) ix, x, xv, 179, 181, 188–81, 194–95, 197–201, 202, 203–7, 208
*Popular* 16
Powell, D. Reid 153
Pratt, Fletcher 132, 140
Priest, Christopher 153
*A Princess of Mars* (Burroughs) 45, 65–66, 69
*Proceedings of the Institute for Twenty-first Century Studies* 144
"Project Nursemaid" 56–58, 93; contribution 57, 58, 210; reception 58
psi (psionics) *see* American psychology and primary communication theme
psychology *see* American psychology and primary communication theme

"Rain Check" 5, 70–73, 74, 75, 103; contribution 70–71, 133, 210
Random House 17
Readercon 196
Red Bank, New Jersey 90, 97, 122, 123–25, 128–29, 130, 139, 143, 191
*Red Book Magazine* 17
Red, White, and Black 166
Reed, Kit 158
Regency Books 150
"Remembering Cyril: An Interview with Judith Merril" (Rich) 192
"'Repent, Harlequin!' Said the Ticktockman" (Ellison) 164
Rich, Mark 117, 118, 119, 124, 125, 129, 130, 131, 141, 181, 192
*Riders of the Purple Sage* (Grey) 41
Rieder, John 13, 23, 32, 65, 77–78, 183
"Road to the Sea" (Ishikawa) 171
Roberts, Jane 144
Roberts, Keith 153
Roberts, Robin 70, 84
Roberts and Vintner 39
Robinson, Kim Stanley 132
Robinson, Spider 151, 164, 176, 177, 179, 194, 204–5, 208–9
Rochdale College xi, 166–67, **168**; and the free university movement 25
Rochdale Medical Clinic 166
Rochdale Summer '69 Festival of Science Fiction and Fantasy 167
*Rocket Dreams: How the Space Race Shaped Our Vision of a World Beyond* (Benjamin) 20
*Romance Range* 16
*A Room of One's Own* (Woolf) 121
Rowlandson, Mary 70, 91
Russ, Joanna 16, 24, 27, 152, 156, 159–61, 196, 209
*The Rustler: A Tale of Love and War in Wyoming* (McElrath) 21, 49, 58

Sagan, Carl 156
Sakyo, Komatsu xiii, 171
*The Sands of Mars* (Clarke) 132
Sargent, Pamela 4, 30
*Saturday Evening Post* 17
*Saturday Review* 132
"The Savage Mouth" (Sakayo) 171
*Savage Perils: Racial Frontiers and Nuclear Apocalypse in American Culture* (Sharp) 11
Sawyer, Robert J. 151
Saxon, Josephine 153
Schlissel, Lillian 21, 51
*Science Fiction Adventures* 17
science fiction: American *see* American science fiction field; Canadian *see* Canadian science fiction field; Japanese *see* Japanese science fiction field
Science Fiction Canada 177
*Science Fiction Hall of Fame, Vol. 1* (Silverberg) 30

*The Science Fiction of Mark Clifton* (Malzberg and Greenberg) 181–82
*Science Fiction Quarterly* 93
*Science Fiction Studies* 177
Science Fiction Writers of America (SFWA, later, SSFWA, Science Fiction and Fantasy Writers of America) 2; SSFWA Author Emeritus Award 196
Scott Meredith Agency 114
Scribner's 17
"Sea-Change" (Merril and C. M. Kornbluth [Cyril Judd, pseud.]) 129–30; contribution 129–30
*The Searchers* (Ford, director) 92
Secondary Universe Conference (Secon IV, 1971) 172, 187
Sedgwick, Catharine Maria 71, 75
Seed, David xiii, 14, 18, 32, 33, 34, 35, 38–39, 209
*Sgt. Pepper's Lonely Hearts Club Band* (The Beatles) 152
*Seth Jones, or, The Captives of the Frontier* (Ellis) 76
"Sex and/or Mr. Morrison" (C. Emshwiller) 158
*SF Magazine* (Japan) 175
*SF: The Best of the Best* 151–52; Japanese translation 175; reception 152, 160
*SFRevu* 204
*Shadow on the Hearth* 3, 5, 15, 18, 30, 33–40, 43, 121, 122, 212; *Atomic Attack*, revised for TV as 35, 39–40; contribution 35, 36–37, 39–40, 212; reception 5, 35, 39–40, 116, 120, 121–22, 188–89, 206
Shaefer, Jack 19
*Shane* (Schaefer) 19
Sharon, Rose (pseud. of Judith Merril) 40, 59, 60, 127–28, 134, 135–36, 137
Sharp, Patrick B. 11, 13, 33–34
Shelly, Mary 96
Shklovskii, I. S. 156
*Shot in the Dark* 114, **116**, 139; reception 116, 131
"The Shrine of Temptation" 80–81, **82–83** 84; contribution 81, 211; and Merril, Judith, LP album narration 175
Silverberg, Robert 30, 144, 160
Simon and Schuster 17, 124
*Sin in Space: An Expose of the Scarlett Planet* (Merril and C. M. Kornbluth [Cyril Judd joint pseud.]) 130–31; *see also* "Mars Child"
Sinusas, Asta 204
*The Skylark of Space* (E.E. Smith and Garby, uncredited) 45
Slotkin, Richard 18, 28, 38
Smart, Elizabeth 203
Smith, Cordwiner 158
Smith, E.E. ("Doc") 45, 46
Smith, Henry Nash 14
Smith, Sidonie 198–99
"So Proudly We Hail" 61, 62; contribution 62; reception 62
*Solaris* (magazine) 176

Sontag, Susan 42
Space 17
*Space and Beyond: The Frontier Theme in Science Fiction* (Westfahl) 12
space frontier *see* American space frontier theme
The Space Frontier Foundation 14
*The Space Merchants* (F. Pohl and C.M. Kornbluth) 130–131
space opera *see* American science fiction field
space science 11, 44–46, 47
*The Space-Time Journal* see *England Swings SF: Stories of Speculative Fiction*
*Space Travel* 17, 46
Spaced Out Library (SOL) *see* Merril Collection of Science Fiction, Speculation and Fantasy
*Spaced Out: Three Novels of Tomorrow* (Merril and C.M. Kornbluth) 3, 206
Speculative Fiction ("SF") 3, 4, 7, 17, 147, 153–54, 156, 162–63, 166, 167, 174, 176, 182, 206, 210, 211
*Speculative Japan: Outstanding Tales of Japanese Science Fiction* (van Troyer and G. Davis) 206
*Sputnik-I* 20
Stableford, Brian 48, 79
*Stagecoach* (Ford, director) 60
Stanton, Domna C. 199
*Star Well* (Pashin) 166
*Startling Stories* 17
Stekel, Wilhelm 99
Stephens, Ann S. 69
"Stormy Weather" 103, 104–5, 106; contribution 106
Street & Smith publishers 16
Streetby, Shelly 65
Students for a Democratic Society (SDS) 156, 165
Sturgeon, Theodore H. (Ted) 113, 114, 125, 140, 158, 161, 173, 182, 188, 191, 193, 196, 203
Sugrue, Daniel 1
*Sunburst* (Gotleib) 99
"The Sunset, 2217 AD" (Mitsuse) 177
"Survival Ship" 49, 50–51, 121, 122; contribution 50; Merril, Judith, LP album narration 175
*Survival Ship and Other Stories* 174, 176; reception 174
Suvin, Darko 177

*Takeoff* (C. M. Kornbluth) 119, 131
Tallentire, Jenéa xi, 159, 179–80
Tatsumi, Takayuki xiii, 175
telepathy *see* American psychology and primary communication theme
*Tesseracts* xiii, 2, 177; contribution 177; volume 1 176, 177–78
"That Only a Mother" 5, 29–33, 40, 43, 68, 114, 116, 120, 212; contribution 30, 68, 211; reception 30, 116, 190, 211

Theall, Donald F. 174
Theatre Passe Muraille 175
"Theodore Sturgeon" 161
The Thin Edge anthology project 150–51
*Thrilling Wonder* 17
*The Tomorrow People* 3, 95, 100–2, 106; contribution 106; reception 102, 210
*Tomorrow the Stars: A Science Fiction Anthology* (Heinlein) 133
Toolis, Lorna xii, xiii-xiv, 164, 165, 167, 173, 178, 185, 194, 195, 196, 202, 204, 209
Toronto: as a place of counter-culture 166–68, 204
*Toronto Globe and Mail* 179, 183
*Toronto National Post* 204
Toronto Public Library x, xii, 2, 25, 147, 167–68, 191
*Totem and Taboo: Some Points of Agreement Between the Mental Lives of Savages and Neurotics* (Freud) 91
Toyota, Aritsune 170
tranquilizer boom 78
"Transformations" 179, 181–83, 184, 185, 190, 196, 197, 202
*Travels by Night: A Memoir of the Sixties* (Fetherling) 168
Trotskyism 25
Tsuruta, Kinya 171
Turner, Frederick Jackson 11, 12, 19, 47
Tutihasi, R. Laurraine 174
Twayne Science-Fiction Triplet series ("Twayne Triplets") 52
*The Twinkling of an Eye: Or, My Life as an Englishman* (Aldiss) 189
*2001: A Space Odyssey* (Kubrick and Clarke, screenwriters) 45

U.S. Indian Claims Commission 84
*Universe Science Fiction* 17

Vance, Jack 158
Vancouver Writers' Festival 196
*Venture Science Fiction* 17, 41, 59, 60, 135, 137
*Village Voice* 204
*The Virginian* (Wister) 19, 21–22, 40, 41, 49, 61
*Visions of Wonder* (Hartwell and Wolf) 152
van Troyer, Gene 206
van Vogt, A.E. 176
Vonarburg, Elizabeth 176, 177

*Waiting for Godot* (Beckett) 154
Walt Disney Productions 20
*The War of the Worlds* (H.G. Wells) 78
Warner Books 174
Watson, Julia 198–99
Way, Katherine 47
*The Way the Future Was: A Memoir* (F. Pohl) 113, 183, 190
*The Way We Never Were: American Families and the Nostalgia Trap* (Coontz) 27
Weart, Spencer R. 13

Webster, Bud 205
Weihs, Ron 175, 181
Weiner, Andrew 176
Weiss, Alan xii, xiv, 89, 181
Wells, H.G. 78
Wells, Orson 141
*Western Story* 16
Westerns xv, 1, 12, 13–14, 15–16, 19–21, 26, 41, 44, 58, 60, 61, 63, 64, 99, 114; and colonial and racial discourse, central vehicle for 13; female writers 15–18, 21, 24, 26, 49, 61, 63, 92; parenting, reproduction, and sex, common themes 58; and women's science fiction, links to women's Westerns 15–16, 17, 23, 49, 60, 64, 92, 133; *see also* American frontier mythology
Westfahl, Gary 12
"What Do You Mean — Science? Fiction?" (1966) 162, 163, 188, 189
"What Do You Mean: Science? Fiction?" (1971) 162–63; contribution 162–63
*What Do You Mean, Science? Fiction? (SF-ni naniga dekiruka)* (Asakura) 175; reception of, in Japan 175
"What Have I Done?" (Clifton) 182
What If...? A Film About Judith Merril (Klodawsky, director) 175–76; reception 176
"Whoever You Are" 66–68, 100–1; adapted for radio (Dewar) and stage (Weihs) 175; contribution 68
*Wilderness Visions: Science Fiction Westerns* (Mogen) 12–13
Wilhelm (Knight), Kate 144, 158, 164, 186
Williams, Tess 196
Willis, Connie 2, 4, 140, 209
Winter, Joe 89
WisCon 20 xvi, 196
"Wish Upon a Star" 49, 51–52; contribution 51
Wister, Owen 19, 49, 61
Wolf, Milton T. 152
Wolfe, Gary K. 11, 45, 46, 54, 144, 150
"A Woman of the World" (Merril [Rose Sharon, pseud.) 40, 41–43, 134–36; contribution 43, 135
"Woman's Work Is *Never* Done!" 43
*Women, Autobiography, Theory: A Reader* (Smith and Watson) 198–99
*Women of Other Worlds: Excursions through Science Fiction and Feminism* (Merrick and Williams) 196
*Women of Wonder* (Sargent) 30
*Women Scientists in Fifties Science Fiction Films* (Noonan) 61, 70
*Wonder Stories* 17
Woods, Susan 177
Woolf, Virginia 121
Worldcon: Clevention (Cleveland), 1955 187, 201; Loncon II (London), 1965 152, 157, 164; Nycon 3 (New York), 1967 187; Torcon II (Toronto), 1973 172; Worldcon, "Interaction" (Glasgow) 2005 xiv

*Worlds Beyond* 17, 50
*Worlds of Tomorrow* 17, 51, 85
writer's block 3, 90, 115, 121–22
Writers' Union of Canada 25
"Writing My Grandmother's Autobiography" (Pohl-Weary) 194–95, 197–98
Wrobel, David M. 13

Yano, Tetsu 169, 170–71
Yaszek, Lisa xiii–xiv, 2, 4, 16, 17, 18, 27, 30, 33, 49, 86, 209
Year's Best anthology series 2, 115, 139, 140, 141–42, 144, 146, 149–50, 163, 186, 188, 189; British edition 149; contribution 141–42; Japanese translation 175; reception 140, 142, 144, 175, 189, 208; and SF12, 150
Young People's Socialist League (YPSL) 25

Zarlengo, Kristina 15, 27, 38
Zend, Robert 203
Zimmer Bradley, Marion 22
Zissman, Daniel A. 1, 25, 27, 28, 202
Zissman, Judith (Judith Merril) 26
Zissman, Merril (daughter of Judith Merril) 1, 121, 143, 202
Zoline, Pamela 153, 154

www.ingramcontent.com/pod-product-compliance
Ingram Content Group UK Ltd.
Pitfield, Milton Keynes, MK11 3LW, UK
UKHW041938140426
5217IPUK00014B/535